House Plants

House Plants

by Mariella Pizzetti
Photographs by Giuseppe Mazza

Translation by Catherine Atthill
and Simon Pleasance

CHARTWELL BOOKS INC.
110 ENTERPRISE AVE.
SECAUCUS, N.J. 07094

ISBN 0-89009-067-X
Library of Congress LC 76-15920
Published by Chartwell Books Inc., a division of Book Sales Inc.,
110 Enterprise Avenue, Secaucus, N. J. 07094

Originally published in Italian by
Arnoldo Mondadori Editore, Milan
© 1976 Arnoldo Mondadori Editore
English translation © 1976 Arnoldo Mondadori Editore

The drawings were prepared by Raffaello Segattini

Printed in Italy by Arnoldo Mondadori Editore, Verona

Contents

Introduction: Plants in the home

PLANTS AND HOW THEY LIVE

Every living organism is composed of cells, and plants are no exception. The vegetable kingdom is made up of unicellular and multicellular individuals and although there are enormous numbers of the former (just think of bacteria), it is the second group which, because of their size and complexity, are usually regarded as plants and which alone are specially cultivated.

The cells are normally organized into highly specialized tissues fulfilling particular functions; it is the way these functions are performed which constitutes the main difference between the vegetable and animal kingdoms. There are various forms of cell but the basic constituent is a fluid known as cytoplasm which contains various cavities and particles. The cytoplasm is enclosed by a membrane which controls the interchange of two solutions: cell sap and the more watery solution which the plant absorbs through its roots. The different particles present in the cytoplasm include chloroplasts which contain the pigment known as

The majestic oak has often been the object of worship and veneration.

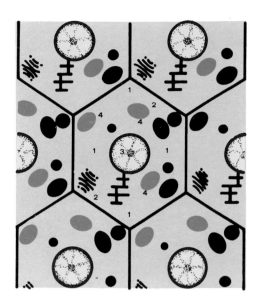

Above: Like all living organisms, plant tissues are composed of cells, the basic structural unit of living matter. The diagram shows 1 cytoplasm, 2 membrane, 3 nucleus, 4 chloroplasts; various other corpuscles.

chlorophyll — nature's strangest and most wonderful creation.

Chlorophyll is the basis of life itself, the first stage in the chain which links the plant cell to man : it is rather like a factory which uses solar energy to separate out the elements of water, combine them with carbon from carbon dioxide in the air and make organic products like sugars and starches, fats and protein. This unique process, known as photosynthesis, can only occur if there is light, and without it no form of life could exist: the substances which nourish the plant pass in an unbroken chain to the organisms of herbivorous animals which eat the plant and from them to carnivores and of course omnivores such as man. In higher plants the interchanges which make photosynthesis possible take place in the green parts, usually the leaves, although in certain environmental conditions the leaves often disappear, their job being done by modified stems or branches.

For a practical understanding of what a plant needs if it is to thrive, a few facts about leaf tissues are obviously indispensable. First in a leaf comes the epidermis, generally covered by a membrane or cuticle of a certain thickness and sometimes

Right: How a plant manufactures food from sunlight.

Below: Section of a *Fagus* (beech) branch, showing growth rings, medullary rays and the vessels which carry the sap.

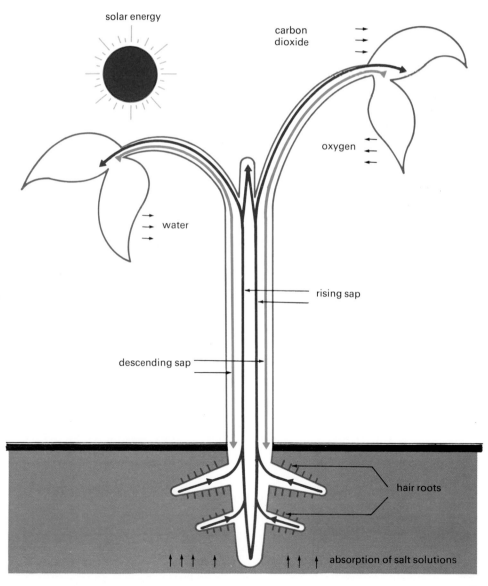

The structure of leaf tissues consists of different types of cells, including cells containing chloroplasts. The illustration clearly shows the stomatic cells which are less apparent in vertical section.

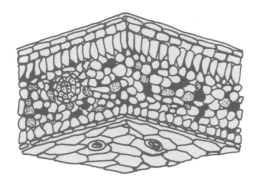

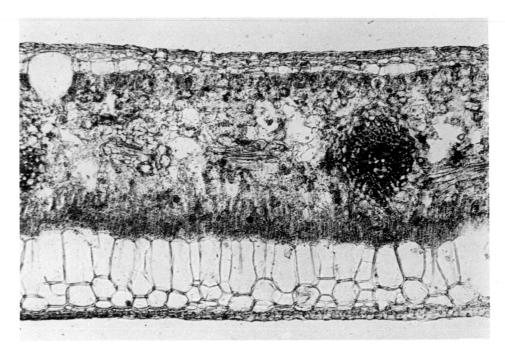

with a waxy bloom. There may be additional features produced as outgrowths to the tissues — for example, hairs, tomentum (a matted, cottony down) or glands.

The epidermal tissue contains essential formations. These are the stomata, microscopic valve-like openings enclosed and controlled by two kidney-shaped guard cells which, according to their content or turgidity, allow or prevent the opening of the mouth-like pores. The word 'mouth-like' is used deliberately as the term 'stoma' comes from the Greek *stoma* meaning 'mouth'. These openings do indeed act as mouths, absorbing carbon dioxide and giving off the oxygen not used up by photosynthesis, so contributing to the plant's nutrition and respiration. They also give off in the form of water vapour excess water absorbed by the roots, which allows further absorption of solutions containing vital mineral salts and their circulation all round the plant.

This phenomenon is most clearly seen in certain plants which actually sweat drops of water from the edges of their leaves if there is too much water in the soil and the heat is excessive.

The guard cells, which contain chloroplasts, are rich in sugars and starches. As this makes their cell sap very dense it increases the osmotic pressure exerted on their membranes so that they become turgid as they absorb water from the moisture around them. During the night, or whenever the plant does not have enough water in the soil or in the atmosphere, the guard cells become less turgid and the stomata contract until they are almost closed, thus restricting transpiration. This mechanism is so perfectly developed that not all plants have the same number of stomata: in plants from humid tropical environments they are very densely distributed and protuberant, while to reduce transpiration in plants from dry climates they are few in number, hollow and often surrounded by hairs which help to close them, or protected by thick, leathery cuticles. These simple facts should always be kept in mind when growing house plants which, as you will see, come mainly from tropical or subtropical climates where the air is often full of moisture. For fine healthy tissues which can perform their functions properly, the stomata must be able to achieve the necessary state of turgidity; copious watering

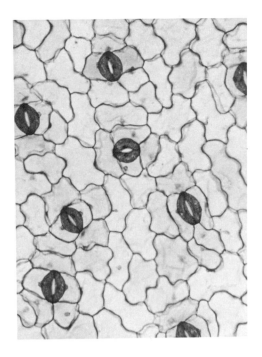

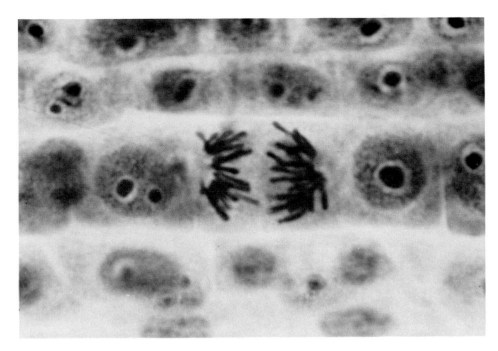

Above: The stomata are essential for the interchange of gases. Stomata on the underside of a leaf show up clearly under the microscope.

Right: Cell division shows the chromosomes: here the chromosomes have already divided and are about to form the nuclei of two new cells.

can never supply or replace this as the root system is unable to absorb and use water in the same way.

A long section on plant cytology or physiology is obviously not called for here but it is as well to know a few facts which may be of practical use, especially when growing plants indoors, in conditions very different from their original habitat. The information already given about epidermal tissue, for example, explains why so much emphasis, often not fully understood, is placed on keeping the air as moist as possible, by all available means, including spraying and washing the leaves regularly, which also help to keep the stomata dust-free.

It is also useful to know that the nucleus of each cell contains a number (constant for each species) of chromosomes, the bearers of the hereditary genes. At the moment of fertilization chromosomes from male and female cells must be able to link up to form homologous pairs if reproduction is to be possible. On the whole nowadays most cultivated ornamental plants are not original species, but crosses or hybrids. However, because the chromosomes must be similar, hybridization generally takes place within the same species; it rarely occurs between different genera and never between different families. Any given species' growing needs will usually be the same for any hybrid bred from it, and can only be partly changed by careful selection aimed at producing more attractive or hardy plants; the hybrids will always reveal their common origin. An orchid cannot be crossed with a daisy to give easy flowering in ideal intermediate conditions. The most that can be achieved by crossing different species or varieties from partially different habitats is increased resistance in certain very delicate species to such things as soil composition or temperature; the basic needs will remain much the same.

Apart from hybridization, occasional natural variations known as mutations can occur. Mutations may be heritable, causing changes in the chromosomes, which then become part of the genetic inheritance and so can be reproduced by seed. But more often they suddenly appear on a single part of the plant and do not affect the reproductive cells; this phenomenon is known as somatic or gemmate

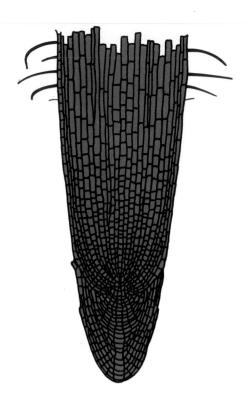

The end of a root showing the root cap, the tip where cellular division produces growth, and the root hairs which absorb nourishment and moisture.

mutation and the forms produced by this process can only be reproduced vegetatively. Many houseplants fall into this category and have a marked tendency to lose the variegation or other modifications which they have acquired with any change in the optimum environmental conditions in which these features were produced. This is known as reverting to type (or species).

It is also useful to know something about a plant's root system, as this often creates difficulties, especially when growing plants indoors. As it would be practically impossible to give special instructions for each plant, the problem is discussed generally here. In its natural habitat, whatever that may be, a plant's root system is never in danger of wasting away or being completely destroyed as it may be if it is grown in a too-small pot, often with insufficient food and an unsuitable or poor growing medium. If the part of a plant above ground is damaged the plant can recover by sprouting again, but it is very difficult for an affected root system to revive, not least because it is usually noticed too late. First in the root comes the rootcap, a hood-like formation which protects the tissues inside it from coming into contact with the soil as they grow; this soon wears the rootcap away, so its cells are continually being renewed. Just below it comes a short smooth section and then the system of root hairs for absorbing water and respiration. The root hairs are constantly changing: during growth the old hairs wear out while new ones form towards the top. The older part of the root generally becomes woody and merely serves to conduct the elements which make up sap.

The root hairs are the most delicate part and need most attention. Soil which is too close-packed may stop the hairs forming; if it is waterlogged so that they cannot perform their essential functions they may 'drown'. With house plants, which are generally used to loose, light soil, rich in humus, it is vital for the root hairs to be able to develop in a light, moist medium with no danger of drowning or rotting.

It would of course be useful to know more about other aspects of plant life, but these are in outline the main points to keep in mind: a healthy root system; care of the epidermal tissues; the need for photosynthesis which supplies the plant with food and life itself; and the fact that in each species the basic needs will not alter appreciably, even when dealing with hybrids or cultivars (that is, cultivated varieties).

WHAT IS A HOUSE PLANT ?

Over the centuries, as man's way of life changed, his original straightforward need to obtain food, which had led to the development of agriculture, became a sophisticated intellectual and aesthetic wish to surround himself with greenery and flowers.

For many centuries the only way to do this was by bringing all too short-lived cut flowers indoors. Meanwhile, with more land available, gardens large and small flourished, and for all we know the humblest of these, now vanished, was just as great a source of joy to its users as the most lavish; aesthetics apart, that of course was what they were there for. As time went by explorers discovered new lands and new plants, plants which clearly did not have the same needs as those of the temperate zones. Familiar plants then, whether originally from Continental Europe, the Mediterranean region, Asia Minor or the Far East, all needed more light, air or space than they could possibly get in an enclosed setting like a house. Moreover many of them were deciduous, with bare, unattractive branches for many months of the year and often dull foliage. They could never compete with cut flowers which could in season be used for indoor decoration. However when the first tropical plants began to reach Europe houses were ill-equipped and too unevenly heated to receive them. They could only be grown in greenhouses and winter gardens which had developed from the orangeries long used for citrus plants during the winter in colder climates. But knowledge was still sketchy and for a long time exotic plants were automatically assumed to be hot-house plants.

Chinese plants, which would happily survive frost, were left to droop in winter temperatures suited only to plants from tropical America. Although it soon became clear that some plants did not take to this treatment and could live in unheated or poorly heated houses, such experiments were usually frustrated by inadequate light and ventilation. Palms and ferns suffered most, though many other plants perished with them. Every living species has had its own humble, little-known sufferings, and house plants are no exception. This situation continued more or less until the end of the Second World War, interrupted by periods when disappointment and scepticism led to the popularity of paper or fabric flowers and then modern horror plastic plants. Then central heating, better-lit modern houses with larger windows and increasing prosperity created a true understanding of what a house plant can and should be. In practical terms nowadays no household need be without ornamental plants. Even prosperity is not a decisive factor. In any house, small or large, old or new, that special corner of greenery depends entirely on the determination and expertise of the people who live there.

The idea that house plants are a hobby of the rich is quite mistaken. Of course people who work long hours and have a great many other worries may feel they could not give plants enough time and attention, but even in their case a well-chosen selection of just a few plants to start with will make things much easier. This careful initial choice is in any case indispensable if the number of unknown plant martyrs doomed to die through errors of judgement is to be kept to a minimum.

What exactly is a house plant? The reply is simple, but it may not sound very encouraging as it rules out many plants which people dream of owning. Strictly speaking a house plant is one which can live more or less permanently in a house with average light and temperature, maintaining its life cycle and growth and providing decoration. These three basic requirements — lastingness, the ability to survive and an ornamental appearance — rule out a great many plants. Above all, to live confined in a pot, the plants must have a limited root system and slow growth, combined with a fairly long life; to survive and grow they must adapt to whatever light, heat and humidity are available; finally to be decorative they need certain qualities – they must be evergreen and have an attractive shape, leaf arrangement or general appearance.

Basically this rules out all annual plants, flowering or not, and all plants which need a lot of air and light before they can flower, for example geraniums. All evergreen plants from temperate zones are excluded, not only because they need more light and air than they could possibly get, but also because their very extensive root systems call for excessively large containers. Also excluded are plants with a definite resting period like those which grow from bulbs, tubers or rhizomes and usually spend months in a state of apparently complete inactivity. It is not impossible to grow them indoors, but they usually have a vegetative period much longer than the time they are actually in flower while they build up their food reserves, and during this period they almost always have cumbersome and not particularly attractive leaves. Tropical varieties, for example many gesneriad tubers or rhizomes, can easily be made to put out shoots indoors but it is difficult to get them to flower if you have not got a greenhouse to provide the light and humidity they need.

Unless you can provide special conditions, for example a very well-lit terrace or balcony, you will have the same problem with all flowering herbaceous plants and shrubs, spontaneous or exotic. They hardly flower indoor at all with the exception of a few species which still need special care and in any case are attractive because of their shape or foliage as well. Understandably this often causes disappointment, as a beautiful coloured flower always has a more immediate impact than a stem's sculptural shape or a leaf's delicate texture. However we should remember that flowering is only one stage in a plant's life; indeed with ornamental plants which have rather inconspicuous flowers it is often vital to remove the flowers as soon as they appear so that the plant does not use up too much energy and suffer a general deterioration in health and appearance. Of course, there is no reason why you should not use flowering plants, bulbs and so on for short-term decoration, but unless you have a garden or balcony where many of them can be planted out for future use, you may as well regard them in much the same way as a bunch of cut flowers. In particular the type of flowering plants bought from florists, or given as gifts, are almost all forced in ideal greenhouse conditions and have reached their moment of glory; they may keep their looks for some time but they will never repeat or improve on them.

Succulent plants are another matter. They mostly come from very hot, sunny climates where they have a clearly defined resting period and they have adapted so that they develop defence mechanisms against drought, direct sunlight and changes in temperature. Without this rest period they will not flower and will grow new unprotected tissues which besides being unattractive can kill off the whole plant. You can keep many succulents in a cool well-lit place in winter, and move them if possible into direct sunlight during the summer, allowing them to make the transition gradually so that the sun does not scorch the delicate tissues before they develop their new protection. Few succulents, especially cacti, will flower successfully if their minimum winter temperature goes above 5–7 °C (41–45 °F).

To sum up: the plants generally classed as 'house plants' are tropical or subtropical in origin; they are most often herbaceous plants, with occasional shrubs; they are usually leafy evergreens; their needs as regards temperature, ventilation and humidity are wide-ranging (this is not true of light, however, but there is unlikely to be too much of that indoors anyway). Given these characteristics, you will almost certainly be able to find a house plant to suit any set of conditions.

PIONEERS OF LIFE

Life originated in the waters of the earth where the first primordial chlorophyll-bearing forms of life developed, the blue-green unicellular algae which many biologists believe go back more than three thousand million years. From these beginnings the vegetable kingdom continued its unbroken evolution for a period of roughly two thousand million years before animal life appeared. It should be explained here that the term 'evolution' does not mean that a form of life developed automatically into more evolved forms, as is often wrongly supposed; in fact more complex forms appeared, lived, reproduced and disappeared or eventually co-existed with existing organisms which either survived in a similar form to their ancestors for a certain period or underwent modifications and then became established. Fungi, lichens, mosses, Selaginella, ferns and conifers and some gymnosperms are examples of plants which survived the upheavals of successive geological eras to become what can now be described as 'living fossils'. Some of them are used as ornamental plants. Meanwhile, in the course of earth's cataclysmic existence over millions and millions of years (if it is not an over-simplification to use our unitary measure of time for such long periods), new plant species appeared, caught up in a process of specialization which then as now had a single purpose: the perpetuation of the species in time and therewith the means of reproduction. From scission they progressed to spores then to seeds,

Diatoms are very ancient unicellular algae which first appeared thousands of years ago and are still commonly found in water all over the world. These minute creatures (they rarely reach 1 mm in size) exist in vast quantities and are a basic component of plankton; this vital source of food for creatures which are then eaten by fish and other animals is the first link in the food chain.

Facing: Present-day forests only give an idea of the spectacular growth of primeval times, but many plants still have their original habit.

and finally from naked seeds to protected seeds — that supreme work of nature we call a flower — which made fertilization and the formation of new organisms easier.

What, you may ask, has all this got to do with house plants? Growing house plants is a very artificial process compared with other types of cultivation, since it is extremely difficult in these circumstances to reproduce the plants' natural conditions as is possible if, say, you have a greenhouse. If you are to succeed you must take care to choose plants whose needs you will be able to satisfy as far as possible. You should therefore take into consideration not only the plant's original habitat today, but often its past evolutionary history too. However developed plants may seem compared to primitive forms, certain genera and species still show some trace of their origins.

Let us therefore briefly consider what the earth must have been like in the Devonian period when ferns appeared, or at the beginning of the Carboniferous eras when they were the dominant form of vegetation. The distribution of dry land and seas was nothing like it is today. The atmosphere was dense and contained more carbon dioxide than now and there was almost constant cloud, giving a dim, misty light. Evaporation from the vast masses of water meant there was a high level of humidity. The soil layer must on the whole have been very shallow as rock erosion was in a relatively early stage. The great tree ferns of that period, some 300 million years ago, have long since turned into coal, but it is not hard to see the ancestry of the graceful smaller ferns which exist today. Few of them have adapted to living in sunlight, and those which have only do well when there is a high level of humidity in the air. Most of them prefer the shelter of woods, and damp, shady, but not waterlogged spots; often they even become epiphytes or 'air-plants'. Probably during those periods the enormous mass of vegetation was partly responsible for purifying the atmosphere and producing more oxygen which helped to make possible the development of new forms of life and the

Fungi and lichens first appeared in the earliest stages of life; many forms, some recently evolved, still survive.

The simple structure of the *Cycas* inflorescence is a reminder that these living fossils are among the oldest and least evolved of plants.

Facing : The appearance of flowering plants marks the advent of a clearer atmosphere, allowing the sun's rays to provide the necessary energy for flowers to open.

appearance of plants with seeds. Plants need a great deal of energy to produce seeds, and even more for the later flower-fruit-seed cycle; this energy could only be produced in the presence of clearer air with a higher oxygen content and therefore stronger light.

There were fishes but no mammals when the *Cycadaceae* first appeared, with their lofty crowns of leaves and their strobili. It is strange to think that cycads would be used to decorate terraces, halls and balconies in the twentieth century, and that the descendants of the conifers, then evolving towards their modern forms, would one day be stunted to produce dwarf 'bonsai'. Cycads and conifers still hate to be imprisoned in stuffy central-heated rooms, conditions which their now fossilized giant ancestors would also have refused to tolerate. Most flowers too need more light and air than they can possibly get indoors if they are to bloom and fulfil their function passing on life. When man appeared, about two and a half million years ago, the Angiosperms (or flowering plants) were already there. Today man has successfully modified and sometimes improved plant species, but he has never been able to make radical changes affecting the species' essential nature, their present needs as regards habitat or the effects of past millennia. Human intelligence unfortunately only has the power to destroy not just ecosystems, but the balance of life and its very foundations, producing by physical or chemical means horrifying mutations which we can only hope will stay in the laboratory and spare Nature.

WHERE HOUSE PLANTS ARE FROM

To satisfy our requirements most house plants, as has been said, come from what are now the tropical and subtropical zones. In these days of rapid travel many people have been to places situated in the belt between the Equator and the Tropic of Cancer to the north and the Tropic of Capricorn to the south. This area is the main source of house plants. Not everyone realizes, however, that over such a large area conditions vary considerably, not just from continent to continent, but because of a whole range of factors; very dissimilar ecosystems exist there side by side. The only common feature of the whole belt is the length of daylight in relation to the amount of darkness. At the Equator day and night each last twelve hours and there are twelve hours of light and twelve hours of darkness all the year round. Gradually, as one gets further away from the Equator, days and nights start to differ in length at different times of the year, the twilight hours are extended and the cycle of the seasons begins. We are used to thinking of the seasons in terms of temperature, and so many of us imagine that the equatorial belt is always unbearably hot: this is not in fact the case, height is the first consideration. Besides the world's major mountain systems, there are smaller (but not necessarily lower) ranges. For example, the mountains of New Guinea, lying between 0° and 5° latitude, include certain peaks higher than the Alps; in Guatemala the Tajumulco reaches a similar height, while in Costa Rica there are mountains of more than 3,000 m, to say nothing of the famous mountains of Kenya and Tanzania (Kilimanjaro) in Africa.

Obviously at higher altitudes the temperature is lower, and so in the equatorial zone there are plants which can not be grown in a warm temperate climate

Map of the principal biomes: 1. Arctic tundra; 2. Northern coniferous forest; 3. Northern deciduous forest; 4. Rainbelt and equatorial virgin forest; 5. Parklands; 6. Semi-desert, scrub etc.; 7. Steppes & prairie; 8. Savannah; 9. Mediterranean maquis; 10. Hot desert; 11. Cold desert; 12. Mountain biome.

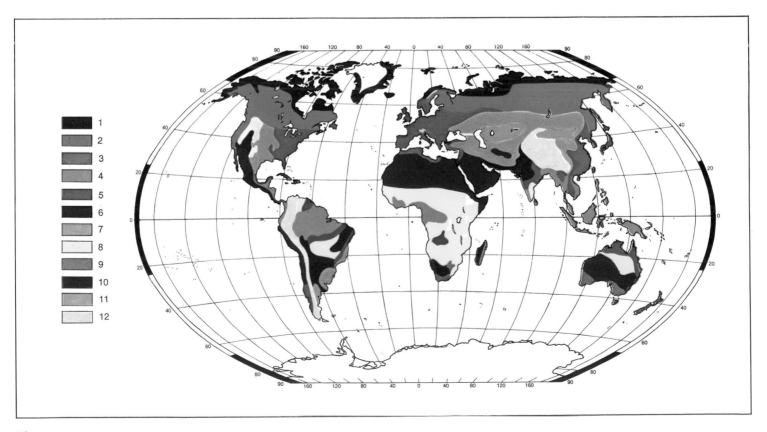

In the equatorial forest plants live together, competing for light which filters down through the foliage of the giant trees. Fantastic creepers struggle upwards; ferns and orchids grow on trees as epiphytes. *Platycerium* is an epiphytic fern.

because the summer is too hot. Then, mainly on the plateaux, there are regions with scanty rainfall, and practically no inland waters at all; here, far from the softening influence of the sea, there is a definite continental climate, with marked contrasts of temperature at different seasons. The seasons are not like ours, but are determined by the amount or lack of rainfall. In these places the vegetation can tolerate drought and is accustomed to remarkably long rest periods.

In a single country there may be various different formations or plant communities, and some familiarity with them will make it easier to understand a plant's needs, which remain the same even when it becomes a house plant. It is not much help if all you know about a plant is that it comes from Mexico, since plants native there include both the *Agave* of the sun-baked plateau and the delicate, velvety *Hoffmannia* from the steamy forests of the Chiapas region. Instead you must know something about the principal formations and the plants' different habitats so that you may compare them with the artificial environment which can be created for pot plants.

When the tropics are mentioned *rain forest*, or virgin forest, is the picture which usually springs to mind. It is unevenly distributed over the different countries and usually covers large areas, forming a belt which lies mainly on the Equator although, in America particularly, it sometimes extends several degrees north or

south. It is usually flat, or with only the occasional mountain. Above all it is hot and moist. The average temperature is normally between 25–30 °C (77–86 °F) with little variation between day and night or between seasons. Rainfall, amounting to over 2,000 mm a year, is evenly distributed and often occurs daily. Major rivers with an exceptional number of tributaries flow through the vast expanses of forest. In Africa in particular there is an enormous amount of inland water of all types – streams, lakes and pools. In Asia these areas are directly influenced by the sea's humidity as the forest there spreads over a number of islands and peninsulas both large and small. The vegetation is predominantly arborescent: gigantic trees with dense foliage form a more or less impenetrable barrier to light. Often little can grow on the ground because of the poor light, but a richly varied flora is constantly striving to reach the light's energy: lianas contort themselves into fantastic shapes to get their share, while epiphytic plants flourish wherever they can find a little humus, on tree trunks or between branches, developing special roots which can even draw nourishment from the humid air. In

Between the equatorial forest and dry formations like the savannah and the steppe the characteristic transitional formations are the tropical river forest where marshes or lagoons often form areas of aquatic forest known as mangrove swamps, or areas of brushwood merging into the vast expanses where rainfall is low and there are only a few sparsely scattered trees.

open spaces on the river banks and sunlit clearings, herbaceous plants grow, taking advantage of the welcome half shade and the moisture in the air. Rain forest is hardly an ideal source of house plants as their needs can usually only be met in hot, steamy greenhouses and by using special potting mixtures; they are very much collectors' items for gardeners who can create the special conditions which these delicate plants demand in greenhouses, enclosed verandas or balconies and terrariums. In any case it is often impossible to buy them. Fortunately the rain forest does not have clearly defined borders, but merges into two transitional formations.

Evergreen tropical forest surrounds the rain forest and sometimes occurs on higher ground within its borders. Here there is always a very high level of humidity, but lower rainfall. The minimum temperature varies between 10–20 °C (50–68 °F) which is not low enough to give the vegetation a real rest period, but which allows a spell of semi-rest according to the pattern of the periodic rainfall. This climate, similar to conditions in a moderately heated greenhouse, produces

Drought-loving plants of the pre-desert formation.

many plants which make good house plants provided that the air is kept humid enough for them. They also need a good light, but out of direct sunlight; in this type of forest the trees, though less dense than in virgin forest, only let diffuse light filter through. At the edge of this formation and where it reaches lower ground *deciduous tropical forest* occurs, often bordering on the savanna. Rainfall is only about 1,000 mm a year and occurs seasonally, with a dry period which generally falls between December and February, although there may be another shorter period at the beginning of summer. The temperature varies considerably between 5·8 °C (43 °F) and 28 °C (82·5 °F). Most of the herbaceous plants and shrubs which live there have some apogeous or hypogeous fleshy tissues which allow them to survive periods of drought, while still drawing on the humidity which, with lower temperatures, is still present in the air even when there is no rainfall. The soil is light and rich in humus since leaves are constantly falling from the trees and decompose quickly during the hot rainy season. These are the classic conditions found in a moderately heated greenhouse with good light, and fairly low maximum temperatures in winter and heat and filtered light in summer when the foliage provides protection against direct sunlight. Plants from this type of forest are suitable for rooms which get plenty of light and are not too hot in winter. Large windows and verandas are often ideal.

The *savanna* usually extends over plateaux. The normal vegetation consists of graminaceous plants (or grasses), interspersed with scattered drought-resisting trees or succulent arborescent plants. The climate is generally continental with less than 1,000 mm of rain a year, a dry season which may last as long as six months, temperatures which reach 32 °C (90 °F) and sometimes long periods with a minimum of 3 °C (37·5 °F). The largest areas of savanna are to be found in Africa, but it also occurs in Australia and South America.

The *steppe* is generally classed as the last distinct formation before the desert, but there are various gradations before real pre-desert conditions set in. Typically the steppe consists of extensive grasslands with xerophytic shrubs and plants; there is minimal rainfall and extreme temperatures, ranging from 3 °C (37·5 °F) to 40 °C (104 °F). The pre-desert areas which feature prominently in the Americas and in Africa are characterized by irregular, infreqent, but at times very heavy rainfall, giving a short-lived flora which springs up, blooms and dies startlingly quickly, producing seeds which remain germinant for long periods until rain falls again. Structurally, the steppe is far from uniform, ranging from extensive plains to weird rock labyrinths eroded by water or thrown up by seismic cataclysms. The heat is tremendous, but there are wide variations between day and night.

Next is the *maquis*, where rainfall is again sparse and occurs mainly in winter, while the summer is hot and dry. The vegetation consists mainly of plants with tough, long-lasting foliage, often aromatic. This formation is typical of the Mediterranean, though there are also examples in Australia, South Africa and on the coast of California.

Last of all comes the *desert*, of sand, rock or stone, where nothing grows except in the oases, in the special microclimates created there by the presence of water-bearing strata reaching surface. Desert plants are all suitable for cold greenhouses, and need high summer temperatures, full sunlight and a very marked resting period if they are to flower. They do not make particularly good house plants, although they will survive in a brightly lit, well-ventilated position with little or no heating. In milder European climates they can be grown outdoors, and some will even survive frost. They always need a spell in the open with more intense light during the summer.

Above: In dry regions succulents reaching tree-like proportions are a characteristic feature; the large candelabra *Euphorbia* are typical.

Below: The Mediterranean *maquis* flourishes beneath age-old pines; sometimes it is treeless scrub.

An example of classification. With the Linnaean system of classification a plant can be identified simply by its generic and specific names, in this case *Ceropegia woodii*.

Division: Spermatophytes

Sub-division: Angiosperms

Class: Dicotyledons

Sub-class: Gamopetales or Sympetales

Order: Contortae sympetalae

Family: Asclepiadaceae

Genus: Ceropegia

Species: woodii

PLANT NAMES

All over the world plants have common or popular names in each country, region or dialect. However all these names in different languages and different accents obviously do not make for easy understanding. In the ancient world, when a relatively small number of plants were known, the rather inefficient system of identification consisted of lengthy morphological descriptions, although by then Greek and Roman naturalists, notably Theophrastus and the Elder Pliny, already felt the need for some method of classification and made attempts to devise one. As geographical knowledge increased, it became clear that an exact system of identifying plants was becoming more and more necessary and that it was not possible to go on as before solely on the basis that the descriptions, although tiresome and vague, were in Latin, the accepted language of scholarship. Many botanists set out to subdivide the vegetable kingdom in various ways. In the sixteenth century Andrea Cesalpino tried to set up a system based on seed characteristics. He was followed by others, including the great Joseph Pitton de Tournefort, who attempted to establish different methods of classification. These men are called pre-Linnaean because they were precursors of the man who really invented plant taxonomy: the Swedish botanist Carl Ritter von Linne (1707–1778), or Linnaeus, to give the Latin form which he adopted as was customary then. After some initial writing, he published his main work, *Species Plantarum*, in 1753. Though far from perfect, this system, based on the structure of plants' reproductive parts, is still the basis of taxonomy today. It involves the brilliant and at that time novel classification of plants into *divisions*, *classes*, *orders*, *families*, *genera* and *species*, so that it is possible to make an exact identification of a plant by using just two names – the genus and the species. The system was therefore termed the binomial system.

Linnaeus's system has several times been rearranged, improved, expanded and adapted to fit Darwin's nineteenth-century theory of evolution, but the basic conception still stands, although some botanists would now like to see a new taxonomy based on modern knowledge of plant physiology and chemistry.

Generic names, which are often further subdivided as new facts are discovered, or survive solely as synonyms, consist mainly of a relatively small number of names already in use in ancient Greek and Roman times; sometimes modern names are coined from Greek and Latin terms or by latinizing the names of certain people or places; occasionally they are drawn from some other language. The species names are usually Latin adjectives describing features of the plant's appearance, form and colour; often they are fairly easy to understand. They are sometimes derived from personal or geographic names (which are used in the genitive case indicating possession) to honour an individual or to show where the plant comes from. A few familiar plants, both indigenous and naturalized, have kept, or nearly kept, their Latin names, e.g. viola, convolvulus, rose, used so commonly that we tend to forget their scientific origin. In other cases the meaning of scientific names in popular use has been so broadened as to include quite different genera. For example, the name *Pinus* has been popularized into pine and often applied indifferently to the genera *Pinus, Abies* (fir) and *Picea* (spruce).

With exotic plants like house plants, the problem is not one of information but of logic. For one thing, strictly speaking, the 'common name' should really be the name used in the plant's place of origin; yet it would be absurd to learn and remember imprecise foreign names, rather than the correct scientific names. For another thing, the result would be total confusion; as tends to happen everywhere with more familiar plants, everyone would have his own set of names and reasons for using them. Take *Ipomoea tricolor*, for instance, the Mexican species known in English as 'morning glory' because the flower opens only during the forenoon. The Italian name is *campanelle*, due to its bell-like shape, but that name is bestowed on common convolvulus as well; the Germans call it *Prunkwinde* because of its climbing habit, while in Mexico itself it is referred to as *manta*. Only by using the scientific name *Ipomoea tricolor* can we be sure what species of plant is meant.

Sometimes the common names are less attractive than those derived from Latin and Greek. The charming *Dianthus* becomes pink, carnation or picotee in English, *oeuillet* in French and *Nelke* in German. Accordingly Indians have every right to refer to *Lagerstroemia* as 'jarool', or the Polynesians to call the sweet potato *umara maohi*. It seems more sensible to keep the scientific names and learn at least some of them, apart from a few names now firmly entrenched in horticultural usage owing to some substitution of synonyms or other errors in the past. After all, it is doubtful whether it is much easier to remember *curuba* than *Passiflora mollissima*, while to call it 'long-tubed passion-flower' would be no more than an inaccurate pre-Linnaean circumlocution.

Ficus religiosa, known in India as the peepul tree, is held sacred by Buddhists because Buddha attained enlightenment while sleeping in its shade. The sunlight filtering through the enormous adventitious roots seems to illuminate this mystic faith.

THE TWENTIETH-CENTURY APPROACH:
from specimen to species

Primitive religion began logically with the natural forces which surrounded people and affected their lives for better or for worse. The sun, the moon, lightning and fire were all elements which could give or destroy life, and so, in most of the inhabited world, were plants. From earliest times each human settlement made a religious cult of one or more types of plants and often regarded as sacred an individual plant, usually a tree which for some reason – usually its age or imposing appearance – had a particular fascination: this in fact happens today in parts of the world where small groups of people still live very close to nature. As time passed this kind of animism evolved and plants, instead of being sacred objects themselves, were consecrated to spirits and gods as a kind of intermediary object of worship. For many centuries a *Ficus carica* (edible fig) known as the 'Ficus ruminalis' stood in the middle of the Roman Forum; it was believed that the she-wolf had suckled Romulus and Remus beneath it and when the tree died it was hastily replaced because its disappearance was thought to mean the end of Rome's good fortune. The Scythians and the Celts held mistletoe sacred from the earliest times. In Greek and Roman mythology nearly every divinity had a plant consecrated to him or her: the oak to Jove, the pine to Cybele, the olive to Minerva, the laurel to Apollo, the vine and the ivy to Bacchus, to name but a few. In India the *Ficus religiosa* is still sacred because it is believed that Siddhartha Gauthama was sleeping under a fig tree when truth was revealed to him and he attained 'bodhi' or Enlightenment and so became Buddha. These beliefs disappeared in monotheistic religions, yet for centuries people were fascinated by certain plants which were often in some confused way regarded as tutelary gods. Until comparatively recently there was a custom, especially in country places, of planting a tree when a baby was born, and such majestic trees as oaks or pines were treated with affection and respect.

Gradually a change of emphasis occurred as the large-scale cultivation of many plant species, especially house plants, became widespread. Nowadays people take a fancy to an entire plant species, not to an individual plant: if someone dear to you gives you a *Codiaeum* as a present, you will think of that person whenever you see a *Codiaeum* of the same kind, even if your original plant has died meanwhile. If you hear some good news while sitting comfortably near a *Dracaena deremensis* you will smile as your mind goes back to that moment each time you see one. No longer do you need a large garden to bring back memories of childhood: children nowadays may not be able to climb about on a *Philodendron* as they could on an oak, but without realizing it they will grow up with the plant and later will have sad or happy memories associated with it; the shape of its leaves will take the place of the oak's majestic trunk or striking branch formation. This is another reason for surrounding yourself with plants whenever possible. If a plant responds to care and attention and lives a long time to become a friend to you, so much the better. If not, try and replace it with a plant of the same sort. It is little things like this which create a world of greenery we can remember amidst the barren concrete of our cities.

In a simple setting *Ficus lyrata* and *Dieffenbachia* make an effective display.

Facing: Large windows provide a suitable setting for large plants; the pots are hidden in tall containers. The large leaves of *Ficus lyrata* contrast with the delicate segments of *Philodendron elegans* against the sky.

1 *Tetrastigma*
2 *Ficus lyrata*
3 *Dracaena fragrans*
4 *Philodendron elegans*
5 *Dieffenbachia amoena*
6 *Dieffenbachia 'roehrsii'*
7 *Philodendron erubescens*

PLANTS AND FLOWERS AS INTERIOR DECORATION

The living room garden

Conditions for growing plants indoors inevitably vary, not only according to the type of plants chosen but also because of all those individual features which give a house or flat its own special character. Geographical location, the age of the house, the way it faces, winter temperature, type of heating, size of rooms and the amount of light they get are all variables which make it impossible to lay down hard and fast rules; each case must be judged on its merits. Only general suggestions can be made and must be adapted to suit particular circumstances.

Light is the essential element for plants, and you may run into problems if your house is fitted not with sash windows but with casement windows opening inwards. These make it difficult to keep plants, as is often done, on a surface in front of the window where they can be given an airing when necessary. With inward-opening windows this ideal solution involves a fair amount of work building some kind of shelf arrangement, possibly collapsible, to take trays of plants; when you want to open the windows you move the whole tray, which is obviously far simpler than moving individual pots. If a room has more than one window, you may be able to sacrifice one and keep it permanently shut. You can create a very pleasant effect in this way with an ordinary or slightly longer window beside a French window leading to a terrace or balcony, a fairly common feature in modern houses and flats. In this situation there will be no need to open the

Below: various *Coleus* and *Dracaena* species.
It is even possible to build a greenhouse on a roof.

1 *Codiaeum*
2 *Dieffenbachia*
3 *Pilea repens*
4 *Cyathea arborea*
5 *Asparagus sprengeri*
6 *Hedera*
7 *Cyrtomium falcatum*
8 *Gynura sarmentosa*

A tropical garden can be created by glassing in
part of a balcony.
1 *Dizygotheca elegantissima*
2 *Tetrastigma voinerianum*
3 *Scindapsus aureus*
4 *Ficus elastica*
5 *Hibiscus rosa-sinensis*
6 *Codiaeum*
7 *Aphelandra squarrosa*

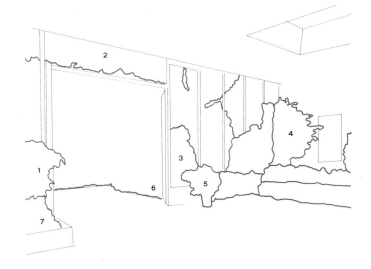

window and you can place trays or containers up against the glass where they will get the maximum light; you can also build the shelf or sill out into the room at right angles to form an 'L' so that the short arm of the 'L' also gets light from the French window; the corner by the window frame will get plenty of light and would be an ideal place for a climbing plant to flower or maintain its fine colouring. This kind of arrangement solves problems and has positive advantages.

One major problem which arises fairly often nowadays is that radiators are frequently fitted under windows to save wall space. If you leave a space for air to circulate between the radiator and the shelf the heat under the plants will not harm them and in fact if they are placed on damp gravel they will benefit from the slightly humid atmosphere which will be created. But if you place plants directly against the radiator you may kill them off, as the direct effect of the hot air will be to dry out the foliage. In these circumstances potted plants must be kept well away from the source of heat. A second problem is that of floor-length curtains. It is true that most house plants prefer indirect light to direct sun, and a light curtain across a south-facing window helps to protect them, especially during the hottest part of the day. However full-length curtains are usually made of heavier material and unless they are left open all the time they will shut out much vital light. If there is room for plants between the curtains and the window sill, a selection of suitable plants can be placed there, getting all the light they need and providing an attractive feature whenever the curtains are left open. The humidity which builds up near the glass panes, especially at night time, is very good for plants too. If you have double-glazed windows, this is the answer for all plants which like low temperatures in winter but cannot stand frost; flowering plants last much longer, and conditions are ideal for succulents which can enjoy plenty of light and a rest period to help them produce brilliant flowers.

Modern houses are usually better lit with more sensible window provision than

Light rooms and French windows provide plenty of light for variegated plants and give scope for pleasing combinations of form and colour.

in the past, but often there is not much free space except in the living room, so it will probably be there that you will wish to create your garden. Where possible, taking into account the points made above, the window sill is undoubtedly the ideal spot. If the sill is fairly low and the window a long picture-window a large plant holder running along all or most of its length can be used. This creates an effect very like a flower bed with a great many plants carefully arranged so that those needing more light are in front and those needing less towards the interior of the room. It is also advisable to put taller plants at the sides instead of scattering them all over the place which gives a rather confused overall effect rather than the desired sense of harmony, and in any case does not produce such good results, as the smaller plants are likely to be suffocated by the others. In this and similar arrangements you should always try to group the plants as close together as you can. Not only does this make them more attractive to look at, but it allows the leaves to transpire more freely, while evaporation from the earth in the pots remains more concentrated and will create a favourable microclimate. In some mysterious way plants placed near one another tend to thrive as if a mutually beneficial sympathy existed between them. However, this does not mean that you should plant them all together in a single large container. It is better to keep them in separate pots. For one thing, some plants, such as climbers, should never be moved because they always 'face' a certain direction, turning their leaves towards the light; this is their natural behaviour and moving them simply means that for a time the plant takes on an unattractively bedraggled appearance while it struggles back to its original position. Other plants however grow naturally straight, though some have a greater tendency to twist stem or leaves towards the source of light.

These should be turned from time to time to stop them leaning too much to one side. The idea that plants should never be moved is quite mistaken: their leaning towards the light depends entirely on the presence of certain hormonal substances called auxins in the growing tissues; these regulate growth and, as light reduces their concentration, the less well-lit side of the plant grows more rapidly and causes the stem to curve. Turning the plant round in the light allows the even distribution of auxins throughout its apical tissues to keep the plant reasonably upright. You should not forget either that one of the plants in your arrangement may develop some disease or die. It is then much easier to remove it or replace it in its own pot, without having to disturb the whole arrangement as you try to tease out the roots of that one plant from the tangled roots of all the others. Whatever type of container you use, the base must always be well drained with a good layer of stones, gravel and bricks so that the water which runs through does not lie in puddles round the pots. The question of drainage, which will be dealt with again in the section on growing techniques, is the first consideration in creating an indoor flower bed.

Often large plants need to stand alone to show off their shape to best effect, and a plant like this can become an effective design element complementing the room and its furnishings. This is particularly true of modern furniture which can often be simple in line to the point of starkness. Or you may have the kind of hall which is difficult to furnish and all too often remains half empty: here large plants with attractive leaves which like the low temperature to be expected there are an ideal way of softening the chilly impression the hall gives as you go into it. *Ficus elastica, Ficus lyrata, Philodendron selloum* and the very hardy *Howea* (also known as *Kentia*) are some well-known possibilities. Obviously plants used in this way should have plenty of foliage or else leaves which grow so that no part of the stem is left bare; climbing species like the popular *Scindapsus aureus* and *Philodendron scandens* which are also very hardy should preferably be placed against or near a wall rather than free-standing in an empty space; as they grow with all their leaves turning in one direction the rear view is fairly uninspiring.

An unusual and elegant decoration.

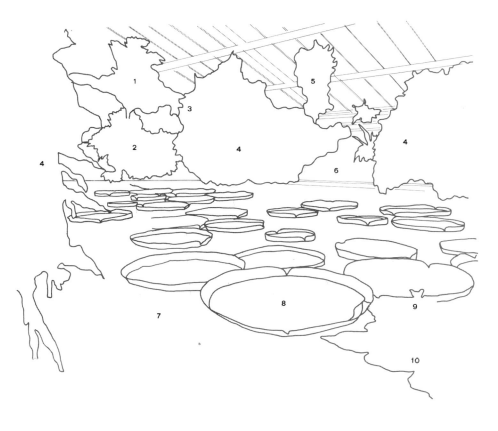

The greenhouses of botanic gardens where plants are grown on a large scale under glass may provide inspiration for the more restricted space of balcony or veranda. *Victoria amazonica* is hardly a house plant, but smaller plants can be grown and will flourish.

1 *Ptychosperma elegans*
2 *Codiaeum variegatum pictum*
3 *Platycerium willinckii*
4 *Acalypha hispida*
5 *Setcreasea pallida*
6 *Pandanus baptistii*
7 *Pistia stratiotes*
8 *Victoria amazonica*
9 *Eichhornia crassipes*
10 *Nymphaea hybr*

Special attention must be given to colour combinations when the plants are used in settings with fabrics, curtains and soft furnishings as well as wood. This might seem an obvious piece of advice, but though easy to remember when dealing with arrangements of cut flowers or flowering plants, it is often neglected when it comes to green plants. Yet there are countless different greens, and indeed house plants are often variegated with white or other colours from all shades of red to silver and brown. If the foliage is all green or variegated with white, plants should be chosen for their colour tone or general shape and they should contrast with rather than emphasize the dominant tints of the other furnishings.

Sansevieria and *Ficus* for example, both being very stiff, upright plants, one or other of them can be used, especially combined with other more delicately-leaved plants, to set off the low and emphatically horizontal lines of much modern furniture. However the two together would be too much, and the effect would be lost. Both have tough leaves, which in *Ficus* are very dark in colour and in *Sansevieria* dark with broad bands of white, or sometimes variegated with bright colours. Each in its own way goes well with pale-coloured furniture and walls, though they look gloomy in a room with blue or dark green wallpaper. If the walls are dark the way to brighten the room is by creating splashes of colour with bright, colourful plants, duly taking into account the available light and heat of course. If the room is dark and poorly heated it is absolutely no use trying to decorate it with a *Codiaeum* which would never survive. In fact if you are concerned with both results and expense, it may sometimes be more satisfactory to use seasonal flowering plants, even if they do have to be thrown out and replaced periodically, and combine them with hardier green plants rather than buying expensive greenhouse plants which will inevitably die in the wrong conditions. When there is adequate light, however, you can use beautiful plants of many colours. For the best effects place them so that they stand out well against a dark or neutral ground. If they are put against strong colours or designs their beautiful leaves and subtle colouring cannot be fully appreciated. This is true of, for example, *Ficus elastica variegata* and many kinds of *Begonia*.

Nowadays a good number of houses have glass-covered sunrooms which can be used as conservatories to produce quantities of marvellous flowers without too much difficulty. If you are lucky enough to have one you could use it as a greenhouse – putting in emergency heating for winter if required – but a better use is to house in it all plants requiring plenty of light and minimum temperatures of about 10 °C (50 °F) which are too low for inside the house itself. Such places are generally more humid too because of the condensation of water vapour on the panes of glass; if the floor is paved with ceramic tiles or some other water-resistant material the humidity can easily be increased still more by frequent sprinkling and spraying.

Modern flats often have a type of semi-enclosed balcony, flush with the outer wall of the building. These balconies are not much use for traditional open-air plants as they are generally not light and airy enough. However it is quite easy and inexpensive to convert them with sliding windows along the outside edge to create an intermediate climate ideal for a great many plants. Although, unlike greenhouses, they are not lit from above, you can grow climbers along the sides and green and variegated plants of different sizes near the windows; you may even get some of them to flower. A further advantage is that as the balcony does not project, its outer edge is over the house foundations and it will be able to bear the weight of fairly large pots and tubs for plants such as *Strelitzia, Passiflora* or *Lantana* which need plenty of space to develop a good root system. Then when you open the French windows onto your balcony, you will create the effect of a garden inside your house.

Flowering plants

All higher plants have flowers of some description. However, usually the term 'flowering plants' is used to mean ornamental pot-plants with showy blooms grown for gardens, patios and terraces and, less often, for indoor display. Hundreds of thousands of these plants are grown every year all over the world. They may be annuals or perennials, and they may either be forced or be left to follow their natural cycle. Although they make charming and popular presents for Christmas, birthdays or other special occasions, their life as ornamental house plants is often all too short. Even in ideal conditions, flowering is only a passing phase and although the right treatment can make flowers last longer they have to die eventually. Moreover as plants are sold when they are at their best, their decorative splendour can then only fade. Usually they have already undergone a series of sudden changes, from the nursery or greenhouse to the florist's shop

The many hybrids of *Cyclamen persicum* are popular ornamental plants for the winter. They will survive and flower again if given cool temperatures and the necessary rest period.

before being shut up in an indoor room, and all this will certainly affect them. Some of these plants are annuals grown from seed each year, which can simply be thrown away once they have finished flowering. Others are perennials which are treated as annuals or biennials because the young plants are more attractive, a better shape, or produce more and better blooms. Others are genuine perennials which you can easily keep for the next year if you have a garden, patio or terrace, and enough patience to help them survive and flower again. With a few exceptions it is practically impossible to make them continue their cycle and flower again indoors, and in any case most of them are not particularly attractive apart from their flowers or fruit and their looks will most likely be spoiled too by the ruthless pruning which must be done. Flowering plants which appear in winter generally find central heating temperatures too high and in a stuffy

Gaily-coloured *Primula obconica* should be treated as an annual and used to provide a temporary
splash of indoor colour.

atmosphere they may quickly die. They also usually need plenty of light. Florist's
cyclamen (*Cyclamen persicum*) would last far longer than it normally does if it
could be kept at a maximum temperature of 13–15 °C (55–59 °F), and the same
applies to primulas and azaleas. Some of the most popular and attractive, if short-
lived, flowering house plants are described below.

Azaleas belong to the *Rhododendron* genus. There are many cultivated
varieties and hybrids, especially those belonging to the *Rhododendron simsii*
species known to gardeners as *Azalea indica*. They need a temperature between
10–16 °C, very good light (away from direct sunlight), frequent watering and a
fairly moist atmosphere. If the air is too dry, leaves and flowers may drop. After
flowering azaleas can often be put outdoors in semi-shade for the summer, when
there is no further risk of frost. They should then be brought back to a well-lit
position with a temperature of about 10 °C (50 °F) and eventually repotted in a

Calceolaria (*below*) is an annual with strangely-shaped, attractive flowers which last just one season. *Hydrangea* hybrids will last many years, especially in a damp climate, if properly tended.

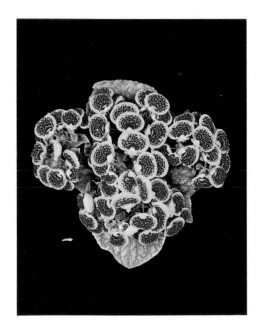

lime-free mixture of sphagnum peat or ericaceous mixture. Often the plant will not flower the year after it has been forced but later the following year. A few cold spring days encourage flowering by stimulating the dormant buds formed during a mild winter. If then taken indoors and kept in a mild place with plenty of light the plant will flower more profusely.

Cyclamen, horticultural hybrids of *Cyclamen persicum*, droop alarmingly quickly once the temperature rises above 16 °C (61 °F) but they thrive at temperatures a few degrees below that, so long as they have plenty of light and humidity. A healthy cyclamen plant in a house should be cause for concern for visitors who are sensitive to cold. Cyclamens need only moderate watering, as over-watering, far from encouraging more flowers, simply causes rotting. Water from below or plunge the whole pot into water so that the corm itself does not get too wet. After flowering, when the leaves die down, the corm should be left

The fine, tuberous-rooted plant *Sinningia speciosa*, commonly known as *Gloxinia*, usually needs greenhouse conditions in order to flower; it likes a very humid atmosphere.

Facing: Solanum capsicastrum is an attractive little shrub when grown as a pot plant. In a mild climate it can be grown in open ground and will reach a large size.

completely dry in its pot in a cool shaded position. In August or September remove it from the old mixture and repot it in a peaty potting mixture with plenty of sand. Water sparingly by plunging the pot into water. In a cool, light position plants may flower again, although they will not make such a fine display as when grown from seed in greenhouse conditions.

Poinsettias (*Euphorbia pulcherrima*) have reappeared in florists in recent years after various attempts at hybridization and grafting to produce low, compact varieties suitable for house plants, instead of the taller varieties which are better as cut flowers, and cannot tolerate dry, poorly-lit house interiors. In 1964 the hybrid 'Mikkelsen' was produced with the help of 'dwarfing' hormones. These compact plants are much more able to tolerate hot dry conditions within reason. Their handsome red bracts surrounding the tiny, insignificant yellow flowers may last two or three months in a light position, provided they are not overwatered, almost until the new leaf shoots start to appear. However it is not easy to get the plants to flower again unless they can be kept in total darkness for at least twelve to fourteen hours a day in October and November. Even the slightest ray of reflected light can prevent their flowering. In spring the plant should be cut right down, repotted in equal parts of leaf mould, manure and peat with a little sand and then left out for the summer in semi-shade or a well-lit, airy position. Bring them indoors again in the autumn and if they get the necessary hours of darkness each day they may flower again.

Primulas like cool, damp climates. The attractive *Primula x polyantha*, which comes in a wide range of colours, makes a good garden plant if grown in a cool, moist spot, sheltered from frosts. *Primula obconica* is more hardy and commoner as a pot plant. It likes frequent watering and plenty of light, but it is no use thinking you can keep it to flower another year. Touching its leaves is said to cause allergies, but this can only apply to a few sensitive-skinned people, otherwise the plant would not be so popular.

Cinerarias (*Senecio cruentus*), available in all kinds of colours, also need fresh air and plenty of water, but they should be thrown away once they have flowered. This is also true of the strangely-shaped *Calceolaria* which are treated as annuals.

The various types and hybrids of *Hydrangea* like a damp, cool position, especially when they have been forced into early bloom, and plenty of frequent watering. Once past their best you can save them by drastic pruning, and repotting in very acid soil, e.g. ericaceous mixture of sphagnum peat; place the pot in a shaded spot out in the open. It is difficult to make hydrangeas flower again indoors and even outdoors they will never have such fine blooms again.

Gloxinia (or *Sinningia speciosa*) is another flowering plant which may disappoint you if you are hoping to make it flower again after the tuber has had a rest period, like cyclamen. This Brazilian plant likes warm temperatures, and modern hybrids have been selected to produce near perfect colours and shapes, but unfortunately it likes so much humidity that it really needs to be grown inside a greenhouse or its equivalent. For a low compact shape the plant needs to be well lit from above, with diffused light to stop the stem growing crooked. If you have room, this is a good plant to grow under artificial light in a glass plant case: at the end of winter place the tubers in a very peaty mixture with the middle bud just showing above the surface, water moderately to avoid rotting and you will find that the plants soon put out shoots and may even flower successfully.

In autumn you can often buy plants which make a colourful show with little red fruit instead of flowers. *Solanum capsicastrum* is a perennial shrub which stays small for some time if kept in a pot. It has sharp-edged tapering dark-green leaves, small white flowers in summer, followed by little round orange berries about the size of a cherry. The plants need a very light airy position. They can be left out in the open during the summer, which also allows the little flowers to be

pollinated. Medium temperatures help the berries to last a long time, but hot dry surroundings encourage pests and make leaves and fruit wither. There are several varieties of *Capsicum annuum* (also known as Christmas pepper). This is an annual which can easily be grown from seed, although it is then more difficult to give it the air, light and humidity needed if its little flowers are to be followed by fruit. These little fruits may be round or shaped like a chilli; colours vary from yellow to purple and red. This is another plant which dislikes excessive heat but needs good light and frequent watering. It makes an attractive decoration which is best bought when the berries are already formed and afterwards thrown away.

It is practically impossible to grow flowering bulbs in a flat, because of the conditions needed in the early stages before the flowers make their rather brief appearance. Hyacinth, narcissus and tulip bulbs must be put into pots and then

Capsicum annuum, as the name suggests, is an annual with small, ornamental round or chilli-shaped fruit. It is easily reared from seed and likes cool conditions to keep its attractive appearance.

left for a time in a damp cool place in the dark so that they can develop a good root system and produce flower-bearing shoots before being moved to a cool, well-lit position. Obviously you can only do this if you have a garden where the pots can be buried or a cool, dark cellar; the average town house or flat may not have such facilities. Without this preparatory stage the bulbs will produce leaves but not flowers. However the hybrid *Hippeastrum* (often known as *Hippeastrum amaryllis*) will tolerate light from the start and will flower indoors with no difficulty. It is more difficult however to keep the bulb in good condition between flowering and its rest period, when the plant has long, untidy leaves and needs nourishment in order to build up new reserves. It is not particularly attractive at this stage and should be kept out of the way in a light, cool position. These problems do not arise with hyacinth or narcissus bulbs specially prepared to

Commonly known as *Hippeastrum amaryllis*, *Hippeastrum vittatum hybridum* readily produces striking blooms when grown indoors and will flower again for many years if well treated.

flower over containers or bulb glasses filled with water instead of bulb fibre: they are so exhausted by producing their handsome blooms that they do not often flower again, even if planted out in the garden, and they have to be thrown away.

Clivia miniata is one of the hardiest flowering bulbs and it has fairly attractive

Right: Hyacinths forced into flower for indoor use, in bulb fibre or water, make a fine display for a short period, but if the bulb's food supplies are allowed to become exhausted the plant must be thrown away.

Below: Clivia miniata is an old-established favourite among flowering plants; a hardy evergreen, it will thrive and flower at low temperatures.

evergreen foliage even when there are no flowers. It is particularly suitable for cool terraces and balconies. This is another plant which needs a rest period in late autumn and winter, in a cool place without any watering, which will be rewarded in spring by the plant's handsome orange flowers.

From this brief account of flowering plants and their needs it is clear that they do not make good permanent ornamental plants. However, with a few exceptions, they are often the least expensive plants to buy, especially if they have been left to flower normally without forcing. It is a good idea to combine one or two flowering plants with the green house plants which are the basis of your indoor garden. Carefully arranged, with well-chosen tints, you can create a gay splash of colour to set off the green foliage and brighten your house. If you have a balcony you should choose plants that will not die when exposed.

FLOWER ARRANGEMENT

Free composition

The art of flower arrangement is not particularly old. In ancient times people may have picked flowers and branches and then placed them in vases, perhaps one of those fine Greek or Etruscan vases which are now seen in museums, but there is no firm evidence that this was a widespread practice. The Greeks and Romans wove crowns and garlands, which they wore on the head or used for decoration or religious purposes, as was also customary in the East.

Modern Polynesians still have their *lei*. But there is more to the art of flower arrangement than weaving garlands. Or even than those beautiful single lilies standing in a vase in the corner which start to feature several centuries later in paintings of the Annunciation. The fact that they were there shows the continuing importance of flowers in art, but not until about 1500 do we find planned flower 'compositions' in both East and West. Since the materials used are by their very nature so ephemeral, we have to rely on paintings for evidence about how and when cut flowers were used in interior decoration. At about that time a wealth of flower paintings suddenly appeared, which are an important source of information. During the same period the influence of distant lands newly explored and new plants recently discovered began to be felt. One can safely say that if Ogier Giselin de Busbecq, ambassador of the Holy Roman Empire at the Turkish court, had not introduced tulips into Europe from Turkey sometime in the mid sixteenth century, many sumptuous and beautiful Flemish still life paintings would never have existed. Scented jasmine was brought to England by John Tradescant who had gone to fight pirates in the Mediterranean. About a hundred years later the camellia arrived, by mistake, it is said, in place of the similar tea plant. Plants began to be transported from one place to another, a process which has gone on ever since. Even today air transport makes it possible for exotic and previously unknown kinds of flowers to go on sale in peak condition.

The traditional bouquet, as new species have appeared and under influence of the East, has gradually given way to richly imaginative arrangements in a variety of styles. Although there are certain guidelines, these are not based on fixed philosophical interpretations like Japanese Ikebana and do not have to observe the set formal requirements of the past; these arrangements are in what is now known as free composition. Some of the rules now followed are pure commonsense. To give a few examples: a dinner-table arrangement should be low and horizontal, as a tall bunch of flowers would obviously get in the guests' way. Similarly the vase or receptacle used should always be a good match for the flowers as regards form, colour and the rarity of the flowers used, as well as the size of the arrangement. A vase which looks fragile (even if it isn't) should not be used for massive-looking flowers like large chrysanthemums or dahlias. Fragile and delicate flowers like lily of the valley look lost in patterned vases which should in any case be avoided as far as possible except for large formal arrangements. A sophisticated flower like an orchid never looks right in a rough pottery vase.

There are other rules concerning how and where the arrangement is to be used and its basic shape or line – horizontal and circular or elliptical, depending on the length of the stems and how they are arranged; or vertical i.e. linear, oval or conical; or irregular, with a more or less diagonal flow. Obviously the best position for an arrangement in a room depends on its basic shape. It is no good putting a round arrangement against a wall: it should stand free where it can be admired in the round. A tall, slender upright arrangement needs to stand on a fairly large base otherwise it will look unstable. Apart from these minor rules, which should come naturally anyway, everything else in free composition depends on the arranger's inspiration and resources. The resources available will depend on a number of factors. If you live in a town you can more easily obtain rare or out-of-season flowers from large florists, whereas if you live in or near the country or have a garden you will be more dependent on the seasons, but you will be able to get branches, decorative foliage, berries and other materials which are hardly ever available in towns. Greenery is a particular problem for the average town-dweller.

Although interior designers always seem to know where to get hold of some, florists do not usually like to stock ornamental leaves. Whenever you go for a country outing you would do well to get in a supply for future needs, at least of ivy branches which are very long-lasting and may even develop roots in clean water.

There are various ways of anchoring flowers in their vase, from the familiar pinholders (or kenzans) to little metal grids. Various absorbent plastic substances into which stalks can be inserted are increasingly popular: Oasis is the best known brand name. This method is ideal for florists as it means they can move vases without spilling any water, and it is vital when there is no other way of getting moisture to part of the arrangement. Its disadvantage is that the flowers do not stay fresh as long. You also have to take care that the Oasis does not dry out, as it is then almost impossible to moisten it again without it crumbling. If you are using a large enough piece of Oasis you can get little glass or plastic cone tubes with a stopper which prevents evaporation but has a hole large enough for the stem to pass through: these are filled with water and fitted over the bottom of the stems which are thus hidden but get more moisture than when Oasis alone is used. These and other accessories can be obtained from florists' sundriesmen. For all vases containing long-stemmed flowers and branches which often will not stand up properly you can use pieces of zinc or plastic-covered mesh wire netting cut to the right shape and size, slightly larger than the top of the vase so that it fits in snugly and the meshes hold the stems in position. If the vase is on the large side another piece of netting may have to be pushed in in the same way near the bottom. Glass marbles can be used to hold flowers upright in a glass vase. Holding the stalks in the correct position with one hand, gently slide in the marbles without disturbing the arrangement and add the water last. It is a good idea to build up a small collection of attractive stones, smooth shiny pebbles and large clean, regular-shaped pieces of gravel, making the most of each visit to the sea or country. These will come in useful for hiding pinholders, balancing them if they are unstable or weighting light vases if they are being used for long flowers or branches which might topple over.

Before starting your composition cut the flowers to the right length, trim the ends, plunge them into a bucket or bowl of water right up to the head if possible and leave them to have a good soak for a couple of hours. Woody stems should be stripped of a couple of inches of bark so that water can get to the internal tissues. If the stems are secreting latex they should be dipped in hot water to seal them. Hollow stems should be trimmed under water so that air bubbles cannot form and prevent water being absorbed. With flowers grown from bulbs the white part below the real stem must be completely cut away or the flowers will not be able to drink at all. Remove thorns from rose stems. After the flowers have had a good soaking you can start your composition, cutting the flowers again to the required length as necessary, but taking the same precautions. If you do this you will not have the problem of changing the water every day; you can simply top up with fresh water as necessary. You must take care that there are no leaves or other parts which might rot under the water. You need only remove the flowers to trim the ends when they start drooping. Some flowers, for example roses or poinsettias, will revive if the stem is trimmed and the whole flower then dipped for a moment into near-boiling water and then plunged straight into fresh water and left for at least an hour. When the central heating is working it is a good idea, if you can

Below: The contrasting shapes of roses and lilies make a delicate composition.

A country-style table arrangement for an informal supper. Insert the flower stalks into artificial moss which also supports the artichoke and other elements.

Facing, above: A classic, triangular-based arrangement which looks best on a long surface, forming an effective contrast with the wallpaper. Place some wire netting or a metal grid in the neck of the vase and arrange the flowers, starting from the focal point at the centre of the vase.

Facing, below: A vertical arrangement for a modern setting.

easily move the flowers, to take them into the bathroom or kitchen at least once a day and spray them lightly all over with water at room temperature. This will make both petals and leaves perk up and will prolong the arrangement's life and your enjoyment of it.

Ikebana

The Japanese art of flower arrangement now known universally as Ikebana is in fact Chinese in origin and was introduced into Japan, in about the seventh century BC, along with Buddhism and ideograms. It was only during the eleventh century that large and highly symbolic floral offerings first appeared in Japan's temples, known as *rikka* or *rikkua* from the Chinese. These huge flower arrangements obviously had no practical use and it was not until much later that smaller-scale arrangements became common both as decoration and for philosophical and contemplative ends with the emergence of that special art form known as ikebana. This is usually roughly translated in the West as 'living flowers' but in fact it means something rather different, as the general aim is to give cut flowers, or plants, new life according to set principles of arrangement. The basic

concept is the arrangement of three main stems of different lengths set at different angles which symbolize respectively Heaven (the longest and most upright), Earth (the shortest, set almost horizontally) and in the centre Man (somewhere between the two as regards height and angle). The three stems must always meet at the base and wavy as well as straight lines may be used to suggest the angle. This arrangement was scrupulously adhered to by the oldest and perhaps most important school, the Ikenobo school, but it has been abandoned by some of the freer, modern schools. Different interpretations have given rise to a great many different rules, all equally binding in their own sphere. These govern such considerations as the angle of flowers or branches, their total number, the position of flowers or buds on a branch in relation to the active male or passive female principle, so that the flower symbolizing woman must be on the lower part of the branch and at least partly hidden by a leaf. Among the many schools which exist today, the two principal ones have given their names to different styles of composition. The Nageire school's main characteristic is that it only uses tall slender vases; the Moribana school only uses low bowls and the flowers are usually arranged to form an imaginary scalene triangle drawn on the kenzan. This

Above: Chabana. The style developed as part of the tea ceremony to express an essential image of perfect beauty. An arrangement of red camellias.

Right: Seika. A classic style with very precise rules. In this Ikebana the search for beauty is expressed in harmoniously balanced elements and pure lines. An arrangement of *Cydonia japonica* branches.
(Arrangement by Mrs Keiko Ando Mei.)

Left: Moribana. Moribana arrangements always convey an immediate sense of the seasons and nature. This Ikebana, composed of blue irises, recreates all the freshness of a landscape with water.

Right: Nageire. In this style the arranger can express his or her personality more freely within the traditional rules. This arrangement of *Malus* branches, tulips and narcissi is a joyful image of spring.
(Arrangements by Mrs Keiko Ando Mei.)

obligatory arrangement may be combined with additional elements which are also governed by set rules. The length of the stems is particularly important as the longest should measure the vase's diameter plus its depth, and the others are in given proportions to this first measurement. The Nageire tall-vase arrangements do not use a kenzan, but a variety of different fixing methods which are often quite difficult. There are basically three classic styles: upright, slanting and cascading. The combination of three main stems is not always used and sometimes the composition is completely abstract. When the three stems are used they are remarkably long, as the longest of them can sometimes be more than twice the height of the vase, with the others again in a set relation to it as regards both height and angle. Genuine ikebana, as opposed simply to free-style composition based on some of its ideas, is a difficult art, almost incomprehensible to the Western mind and its sense of what is beautiful, particularly in the case of abstract compositions which for us may not have an obvious aesthetic appeal.

Dried arrangements and other materials

Dried flowers are by no means a modern invention and were in fact very popular during the nineteenth century. Arrangements which consist solely of dried or preserved flowers and leaves can be rather dull, particularly if instead of including brightly coloured flowers like *Heliychrysum*, only pale or, worse still, artificially dyed flowers are used. The result will look much the same as a bunch of artificial flowers and can easily become dingy with dust and hard to clean. For dried arrangements you can either buy bunches of flowers ready dried or dry them yourself in a number of ways. The simplest is to hang the cut flowers up by their stems in a shaded, airy place, the ideal method for many types of grass including the lovely, delicate *Briza* and for many *Compositae*. Other flowers can be dried

This page and facing: Arrangements of dried flowers and other plant materials follow the usual rules of free-style arrangement: they may be classic in style or more informal.

with borax, while sturdier foliage should have the stem ends dipped in a mixture of glycerine and water. Dried flower arrangements should follow the basic free-style principles as regards form and the use of colour. However more interesting effects can be achieved by combining dried materials with fresh flowers. The light silvery pods of honesty (*Lunaria*) can be used to set off brilliantly coloured flowers like roses, carnations or dahlias or it can be combined with pastel shades to create a delicate symphony of colour; stiff *Typha* goes well with slender irises; feathery *Cortaderia* can be used as a background for expensive camellias or wild flowers creating two quite different effects. You can also use parts of plants which are naturally dry and do not need special treatment — branches, twisted roots, moss-covered logs or pine cones. If using pine cones, which are open when dry,

make sure you do not get the base or scales wet or you may unexpectedly find them partly or completely closed. Then again you can use rocks and stones of various shapes, and even shells and fruit.

Fruit and some kinds of vegetables combined with flowers and branches make a very attractive arrangement, although a few problems may arise. The display will be a considerable size so you may have difficulty finding a suitable container. Then as the fruit may be fairly heavy you must make sure that it is well secured. Fruit in a variety of colours and shapes arranged on a flat base, perhaps with some vegetables or greenery, makes a particularly attractive table decoration. If the table is stripped pine or a similar style you can create a pleasant, homely effect by using a low basket as no water is needed. If you want to include flowers, use a small container hidden under bunches of grapes or trailing ivy so that the flower stems are in water without the fruit getting wet. It is best to avoid very ripe fruit which will soon be past its best in a warm place and which may give off fumes harmful to the flowers, especially if apples are included. Harvest-festival-type arrangements of vegetables have a fine country look, though obviously you should keep strong-smelling onions and garlic for outdoor meals. As the most handsome and brightly coloured vegetables — tomatoes, aubergines, peppers — are summer produce, they can be used as an ornamental addition to those warm *al fresco* evenings: you can even sprinkle a little parsley from your table decoration over your charcoal-grilled steak.

TERRARIUMS, MINIATURE GARDENS AND BONSAI

Terrariums should not be confused with vivariums. A vivarium is the opposite of an aquarium: while an aquarium recreates the conditions of aquatic life, a vivarium reproduces part of a land environment in a suitable, enclosed setting with all the proper geological features, fauna and flora. Zoos and some keen private individuals may keep vivariums for the purposes of study and information: the aim is to observe the life and habits of animals which are too small or too dangerous to be kept any other way. A vivarium may contain insects, small amphibians, tortoises, reptiles, small rodents and even small birds. To study them in conditions similar to their natural habitat the correct light, ventilation, temperature and humidity must be provided, in the same way as a well-kept aquarium should supply as far as possible a biologically balanced environment. Vivariums can thus reproduce desert, rocky or marsh conditions. Naturally they are not very common because of the problems of size and maintenance: the base must be at least one metre by two and the height depends on the habits of the animals inside. A glass case is generally used with close mesh netting over the top or sliding glass panels with air vents if a humid atmosphere is required. To create a vivarium is a specialist job, and in the average flat or house light is an insuperable problem. While fish and aquatic plants only need a fairly small amount, which can usually be supplied adequately by fluorescent strips, animals and land plants need much more light and even direct sunlight; artificial lighting can only be subsidiary. Moreover overhead lighting is necessary to prevent the plants leaning too much in one direction and to stop one side of the case overheating. All these considerations make it difficult to find the right place for a vivarium.

A terrarium, on the other hand, is a collection of plants, usually tropical and moisture-loving, attractively arranged in a transparent container which forms an enclosed or almost enclosed environment. With little or no ventilation, a moisture-laden atmosphere is created as the leaves transpire and the potting mixture dries out: this vapour condenses and is returned to the soil to complete the cycle. The system dates from 1838 when a London doctor and natural

A terrarium in a glass bowl. Choose plants which do not grow very tall and have a fairly small root system, such as *Cryptanthus bromelioides tricolor*.

scientist, Nathaniel B. Ward, observed that seeds present in the soil in a hermetically sealed container, in which he had buried a chrysalis he wished to study, germinated and grew vigorously. Further experiments showed that a great many plants, especially tropical plants, could live for long periods in sealed containers provided these were transparent and let in the light necessary for photosynthesis. These containers, known as 'wardian' cases after their inventor, proved enormously useful for transporting tropical plants which would previously have died because of the lack of light and the salty air during long sea voyages, and which had to be transported in large quantities to allow for the heavy losses. The mutiny on the *Bounty* was in fact caused by a revolt of the crew against Captain Bligh and the intolerable conditions which were created when he overloaded the ship with bread-fruit trees (*Artocarpus incisa*) to be transplanted to the West Indies. Wardian cases helped tea to become a cultivated crop in India and made quinine and banana plantations possible in all tropical countries. Gradually this useful device for transporting plants became a fashion. Small and elaborately designed sealed glass cases appeared in Victorian drawing-rooms, usually containing ferns which like plenty of humidity and needed to be protected against the fluctuating temperatures of houses then. Central heating marked the end of the vogue. In well-heated houses the amount of transpiration and evaporation inside wardian cases meant that the glass panes were always steamed up so that the plants could not be seen and light could not get in; moreover in these conditions the plants tended to rot and be attacked by fungi.

The first variation on the theme appeared in England and America with the creation of gardens in bottles, using large ten-gallon jars and carboys designed for different purposes. Some ventilation was possible if required by removing the stopper. Potting mixture to cover the base was poured in through a funnel and plants were inserted with small long-handled tools such as tweezers or miniature hoes. This demanded some patience but once the plants were in position they needed little further attention and had enough room to grow and spread. The main snag was that with round containers the curved glass distorted the image. Bottle gardens never really caught on except in England and America and they are not particularly common nowadays, as plastic containers have on the whole replaced glass jars which are now hard to find. The containers now used tend to be far smaller so the display is not usually very long-lasting as the plants do not have room to grow; they tend to grow crooked because they hardly ever have overhead lighting, and they grow faster because of the humidity. However if you are interested in creating a garden in a bottle, this is the procedure. The soil used must be completely sterile so it is best to use a specially prepared commercial potting mixture. First put in a drainage layer of gravel, then the potting mixture. If the container has too narrow a neck for you to get your hand inside pour the gravel and potting mixture in through a stiff cardboard tube. Choose moisture-loving, slow-growing plants and use small cuttings which have already formed roots. Remove them from their pots and wash the roots so that the old soil cannot contaminate the fresh potting mixture. Make small holes in the earth with your hand or small tools if the bottle neck is too narrow and place a plant in each, spreading out the roots well and pressing the soil lightly over them. Taller plants should be positioned in the centre. After planting spray lightly with water. All you have to do then is check for mildew and give an occasional light watering, about once a month if the container has a lid. Remove the lid from time to time and take it off altogether if there are any signs of disease.

You might get more enjoyment from creating a miniature garden in a glass tank similar to a fish tank with a sliding top or side, and possibly additional fluorescent lighting above to help the plants grow upright. This type of container is often used for orchids, which may even flower in this setting, or for plants too delicate for ordinary indoor conditions. These should be left in their own pots so that they can

A garden in a large, narrow-necked bottle. You can achieve the apparently impossible if you use suitable tools and follow the sequence below:

1 Pour in soil through a funnel of stiff cardboard
2 Arrange with a spatula
3 Gently lower in a small plant
4 and 5 Plant, using a long-handled miniature spade or spoon and a stick
6 Finally attach a piece of string to a rigid support so that the glass does not get dirty, and water by capillary action.

have the individual attention they need. Orchids need what amounts to a proper little greenhouse with its own heating, thermostat, vaporizer and so on, often known as an 'orchidarium' by analogy with 'aquarium' and 'terrarium', although there is no such thing as an ecosystem composed solely of orchids. Even if you are not interested in such specialist plants you can make a proper miniature garden in a tank of this type. As with smaller containers, put a drainage layer on the bottom, cover it with potting mixture and plant the plants directly in this. If there is room you can even sketch in a landscape, with rocks, moss and even bowls of water containing tiny aquatic plants.

Another attractive and easy-to-make type of miniature garden is composed of epiphyte plants growing in the knots and crevices of old logs or better still old roots which are less likely to rot. Bromeliads, ferns and many epiphytic cacti are suitable choices. The wood should be fairly gnarled, with natural cavities; additional holes can be made as necessary. According to its shape, the log or root can be laid flat on a tray with a drainage layer of gravel to prevent the wood getting wet and rotting, or it can be stood upright in a taller container half filled with gravel for drainage and also to weight down the arrangement. In either case you can add a shallow layer of moss-covered earth all round, for other land plants. Remove the epiphytes from their pots and slip their roots into the holes and crevices with a mixture of wet sphagnum moss and peat. Osmunda fibre is often recommended for this but it is not easy to get hold of, and it then has to be broken up into small pieces and moistened. You will find it fairly hard keeping sphagnum moss moist in a centrally heated house. Watering must be done with a spray.

Bonsai is a special kind of miniature gardening. This Japanese (or rather originally Chinese) art of cultivating dwarfed trees dates from about the thirteenth century. It demands a great deal of time and skill: ten or twenty years may not be long enough to grow a striking, well-shaped tree from seed. This is reflected in the commercial price of bonsai, but if you choose to start from scratch you need plenty of time ahead of you and boundless optimism. It is rarely possible to start with a cutting or a seedling – gathered in the wild. Growing from seed is more or less the rule, especially for conifers, which cannot stand having their roots

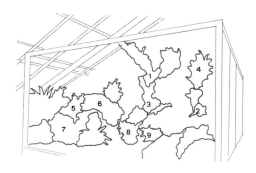

Tropical terrariums can be created in a green-house, giving all the pleasure of a small-scale collection. Orchids and epiphytes here include:

1 *Cryptocereus anthonyanus*
2 & 4 *Vanda* hybrids
3 *Phalaenopsis* hybrid
5 *x Laeliocattleya*
6 *Adiantum*
7 various *Paphiopedilum* species
8 *Odontoglossum grande*
9 *Masdevallia coccinea*

exposed during transplanting and which suffer from any kind of transplantation. Before laying out money on bonsai or starting to grow them, remember that though they can be evergreen or deciduous, they are always native to cold or temperate climates and will not tolerate the artificial heat and airless atmosphere of the average house or flat. The commonest trees used are conifers in particular, then flowering cherries, *Ginkgo*, certain species of *Ficus* and sometimes olive trees.

The basis of bonsai culture is judicious and patient pruning of the roots to create a compact system with plenty of small roots, cutting away the bulky main roots. At the same time the most vigorous shoots should be cut back by pinching out the tips. If the tree does not develop into the desired shape, the branches can be wired to train them into the correct position; they must never cross or be bunched together. With these aims in mind, starting from seed, sow the seed in small clay or plastic pots with several drainage holes; a perforated plastic container can be used, or even the dried skin of half an orange, pierced in a number of places. A peat pot would be ideal, allowing the roots to grow through, but there is always the problem, unless using a plastic pot, of keeping the soil slightly moist all the time. When the seed germinates, which may take a long time with tree seed, you must take note of how the roots emerge. If they appear through the holes in the container there is no problem; if using a clay pot repotting will be necessary. In the first year the roots should be pruned once or twice; if more appear they should be cut back when they become too vigorous. In the second year prune twice. In the third year the plant can be transplanted to its

Ginkgo biloba, (*above*) and various conifers are ideal for bonsai culture; olive and even rosemary may also be used.

permanent container which should be a wide, shallow glazed pot. After that you will have to remove the plant from the pot, prune the roots and repot it in the same container at least once. You can take this opportunity to move the collar, where roots and trunk meet, a little higher or to slip in stones round which the roots can grow. Finally you will have something that looks like a bonsai tree.

Above: The strange flower of one species of *Huernia*.

Below: Conophytum velutinum properly grown produces attractive, daisy-like flowers between the two fleshy leaves.

SUCCULENTS

In horticultural terms succulents are plants capable of storing large reserves of water in their tissues so that they can survive periods of drought. They are xerophytes from regions where there are long dry seasons affecting both ground and air. Some species can survive in very dry ground but need a high level of atmosphere humidity: these include some epiphytes and mountain plants. There are many keen growers of succulents attracted by the plants' curious shapes, which are perhaps at times more exotic than beautiful. Often these enthusiasts become real collectors, and it certainly is true that displaying a large number of succulents together shows up the differences between families, whereas a few isolated specimens make little impact. To cater for this popular hobby succulents are grown from seed and sold as young plants. Often it is difficult to put a name to them, as it is very easy to cross cultivated species and the enormous number of varieties produced cannot always be readily identified. It is worth knowing something about the families which include succulent species, if only to appreciate their wide range.

Aizoaceae: These are all succulents *par excellence*. They are native to South Africa, although some species will grow spontaneously elsewhere. Many of them used to be classed as belonging to the extensive *Mesembryanthemum* genus which has gradually been reduced to a single species. These creeping plants, which tend to be rather unwieldy and so do not make good pot plants, are often found in gardens near the Mediterranean coast: the main genera are *Carpobrotus*, *Clottiphyllum* and *Lampranthus*. Unfortunately their stems tend to dry out while the tip is still green, so they have to be renewed periodically by propagation. Small or dwarf genera must be grown in pots; they tend to rot very easily and require long rest periods at low winter temperatures. The commonest of them include *Carruanthus* and *Faucaria*, which have fleshy decussate leaves with very short internodes; *Pleiospilos*, sometimes called 'living stones', and *Conophytum* which have two very fleshy, sometimes elongated, hemispherical leaves; *Lithops* and *Fenestraria* which simply have stems, divided in the middle in *Lithops* and having shoots in *Fenestraria*: most of the plant is underground, but it has translucent spots on the upper part through which light is absorbed. These species are known as 'living stones' and are a fine example of plant mimicry, providing protection against animals as well as against climatic conditions. They are not easy to obtain and are rarely successful as house plants.

Amaryllidaceae: The most prominent member of this family is the genus *Agave*. Some species now grow spontaneously round the Mediterranean, although the genus is native to the semi-desert regions of America. Usually the plants are too big for house plants except in their early stages.

Apocynaceae: It is sometimes possible to buy *Pachypodium*, also known as Madagascar palm, a plant with a fleshy, prickly stem and leaves which show that it is related to the oleander. Although it grows quickly it never of course turns into a tree while in a pot. It cannot stand frost but is easy enough to grow with plenty of light and summer sun.

Asclepiadaceae: All members of this family are more or less fleshy. The true succulents include the genera *Caralluma, Huernia, Hoodia* and *Stapelia*: these have aphyllous stems, and many of them have exotic flowers which give off an unpleasant odour to attract the carrion-feeding insects which pollinate them. They all come from South Africa and are fairly easy to grow although they are liable to be attacked by mealy bugs.

Above: The strange, contorted stems of *Chamaecereus silvestri* have earned it the nickname 'peanut cactus'.

Bromeliaceae: Some genera of this family are inaccurately described as succulents when often they simply have tough leaves but are not xerophytes. However *Dyckia, Hechtia* and *Puya* can be classed as true succulents: they live in dry rocky environments in South America. They are usually too unwieldy to be grown in pots, except as young plants, particularly *Hectia argentea* and *Dyckia brevifolia*. They cannot stand frost but are fairly easy to grow.

Cactaceae: These are all succulents, although the epiphytic types from the tropical rain forests, which need a humid atmosphere, should really be classed separately. The rest are generally known as cacti and most of them are well equipped with spines, prickles or glochids. All species bear the characteristic tufts known as areoles. They are all American in origin except for a few epiphytic species common in Madagascar. There are some 1,500 species and countless varieties both common and rare. The flowers are usually striking but only appear if the plant has a long winter rest period in dry, cool conditions. Some common cacti are *Astrophytum, Cephalocereus, Cereus, Cleistocactus, Echinopsi, Echinocereus, Espostoa, Ferocactus, Gymnocalycium, Lobivia, Mammillaria, Opuntia* (including the so-called 'prickly pear' which now grows spontaneously in Mediterranean regions) and *Parodia*. Some delicate species are sold grafted on to more robust plants; this can create an interesting effect when the colours are strongly contrasted, for example when red or yellow *Gymnocalycium* species are grafted on to green *Cereus triangularis* or pale yellow or white *Chamaecereus silvestri*. How such forms are obtained is a Japanese trade secret. It is often said that the plants undergo gamma ray treatment, and certainly the chlorophyll is completely destroyed and the plant can never root again even if it already had

Right: Lithops salicola has beautiful white flowers, but the small silver-grey plant has a curiosity value of its own.

All *Echeveria* like plenty of sun and readily produce attractive flowers in the right conditions.

shoots before the treatment. This destruction of life has alarming implications and the results are not totally satisfactory; the colours soon fade unless they have the right amount of light and the plants die off fairly quickly.

Compositae: Succulents belonging to the daisy family are known almost interchangeably as *Senecio* or *Kleinia*. Decidedly odd in shape, they include the leafless stems of *Kleinia stapeliiformis*, which branch out underground, and the slender creeping stems of *Kleinia radicans* and *Senecio herreianus* which have almost round leaves like little green peas. These plants are all South African. They cannot stand frost and the most delicate of them do not like full sunlight in summer either. They sometimes have yellow or scarlet flowers which look just like dandelions.

Crassulaceae: All these plants are succulents, but they have such different habitats, origins and requirements that few of them can be grown successfully as house plants. These few include some tropical *Sedums*, Mexican *Echeverias* and certain *Crassulas*. Some viviparous species of *Kalanchoës* are interesting, although they can become rather a nuisance. Young plants form along the edges of leaves, and as they fall off they quickly take root; sometimes they even start to develop little roots before they drop. These plants all like very strong light. Eventually they get straggly and untidy, so they need to be divided from time to time which can be done without difficulty.

Euphorbiaceae: Most species are succulents, with some exceptions like the poinsettia *Euphorbia pulcherrima*, which is grown for its splendid red bracts. Many closely resemble cacti, but they secrete an irritant white latex if damaged at all and do not have areoles. The African species are probably the most common, although there are species from Asia and America too. The commonest include *Euphorbia canariensis, candelabrum, erythreae, ramipressa, triangularis* and the famous 'crown of thorns', *Euphorbia milii*, better known by its old name *Euphorbia splendens*, which has a thorny stem with small bright red bracts and needs more heat and moisture than the others.

Liliaceae: This family includes many succulent species divided into relatively few genera. Some make ideal house plants as they do not need direct sunlight. *Aloes* are the African equivalent of *Agaves*. Many of them are too large, but there are some small species and others which can be kept within bounds by periodic propagation when shoots form at the base, as frequently happens. They include *Aloe brevifolia, jocunda, eru, hobilis* and *saponaria*. *Casteria* and *Haworthia* are naturally small although they sprout readily. Their leaves, which form rosettes, may have translucent patches or be decorated with white verrucae. They do not like direct sunlight, especially in summer, and can survive with relatively little light although this may make them straggly and less attractive.

Portulacaceae: Only one genus can be classed as succulents: *Portulacaria afra*, a shrub with small green, fleshy leaves. Small specimens look rather like distorted bonsai and can effectively be used in the composition of miniature gardens. They grow slowly and often shed many leaves in winter, but apart from that they can tolerate quite a hot atmosphere.

Vitaceae: Some species of genus *Cissus* are not climbers although they belong to the vine family. They are genuine rarities often not found even in the most specialized collections. *Cissus quadrangularis* is the commonest species. It climbs by means of tendrils and has fleshy stems divided into a number of joints

Gymnocalcium mihanovici grafted onto *Cereus triangularis* is given a special treatment which produces the unnatural red colouring and prevents further rooting.

which are angular as the name suggests, and small deciduous leaves. It likes the sun if it is used to it, but the epidermal tissues may easily scorch if the plant is exposed to sunlight after a period out of it. It needs moderate warmth and will survive a fair amount of neglect. It makes quite a good house plant provided it has a support, but is perhaps best grown with other plants, as on its own it tends to look rather spindly.

This list obviously does not include families and species which are extremely rare, and difficult if not impossible to grow in normal conditions.

WATER PLANTS

There are specialist books describing all aspects of aquariums, their construction, contents and even the plants which can be grown in them, so this ground will not be covered again here. It is well-known that fresh-water aquariums need plants because their capacity for photosynthesis, which varies from species to species, helps to oxygenate the water. Plants also help to eliminate the fishes' organic waste by absorbing nourishment from it through their roots. In fact they help to establish and maintain the biological balance necessary for animal life. However, on their own, plants are far more self-sufficient than animals, so it is possible to create a water environment consisting entirely or mainly of plants rather than fish.

In ordinary unscientific terms, aquarium plants are plants which live completely or partly under water and so can only be fully appreciated when grown in a transparent container. This rules out many aquatic plants, such as floaters whose ornamental value lies entirely in the leaves and flowers showing on the surface. The plants come from a wide range of botanical families. Just as some trees make good house plants in their early stages, so some water plants which eventually become floaters or bog plants can be used in aquariums while still at their underwater stage. They are often extremely interesting to observe and can be quite as attractive as land plants, if not more so. If you do not want to set up a proper aquarium, a square or rectangular tank of the right size standing on a piece of furniture makes an attractive decoration, if properly looked after and filled with plants suited to the tank's position and other factors. Some species can be grown in round goldfish bowls, but remember that the curved glass will distort the image and that the water level must be kept fairly low so that there is a large enough surface area in contact with the air, not just the comparatively small bowl neck.

An aquarium containing plants only needs much the same care and attention as a small greenhouse. Choose species suitable for the available light and heat: tropical and sub-tropical plants are a better choice than those from the temperate zones because although they need more warmth they can make do with less light and air. Aquarium plants are not usually very fussy about their growing medium. Many do best on a layer of peat or mud, covered with sand so that the water does not get dirty; however this has its disadvantages, including the unpleasantly murky look the water may take on, so it is probably better to use coarse shingle, preferably limefree. If there are fish in the tank their waste products gradually create a steady supply of manure. Otherwise fertilizer tablets can be used; they are buried in the bottom and release vital mineral salts as they gradually dissolve. Only a few aquatic plants need hard or alkaline water and those which do, for example *Myriophyllum*, in any case usually need too much light to be grown successfully indoors without encouraging the growth of algae which can then kill off the plants. Most plants need soft acid water which should be boiled and carefully decanted, leaving behind the mineral deposits which settle at the bottom of the container. You can add distilled water. Ideally you should measure the water's pH

Above, top: Cryptocoryne lingua needs more light than other species of the same genus.

Above, bottom: A species of *Hygrophila polysperma* suitable for cold aquariums which is hardy and easy to propagate.

Below: An *Echinodorus* hybrid which does well in a warm light position.

value, that is its acidity or alkalinity, but this is not strictly necessary except for particularly sensitive species. More important is the possible incompatibility of different genera from different ecological environments. Aquarium owners often complain that in carefully controlled conditions, with identical amounts of light, heat and so on, some plants still die. You may find that plants recommended for aquariums do not grow well on their own, and in this case the amount of oxygen they produce is not an important consideration.

Cryptocoryne, belonging to the *Araceae* family, and possibly the most attractive genus and the easiest to grow, has fairly tough leaves and is not one of the best oxygenators. These plants, which come originally from tropical Asia, can in most cases tolerate fairly poor light. In nature they are usually found in pools and ricefields where the water level rises and falls according to season, so they are almost amphibious. The inflorescences characteristic of this family hardly ever appear in cultivated plants, and in fact available varieties are usually hybrids between different species. They include: *Cryptocoryne affinis* which has lanceolate leaves, green on the upper face, red below; *Cryptocoryne balansae* with easily recognizable narrow, wrinkled, blistered-looking leaves; *Cryptocoryne nevillii* a ground-cover plant only 10 cm high; *Cryptocoryne willissi* with reddish-brown leaf ribbing. These plants do not like to be mixed indiscriminately, and some space should be left even between members of the same species; however they will tolerate other Asiatic plants and most water ferns fairly well. The water temperature should be between 15 and 28 °C (59 and 82 °F), and the water should be soft and acid. *Cabomba* is another plant which can be grown on its own, for quite different reasons. The plant is a good oxygenator and has leaves arranged in pairs, with blades which consist of a great many needle-like green segments forming a fan shape. The *aquatica* species comes from Brazil and Guyana, and *Cabomba caroliniana* from the eastern United States. It likes very strong light, but often fails in aquariums because its main requirement is almost completely still water with no filters or air pumps. It is an ideal plant to grow on its own, with good light, soft water and a temperature of 18–25 °C (65–77 °F), or with species of *Sagittaria* which have similar requirements and make a suitable partner as regards appearance. As a member of the family *Nympheaceae*, its dislike of moving water is quite understandable. *Aponogeton* are beautiful plants which include one of the strangest forms of plant life: *Aponogeton fenestralis* from Madagascar, which consists of a fine tracery or ribbing with no chlorophyllous leaf tissues at all. This very delicate plant is almost unobtainable and must be kept on its own in still water containing some humus, changed fairly often. There are many other much sturdier species of *Aponogeton*, a number from Madagascar and others Asiatic in origin. They can be distinguished by the different kinds of inflorescence: in the African species the spike is forked, while in Asian species it is simple. Generally plants available commercially are hybrids and for best results they all need a rest period between November and February when the tubers should be kept at 10–13 °C (50–56 °F), then brought back to 20–26 °C (68–79 °F); the tuber should be slightly hollowed out and then planted shallowly so that the hollow is uncovered. There are other good ornamental plants. *Synnema triflorum* from tropical Asia, like other members of the family *Acanthaceae* such as *Hygrophila*, tends to grow too long, a common fault in the land species too, but it will keep its shape with careful pruning and makes a good companion for many species of *Cryptocoryne*; *Echinodorus* is undemanding but likes strong light.

Ludwigia, surprisingly enough a member of the same family as *Fuchsia*, the Onagraceae, goes well with the Asiatic plants; if the light is good it often goes a

The delicate, feathery segments of *Cabomba* offset the slender leaves of *Echinodorus. Cabomba* likes completely still water: often even an air pump may be enough to kill it.

red or reddish colour, but it cannot stand alkaline water. *Sagittaria* and *Vallisneria* with their many respective hybrids are good standbys: although they cannot be crossed with each other, their long slender leaves, arranged to form rosettes, are remarkably similar. You will hardly want to pack your house with tanks of water plants, so it is important to know how to make a wise initial choice of a few suitable species.

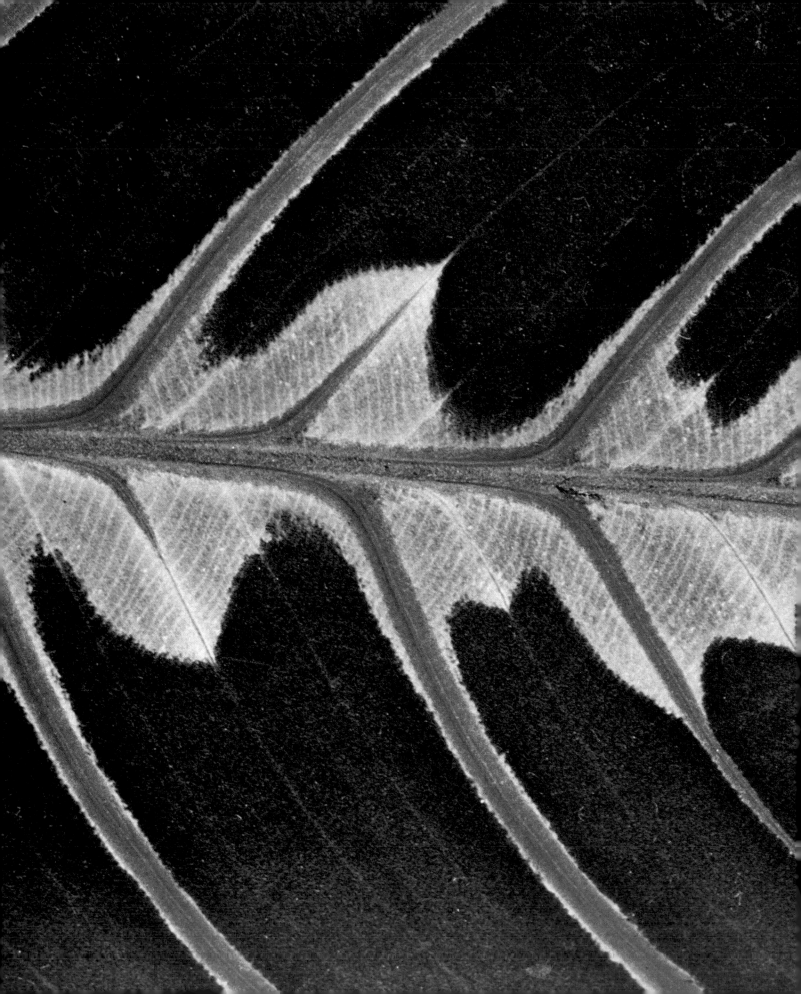

House Plants

ABUTILON MEGAPOTAMICUM (Malvaceae)

Etymology: The generic name comes from the Arabic term used to describe a plant similar to mallow.

Description: An evergreen shrub with slender, arched branches which lie flat but rise at the tip. The rather small, alternate leaves are lanceolate-acuminate with crenate margins. The flowers are pendulous with a showy, red calyx with fused sepals from which the lemon yellow petals emerge. In all members of the family, the filaments of the stamens fuse to form a little column round the style and in this species they extend showily beyond the petals.

Habitat: From Brazil. The species name *megapotamicum*, or 'of the great river', refers to the Rio Grande.

Minimum winter temperature: 10–13 °C (50–55 °F). The leaves shrivel and drop if the winter temperature is higher.

Light: As much as possible to encourage flowering, which may occur almost continuously if the temperature is right. The plant will tolerate all but the hottest direct sunlight. Suitable for cool, well-lit positions.

Environmental humidity: Average humidity is adequate if the temperature is not too high, but in warmer conditions a moister atmosphere is required to keep the foliage in good condition.

Watering: Plentiful in summer, less frequent in winter.

Soil: A well-drained, humus-rich mixture composed of equal parts of compost, well-rotted leaf mould and sand. Give weekly applications of fertilizer containing a high proportion of phosphorus throughout the growing season.

Propagation: By stem cuttings, preferably taken in spring or early summer, kept at 18 °C (64 °F), under a plastic cover. Frequent airings are necessary and the cuttings should be uncovered gradually. Prune at the end of winter to obtain bushy specimens.

Varieties: A variety called *variegata* is available which has irregular markings in shades of white and yellow. This is more decorative but is slightly more delicate.

ACALYPHA GODSEFFIANA (Euphorbiaceae)

Etymology: The name comes from the Greek *akalephe*, Hippocratus's name for nettles which Linnaeus applied to this genus because the leaves of many of its species are like some members of the *Urticaceae*.

Description: A shrub-like, bushy plant which has short-stemmed, ovate-acuminate leaves with a serrate or crenate margin bordered by a broad yellow or cream band. The inconspicuous flowers are greenish-yellow in colour. This is essentially a foliage plant.

Habitat: From New Guinea.

Minimum winter temperature: 12–15 °C (53–59 °F).

Light: The plant needs good light and an airy position.

Environmental humidity: A high level, if possible, increased by spraying and sprinkling; this will also discourage mites and scale insects.

Watering: Frequent during the growing period, much reduced in winter.

Soil: A humus-rich, well-drained mixture composed of two parts of leaf mould to one of peat with a little extra sand.

Propagation: By semi-woody cuttings taken in spring and kept at a temperature of at least 21 °C (70 °F), under a plastic cover, which should be removed gradually after about a month when roots develop. For a neat, compact shape, the plant should be clipped and pruned at the start of the growing season and during growth as necessary.

Varieties: Various forms of the species *Acalypha wilkesiana* are also available. These have leaves with red variegations and markings and are grown in exactly the same way as the species described here.

ACALYPHA HISPIDA (Euphorbiaceae)

Description: A shrubby plant with large, green, downy, alternate leaves, ovate-acuminate in shape, with crenate margins. It is cultivated for its attractive flowers which are grouped in pendulous spikes and grow much longer than the leaves. The little red flowers, which do not have petals, grow closely clustered together. The male flowers have as many as sixteen stamens, giving the inflorescence as a whole a feathery appearance.
Habitat: From India and Burma.
Minimum winter temperature: 13–16 °C (55–61 °F).
Light: To encourage flowering, the plant needs strong, diffuse light, out of direct sun, and a very airy position.
Environmental humidity: As high a level as possible, following all the usual procedures to increase the level. Do not spray the inflorescences.
Watering: Frequent and plentiful in summer, less often in winter. Combine with applications of liquid fertilizer during the growing period.
Soil: Rich and well-drained, composed of equal parts of compost, leaf mould and peat with some extra sand to improve drainage. Effective drainage is vital and a good drainage layer on the pot bottom is necessary to prevent waterlogging.
Propagation: By woody cuttings with a heel or semi-woody cuttings cut off just below a node. Cuttings are preferably taken in spring and kept under a plastic cover at a temperature of about 24 °C (75 °F) with an occasional airing to prevent a damp stagnant atmosphere and condensation.
Varieties: A number of hybrids are available which can be grown in the same way. In summer all *Acalyphas* can be left outdoors in a semi-shaded position.

ADIANTUM CUNEATUM (Polypodiaceae)

Common name: Maidenhair fern.
Etymology: The generic name comes from the Greek *adiantos*, meaning 'dry', and occurs as early as Theophrastus's *Historia plantarum*, probably describing the way water runs off the plant's leaves without being absorbed. The common name 'maidenhair' is indiscriminately applied to all species, but should really just be used for *Adiantum capillus-veneris* which grows spontaneously all over Europe.
Description: Rhizomatous ferns with pinnate, feathery fronds. The cuneate lobed segments open out into the characteristic fan shape. The fronds sometimes grow as long as 50 cm (20 in). There are a great many varieties, and in general the species is readily available in nurseries and florists' shops.
Habitat: From Brazil.
Minimum winter temperature: About 15 °C (59 °F).
Light: Moderate, diffuse light, out of direct sun.
Environmental humidity: A very high level, increased in every way possible. Because the genus likes such a moist atmosphere the plants need near greenhouse conditions and may be difficult to grow as house plants.
Watering: Frequent all the year round. The potting mixture must be kept damp, but never allow to become waterlogged.
Soil: Very porous, so that the mixture stays moist but lets water drain through easily. You can either use a mixture of partly decayed leaf mould, sphagnum moss and peat, or moss mixed with a little leaf mould. The rhizomes should be shallowly planted in shallow pots, with a good drainage layer. Stand them in trays containing a layer of damp gravel or perlite.
Propagation: By rhizome division, making sure that each segment bears two or three buds. Plant in small pots with moss or sphagnum and keep moist at a temperature of 18–21 °C (65–70 °F).

ADIANTUM TENERUM (Polypodiaceae)

Description: This species has fronds with meltoid segments which are not laciniate in the parent species. However there are so many cultivated varieties that the parent species is rarely encountered. The plant's main characteristic is the red or reddish colour of its young fronds which later turn paler or darker green.

Habitat: The species originally comes from an extensive region stretching from Florida to South America.

Minimum winter temperature: 10–13 °C (50–55 °F). In a moister atmosphere plants tolerate slightly higher temperatures.

Light: Moderate, diffuse light out of direct sun.

Environmental humidity: As high a level as possible.

Watering: Frequent. Do not let the soil get waterlogged as this can do irreparable harm to the rhizome.

Soil: Porous and well-drained. Leaf mould, crumbled sphagnum and peat make a suitable mixture. Put a deep drainage layer, perhaps incorporating some charcoal, in the bottom of the pot.

Propagation: By rhizome division. Plant shallowly in small pots of damp sphagnum or moss, and keep at about 15 °C (60 °F).

Varieties: Some slightly hardier varieties are more readily available, including *A. tenerum* var. *scutum roseum* which has rosy-pink young fronds. Others are more attractive but more delicate, e.g. *A. tenerum* 'Farleyense' which has superimposed segments with curly, lobed edges giving the plant a feathery appearance.

Soil: As porous as possible, composed of fern roots with a little immature leaf mould and some sand. Use small pots, so long as this does not make the plant top heavy, with a good deep drainage layer.

Propagation: As with other members of the family, once the rosette of leaves has flowered it dies down. Meanwhile shoots will have developed round the base and these can be removed and used to produce new plants. It is best to wait until they have developed roots, but they can be treated as cuttings and grown in small uncovered pots with a porous, almost dry potting mixture.

AECHMEA FASCIATA (Bromeliaceae)

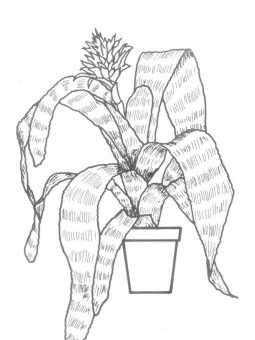

Etymology: The name comes from the Greek *akmé*, or 'point', which refers to the sharply pointed tips of the calyx.

Description: The plant appears to be stemless. The leaves are arranged in a rosette, closely overlapping to form a spiral with a round, hollow central section which the inflorescence grows out of; this is a characteristic feature of several genera of the family. In this species the leaves are stiff, about 10 cm (4 in) wide and 45 cm (18 in) long, with spines along the edges. They are greyish-green in colour with horizontal stripes of silvery grey. The inflorescence, which sometimes reaches a height of 40 cm (16 in), consists of a large number of pink, spiny bracts which may last as long as six months; the small pale blue flowers which grow among them are only short-lived.

Habitat: From Brazil. In nature the plants are epiphytes, but in cultivation they are always treated as terrestrial.

Minimum winter temperature: 16–18 °C (61–65 °F).

Light: The plants are usually bought already in flower, in which case they only need moderate light to thrive. You are unlikely to produce flowers in the plants from scratch in normal indoor conditions, as very strong light and a very humid atmosphere are necessary.

Environmental humidity: The level need not be increased, particularly in winter.

Watering: Regular in summer, infrequent in winter. Remember that like most bromeliads, whether epiphytic or terrestrial, these plants are liable to rot round the collar if they always have damp soil round them. This means that it is not a good idea to keep the central 'vessel' full of water as occurs in nature unless you are sure that the collar is free of damp soil. Otherwise the plant will not tolerate this double dose of moisture both inside and around it.

Soil: As porous as possible, composed of fern roots with a little immature leaf mould and some sand. Use small pots, so long as this does not make the plant top heavy, with a good deep drainage layer.

Propagation: As with other members of the family, once the rosette of leaves has flowered it dies down. Meanwhile shoots will have developed round the base and these can be removed and used to produce new plants. It is best to wait until they have developed rudimentary roots, although they can be treated as cuttings and grown in small pots with a porous, almost dry potting mixture. Do not cover the pots.

AECHMEA FULGENS VARIEGATA
(Bromeliaceae)

Description: The standard species has the genus's characteristic rosette form. The leaves are dark green, with a greyish sheen and spikes of inflorescences branch out from the base, bearing flowers with small purple petals at the tip of the red, swollen, oval, persistent calyx. The attractive and showy variegated variety is much rarer.

Habitat: The standard species comes from Brazil.

Minimum winter temperature: 13–16 °C (55–61 °F).

Light: The standard species needs only an average amount of light as it is unlikely to flower successfully indoors. The variegated variety needs more light to keep its markings intact.

Environmental humidity: The plant tolerates a dry indoor atmosphere.

Watering: Regular in summer, much less frequent in winter.

Soil: A very porous, well-drained mixture is needed to prevent rotting. A mixture of crumbled fern roots, leaf mould and sand is suitable. For very dry conditions a little peat can be added.

Propagation: By means of the shoots which develop round the base of the main rosette. These can be broken off and potted once roots have developed, or planted in barely damp sand and peat to take root.

AEONIUM (Crassulaceae)

Etymology: The name comes from the Greek *aionios*, or 'immortal'. The plants which now make up this genus were formerly included in the genus *Sempervivum*, but were classed separately because of their different botanical characteristics, including the fact that they have a stem.

Description: All species belonging to this genus are succulents. Their leaves form rosettes of various shapes and colours. A great many species are semi-rustic and can be grown outdoors in a mild climate, as they can survive freezing temperatures. Some, such as *Aeonium decorum* and *Aeonium haworthii*, will happily spend the winter indoors in a cool position with plenty of light. *A. decorum* forms a small bush, with many branches ending in rosettes of small fleshy leaves which take on a bronze colour in the sun. *A. haworthii*, is a bushy semi-woody plant with rosettes of obovate-acute leaves, fringed with fine hairs and edged with red.

Habitat: Most species come from the Canaries, except for a few which are native to North Africa, particularly Morocco.

Minimum winter temperature: 5–7 °C (41–45 °F). At higher temperatures many leaves will shrivel.

Light: Maximum possible, as for all succulents. In summer the plants do well outside in a semi-shaded position.

Environmental humidity: They readily tolerate dry air.

Watering: Regular in summer, but very sparing in winter. If conditions are warmer than suggested, spray the leaves occasionally rather than watering more frequently.

Soil: Porous and well-drained, composted with about three parts of well-rotted compost to one of sand.

Propagation: Take stem cuttings in summer, or remove a leaf and lay it on slightly damp sand. The stem cuttings too should be kept in an almost dry sandy potting mixture.

AESCHYNANTHUS MARMORATUS
(Gesneriaceae)

Etymology: This genus is sometimes known by its old name *Trichosporum*. The name *Aeschynanthus* comes from the Greek *aischyne*, or 'shame', and *anthos*, or 'flower'. The name was chosen by W. Jack who perhaps wanted to suggest that the red flowers of most species are blushing for shame or modesty.

Description: Like most other species, the plant is an epiphytic suffrutescent plant with branches which lie flat with rising tip. The opposite leaves are fairly large and tough, and lanceolate-acuminate. They are delicately patterned with a network of yellowish lines showing through the transparent-looking epidermis. The same markings show up pale green on the reddish-brown underside of the leaves. Unlike in other species, the flowers are inconspicuous, greenish in colour with brown markings.

Habitat: From Thailand.

Minimum winter temperature: About 16 °C (61 °F), although if kept completely dry the plants will tolerate temperatures several degrees lower.

Light: Good light is needed to maintain the markings, but it should be diffuse, away from direct sun.

Environmental humidity: Should be increased in every way.

Watering: Frequent in summer, very well spaced in winter depending on the temperature. Water must never be allowed to gather round the roots. Use small pots, or for best results grow in a hanging basket.

Soil: As light and porous as possible, composed of equal parts of leaf mould and peat with a fair amount of sand or perlite.

Propagation: By herbaceous or semi-woody cuttings at any time of the year. The cuttings must be kept at a temperature of at least 22 °C (72 °F) and planted in damp sand or potting mixture. They need not be covered.

AESCHYNANTHUS SPECIOSUS (Gesneriaceae)

Description: An evergreen suffrutescent plant which grows vigorously but has a rather untidy appearance. The branches which are flat with rising tip may grow as long as 60 cm (24 in). The large, green, tough leaves are lanceolate. The flowers are very showy and may grow in terminal clusters of up to twenty. The calyx is fairly short for this genus, with a long, curved and swollen tubular corolla with bilabiate limbs from which the stamens emerge. These are an orange-pink or flame-red colour, and the mouth of the corolla is yellow with red-brown markings.

Habitat: From Java.

Minimum winter temperature: 16 °C (61 °F).

Light: Very good, out of direct sun. This encourages flowering, which will not occur in a shady position.

Environmental humidity: As much as possible. Because of this requirement it is easier to produce flowers in a greenhouse than indoors.

Watering: Plentiful in summer, with applications of liquid fertilizer throughout the growing period. Much less frequent from November to February, although the level of environmental humidity should be kept high.

Soil: As for all epiphytes the soil must be very porous so that water never collects. A suitable mixture would be leaf mould mixed with sand and peat and possibly a little crumbled sphagnum moss. The pots should be as small as possible (so long as this does not make the plants top heavy) with a good deep drainage layer.

Propagation: By cuttings taken from non-woody stems and planted in a damp, sandy mixture kept at a temperature of at least 24 °C (75 °F). Cuttings need no protection and can be taken at any time of year, though it is best to wait until growth has started.

THE AGLAONEMA GENUS (Araceae)

Etymology: The name comes from the Greek *aglaos,* or 'shining', and *nema*, or 'thread', describing the flower's stamens.
Description: Small, evergreen herbaceous plants. One cultivated species is stemless, or almost so. All species readily become bushy in shape by means of shoots which develop at the base. The leaves have long petioles which are sheathed at their base; they have unbroken margins and are usually oblong or lanceolate and often variegated. The inflorescences are characteristic of the *Araceae* family, but in this genus are generally inconspicuous. They consist of a spadix, on which the small unisexual or bisexual flowers grow, partly enclosed by a bract known as a spathe. Flowers appear fairly easily in cultivated plants, but they are usually white or green and so not very striking, although in some species they are followed by attractive red or yellow berries.
Habitat: There are some fifty species, all originally from South-East Asia, from India to the Philippines and China. The genus can be described as the Asiatic equivalent of the American genus *Dieffenbachia*, which belongs to the same family. In such a huge and varied cosmopolitan family – consisting as it does of about 120 genera, over a thousand species and countless hybrids, found in terrestrial, aquatic, marsh and epiphytic forms – it is hardly surprising that some genera have more or less exact equivalents in different continents.
Minimum winter temperature: 13–16°C (55–61°F) for Far Eastern species. Others will tolerate moderate light, although variegated species need more to preserve their markings.
Environmental humidity: Normal, but the leaves must be washed and sprayed, especially in winter.
Soil: Light and well-drained, composed of equal parts of composted farmyard manure and leaf mould with some peat and sand. Roots and stems are fleshy, so make quite sure that the potting mixture never gets hard-packed or waterlogged.
Propagation: By cuttings taken from the tips of defoliated stems. You can also grow new plants from sections of bare stem consisting of at least three nodes from which the new growth will develop. These fragments can either be planted vertically or laid flat and half-covered with soil. In either case the potting mixture should be very porous and sandy and kept just moist, never wet. Cuttings can be taken in any season; they require a temperature of 21°C (70°F), but need not be covered. However the best time of year is the beginning of summer when growth has started. *Aglaonema costatum* is propagated by rhizome division, so long as the rhizome has at least two buds. When a plant produces fruit successfully new plants can be grown from the seeds, which take at least three months to germinate in a barely moist seed mixture kept at a temperature of 18–20°C (65–68°F).

AGLAONEMA COMMUTATUM (Araceae)

Description: The stems may grow as long as 1 m (3 ft 3 in) or more, but as they grow they lose the bottom leaves, leaving the lower section bare. They tend to grow crooked and so often need to be attached to firm supports. The plants put out new shoots readily. The leaves are oblong, with silvery grey, striped markings on a dark green ground, following the veins on either side of the mid rib. The smooth, tough-looking leaf epidermis is easily washed from time to time. The spathe is cream-coloured with a whitish spadix. The inflorescences, which develop fairly often in cultivated plants, have no particular decorative value themselves, but are often followed by red or yellow berries which are an attractive feature.
Habitat: From a large area stretching from Malaysia to the Philippines. The species occurs in a variety of forms with different amounts of variegation.
Minimum winter temperature: About 13°C (55°F).
Light: The plants tolerate poor light, but flower more easily in brighter conditions.
Environmental humidity: As high a level as possible. This will encourage fruit which may not develop in dry conditions.

AGLAONEMA COSTATUM (Araceae)

Description: More or less stemless, or with very short internodes. The leaves are very dark green, ovate in shape, with irregular white speckling and an ivory-coloured midrib. The plant readily puts out new shoots and may grow large and bushy.

Habitat: Originally from India, but local varieties can be found as far afield as Malaysia and the Moluccas.

Minimum winter temperature: 13–15 °C (55–59 °F). The species tolerates warmer conditions if humidity is increased.

Light: It tolerates moderate light, but will lose much of its speckled marking and in very poor light only the midrib will stay white.

Environmental humidity: Increased according to temperature, by washing and spraying the leaves.

Propagation: As the plant is almost always stemless, cuttings are out of the question. Divide the clump instead, making sure that each section of the rhizome has a certain number of buds. Plant in a very peaty mixture kept almost dry.

AGLAONEMA MODESTUM (Araceae)

Description: This very hardy plant has long stems, which in cultivated specimens may reach 1 m (3 ft 3 in) or more, but it is more likely to lose leaves and grow crooked than other species. The leaves are dark-green, ovate-acuminate or lanceolate, with clearly visible, slightly hollow secondary veins. The petiole is long and often hangs downwards so that the leaves are turned outwards. This occurs particularly in adult plants. The young plants are more attractive and readily put out new shoots. Even if cut right back the plant sprouts again vigorously, so periodic pruning is a good idea. The stems you remove can be treated as cuttings to provide a constant supply of new, well-shaped plants.

Habitat: From China, hence the common name 'Chinese evergreen'.

Temperature: This hardy species likes cooler conditions than other members of the genus. It does well up to about 10 °C (50 °F), but is prone to infestation by mealy-bugs at higher temperatures.

Light: With its dark-green unmarked leaves, the plant can tolerate poor light, but turn it from time to time to prevent the stems growing crooked.

Remarks: This plant is particularly suitable for growing by hydroponics.

AGLAONEMA OBLONGIFOLIUM (Araceae)

Description: The parent species which has completely green leaves is not available in a cultivated form, but the variety 'Curtisii' is not hard to come by. This is a slow-growing plant. Its elliptical, acuminate leaves are greyish-green with silvery-grey, crosswise stripes slanting towards the tip and reaching almost to the leaf margin. A number of cultivated varieties with even more pronounced markings are derived from this compact, attractive plant.
Habitat: The parent species is from the tropical forest of Malaysia.
Minimum winter temperature: About 16 °C (61 °F), higher than for other species.
Light: Good, to maintain the plant's variegated markings.
Environmental humidity: High. The leaves must also be washed and sprayed. If conditions are too dry leaves drop and the plant loses its compact shape.
Watering: The plant's semi-rest period is less pronounced than in other species. Water sparingly between November and February, then gradually resume regular watering.

AGLAONEMA 'PSEUDO-BRACTEATUM' (Araceae)

Description: A medium-sized plant, normally reaching 50–80 cm (20–32 in) in bought specimens. Stem tips and petioles are white with green marbling. The long ovate-acuminate leaves are green with profuse, irregular markings of pale green, cream and white which show through on the underside. The petioles are usually long, but the plant is of upright habit although the stems sometimes display the usual tendency to grow crooked.
Habitat: The origin of this hybrid or mutation is not known. Its striking appearance and hardy disposition make it one of the most readily available forms of the genus.
Minimum winter temperature: 13–16 °C (55–61 °F).
Light: With inadequate light the plant loses some of its markings and the stems get leggy. Good, diffuse light is required.
Environmental humidity: The leaves must be washed and sprayed to discourage scale insects and keep the tissues in good condition.

AGLAONEMA ROEBELINII (Araceae)

Description: The species used to be classed as belonging to the *Schismatoglottis* genus and is sometimes still found under that name. It has fairly large ovate-acuminate leaves. On the whole its colouring is rather dull; the broad silvery markings which cover most of the leaf blade except the edges do not show up well against the greyish-green background. It is a good species to use in combination with other more brightly coloured plants and its slow growth means that it keeps its compact shape for some time.
Habitat: From the forests of Malaysia and Borneo.
Minimum winter temperature: About 16 °C (61 °F).
Light: Moderate light is adequate.
Environmental humidity: A much higher level is required than for other species, increased in every possible way, since the plant's strong colours depend on environmental humidity rather than light.
Watering: Even during the semi-rest period water fairly frequently, but make sure that the soil does not get waterlogged and cause the fleshy roots to rot.

ALOCASIA INDICA METALLICA (Araceae)

Etymology: This genus used to belong to the *Colocasia* genus which it closely resembles, and was given the similar-sounding name *Alocasia* when it was classified separately.
Description: All plants belonging to this genus of some fifty species and numerous hybrids are evergreen perennials which really need hothouse conditions. *Alocasia odora*, one of the largest plants, will tolerate lower temperatures and in mild climates can be grown out of doors in a sheltered position. *Alocasia indica* variety *metallica* is a very similar, smaller, attractive-looking plant. The leaves, which initially appear at the base, grow in a rosette from the rhizome buds and eventually form a short stem as they wither. The long petioles are sheathed at the base and winged in the lower section. The leaf blade is peltate and sagittate with very pronounced venation. Where the petiole joins the leaf two veins branch off from the midrib towards the tip of the lower lobes. The leaf is dark green with metallic glints on the upper face and a purplish red underneath. In *A. odora* the leaves are bright green.
Habitat: From eastern India and Malaysia. *Alocasia odora* comes from Formosa and the Philippines.
Minimum winter temperature: About 16 °C (61 °F).
Light: Excellent, away from direct sun. The plant tends to grow towards the light so should be turned from time to time.
Environmental humidity: High, increased as much as possible. Wash and sponge the leaves in winter to discourage mealy bugs.
Watering: Frequent in summer, sparing in winter. The plants have a semi-rest period when they lose some of their aerial parts.
Soil: A coarse, porous mixture composed of equal parts of leaf mould and peat with some sand or perlite. Good drainage is needed.
Propagation: By rhizome division in spring, making sure that each piece bears at least one bud. Maintain a temperature of about 21 °C (70 °F) and water moderately until the roots are properly developed.

ANANAS COMOSUM (Bromeliaceae)

Etymology: South American Indians called the plant *nanas* and M. Adanson adopted this as its scientific name at the beginning of the eighteenth century.

Description: This plant, often known by its old name *Ananas sativus*, is extensively grown in the tropics not for ornament but for commercial production of its popular fruit, the pineapple. It consists of a rosette of grey-green leaves growing directly from the root, curved on the outside with spines along the edges. The inflorescence which produces the fruit grows from the centre of this rosette. In some species the leaves are greyish, in others a bronze colour, but they are always very long and untidy. Young specimens and dwarf forms, especially of variegated varieties, can be grown in pots. In hot, moist greenhouse conditions they may even produce fruit on a small scale, although this is unlikely to occur in normal indoor conditions. After the first year the leaves get long and narrow and the plant loses its compact habit.

Habitat: From Brazil.

Minimum winter temperature: 16–18 °C (61–65 °F).

Light: Excellent, especially for variegated species, but keep out of very hot direct sun.

Environmental humidity: As high a level as possible.

Watering: Plentiful in summer, sparing in winter.

Soil: Porous and well-drained, consisting of two parts of partially rotted leaf mould to one of peat, with a good proportion of sand for good drainage. Use the smallest pots you can.

Propagation: If new shoots form round the base they can be used to propagate new plants, but they do not often occur indoors. Another method of propagation involves slicing off the crown of leaves which grows at the top of the fruit. Allow the fleshy part to dry out and then plant it in a sandy, almost dry potting mixture and keep at a temperature of at least 24 °C (75 °F). Simply spray the leaves until roots develop.

THE ANTHURIUM GENUS (Araceae)

Etymology: The generic name comes from the Greek *anthos*, or 'flower', and *'oura'*, or 'tail'. This refers to the spadix, which in many species is slender and erect or curling; it grows out like a small tail above the spathe, which does not enclose it.

Description: The genus consists of some 600 species with many more varieties and hybrids. However, relatively few species are cultivated; many are difficult to grow even in greenhouse conditions, and the foliage and general appearance of some species are rather straggly and not particularly attractive. The plants may be epiphytic or terrestrial. Most are herbaceous, though some are tree-like and others are suffrutescent, or woody in parts. Habit, foliage and proportions vary from species to species, but all have fleshy roots which need porous, well-drained soil, even in those plants which are not epiphytic in nature. The leaves may be entire or lobed, and sometimes have deeply slashed margins; many are palmate, and some are ribbon-shaped. Some have sunken veins with a corrugated surface between them. The leaf tissue is smooth or velvety. The inflorescences, consisting of the spadix, may grow inside the spathe or above it. The spathe may be inconspicuous or brightly coloured, and because of this a quite unscientific distinction is made for the convenience of growers between flowering and foliage species of the genus. Only those foliage plants which have attractive leaves apart from their inflorescences make good house plants.

Habitat: The genus originally comes from the tropical rain forests of Central and South America. Although some species grow at surprising altitudes, the main problem of cultivation is the high level of environmental humidity required, which is often impracticable even in a greenhouse.

Minimum winter temperature: About 16°C (61°F) for most cultivated foliage species.

Light: These forest plants tolerate moderate light and cannot stand direct sun.

Environmental humidity: Maximum, increased in every way. Plants with smooth foliage can be washed and sprayed, but hard water will mark velvety leaves. Even using distilled water any drops which collect on the epidermis are likely to cause fungus diseases, which appear as brown or yellow marks so that any damaged leaves must be removed.

Watering: Plentiful in summer, regular in winter. Never let water collect at the bottom of the pot or allow the soil to get heavy and waterlogged as this can damage the root system badly.

Soil: Very porous and well-ventilated, so that water runs through easily. You could use a mixture of equal parts of partly rotted leaf mould and peat with some crumbled sphagnum, sand or perlite, and lumps of charcoal. As aerial roots gradually form on the stem it is often a good idea to surround the base with a pad of sphagnum so that the aerial roots can grow into it and absorb moisture from it. However, see that the sphagnum is not too close-packed, as this may encourage rotting; leave it loose and well-ventilated.

Propagation: By stem cuttings, especially when the plant has plenty of bushy stems. Plant the cuttings in a very light and permeable mixture consisting of equal parts of peat, crumbled sphagnum, and sand or perlite. Keep moist but never waterlogged, at a temperature of 21–24°C (70–75°F). If conditions of maximum environmental humidity can be created it is best not to cover the cuttings, as this can encourage fungus disease, especially in species with velvety foliage. *Anthuriums* can easily be grown from seed if available, but the seeds only remain fertile for a very short period, as with most tropical plants, and growth is very slow. The seeds should be shallowly planted in crumbled sphagnum at a temperature of about 21°C (70°F).

ANTHURIUM COMTUM (Araceae)

Description: The species has smooth, short-stemmed dark green leaves, lanceolate-acuminate in shape, arranged in a rosette, with pronounced venation. Specimens available commercially probably do not belong to the parent species, but are more likely to be hybrids produced in conjunction with hardier species which do not need warm humid greenhouse conditions; they may even be young plants of closely related species, since when young many of them are heterophyllous, that is to say they have differently shaped leaves on the same plant. The species' distinctive characteristic is the inflorescence – a slender pink spathe with violet spadix – but as only adult plants flower, and even in greenhouse conditions do not do so readily, it is not easy to obtain this proof.

Habitat: From southern Brazil.

Minimum winter temperature: 16–18 °C (61–65 °F).

Light: A good diffuse light, well away from direct sun. As flowering is so unlikely to occur, the light may be more moderate than for other species.

Environmental humidity: High, and increased in every way, by spraying and washing the leaves often to keep the tissues turgid and glossy.

Watering: Plentiful in summer, very sparing in winter. Remember that rotting is the *Anthurium*'s worst enemy, because of the very fleshy roots.

Soil: Very porous and well-drained. You can use equal parts of partly rotted leaf mould, peat, crumbled sphagnum, and sand or perlite. Create a good deep drainage layer, perhaps using wood chips and lumps of charcoal.

Propagation: By stem cuttings from shoots bearing several aerial roots. Or by dividing the rosettes of leaves when more than one has formed. No covering is required in either case. Plant in porous soil, sterilized if possible, perhaps consisting of peat and sphagnum with some perlite, kept at about 24 °C (75 °F).

ANTHURIUM CRASSINERVIUM (Araceae)

Description: This species has tough, green, glossy, rather fleshy leaves arranged in a rosette. The leaf blade is elliptical in shape with undulate margins. The venation is pronounced and stands out on the underside. In due course the lower leaves drop and a sturdy stem forms on which roots appear, often reaching right down to the soil. The plant grows slowly, but may become very large. Usually only young specimens are available commercially, or hybrids which keep their compact habit longer and have shorter leaves than the parent species, in which the leaves of the adult plant may be as long as 1 m (3 ft 3 in).

Habitat: From the area round the Panama canal, also found in inland Venezuela.

Light: Diffuse, out of direct sun. The light need not be particularly intense, but in a bright position the plant grows more attractively.

Environmental humidity: High, to keep the leaf texture healthy. Spraying and washing are required in winter.

Watering: Plentiful in summer, well spaced from November to the end of January, regular the rest of the year, though taking temperature into account.

Soil: Humus-rich and porous, composed of two parts leaf mould to one of peat with some sand to increase drainage.

Propagation: In old plants adventitious stems sometimes form and can be used as cuttings. Old plants which have become ungainly can be put down, leaving some roots under the rosette of leaves; pot in a very damp, porous mixture of peat and crumbled sphagnum. The old stem will put out new shoots. The operation can be performed at any time of year, though it is best to wait until the growing season starts. The new plants need a temperature of about 21 °C (70 °F), but need not be covered.

ANTHURIUM CRYSTALLINUM (Araceae)

Description: This species has velvety, cordate, ovate heavily textured leaves which are dark or reddish green when young. The veins are emphasized by glittering silvery-white stripes which look as if they contained tiny fragments of crystal. There are many related species which are practically identical in appearance when young; as only young plants are sold, because of their more convenient size and better looks, you can hardly ever be quite sure which species you are buying. So growing these plants is chancy—hardiness depends on the different habitats of the different species.

Habitat: The true *A. crystallinum* comes from the rain forests at the foot of the Andes between Columbia and Peru. *A. magnificum* and *A. forgetii* are also Columbian species, but from the tropical forest. *A. clarinervium* is from the Chiapas forests of Mexico, and is used to more clearly differentiated seasons.

Minimum winter temperature: About 16 °C (61 °F).

Light: Diffuse, but not very strong, out of direct sun: the ideal place is a north-facing window.

Environmental humidity: Very high, but spraying the leaves can leave marks or encourage fungus diseases.

Watering: Plentiful in summer, sparing in winter.

Soil: Very light and porous, usually composed of equal parts of peat, leaf mould and crumbled sphagnum with some sand or perlite. Because the species is so prone to fungus diseases use sterilized leaf mould or a sterile, ready-prepared potting mixture.

Propagation: By stem cuttings. No covering is required, but plant in a very porous mixture such as sphagnum. Keep just moist at a temperature of about 24 °C (75 °F). The top part of the stem usually bears some roots which make the operation more likely to succeed. Cutting back the stem will encourage new stems to grow, and if the plant has more than one stem it can be divided at the start of the growing season; keep warm and carefully remove all dead roots. As a precaution dust the cuts with a sulphur-based fungicide powder.

APHELANDRA SQUARROSA (Acanthaceae)

Etymology: The name comes from the Greek *aphéles*, or 'simple', and *andrós*, or 'man', because the anthers have a single loculus.

Description: Evergreen plants with large, entire, acuminate leaves which are dark green on the upper surface with conspicuous ivory stripes along all the veins, and pale green on the underside. The leaves are arranged in pairs at each node on erect stems. The bilabiate, yellow flowers grow from a closely overlapping arrangement of bracts which are also yellow, forming a spike. There are two main varieties: *Aphelandra leopoldii*, which is in fact the same as the parent species, may grow as tall as 1 m (3 ft 3 in). *Aphelandra louisae* is smaller, with more pronounced variagation and brighter yellow flowers and bracts. Crossing them has produced the cultivar 'Fritz Prinsler' from which two further varieties, the compact 'Diana' and 'Brockfeld' have recently been developed.

Habitat: From Brazil.

Minimum winter temperature: About 16°C (61°F), but they tolerate warmer conditions.

Light: Excellent, but diffuse, out of direct sun. The plants are usually bought already in flower; they need a well-lit position to help the inflorescences last well, and to encourage new flowers to appear.

Environmental humidity: As high a level as possible, combined with spraying and light sponging of the leaves. Like all *Acanthaceae*, these plants readily lose their lower leaves and are liable to become infested by scale insects. Increased humidity means that the leaves are far less likely to wither and drop, and discourages the parasites, which are washed away while still at the unprotected larval stage.

Watering: Very plentiful in summer, but less frequent in winter when watering should be combined with measures to increase environmental humidity. Liquid fertilizer should be given when flower buds appear and, less frequently, during the growing season. If fertilizer is given at other times the leaves will grow well, but at the expense of flowers. *Aphelandras* flower best in fairly small pots; effective drainage is essential and the soil must never become waterlogged.

Soil: A humus-rich, very well-drained potting mixture: composted farmyard manure, well-rotted leaf mould, peat and sand in equal parts make a possible basic mixture. If you want to include a small amount of fertilizer in the mixture make sure it is rich in phosphate with a minimum of nitrogen.

Propagation: The young plants are more compact and attractive, so it is a good idea to take stem cuttings from time to time; plant the stem tips to root in a light mixture composed mainly of peat and sand. Keep at about 24°C (75°F) under a plastic cover which should be removed gradually. For quicker, surer rooting, try and keep the soil at a higher temperature; this can be done by standing the pot with its cover on a shelf over a radiator. The cuttings will need frequent airings.

ARAUCARIA EXCELSA (Araucariaceae)

Etymology: This genus and family, belonging to the *Coniferae*, are called after the Araucanos Indians of central Chile; the main species was native to their territory.

Description: In its natural setting the species is a large tree sometimes 50 m (165 ft) high. Obviously young specimens grown in pots never reach this size although as they get larger they can be grown outdoors in open ground in a suitable climate. Similar in shape to a fir tree, the plant is erect with a straight stem from which the verticillate branches radiate, forming whorls of between three and eight horizontal branches, which in a healthy plant grow parallel to the ground. The many needle-like, persistent leaves are short and often slightly curved; they are rather prickly and green or blue-green in colour. House plants are usually five or six-year-old specimens, less than 1 m (3 ft 3 in) in height, on average, with regular branches and short internodes.

Habitat: From Norfolk Island which lies to the West of Australia, between New Zealand and New Caledonia. The species was discovered by Captain Cook and brought into cultivation in 1793.

Minimum winter temperature: The plant can survive freezing temperatures but does best in cool, frost-free conditions in an unheated or almost unheated room.

Light: As strong as possible, out of direct sun.

Environmental humidity: At the correct temperature there is no problem. As the plant cannot stand warmer conditions anyway, there is little point in trying to increase the humidity to counteract the effects of a dry central-heated atmosphere.

Soil: Very well-drained, composed of equal parts of compost, well-rotted leaf mould, sand. Use the smallest pot possible, so long as the plant does not topple over, and provide an effective drainage layer.

Propagation: By apical stem cuttings or grafting, performed on plants specially grown for commercial purposes. Where the cut is made new shoots develop and can eventually be used for propagation. However this difficult technique is not recommended for house plants if you have only a single specimen of the species.

ASPLENIUM NIDUS (Polypodiaceae)

Etymology: The generic name comes from the Greek *splen*, or 'spleen', because one species was believed to be an effective cure for disorders of the spleen and liver. The species' full horticultural name is *nidus-avis* because the fronds are arranged in a rosette which looks rather like a birds' nest.

Description: Although the genus has over 600 species all over the world this is the only one grown for ornamental purposes. In nature it is epiphytic and has entire, oblanceolate fronds with undulate margins. The green, delicately textured blade grows out from a black central rachis or stem. The plant grows up to 1 m (3 ft 3 in) tall. The leaves grow in a crown directly from the rhizome, but may dry out and form a kind of short, brown, scaly stem.

Habitat: A very large area stretching from India to as far as Japan and Australia.

Minimum winter temperature: 10–16 °C (50–61 °F); at lower temperatures brown spots may appear on the fronds, while in warmer conditions the air is too dry and may make the plant wither.

Light: Fairly moderate and diffuse, out of direct sun.

Environmental humidity: As high as possible; wash and spray cautiously, making sure that the water does not trickle down and collect in the middle of the rosette.

Watering: Regular all the year round. Make sure the soil is well-drained: waterlogging would damage the rhizome.

Soil: Very light, airy and porous, composed of leaf-mould or sphagnum, peat and sand. Make a deep drainage layer and use the smallest pots you can.

Propagation: This is not always possible as new rosettes of leaves are unlikely to grow from the rhizome in indoor conditions. If they do, remove them and repot with a small piece of the rhizome in a sterile mixture containing some sand and perlite. Keep moist under a plastic cover which should be removed gradually once roots have formed.

THE BEGONIA GENUS (Begoniaceae)

Etymology: Linnaeus gave the genus its name in honour of Michel Begon (1638–1710), governor of Santo Domingo and a great patron of botanical studies.

Description: It is estimated that this enormous genus has more than a hundred species, as many varieties, and countless cultivars. All are purely ornamental and have no practical use, but the beautiful appearance of many species and the ease with which they can be grown from seed or from cuttings make them one of the commonest and most widely cultivated genera. The species all originally come from the tropical and subtropical regions of both the Old and New Worlds. Their range of form, size and habit makes classification difficult. The single characteristic they have in common is that they are all monoecious, bearing unisexual flowers on the same plant. The male flowers are usually caducous, and the female ones persistent with an ovary which becomes a winged fruit capsule, triangular in section, containing many very fine seeds. The cultivated varieties of tuberous-rooted begonias with double or multiple blooms differ from the normal flower form, and the sexual parts in most of them are transformed into petal-like organs: they only acquire the general characteristic if they revert to the simple form. There is no scientific classification of the genus, but for practical horticultural purposes begonias are usually subdivided into four categories based not on leaf shape, size or habit, but simply on the type of root system. According to this widely accepted division there are:
(a) bulbous species (with bulbous-tubers to be precise).
(b) tuberous species (this category includes some semi-tuberous types which are assumed to be hybrids rather than true species).
(c) rhizomatous species.
(d) fibrous-rooted species.
This classification is complicated by the fact that during the last century many hybrids were given Latin names which did not indicate parentage, so it is now often impossible to identify the true botanical species. Many species grow best in greenhouses, while others do well outdoors. Only certain rhizomatous and fibrous-rooted begonias are really suited to be ornamental house plants.

Minimum winter temperature: Varies greatly from species to species, but in general should not go below 13 °C (55 °F).

Light: All begonias are undergrowth plants and so cannot tolerate direct sunlight. However, rain forest species need less light than species from the deciduous tropical forest which are used to strong light in winter when most of the trees are bare.

Environmental humidity: Practically all members of the genus like a high level of humidity, although if the atmosphere is still and poorly ventilated they are liable to attack by mildew and fungus diseases, especially oidium.

Watering: Some species clearly have succulent tissues while in others only the tuberous or rhizomatous root system and the stems or veins have this characteristic. Water generously in summer, but less frequently in winter to prevent rotting. Tuberous species have a period of complete rest with no watering.

Soil: Whatever their natural habitat, all species are accustomed to humus-rich, porous soil with a constantly renewed supply of humus caused by the decomposition of organic detritus. Because they tend to be succulent they always need a well-drained mixture. Leaf mould and peat are the basic ingredients of a suitable mixture.

Propagation: Some begonias are among the easiest of plants to reproduce. The fine seeds can make growing from seed rather tiresome, but the regenerative powers of the tissues make it easy to grow new plants from stem cuttings of fibrous-rooted species, from pieces of rhizome or leaf cuttings of rhizomatous species, and by tuber division with tuberous species. The vital consideration is to avoid overwatering which can cause rotting and fungus diseases.

BEGONIA 'CLEOPATRA' (Begoniaceae)

Description: This cultivar which is quite commonly sold as a house plant has rhizomes which spread horizontally but are erect at the tip. In pots they tend to become decumbent when they reach the rim, but before this they can be kept fairly upright with supports. The leaves are long-stemmed, with red markings and tiny silvery bristles. The palmate, oblique, irregularly lobed leaf blade is a rather pale green with chocolate brown speckling, sometimes giving an overall bronzy hue. The epidermis is velvety. In greenhouses tall inflorescences with a large number of little pink flowers appear readily, but it is not easy to produce flowers indoors.

Habitat: The variety is a cross between two cultivated varieties, 'Maphil' × 'Black Beauty'. 'Maphil' is a descendant of *Begonia boweri* from the forests of southern Mexico. Neither parent needs high temperatures.

Minimum winter temperature: 13–16 °C (55–61 °F).

Light: Diffuse but strong. The plant will tolerate moderate light, but will not then flower successfully.

Environmental humidity: Fairly high, taking care that the leaves are not marked by spraying.

Watering: Plentiful in summer, well spaced in winter. The water must drain through easily and not collect at the bottom of the pot.

Soil: Light, composed of equal parts of well-rotted leaf mould and peat with some sand or peat.

Propagation: There are a number of possible methods. You can remove the tip of the rhizome or a piece of the rhizome, without leaves on it. Alternatively you can take a leaf cutting, with a small piece of the petiole attached to the base; a new plantlet will develop from this if it's placed in very porous, barely moist soil. In all cases the soil must be very porous and barely moist to discourage rotting; for the same reason the cuttings should not be covered. The plants do not like being transplanted, and so if the rhizomes get too long it is simplest to take cuttings.

BEGONIA MASONIANA (Begoniaceae)

Description: Although rather difficult to grow, this is one of the most beautiful species and so is fairly common in nurseries. It has rhizomes which spread horizontally and from which the long hairy reddish petioles grow. The leaves are more or less round. The upper surface is covered all over with little reliefs with a short red hair growing from the centre of each. There are intersecting broad brown bands along the main veins: they do not reach right to the edge and stand out against their green background, forming the pattern which has earned the plant its common name of 'iron cross' begonia. In greenhouse conditions it often produces tall inflorescences of small greenish-white flowers, but it is unlikely to flower indoors unless a great deal of light can be provided.

Habitat: The plant was fairly recently introduced into England from Singapore; its true habitat is not known, but is thought to be Indonesia or Malacca.

Minimum winter temperature: About 16 °C (61 °F).

Light: Good, diffuse light; it cannot stand sun.

Environmental humidity: Increase in every way, especially by standing the pot on moist gravel. Never let water collect round the base and do not spray, as this may cause fungus diseases.

Watering: Regular in summer, well-spaced in winter. Never let the soil get waterlogged, as this may kill off the rhizome.

Soil: Porous and humus-rich, composed of equal parts of leaf mould and peat with a good proportion of sand or perlite to increase drainage. Avoid an ordinary mixture as the plants, like all begonias, much prefer an acid soil. Some ericaceous mixture could be added to good effect.

Propagation: By rhizome division or leaf cuttings which are placed, with a small piece of the petiole attached, in a well-aerated, just moist mixture. They need not be covered but like a moist atmosphere, a temperature of 24 °C (75 °F) and almost dry soil. Cuttings can be taken at any time of year.

▲ *Begonia rex cultorum*

BEGONIA REX CULTORUM (Begoniaceae)

Description: These handsome, exceptionally decorative plants form a whole group of hybrids. Many of them have been named, but are unlikely to be sold under the correct name except in specialist nurseries. The numerous cultivars have a horizontal growing rhizome, sometimes erect for a short section, with very oblique, acuminate leaves with dentate, lobed or serrated edges. The upper surface is variegated in a wide range of colours – green, pink, red or silver. In some the whole leaf is silver with pink or red glints. In some forms the leaf base is attached to the end of the petiole to form a spiral.

Habitat: All these hybrids derive from the true *Begonia rex*, originally from Annam, crossed with various other species, particularly *Begonia diadema*, a fibrous-rooted Indonesian species with satiny, deeply incised green and silver leaves, which is clearly the ancestor of several cultivars.

Light: Good but diffuse; types with red colouring need more light.

Environmental humidity: As high as possible, but with good ventilation. Do not spray the leaves.

Watering: Regular in summer, well spaced in winter. Old varieties used to lose their leaves during the rest period and this still quite often happens. In this case the rhizome should be given the bare minimum of water to prevent it drying out and it will produce new growth when spring comes.

Soil: A light, acid mixture of well rotted leaf mould and peat with some sand. Do not let the soil get sodden and clogged as this can drown the delicate roots and make the rhizome rot.

Propagation: By rhizome division or leaf cuttings. Leaf cuttings may either be taken with a piece of the petiole attached as for other species.

▲ *Begonia rex cultorum*

BOWIEA VOLUBILIS (Liliaceae)

Etymology: The genus is called after James Bowie (c. 1789–1869) who collected plants in Brazil and South Africa for Kew Gardens in London.

Description: The genus consists of a single type, one of the strangest of all plants. Although it is not common it is worth growing if you can find it, as it is an easy plant as well as a curious one. It is a South African succulent with a large round green bulb which produces a slender, turning green stem with numerous forked softwood twigs producing small green inconspicuous flowers at the tip. Both stem and branches are completely leafless and they are responsible for the production of chlorophyll. The plant generally has a summer rest period, especially when adult.

Habitat: South Africa, in very sandy, well-drained soil, sometimes in the savanna.

Minimum winter temperature: About 13 °C (55 °F), but can be warmer.

Light: Good, diffuse; it does not like direct sunlight.

Environmental humidity: Increased in winter in warm conditions, otherwise mealy-bug infestation is likely to occur.

Watering: Regular in winter, but allow the soil to dry out well in between. Water at less frequent intervals during the summer when the stem begins to dry out. For a period give no water at all, and then start again in about October when new growth appears.

Soil: Humus rich, but with no unrotted organic matter. Use equal parts of very rotted leaf mould, compost and sand. The bulb should be planted with soil only half way up, and needs very effective drainage.

Propagation: Usually by seed, which is hard to get. Sometimes adventitious bulblets form round the main bulb and these can be removed and repotted singly. For the first two or three years the plant does not need a rest period, but cautious watering is required.

THE CALADIUM GENUS (Araceae)

Etymology: The origin of the name is not certain, but it probably comes from the Malay *Kaladi*.

Description: Perennial, herbaceous foliage plants which are deciduous and have a winter rest period. They have tuberous roots. The large leaves, usually sagittate, but sometimes lanceolate, are borne on long petioles which grow directly from the tip of the buds on the tuber. In the greenish inflorescences the spadix is shorter than the spathe; they never appear except in greenhouse conditions, and are fairly inconspicuous. The leaves are very fine, with brightly coloured speckled and variegated markings. The plants grown nowadays are all hybrids descended from *Caladium bicolor* crossed with one of the few species belonging to the genus. The hybrids with lanceolate leaves inherit this feature from *Caladium picturatum*.

Habitat: From South America, particularly Brazil, but one variety of *C. bicolor* is from the W. Indies.

Light: Very good, to maintain the colouring, but shielded from direct sun. Plants with red markings need brighter conditions.

Minimum winter temperature: In winter the tubers should be kept dry in their pots at about 16 °C (61 °F) until it is time to start them in growth again.

Environmental humidity: During the growing period humidity should be increased in every way, including spraying the foliage.

Watering: The tubers should be brought into cultivation during February or March, and at first they only require fairly moderate watering until the first shoots appear and grow a few centimetres. The tubers should be repotted until they reach their final size. Each time allow a period for the plant to settle down and then water more frequently, and during the summer more generously. When the leaves start to die down, gradually give less water and stop altogether in autumn.

Soil: At the start of cultivation the tubers should be planted in the smallest possible pots and partially covered with a mixture consisting of equal parts of compost, leaf mould and sand. For tall plants the tuber should be placed with the tip on the uncovered side; if you want a lower more bushy plant put it the other way up. During this period the temperature should be as high as possible, up to 40 °C (104 °F) in theory. At the first repotting some peat can be added to the mixture so long as there is a good, deep drainage layer. A small amount of well-composted farmyard manure can usefully be added at the final repotting. Avoid fertilizers containing nitrogen which encourages the green parts.

Propagation: In nurseries *Caladiums* are grown from seed, but usually propagation is by tuber division. Before bringing the tubers into growth cut them into pieces, each bearing at least one bud. Dust the cuts with a sulphur-based fungicide powder to prevent rotting. Keep the atmosphere dry until you are sure the cuts have healed.

THE CALATHEA GENUS (Marantaceae)

Etymology: The name derives from the Greek *Kaláthos*, 'basket', although the reasons are somewhat blurred; some authors suppose that the plant is so called because in some species the flowers grow on inflorescences resembling baskets; others maintain that the natives of Latin America used the leaves for basket-weaving.

Description: The genus includes some 130 species of perennial, leafy, evergreen plants, some of which are grown both in the hothouse and indoors, although they are particularly tender; in horticultural jargon they are often muddled with the genus *Maranta* and offered for sale as such. The roots are rhizomatous or tuberose; the long-stemmed leaves grow directly from the stem in clusters. Varying considerably in both shape and texture, the leaves may be leathery or velvety, but are invariably marked with patterns and blotches which make them very decorative. The inflorescences, which, incidentally, never appear indoors and rarely in the hot house unless the plant is very well-developed, are usually dully coloured.

Habitat: The genus comes from the shady, tropical forests of South and Central America; many species come in particular from Brazil, while others are natives of Colombia, Peru, and even southern Mexico.

Minimum winter temperature: 16–18 °C (61–65 °F).

Light: For all the species little light is needed; strong light will often cause the leaves to curl and it will be necessary to place the plant in a shadier spot for it to resume its normal appearance. Strong light is thus less important than the duration of exposure: all the species are subject to nyctonastia, that is, their leaves straighten when in the dark; this, however, occurs in the natural habitat where day and night last more or less the same number of hours. In effect this movement occurs about every 12 hours, and if exposure is extended artificially, the stems straighten even under light, before it grows dark. Absence of this movement may be attributed, to low environmental humidity or attacks from parasites, mites in particular; healthy plants should be regularly checked as a result.

Environmental humidity: The level required by all the species represents the major problem for indoor cultivation, and should be increased by any means available.

Watering: Water plentifully in summer, less often from November to March, and regularly at other times. It is important that the rhizomatose roots should not be damaged by too much moisture, because even if the aerial growth wilts the plant will grow new shoots if the rhizomes or small tubers are healthy.

Soil: Light, porous and very acid; made up, for example, of leaf-mould and peat in equal parts with sand or perlite added. Keep well drained; the soil must never form clods because it is too wet, or be too loose or thin.

Propagation: Unlike other genera of the same family, reproduction occurs solely by division. A temperature of at least 24 °C (75 °F) is required; it is advisable to keep the new plants under plastic covers to increase the humidity until they are evidently sturdy; they should be aired every so often to avoid too much condensation, and the covers should be removed gradually. If there is no foliage, and just the roots are divided, no cover will be necessary, but the soil must be very porous, and the humidity level low but constant.

CALATHEA INSIGNIS (Marantaceae)

Description: This very bushy plant is rather small and compact. Its leaves are linear-lanceolate, acuminate, with slightly wavy edges. On the upper blade, on both sides of the central nervation, there is a pattern consisting of dark green patches which are oblong and irregular, but almost always alternate, one being long and the other short. The former reach almost to the edge, while the latter look like small olives. The lower blade is very dark violet-red; the leaf-clusters grow fairly upright from a sheath which subsequently withers.

Habitat: From Brazil.

Remarks: Although it still needs light and humidity, this is perhaps the easiest species to grow indoors. The foliage should be regularly washed and sprinkled, but it appears to be less liable to red-spider attacks than other species of the same genus.

CALATHEA MAKOYANA (Marantaceae)

Description: Prized for its beauty, this plant is now one of the commonest of the genus, although by no means easy to grow. The leaves, on their long stems, are oval or elliptical; on both blades there is a pattern which, though not regular, is fairly symmetrical, on both sides of the main nervation, with dark-green olive-shaped markings alternating with longer, often slightly sickle-shaped forms reaching almost to the edge. The surface between the variegations is pale and verging on transparent, criss-crossed with very fine green lines; on the lower blade both the pattern and the texture of the surface are repeated in reddish green, which may be shaded with dark red.

Habitat: From Brazil.

Remarks: This species is very liable to attacks from mites and needs a very high level of environmental humidity; the light should be moderate but slightly stronger than for other species if specimens with upright foliage are to be obtained: plenty of humidity and light from above produce hothouse specimens of considerable height which are tricky to keep indoors for this reason.

CALATHEA ORNATA (Marantaceae)

Family: This is a very variable species with two major varieties.

Description: The variety *roseo-lineata* has ovate leaves with a dark-green surface on which there are thin pink lines running from near the central vein to just short of the edge. They are as if drawn and as the leaf ages they turn white. The variety *sanderiana* has broader, dark olive-green leaves and the pink lines almost reach the margin. The other side of the leaf is darkened in both varieties.

Habitat: From Guyana and Colombia.

Remarks: In the photo: *Calathea ornata var. roseo-lineata* is a pretty plant which needs a high level of environmental humidity.

▲ *Calathea ornata roseo-lineata*

CEROPEGIA WOODII (Asclepiadaceae)

Etymology: The name derives from *kerós*, 'wax' and *peghé*, 'fountain' probably both because of the waxy appearance of the flowers and leaves and for the fact that the stems spring from the tuber like sprays from a fountain.

Description: This small plant is very common in Anglo-Saxon countries where it is sometimes called the necklace of hearts because of the shape of its leaves. Its tubers reach an average size of 2 cm (1 in) or slightly more; they produce slender stems which bear well-spaced small leaves which are opposite, heart-shaped, and grey-green with silvery nervations; other small aerial tubers may appear at the axil, although in the natural state these are creeping plants and the tubers take root in the ground. The small flowers are quite unusual, and hence attractive: they have a long tubular corolla which is swollen at the base and are violet in colour.

Habitat: From South Africa.

Minimum winter temperature: About 10°C (50°F) to allow a semi-dormant period.

Light: Plenty of light is required; the plant will only flower if exposed to a lot of summer light, but not direct sunlight.

Environmental humidity: Fairly high, especially in winter, but avoid stagnating water and provide plenty of ventilation.

Watering: Water regularly in summer and sparingly in winter, so that wet soil does not cause the tubers to rot; the plant's needs should be met by atmospheric humidity.

Soil: Humus-rich and well-drained, made up of leaf-mould, sphagnum and sand in equal parts. Hanging baskets are ideal, but they may also be grown in wide, shallow pots with good drainage; the tubers should not be completely buried and the slender stems will need supporting.

Propagation: By means of the tubers, whether already rooted or aerial, placed quite simply on top of the soil, which should be moist but never too wet, and pressed lightly into it without covering them.

CHAMAEDOREA ELEGANS (Palmae)

Etymology: The name derives from the Greek, very probably from *chamaí*, 'dwarf' and *dóry*, 'tree, treetrunk'; in fact many of the species are not very tall. This species in particular is still often sold as *Neanthe bella* or *Collinia elegans*, although some authors hold that these are different species or at least local varieties of the same species.

Description: This small palm may grow to a height of 1·50 m (5 ft) or more, but smaller specimens are usually sold. It has pretty, curved and pinnate fronds which may reach a metre (yard) in length, each segment being 2–3 cm wide and 10 cm long (4 in). The trunk is often solitary, but it may produce subterranean stolons; in the family only species with this feature can be reproduced by division; all species with a single stem are reproduced by seed.

Habitat: The typical species comes from Mexico, although there is a Guatemalan variety which seems to be even smaller; specimens for sale probably belong to the latter group, or are intermediate forms.

Minimum winter temperature: 13–16 °C (56–61 °F).

Light: Although moderate light will suffice the plant will become more handsome under good light conditions and produce racemes of small yellow flowers and, in some cases, small fruit.

Environmental humidity: Fairly high; also sprinkle the fronds.

Watering: Water regularly in summer and sparingly in winter.

Soil: Humus-rich, made up of compost with sand and peat added for good drainage. The pots should be quite small, and, if anything, taller than they are wide: the growth will often push the stem upwards with the appearance of the first roots beneath the surface; repotting is called for in such cases.

Propagation: By seed, but growth is slow, and the seed must be very new. A simpler way is by division when there is more than one stem; repot each division with its root system intact at about 21 °C (70 °F) at the start of the vegetative period in spring.

THE CISSUS GENUS (Vitaceae)

Etymology: The name derives from the Greek *kissós*, 'ivy' and refers to the fact that most of the species are climbing plants.

Description: As a rule the genus consists of suffruticose plants, some of which are evergreen, with single leaves, or leaves composed of three smaller, alternate leaflets with tendrils at the axil used for training the sarmentose branches along supports. The inflorescences have dullish flowers and appear at the axil of the leaves; they are followed by berry-like fruit. Among the more than 200 species in the genus, some are herbaceous, while others, though climbers, are succulent and like compact soil; then there are others, hardly cultivated at all, which are very carnose shrubs with broad stems, flask-shaped at the base, peculiar to exceptionally arid places. Among the species usually grown indoors, two pose few problems and are adaptable, while a third is extremely delicate and is in fact best suited to the hothouse.

Habitat: Various species occur in every tropical and subtropical corner of the world.

Minimum winter temperature: 10–18 °C (50–65 °F) depending on the original habitat.

Light: Plenty of diffused light, but slender-stemmed climbers must not be exposed to direct sunlight; succulent species like as much light as possible, including direct sunlight.

Environmental humidity: Plenty of humidity in general, and a high level for certain species.

Watering: Water plentifully in summer and sparingly in winter; all species of *Cissus* need a semi-dormant period, and some may even shed their leaves if the conditions are not right.

Soil: Humus-rich and well-drained for all species; fairly light and acid, varying with the natural habitat.

Propagation: Usually buy cuttings taken from the top of a semi-mature stem which is not too herbaceous, nor too tender, so as to avoid rot. The climbers with their flexible stems may also be reproduced by soil layering.

CISSUS ANTARCTICA (Vitaceae)

Description: A climbing plant with slender stems with tendrils, single, shiny, dark-green, acuminate, cordate-based leaves; the margins are dentate or crenate and the depressed veins stand out. The stems are tomentose or downy.

Habitat: From Australia, originally native to the forests of New South Wales.

Minimum winter temperature: 10–13 °C (50–55 °F); in intense heat with little ventilation it is easy prey to scale.

Light: Very tolerant, even in moderate light.

Environmental humidity: It usually suffices to maintain the humidity level by sprinkling and spraying the foliage with an atomizer.

Watering: Water plentifully in summer in well-exposed places, and regularly in less well-lit places; water moderately in winter.

Soil: Humus-rich mould made up of compost with one-third advanced leaf-mould added and a little sand.

Propagation: By cuttings taken from the top of a non-tender, semi-mature ligneous stem and placed in sandy mixture at a temperature of about 18 °C (65 °F) under glass or plastic covers which can be gradually opened to air the cuttings and avoid stagnation and condensation, which would rot the leaves. They may be taken at any time of year, but most safely at the start of the vegetative period, or in late summer if taken from more mature wood.

CISSUS DISCOLOR (Vitaceae)

Description: This suffruticose climber has slender, flexuous, reddish branches; it is especially delicate as well as being extremely beautiful. The oblong leaves, which are cordate from the base and have short red stalks, give a relief effect between the green depressed veins; the relief is silvery in colour while the central part along the main nervation is shaded violet to red and looks velvety. The underside of the leaf is dark reddish-violet, tending to brown.
Habitat: From the tropical forests of Indonesia and Cambodia.
Minimum winter temperature: 16–18 °C (61–65 °F).
Light: Diffused, not in direct sunlight, but fairly strong to preserve the colouring of the plant; in poor light the leaves will lose their velvety look and turn an almost uniform green.
Environmental humidity: As high as possible; this plant is really best-suited to humid hothouses, but it will not tolerate stale air, which gives rise to cryptogamic diseases and scale insect attacks.
Watering: Water regularly in summer, sparingly in winter, when it can easily lose its leaves and become deciduous if there is insufficient humidity and heat.
Soil: Light and porous made up of leaf-mould and peat in equal parts with sphagnum and sand added to keep it fresh and moist. Must be very carefully drained.
Propagation: By cuttings taken from young growth; pieces of woody defoliated stem may also be used pressed lightly into sphagnum or peat which is barely moist: these pieces will develop roots at each node. The flexible stems may be trained across damp mould by way of soil layering, and removed when they have rooted. The temperature required is about 21–24 °C (70–75 °F), and the best time is late spring, when the vegetative period commences, and it is often necessary to prune the old and leafless branches.
Remarks: If there is a good deal of environmental humidity this species may be grown with its branches hanging, but it is generally more advisable to provide supports for the sarmentose branches.

CISSUS RHOMBIFOLIA (Vitaceae)

Description: This very common plant is easily run to earth under its old name: *Rhoicissus rhomboidea*. The sarmentose branches, covered with brown down, may be left hanging, and the plant can be left in a hanging basket as long as it is well pruned, because, as a climber, its vigorous growth would otherwise require sturdy supports. The leaves are composite, formed by three stemmed leaflets which are rhomboid in shape, dark-green in colour, and have depressed veins. The young growth is covered with a light-coloured down which makes an attractive contrast.
Habitat: From Central America, and northern parts of South America.
Minimum winter temperature: About 10 °C (50 °F), or slightly more, but it will tend to wilt in strong heat with little ventilation.
Light: Being a green plant, it will grow happily in moderate light.
Watering: Water regularly in summer and sparingly in winter.
Soil: No specific requirements: it may be made up of compost with a little leaf-mould and sand added to prevent it clodding too much.
Propagation: By cuttings taken from young branches which take root easily in spring and summer, with a temperature of about 20 °C (68 °F) in a porous and sandy soil mixture.

CITRUS MITIS (Rutaceae)

Etymology: The name of the genus comes from the Latin *citrus*, 'citron', which Linnaeus and others after him extended to the whole genus, including those species commonly known as 'citrus fruit'.

Description: This is a small tree with spreading as well as upright branches, and green, entire and oval leaves with slightly alate stalks. The plant is completely defenceless and in summer has small, white, scented, solitary flowers at the tip of the branchlets, followed in winter by small, spherical, orange fruit, like oranges with very acid pulp. Although not really an indoor plant, given that it is semi-hardy and can be grown outdoors in milder European climates, at least when the specimen involved is already lignified, it is often found in shops in winter, in fruit, ready to decorate well-lit rooms which must not be too warm, because too much heat will cause the fruit to drop off. This evergreen plant is thus quite decorative, but it is best kept outside in summer so as to flower and be pollinated; bring it back inside when the fruit have formed.

Habitat: From the Philippines.

Minimum winter temperature: 5–10 °C (40–50 °F).

Light: Very strong, including direct sunlight, but more important is good ventilation and a cool place.

Environmental humidity: Not particularly called for at the temperatures indicated.

Watering: Water regularly in summer and quite sparingly in winter, so that the soil may dry out between one watering and the next.

Soil: As for all citrus fruit, the soil must be very humus-rich, consisting of compost with a little sand added to avoid stagnating water. During the summer, add a little liquid fertilizer or manure and replace the upper soil layer every two years with composted farmyard manure to help the flowering and fruit.

Propagation: This is difficult and slow if cuttings are taken. Air layering may be carried out on lignified branches.

▼ *Codiaeum variegatum 'punctatum aureum'*

CODIAEUM VARIEGATUM (Euphorbiaceae)

Etymology: The name is of uncertain derivation: some authors maintain that it comes from the local Malayan name *kodiho*. In horticultural practice these plants are known by the name *Croton* which is another genus of the same family.

Description: All the plants on sale nowadays come from the species *Codiaeum variegatum* in the variety: *pictum*. These plants are shrubs which may grow quite large in the wild, but, when cultivated, usually reach a metre in height; the leaves are invariably single, alternate, smooth and leathery and come in a great variety of shapes and colours. When young, they have green leaves with white or yellow variegations which gradually turn somewhat red, or pink or orange. The flowers which grow on long, slender inflorescences in spikes, are small and inconspicuous. One of the sturdiest varieties is *punctatum aureum*, with slender green leaves speckled with off-white or pale yellow.

Habitat: The various forms of the species are found over a huge area from southern India and Ceylon throughout Malaya to the Sunda Isles.

Minimum winter temperature: 16–18 °C (61–65 °F).

Environmental humidity: As high as possible.

Light: Very strong, specially with the red-leaved forms.

Watering: Water plentifully in summer and regularly in winter.

Soil: Humus-rich and porous, it may consist of equal parts of mature leaf-mould and peat, with sand added.

Propagation: By cuttings from semi-mature wood in winter, with glass or plastic covers, at a temperature of about 24 °C (75 °F) or more. Air layering on mature wood is often preferable on large, leafless specimens.

CORDYLINE TERMINALIS (Liliaceae)

Etymology: The name comes from the Greek *kordýle*, 'club' because of the shape of the roots in certain species.

Description: This is a shrubby evergreen plant grown for its foliage; it has white, stoloniferous roots which differentiate it from the related *Dracaena* which does not have stoloniferous roots, these being yellow or brownish-red in colour. The leaves of the typical species are oblong-lanceolate, bronze-green with pink or red shading when young, but the numerous varieties on the market today have leaves which are white, pink or red when young, and keep red margins when fully grown. The variety *tricolor* has broader leaves with red, pink and cream-coloured variegations.

Habitat: From the East Indies and Pacific Islands.

Minimum winter temperature: About 16 °C (61 °F).

Light: Very strong, diffused, but not direct sunlight, so as to keep the red colouring of the leaves.

Environmental humidity: Fairly high; the leaves should be frequently sprayed with an atomizer and sprinkled.

Watering: Water plentifully in summer and regularly in winter, so that the soil does not become too saturated, which would endanger the carnose roots; never let the water collect at the bottom of the pot.

Soil: Made up of leaf-mould with peat, sand and possibly a little shredded sphagnum added to keep the roots moist and fresh and to prevent the water stagnating, which will cause rot.

Propagation: By cuttings from the uppermost parts, under plastic covers in very sandy soil at a temperature of 21 °C (70 °F); air them every so often and remove the covers very gradually. Cuttings may also be taken from pieces of defoliated stem, placed vertically in the soil or laid across it horizontally, with the same soil and temperature, but without covers: the new plants will grow from the nodes. The old stem will produce new shoots which can be kept or used later as cuttings.

99

CROSSANDRA INFUNDIBULIFORMIS
(Acanthaceae)

Etymology: The name comes from the Greek *krassós*, 'fringe' and *andrós*, 'male', because of the fringed anthers.

Description: This is a small evergreen shrub with entire, ovate, acuminate, dark-green leaves with depressed veins. The flowers grow on a spiked inflorescence; they are tubular and bilabiate, scarlet or orange in colour; they appear amid evident bracts arranged in squares, and closely overlap with them.

Habitat: From India; in the wild state they may reach one metre in height, but when cultivated grow in pots to between 35–50 cm (14–20 in).

Minimum winter temperature: 13–15°C (55–59°F).

Light: Plenty of light, but not direct sunlight. Strong light together with good ventilation is essential for flowering, which is this plant's only decorative attribute.

Environmental humidity: Fairly high, using whatever means possible, but do not sprinkle when flowering.

Watering: Water plentifully in summer, with liquid fertilizers, especially of the phosphorus type; water moderately in winter when the temperature should not be too high and the air as humid as possible.

Soil: Very humus-rich soil, made up of leaf-mould and peat with a little compost and sand added.

Propagation: As happens with all the *Acanthaceae*, the lower leaves drop off and the stem remains bare; it is thus advisable to root top-cuttings every so often, in very sandy soil, with covers which should be removed at intervals to air the plants, and then removed altogether but gradually as the roots develop; the temperature should be about 24°C (75°F) and the soil must not be too wet to avoid cryptogamic diseases. Several cuttings are usually planted together to give a better effect; the old stem will also produce new growth.

THE CRYPTANTHUS GENUS (Bromeliaceae)

Etymology: The name comes from the Greek *kryptós*, 'hidden' and *ánthos*, 'flower' because in most species the sessile flowers remain hidden near the centre of the plant.

Description: This genus, which includes some 15 species and many varieties, some of which are wild, and others produced by crossing, consists almost exclusively of evergreen, herbaceous, dwarf or, if not dwarf, small plants; they are all acaulescent and the leaves grow in characteristic rosettes, usually flat in shape; only some species have the central 'vase'; in others the leaves are so flat and even outward-turned that there is no central cavity and water runs off them with no trouble. Many, in fact, are epiphytes in the wild state, or at least grow in very thin layers of soil, and need little water round the roots. The leaves are often a very beautiful colour, but usually need a lot of light if the colour is to be preserved.

Habitat: The entire genus is from Brazil: the favourite haunts of most of the species are the intersections of branches of tall trees in tropical forests, but they will sometimes also grow on rocks around clearings.

Minimum winter temperature: About 16°C (61°F), but if kept very dry some species will tolerate slightly lower temperatures.

Light: Diffused, avoiding direct sunlight, but enough to preserve the colours of the leaves. Should the colour fade, simply place the plant in a better-lit spot and within a fortnight the colours will have returned.

Environmental humidity: As high as possible, combined with sprinkling and spraying, given that these plants can absorb directly through the leaves as can almost all the members of this family.

Watering: Water regularly in summer, allowing the soil to dry out slightly between waterings, and very sparingly in winter. The actual shape of the plant often stops the water reaching the soil, except in very small amounts; in this case it may be advisable to immerse the pot in a container filled with water every so often. Great care should be taken when so doing, however.

Soil: Very soft and well-drained, made up of leaf-mould and peat in equal parts, with sand added; if these plants are grown on trunks or pieces of hanging wood, a certain amount of sphagnum will be needed to absorb and maintain the moisture; watering in such cases will be by sprinkling or intermittent immersion in water.

Propagation: This is made very simple because of the large number of shoots produced both from the sides and from the centre of the rosette; these can be removed without harming the plant. They can be potted in peat and shredded sphagnum or moss, but the rooting process is a slow one and they often continue not only to live but also to reproduce without having taken root, on nothing more than the atmospheric humidity. It is obvious that covers are not required because these would rot the tender young shoots, but the temperature should be around 21°C (70°F) and the soil should be kept just moist. If these conditions are met, reproduction can be carried out at any time of year.

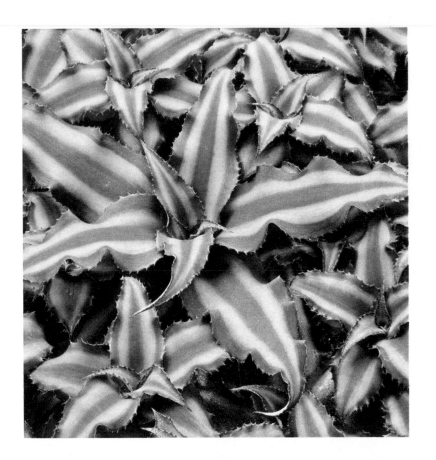

CRYPTANTHUS BIVITTATUS (Bromeliaceae)

Description: This usually acaulescent plant is fairly small; it has linear leaves arranged in rosettes which are very flat and hence often outward-turned; the margins have thorns and are almost always slightly wavy: the surface is olive-green with two paler, lengthwise stripes. There are several varieties: the commonest is *Cryptanthus bivittatus*, var. *roseo-pictus* which is also the smallest variety, in which the two stripes are cream-coloured with pink shading; the colours will fade if there is little light and humidity. The plants produce offshoots at the sides and also large numbers of shoots from the centre of the rosette; these latter often drop off of their own accord or at the slightest touch.
Habitat: All the varieties are from Brazil.
Light: Diffused, not direct sunlight, but plentiful if the colours are to be kept.
Environmental humidity: As high as possible, with the added use of sprinkling and spraying.
Watering: Water regularly in summer and sparingly in winter.
Soil: In the wild state they grow either on the ground or as epiphytes; when cultivated they are usually grown in the ground; they must however have fairly soft and permeable soil, which goes for the whole genus.
Propagation: By removing the off-shoots and potting them in sphagnum and peat. The rooting process is very slow, but the plant will in no way suffer from a temporary absence of roots and will even survive for some time without any, as long as the soil is kept almost dry.

CRYPTANTHUS BROMELIOIDES TRICOLOR (Bromeliaceae)

Description: This is the tallest species in the genus; its upright leaves, slightly wavy at the margin, form a rosette which may also briefly become caulescent. The wild species with its bronze-green leaves is never cultivated, but the variety *tricolor* is very common and one of the finest plants in the whole family. The leaves are irregularly variegated lengthwise in ivory-white which, in good light, becomes crimson-pink (sometimes very intense at the margins and base). Outside the greenhouse the pinkish hue often disappears, or at least fades; but the plant is still very pretty and tillers quite readily, forming large clumps.
Habitat: The typical species is from central Brazil; the variety *tricolor* is a mutation.
Watering: Temperature and humidity requirements are as for the other species; but this species likes to be watered more frequently than the others, in addition to having a high humidity level. The pots should be as small as possible.
Propagation: From the side-shoots in well-drained soil made up of peat and shredded sphagnum; the environmental humidity should be higher than for the other species to stop the leaves curling, and covers may also be used to keep it at a good level; the plants should however be frequently aired to avoid stagnation which will cause rot.

CRYPTANTHUS FOSTERIANUS (Bromeliaceae)

Description: When fully grown this species has a large rosette of leaves which may reach 50 cm (20 in) in diameter and is rather flat; the leaves are coppery-green with uneven horizontal grey and ochre-yellow markings. Given, however, that only young are found in the shops and therefore rather small specimens, this species is often confused with *Cryptanthus zonatus*, and in particular with the variety *zebrinus* which is very like it, but smaller still, with dark-green leaves with pale ochre and brown markings and stripes and often with silvery highlights. Both species flower very easily, with small white blooms growing from the centre and at the axil of the innermost leaves; they produce plenty of sideshoots which turn into runners (stolons) with a new rosette at the tip, before the one that has flowered dies.

Habitat: Both species come from Brazil, and are found in the mountainous regions west of Recife where they often grow in cracks in rocks.

Remarks: Light, humidity and watering are as for the whole genus, but the soil must be slightly richer in humus, though still very well-drained, and also contain a little leaf-mould. Reproduction is virtually obligatory, given that the off-shoots do not manage to take root in the pot because of the long stolons, and have to be removed and potted when the leaf rosette which has flowered starts to wither.

CTENANTHE LUBBERSIANA (Marantaceae)

Etymology: The name of this genus comes from the Greek *kteis*, 'comb' and *ánthos*, 'flower', after the form of the inflorescences, which in some species have bracts.

Description: These perennial, herbaceous plants have slender stems which grow from clusters of caulinar leaves which, in turn, have more leaf-clusters at the nodes, often fan-shaped before growing out or bifurcating. The leaves have a long stalk and are oblong-linear; the upper blade is green with irregular pale-green and yellow variegations; the lower blade is light green. Several species in the genus — including this one — may produce roots at the nodes and thus be reproduced by cuttings, as well as ordinary division of the stoloniferous roots.

Habitat: From the tropical forests of Brazil.

Minimum winter temperature: About 16 °C (61 °F).

Light: This plant is not particularly demanding and will tolerate moderate light; never expose to direct sunlight; too much indirect light will also cause the leaves to curl.

Environmental humidity: As high as possible; wash the leaves frequently, to prevent attacks from mites.

Watering: Water plentifully in summer and sparingly in winter; never saturate the soil, which would cause the roots to rot.

Soil: Acid and porous, in no event calcareous, made up of leaf-mould and peat in equal parts with sand and possibly a little sphagnum added.

Propagation: By division at the end of the dormant or start of the vegetative period, being sure that each division has at least two shoots, or by stem-cuttings taken immediately below a node and put in light soil made up of peat and sand, which must be kept moist. Both operations require a temperature of about 21–24 °C (70–75 °F) and plastic or glass covers to give enough humidity for the foliage; these covers should be removed very gradually so that the plant does not wither when exposed to the dry air outside.

CTENANTHE OPPENHEIMIANA (Marantaceae)

Description: Although very vigorous in the wild, this species does not readily produce large specimens when cultivated, especially outside the greenhouse, where it may behave quite whimsically. Long-stemmed leaf-clusters grow from the stoloniferous roots; these may also be on a short, usually curved stem; the leaf is lanceolate, the upper blade dark-green with diagonal, large, silvery stripes running from the central nervation; the lower blade is very dark red. Large clusters may be produced in perfect conditions. There is a variety, *tricolor*, which is extremely beautiful, with narrower, fan-shaped green leaves, grey-green and ivory-coloured variegations which often have pinkish highlights.
Habitat: From Brazil.
Minimum winter temperature: 16–18 °C (61–65 °F).
Light: Diffused and not too strong for the typical species, which must never be exposed to direct sunlight; stronger for the variety *tricolor*, to keep the colouring as bright as possible.
Environmental humidity: Very high; these plants are in fact best suited to the hothouse; the leaves must be sprayed and washed frequently.
Watering: Water plentifully in summer and regularly in winter; be sure that the water never stagnates at the bottom of the pot, which would cause the roots to rot.
Soil: Very porous and well-drained, made up, in equal parts, of mature leaf-mould, peat and sand. Excess water must be able to run through the soil at once.
Propagation: By division, if possible at the start of the vegetative period, at a temperature of about 24 °C (75 °F); keep the new plants under covers to assure constant humidity, but do not let the water stagnate; air frequently and remove covers gradually when the plants are obviously well established.

THE DIEFFENBACHIA GENUS (Araceae)

Etymology: This genus is named after I. F. Dieffenbach (1790–1863) who was put in charge of the imperial palace gardens of Schönbrunn, in Vienna in about 1830.
Description: Perennial, evergreen, often bushy herbaceous plants with upright, carnose stems which often become twisted, bent or semi-prostrate at the base. The leaves are oblong or lanceolate, acuminate at the tip, and often variegated; the central nervation is very prominent and the lateral veins depressed, with the leaf surface often corrugated in between. The stalks are long, with sheaths running half way up from the base; once the new leaf, which is curled, has fully emerged, the protective part opens out, becoming alate, while the upper part remains semi-cylindrical. The inflorescences are typical of the family, consisting of a spadix and a convolute spathe; cultivated plants may also flower, but this does not add to their ornamental value, since the flowers are rather dull, usually whitish or greenish, and small. The roots are very carnose, and the soil must therefore be very porous. Any part of the plant will, if damaged, emit irritating and sometimes poisonous sap; when taking cuttings be careful not to touch the mucous membranes, especially of the mouth and eyes. In fact one plant, which is hardly ever cultivated – *Dieffenbachia seguine* – is called the 'dumb-cane' in English-speaking countries because if its sap comes into contact with the mouth it paralyzes the vocal organs for several days; this name is often used to cover other species, although they are much less toxic.
Habitat: The entire genus comes from tropical America.
Minimum winter temperature: From 15–18 °C (59–65 °F), depending on the species.
Light: Usually quite strong, especially for variegated forms, but not direct sun.
Watering: Water plentifully in summer and very sparingly in winter. Too much water during the dormant period will cause the bottom leaves to drop off at a faster than normal rate.
Environmental humidity: As high as possible, but they will grow well in dry indoor conditions; wash the leaves, not least to prevent attack from cottony scale insect, to which they are particularly liable.
Soil: Very well-drained and porous, made up of mature leaf-mould with peat, chestnut detritus and sand added to assure the best possible drainage. Root rot is the most common cause of death for these plants.
Propagation: All the species have very strong regenerative properties and can be reproduced by apical cuttings with no special precautions in summer at a temperature of about 24 °C (75 °F); keep the soil almost dry until the plants have definitely taken root. Pieces of bare stem with two or three nodes may also be used for reproduction, either planted vertically or laid horizontally, half-buried, in moist and very porous soil, such as sand or perlite. The roots and new plants will form at the nodes, but the process is much slower than if cuttings are used. The old plants, cut back to the ground, will produce new stems and will often tiller. As all the species lose their bottom leaves, systematic reproduction is recommended.

DIEFFENBACHIA AMOENA (Araceae)

Description: This species is one of the commonest and most vigorous; the herbaceous stem is thick and succulent, the big, long-stemmed leaves are dark-green, oblong-acuminate, irregularly variegated and marked with white along the lateral veins. Although it sheds its bottom leaves it can grow to a height of 2 m (6 ft), even when cultivated.
Habitat: It grows along water-courses and in forest clearings in a vast area stretching from Central America to Colombia.
Minimum winter temperature: 13–16 °C (55–61 °F).
Light: It will grow with average light, but under strong light the variegations will be sharper; they tend to fade if the light is poor.
Environmental humidity: It grows fairly well in ordinary indoor conditions, and does not need special attention, apart from washing and sponging the foliage.
Watering: Water plentifully in summer and sparingly in winter.
Soil: Humus-rich and well-drained; it also grows in fairly compact soil as long as it is well watered; a little compost may be added, especially for larger, more adult specimens.
Propagation: By reproduction, as for all the other species.

DIEFFENBACHIA BAUSEI (Araceae)

Description: A fairly compact plant, with large, acuminate leaves, greenish-yellow throughout with irregular dark-green or white markings and green margins.
Habitat: This is a hybrid (*Dieffenbachia picta × weiri*), and has the same requirements as the typical species.

DIEFFENBACHIA PICTA (Araceae)

Description: This herbaceous plant has a large carnose stem, with very long stalks which often become pendent; the oblong, acuminate leaves are bright with irregular white blotches on the upper blade near the large central nervation. The typical species sheds its bottom leaves and has stems which tend to twist a great deal; for this reason it has been replaced by varieties and hybrids which are less twisted and more compact.

Habitat: From Brazil, but several wild varieties grow over a vast area stretching as far as Venezuela, through Guyana and Columbia.

Variety: *Dieffenbachia picta* 'Superba' is more compact than the typical species, tends to shed its leaves less and has more extensive and brighter-coloured cream-white variegations.

Dieffenbachia picta 'Rudolph Roehrs', also and perhaps better known as *roehrsii*, is a mutation with closely-set internodes, especially when young, and brightly coloured oblong, acuminate leaves; the upper blade is almost completely yellow or greenish-yellow when fully grown, and only the margins and central nervation are green; irregular white markings appear usually on older leaves, and the stalks also have a white marbled effect.

Remarks: Both the typical species and the varieties require a minimum winter temperature of about 16 °C (61 °F), and the other requirements are the same as for the entire genus.

▼ *Dieffenbachia 'roehrsii'*

DIZYGOTHECA ELEGANTISSIMA (Araliaceae)

Etymology: The name comes from the Greek *dis*, 'twice', *zygòs*, 'union' and *théke*, 'jewel case', because the anthers have twice the normal number of loculi. This species is more commonly known by its old name: *Aralia elegantissima*.

Description: In the wild this plant is arborescent and reaches a height of 7 m (23 ft) or more; however, only young, non-ramified specimens with semi-ligneous stems are cultivated; the slender leaves, consisting of an extremely long petiole and thin, dentate segments grow directly from the stem; when young they are reddish-brown, but turn dark-green with salient veins in each segment. Two or three specimens are often grown in the same pot to give a more compact effect; despite this, and because they are shrubby, they start to shed their basal leaves quite soon as the process of lignification gets under way; this is particularly noticeable indoors because of poor ventilation and the dry conditions.

Habitat: From the New Hebrides archipelago in the Pacific.

Minimum winter temperature: About 15 °C (59 °F), but the plants must be well ventilated.

Light: Very strong but diffused, and never in direct sunlight.

Environmental humidity: As high as possible.

Watering: Water often in summer and very sparingly in winter, but be sure to provide good environmental humidity; the water must never be allowed to collect at the bottom of the pot.

Soil: Humus-rich and well-drained soil, consisting of compost, mature leaf-mould and peat in equal parts, with sand added.

Propagation: Reproduction by cuttings, although this may be tricky, with a temperature of about 24 °C (75 °F) under glass or plastic covers, but the plants must be frequently aired. With lignified plants air layering may be carried out at the node nearest the last leaf, but this is a slow method and may take at least 8 months.

Remarks: These plants are especially vulnerable to parasites.

THE DRACAENA GENUS (Liliaceae)

Etymology: The name comes from the Greek *dràkaina*, 'female dragon' which is explained by the fact that the resinous reddish sap used for making the dyes known as 'dragon's blood' came from the species *Dracaena draco* from the Canary Islands.

Description: This genus, which includes more than 40 species, is on the whole very akin to the genus *Cordyline*, and is often confused with it to the extent that in horticultural jargon some types of *Cordyline* are still called *Dracaena* although they have been part of the other genus for some time. They are evergreen, shrubby or arborescent plants, almost all with sword-shaped, linear or lanceolate leaves growing in rosettes at the tip of the stems; these may be petiolate or sessile, with the base or stalk sheathed, and are often variegated and very decorative. The flowers grow in inflorescences, generally in panicles, and are greenish-white or yellowish, followed by berries, although, when cultivated, these seldom appear, especially indoors.

Habitat: All species come from the tropical and sub-tropical regions, especially of Africa, although they also grow in other continents.

Minimum winter temperature: Varies depending on the species, 10—16 °C (50—60 °F).

Light: Good, especially for brightly variegated species, but always diffuse, and never in direct sunlight.

Environmental humidity: The more delicate species require good atmospheric humidity; the hardier types should have the foliage washed and sprinkled to keep the plant looking healthy. Species of *Dracaena* are not usually attacked by parasites, so preferably keep the humidity lower rather than risk stagnation which may cause rot, especially in winter.

Watering: Water plentifully in summer and sparingly in winter; the water should be able to run off, and must never stagnate, so good drainage is called for. The pots should be fairly small to avoid endangering the stability of the plant.

Soil: Most species like a porous, humus-rich soil consisting of compost, leaf-mould and peat in equal parts, with sand added to improve drainage.

Propagation: By reproduction, either by cuttings or air layering, depending on how ligneous the stem is; cuttings should in fact be taken from herbaceous or semi-herbaceous parts, either apical or pieces of leafless stem. The soil should consist of sand and peat and kept just moist so that the cutting does not rot; covers are not necessary but a temperature of at least 21 °C (70 °F) is required. The old plants from which the stem has been cut will easily produce branches lower down; these can either be kept or removed when still small and used as cuttings to produce graceful little plants.

DRACAENA DEREMENSIS (Liliaceae)

Description: In the wild this plant is semi-arborescent, growing to 4 m (14 ft) or more; in pots it obviously stays smaller. The leaves are sword-shaped, semi-upright, narrowing at the sheathed base, and growing spirally from the stem; it may also develop branches. The typical species is not usually cultivated, but there are many varieties which make excellent indoor plants. The commonest is the variety 'Warneckei' the leaves of which have narrow, green margins with two fairly conspicuous lengthwise white stripes; the centre of the leaf between the stripes, is light green with white and pale green markings. There are also various mutations, some of which have a single white central zone between the two green margins.
Habitat: From tropical Africa.
Minimum winter temperature: Varies from 13–18 °C (55–65 °F).
Light: Fairly strong, to preserve the variegations.
Environmental humidity: Grows well in dry conditions, but it is as well to wash and sprinkle the foliage to stop the tips of the leaves withering.
Watering, soil and propagation: As for the rest of the genus.

DRACAENA FRAGRANS (Liliaceae)

Description: An arborescent evergreen which may grow to 6 m (20 ft) in height; it develops branches and has clusters of sessile, green, outward-turned leaves growing at the extremities of the branches and stems. The typical species is not usually cultivated, although it often produces shoots which can vegetate in water and live for several years, although they will inevitably die sooner or later. Certain varieties are used as indoor plants, such as the *massangeana*, with its very outward-turned and pendent leaves which have sharp pale-green and yellow variegations in the central part; the variety *victoriae* has broad and likewise pendent leaves, striped with silvery grey in the green central part, and cream-yellow or ivory-coloured margins.
Habitat: From Guinea and Nigeria.
Minimum winter temperature: About 16 °C (60 °F), and slightly higher for the variety *victoriae*.
Environmental humidity: Higher than for the other species, with frequent washing and sprinkling of the foliage. The other requirements are the same as for the genus as a whole, as are the methods of propagation.

DRACAENA GODSEFFIANA (Liliaceae)

Description: This plant has a completely different growth-pattern from the other species and never reaches a metre in height. It is a shrub which is almost invariably tillered with slender stems rarely growing upright, and usually zigzagging, with angular formations at the nodes where two or three verticillate, elliptical and acuminate leaves grow; the surface is leathery, light green, with strong yellow markings when young, becoming dark-green with white blotches when fully grown.
Habitat: From the Congo.
Minimum winter temperature: 16–18 °C (60–65 °F).
Light: Plenty of light; in poor light it tends to shed its leaves; avoid direct sunlight, however, even more carefully than for the other species.
Environmental humidity: High, using any means available; this plant is in fact better suited to the greenhouse than indoors.
Watering: Water plentifully in summer, and sparingly in winter, but assure good atmospheric humidity; the plant has underground ramifications which enable it to tiller; if the water is allowed to stagnate, rot will ensue. For the same reason there must be good drainage.
Soil: Lighter and more porous than for the other species; use little, or no, compost and increase the percentage of peat. The soil must never clod; if the leaves begin to fall, do not hesitate to change the soil, reduce the amount of watering and increase the environmental humidity until things have righted themselves.
Propagation: Cuttings are tricky, requiring plenty of warmth to take; by division in late spring with a temperature of at least 21 °C (70 °F) and high atmospheric humidity; do not use covers which will cause stagnation and make the leaves fall off. The soil must be kept fairly dry until the growth is well underway, but spray frequently.

DRACAENA SANDERIANA (Liliaceae)

Description: This is the most graceful and least gaudy species, with the growth-pattern typical of most of the genus; the stem is slender and remains herbaceous; the leaves are linear, sheathed, well-separated from one another, linear or lanceolate, acuminate, growing spirally and often wavy. The surface is green with white margins and, again, the basal leaves tend to wither, leaving the stem bare. Two or three plants are usually grown in the same pot to make up for its slender appearance and form a denser growth; because of its adaptability it is often grown in mixed pots to give dimension to the overall effect.
Habitat: From the Congo.
Minimum winter temperature: It is very adaptable and should be kept between 15–18 °C (60–65 °F) or more.
Light: As plentiful as possible, from above, so as to prevent the stems from becoming twisted; it may be necessary to turn the pot every so often. In other respects its cultivation is the same as for the genus as a whole.

DRACAENA STRICTA (Liliaceae)

Description: This arborescent plant has, strictly speaking, been now ascribed to the genus *Cordyline*, but given that in horticultural circles it is still called by its old name, it is included as a *Dracaena* despite the inevitable and strictly botanical differences. It is a semi-hardy plant which is arborescent in the wild, with a slender trunk which is sometimes ramified, and linear leaves which, in time, form an apical rosette on the bare stem. It is suitable only for places which are not heated much, or at all, such as hallways or stairs, and may be grown outside in mild climates. There are one or two varieties which are more decorative than the typical species, such as the variety *discolor* with its bronze-coloured foliage.
Habitat: From Australia.
Minimum winter temperature: About 7 °C (45 °F), although it will survive occasional fluctuations either side of this; it will wither if kept too warm and needs good ventilation.
Light: Does not need to be strong; but avoid direct sunlight.
Environmental humidity: No special requirements.
Watering: Water regularly in summer and sparingly in winter.
Soil: Porous but quite heavy. It may be made up of compost and mature leaf-mould in equal parts with some sand added.
Propagation: By air layering on leafless plants with lignified stems; by cuttings on semi-herbaceous parts, including the side-shoots or shoots at the base which sometimes appear on old plants. The best time is spring, and there are no special precautions to be taken, except that the soil should not be over-watered until the plant has taken root properly.

ELETTARIA CARDAMOMUM (Zingiberaceae)

Etymology: The name comes from *elettari*, the plant's native name in Malabar, its place of origin.
Description: A herbaceous, perennial with rhizomatous creeping roots from which the lanceolate and acuminate leaves grow, forming a long sheath; this produces what appears to be a hollow, cylindrical stem. The plant as a whole is aromatic and when rubbed the leaves give off a pungent odour. In cultivation the plant does not produce flowers or fruit, but in nature its spikes of yellow flowers produce capsules containing seeds which give the spice cardamon.
Habitat: From the Cardamon mountains, on the south-west coast of India, where it grows at heights of 1,000 m. It is often confused with the *Amomum* genus from Java, which will only grow in hot, moist greenhouse conditions.
Minimum winter temperature: 13–15 °C (55–59 °F). It will tolerate short spells at lower temperatures, but does not like warmer conditions.
Light: Good, diffuse light, out of direct sun. In summer it can be left outside in a semi-shaded position.
Environmental humidity: Very good, especially at warmer winter temperatures when watering is less frequent.
Watering: Frequent and plentiful in summer, well spaced in winter. To prevent the rhizomes rotting do not let the soil get waterlogged.
Soil: Very well-drained, composed of one part compost to two parts of well-rotted leaf-mould and a fair amount of sand. A good deep drainage layer is needed.
Propagation: By rhizome division in late winter. A temperature of about 18 °C (65 °F) is needed.

110

EPISCIA CUPREATA (Gesneriaceae)

Etymology: The name comes from the Greek *epískios*, 'shady', because of the natural habitat of these plants, which is the undergrowth in tropical forests.

Description: All the species in this genus are stoloniferous, creeping, perennial, herbaceous plants with opposite, variously variegated leaves and axillary flowers, solitary or otherwise, with a tubular corolla, generally of a reddish shade. *Episcia cupreata* has pubescent, copper-green leaves with metallic highlights and silvery variegations; the flowers are scarlet. As in all the other species, new plants appear at the tip of the stolons and take root if in contact with the ground; the plant may also be suspended, with the stolons pendent. There are many cultivated varieties, almost all of which derive from the variety *variegata* which has bright silvery variegations along the veins; 'acajou' has almost brown leaves; 'Harlequin' is similar but has smooth leaves, and 'Metallica' has almost copper-coloured leaves with pinkish central nervations.

Habitat: Grows wild throughout most of Central and South America; the species *cupreata* comes specifically from Colombia,

Minimum winter temperature: 18 °C or more (65 °F).

Light: Plenty of light, diffused. In poor light the internodes tend to lengthen and the plant will die; it will also fail to flower.

Environmental humidity: As high as possible, but do not spray the downy leaves too much or when the flowers appear.

Watering: Water plentifully in summer and sparingly in winter. Use pots which are wider than they are deep, and not very large.

Soil: Porous, acid: equal leaf-mould and peat with some sand.

Propagation: Very straightforward by cuttings, using the young plants which appear at the tip of the stolons; do not use covers; plant in peaty soil at a temperature of about 21 °C (70 °F). Do not over-water, which will cause rot. If the stolons are removed as they appear, the leaves will grow very large and the plant may be trained upwards with the help of supports.

EUPHORBIA FULGENS (Euphorbiaceae)

Etymology: This genus is named after Euphorbus, physician to Juba II, king of Numidia, who lived from c. 50 B.C. to 23 A.D.

Description: A shrubby evergreen plant with slender falling branches, green, alternate, lanceolate leaves with long stalks, the inflorescences are cyathia in axillary cymes, surrounded by five, scarlet, involucral bracts. The plant flowers in winter and is in fact best-suited to the greenhouse, although with plenty of light it will also turn into a fine indoor plant.

Habitat: From Mexico.

Minimum winter temperature: 16–18 °C (60–65 °F); like many plants in the same family it is very sensitive to temperature changes; the temperature should thus be as constant as possible and follow the normal difference between day and night.

Light: Plenty of light to have flowering plants.

Environmental humidity: As high as possible, but must be well ventilated; the plant tends to be succulent, and may thus rot or be attacked by powdery mildew or other fungal diseases.

Watering: Frequently in summer and sparingly in winter; the plant should be kept almost dry for about 3 months after flowering, then repotted and pruned to allow tillering and the appearance of new branches. Clip it two or three times in summer.

Soil: Humus-rich and acid, made up of mature leaf-mould with a good amount of peat and a little sand to improve the drainage, which must be very good to avoid rot. In autumn watering may be augmented with liquid fertilizers, mainly of the phosphorus variety, and when the plants are repotted also add a small amount of manure or organic fertilizer.

Propagation: By apical cuttings in soil made up of sand or perlite kept just moist, at about 24 °C (75 °F); it is preferable to take the cuttings from the new growth in June. Indoors it is best not to use covers because, for lack of ventilation, the plants may shed several leaves, given the succulent nature of the stems.

THE FICUS GENUS (Moraceae)

Etymology: The name is the Latin one used for *Ficus carica*, the plant which produces edible figs and has been familiar since Antiquity throughout the Mediterranean, where it grew naturally or was naturalized from the Near East.

Description: This is one of the most polymorphous genera in the entire Vegetable Kingdom and various estimates put the number of species belonging to it between 700 and 900. It includes arboreal, shrubby, semi-herbaceous and sometimes climbing plants; many have extremely odd formations, such as tabular (i.e. supporting) roots at the base of the trunk, or adventitious roots forming from the branches which, having reached the ground, then form new stems, so that a single plant may look like a whole coppice. There are also species belonging to the somewhat restricted category of so-called 'strangling trees'; these start off as epiphytes; when they reach the ground they form roots and a kind of trunk which chokes and then kills the host plant. The shape of the leaves varies considerably, as does the size; the only denominator common to the whole genus is the distinctive inflorescence, one of the strangest there is, completely enclosed in round or pear-shaped receptacles with holes at the top. The unisexual and extremely numerous flowers grow in the cavity inside this inflorescence, which is called a synconium; the male flowers are usually near the orifice, which is called the ostiole, while the female flowers are in the inner part, on the sides and at the bottom; when pollination has occurred infructescence takes place which, in the *Ficus carica*, results in the edible fig.

Habitat: All species come from the tropical and sub-tropical regions of the world, although fossilized remains found in Greenland and Moravia indicate that, presumably before the Ice-Age, which limited the area in which they grew, some species spread quite far northwards.

Minimum winter temperature: Very variable from species to species, with some even tolerating spasmodic frosts.

Light: Requirements likewise vary greatly from species to species, but in Europe the cultivated species do not usually tolerate direct sun.

Environmental humidity: Variable, but usually quite high.

Waterng: Generally speaking almost all the species, and in particular the arborescent ones kept as young specimens, should be watered plentifully in summer and sparingly in winter.

Soil: For almost all the species this should be rich with plenty of humus, made up of two parts of leaf-mould, one of well-fertilized soil, with peat and sand added to keep it ventilated and well-drained. All the species of *Ficus* require fairly small pots corresponding to the height of the plant, because in pots which are too large the soil may tend to clod, and choke the roots.

Propagation: Reproduction is by air layering, cuttings or soil layering, depending on the degree of lignification or the growth of the plant concerned. Air layering may be used with all old specimens which have lost a certain amount of foliage, on mature wood, but the roots sometimes take several months to appear. Cuttings, which may be taken from parts which are not at all lignified, are also slow to take root, and in some cases pose problems, especially indoors where there is usually not enough basic warmth. The safest method is soil layering for the climbing species, cuttings of which are often slow to develop and not always straightforward.

FICUS BENJAMINA (Moraceae)

Description: Arborescent in the wild, it has weeping branches, dark-green, ovate leaves which are somewhat narrow and long and acuminate at the tip. In parts of Italy it is grown outdoors, and is used in Sicily for lining roads; young specimens, and especially some varieties grown for their attractive habit, may be used to decorate well-ventilated, well-lit and not overheated rooms.

Habitat: From India and Malaya.

Minimum winter temperature: For young specimens about 10 °C (50 °F); older plants may tolerate slightly lower temperatures.

Light: Plenty of light, but not too much; young potted plants must be kept out of direct sunlight, and need good ventilation.

Environmental humidity: Fairly high, especially in warm indoor places; otherwise they will shed many leaves and the branches will be bare.

Watering: Water plentifully in summer and sparingly in winter.

Soil: Leaf-mould and compost with a little peat and sand added; it is important that the soil is never saturated with water, and does not clod.

Propagation: Usually, with lignified specimens, by air layering; cuttings taken from semi-mature wood do not root easily indoors; they should be placed in sandy soil, in pots which are as small as possible, under glass or plastic covers at a temperature of about 21 °C (70 °F). The covers should be removed gradually, and the plants should be aired every so often.

FICUS DIVERSIFOLIA (Moraceae)

Description: A shrubby evergreen plant with small, obovate or lanceolate, leathery, dark-green leaves at the axil of which appear numerous tiny fruit which are green to begin with, passing to yellow or orange, and solitary and pedunculate. The fruit are produced all year round and give the plant a very decorative effect; in English-speaking countries it is called the 'mistletoe-fig'.

Habitat: It grows over a fairly vast area from India to Indonesia; there are also several local varieties.

Minimum winter temperature: About 13 °C (55 °F); in high temperatures it is necessary to increase the environmental humidity quite a lot to avoid the shedding of leaves and the appearance of the Red Spider.

Environmental humidity: As high as possible in winter, depending on the temperature, to make up for reduced watering.

Watering: Water plentifully in summer and sparingly in winter.

Soil: No special requirements as long as the soil is humus-rich and porous, consisting principally of leaf-mould with peat, sand or perlite added to stop the soil becoming too compact.

Propagation: By cuttings from semi-mature wood on young growth; these take very easily compared with cuttings from other species. A temperature of 21 °C (70 °F) or more is needed, as well as a plastic cover which should be removed when the roots have taken; the best time of year for this operation is the summer.

FICUS ELASTICA (Moraceae)

Description: This is undoubtedly the commonest species, although it is called 'Ficus' somewhat improperly. In the wild it is a large tree which may grow to 30 m (95 ft), with many branches. It contains a latex which is extracted by making cuts in the trunk; it is a kind of rubber, but not one of the most important. The leaves are oblong, shiny and leathery, and dark-green. The plants used indoors are very young specimens, although they can sometimes grow to a fair size and develop branches without any trouble. The commonest type used nowadays is not the typical species but the variety *decora*, which is smaller and more compact; the leaves are larger, the central nervation light-coloured and the lower blade reddish, as are the stipules which enclose the new leaves; there is also a variety: *variegata*, which has grey, pale green and cream-yellow markings; it has been improved in certain varieties such as 'Schrijvereana' and 'Doescheri'; the first, derived from the variety *decora* has inherited the larger leaves and red stipules and stalks.
Minimum winter temperature: The typical species does not require a lot of warmth and will tolerate temperatures dropping now and then to almost 0 °C (32 °F) when it is fully grown and lignified; but the variety *decora* and young plants need a temperature of about 16 °C (60 °F) and the variegated varieties even slightly more.
Environmental humidity: Should be raised when the winter temperature is increased; the foliage should also be sponged.
Light: Plenty of light, and as much as possible for variegated forms.
Watering: Water regularly in summer and sparingly in winter; the water must never stagnate at the bottom of the pot.
Habitat: The typical species is from India.
Soil: Very well-drained and ventilated, made up of mature leaf-mould, peat and sand; it must never be allowed to clod or become saturated with water; the shedding of leaves is most often due to the roots being choked.
Propagation: In nurseries *Ficus elastica* is propagated by cuttings of semi-mature wood, with a couple of leaves which are curled around the stem and kept in place with an elastic band to maintain better humidity and give better ventilation; indoors, however, it is not easy to use this system, which requires all-round warmth and a temperature of about 24 °C (75 °F); another common problem is the revival of older defoliated plants which have lignified; here air layering is normally used. The older plant will usually produce new branches below where the cutting is made, once the air layering has been removed.

FICUS PANDURATA (Moraceae)

Description: This species, also known as *Ficus lyrata*, is likewise a tree which may grow to 12 m (40 ft); when potted it may also grow to a fair height, although obviously not that high. In other respects, even before it develops branches and is hardly a metre in height, it is quite a bulky plant because of the leaves which are very large even while the plant is still young. These have a distinctive shape which recalls that of a stringed musical instrument; they are dark-green and quite wavy at the margins; the surface is corrugated between the secondary nervations. As an isolated specimen this plant is well suited to spacious and well-ventilated rooms.
Habitat: From tropical Africa.
Minimum winter temperature: About 13 °C (55 °F).
Light: Plenty of diffused light, but not direct sunlight.
Environmental humidity: Must be increased when central heating is turned up, especially for young specimens.
Watering: Water regularly in summer and sparingly in winter.
Soil: Humus-rich, made up of two parts compost, one part mature leaf-mould with peat and sand added. Large specimens can obviously not be repotted, and so will need the upper layer of the soil replaced each year; also, make sure that the drainage hole is never blocked up.
Propagation: Usually by air layering on defoliated specimens: the old stem will produce branches.

FICUS PUMILA (Moraceae)

Description: This species, usually known in horticultural circles by the old name of *Ficus repens*, is a climber with tiny dark-green leaves, the sarmentose stalks of which climb over any kind of rough surface with which they come in contact by means of clinging roots, not unlike ivy roots. The plant is quite dimorphic, given that at a certain stage in its life it starts producing rigid, fertile, fruit-bearing branches which are non-climbing, with considerably larger leaves, giving the impression of there being two different plants co-existing. But this phenomenon almost never occurs in potted plants, whether adult or not, and only plants grown in the ground outside will usually produce fruit-bearing branches.

Habitat: From the Far East, i.e. China and Japan, and also from parts of Australia.

Minimum winter temperature: This is a semi-hardy plant and, particularly in the adult stage will tolerate intermittent frosts; on the other hand it will not tolerate winter temperatures in excess of 18–20 °C (65–70 °F); higher temperatures will kill it.

Light: This is an extremely versatile species, which grows well in moderate light; when potted do not expose to the sun's rays; in the open old, sturdy plants, particularly if growing against moist walls, will tolerate direct sunlight.

Environmental humidity: As high as possible. Dry air will cause the leaves to wrinkle and fall off, and if this spreads throughout the plant, there is no way of saving it.

Watering: Water frequently and plentifully all year round.

Soil: Humus-rich and fresh, made up of two parts of compost, one part mature leaf-mould and one part peat. It should always be moist, but never saturated, which would choke the roots.

Propagation: The simplest system is soil-layering, placing a pot near the mother plant and slightly burying one or more branches until they have rooted, keeping the soil constantly moist. You may also remove and pot parts which have been naturally soil-layered.

FICUS RADICANS (Moraceae)

Description: A climbing species with slender sarmentose branches and ovate-acuminate, average-sized leaves. The typical green-leaved species is not cultivated, but the variety *variegata* is obtainable: the leaves of this plant have wide margins coloured white, and are sometimes even completely white. It is an extremely delicate plant, best-suited, in fact, to the hothouse; it is unlikely to survive for long indoors.
Habitat: From India and Malaya.
Minimum winter temperature: 16–18 °C (60–65 °F).
Light: Plenty of diffused light; in no event expose it to direct sun.
Environmental humidity: As high as possible, using any means available; the fact that it urgently needs a humid environment is the major difficulty encountered in growing this plant, which is a very handsome one.
Watering: Water plentifully all year round; the water must never stagnate or saturate the soil, but it is just as dangerous to let the soil dry out, even for a short while.
Soil: Very porous, so that it will retain moisture without forming clods; it may consist of equal parts of leaf-mould and peat with a little sand and shredded sphagnum added.
Propagation: The simplest system for reproduction is soil-layering, by placing pots filled with a suitable soil mixture next to the pot containing the mother plant, and slightly burying one or more branches; keep well moistened at all times. When the roots have definitely taken, which requires a temperature of at least 21 °C (70 °F) for some time, the branches may be removed, but it is still necessary to keep the area around the new plant well moistened for some time; glass or plastic covers may be used to this effect if necessary.

FITTONIA ARGYRONEURA (Acanthaceae)

Etymology: Named after Elizabeth and Sarah Mary Fitton (fl. first half of the 19th century), authors of 'Conversation on Botany'.
Description: A perennial herbaceous plant, creeping and putting out roots at the nodes, with oval and opposite leaves which are slightly cordate at the base, bright green, and covered by a tight criss-cross pattern of white veins. The stalks and stems are slightly pubescent and the inflorescences consist of small spikes of green bracts, with the inconspicuous flowers growing among them. This species is considered by many authors to be simply a variety of the very similar *Fittonia verschaffeltii* which has the same habit but dark olive-green leaves with a slightly velvety look about them which are covered by a network of crimson-pink veins.
Habitat: All come from Peru.
Minimum winter temperature: 16–18 °C (60–65 °F).
Light: Coming from tropical undergrowth they tolerate moderate and diffused light, but should nonetheless not be exposed to too poor light, which might cause abnormal elongation of the internodes and leaves, which are much smaller than normal.
Environmental humidity: Should be high, using any means available (the plants are really best-suited to the hothouse).
Watering: Water plentifully and regularly all year round.
Soil: Light, but such as to keep a certain degree of freshness and moisture; it may be made up of two parts peat and one part leaf-mould with a little sand and shredded sphagnum added.
Propagation: Like all members of this family the *Fittonians* tend to grow longer stems as they shed their leaves. It is thus advisable to reproduce them periodically by taking top-cuttings, putting more than one cutting to a pot and placing under glass or plastic covers at a temperature of about 24 °C (75 °F). They will take root in no time (slightly more than a week), but the covers should be removed very gradually so that the leaves do not dehydrate on sudden contact with the dry air outside.

117

GASTERIA MACULATA (Liliaceae)

Etymology: The name comes from the Greek *gastér*, 'belly', because of the swollen base of the flowers.

Description: Although they belong to the succulents, all the plants in this genus make good indoor specimens which, though not over-brightly coloured, are very sturdy. They are almost invariably acaulescent, but tiller easily; they have rigid, leathery leaves which are variously marked and sometimes warty, and may grow in two rows, hiding each other alternately, or, with time, develop into rosettes. The species *Gasteria maculata* has opposite, almost upright, imbricate leaves which are dark-green with slightly prominent white markings. It is one of the commonest species and can form large clumps.

Habitat: The whole genus comes from South Africa.

Minimum winter temperature: Ideally about 10 °C (50 °F), but it will also tolerate higher temperatures.

Light: It will tolerate quite poor light, and dislikes the direct sun which turns the leaves bronze-coloured and blurs the variegations.

Environmental humidity: It grows perfectly well in dry conditions.

Watering: Water regularly in summer, letting the soil dry out between waterings, and very sparingly in winter, when the greatest danger is rot.

Soil: Very well-drained and non-organic, made up of very mature compost with about 1/4 of sand added. Drainage must be such as to prevent the water from stagnating and given the plant's behaviour, it is advisable to use pots which are wider than they are deep. If the tough, fleshy roots grow out through the drainage hole they can be cut back when repotting, or the plant can be divided.

Propagation: By division, at the start of the vegetative period, or by removing individual side-shoots, which can be potted one to a pot.

GUZMANIA LINGULATA (Bromeliaceae)

Etymology: The genus is named after the 18th century Spanish naturalist Anastasio Guzmann.

Description: This is a herbaceous perennial plant grown for its decorative foliage and the brightly-coloured inflorescences with bracts which grow at the centre of the rosettes of linear or sword-shaped leaves; these are sometimes streaked with reddish-brown or white. The species *Guzmania lingulata* is typically epiphyte and has metallic-green leaves; the inflorescence of red bracts opens like large petals, while the central bracts, from which the white flowers emerge, are orange with yellow tips.

Habitat: It grows over a vast area in the shady forests of Central America, Bolivia, Ecuador and Brazil.

Minimum winter temperature: About 15 °C (60 °F).

Light: Plentiful, to keep the colours of the bracts intact for as long as possible; unlikely to flower outside the greenhouse.

Environmental humidity: As high as possible, especially in winter, when it should be watered sparingly.

Watering: Water plentifully in summer and sparingly in winter; drainage must be extremely good and the water must never stagnate at the bottom of the pot.

Soil: These plants, though epiphytes, are usually treated as if growing in the ground; they need a very porous and humus-rich soil, made up of peat, shredded sphagnum and fern roots, with a little mature leaf-mould and sand added; the necessary food can be provided by using small but regular amounts of fertilizer.

Propagation: *Guzmania* does not most readily produce offshoots at the base, but if the plant is fully-grown these may appear at the last flowering when they can be removed and potted in barely moist soil at about 21 °C (70 °F).

Remarks: Particularly in specialized nurseries it is sometimes possible to find other species with quite different inflorescences such as hybrids of *G. monostachia* or *G. dissitiflora* (see photo).

▼ *Guzmania dissitiflora*

▲ *Guzmania lingulata*

HOWEIA FORSTERIANA (Palmae)

Etymology: Known equally correctly as *Howea*, and also called *Kentia* in horticultural practice, this plant is named after its place of origin: Lord Howe Island, in the Pacific Ocean.

Description: Arborescent in the wild, given that it may reach a height of 18 m (60 ft), young specimens of this palm are cultivated because they stand up well to adverse conditions and make a fine indoor plant. The stipe, which is usually short in cultivated specimens, is strong and rigid, and carries a cluster of pinnate fronds with acuminate segments on long stalks which are upright at first and become slightly outward-turned; they are dark-green in colour. It grows very slowly and often produces just one or two fronds a year.

Habitat: Lord Howe Island, east of Australia.

Minimum winter temperature: By no means a demanding plant, it will survive well in 10 °C (50 °F), although it will also tolerate higher temperatures; it is not affected by fluctuations in temperature.

Light: It dislikes direct sunlight, but thrives under fairly strong light; it may also be kept in quite poorly lit places.

Environmental humidity: No special requirements, but sponge the fronds frequently to remove dust; this improves the appearance and health of the plant.

Watering: Water fairly plentifully from spring to autumn, and sparingly in winter, depending on the ambient temperature.

Soil: Humus-rich and well-drained, made up of compost with mature leaf-mould and a little sand and peat added. The water must never be allowed to stagnate.

Propagation: Only by seed, which is usually imported and must be fresh. Because it is hard to come by and entails a lengthy process, it is not recommended for amateurs.

HYPOESTES SANGUINOLENTA (Acanthaceae)

Etymology: The name derives from the Greek *ypò*, 'beneath' and *estia*, 'dwelling house', alluding to the fact that the calyx is covered by the bracts.

Description: A herbaceous, perennial, branchy plant with small, green, ovate-acuminate leaves; the upper surface is unevenly covered with red dots. The opposite leaves are slightly rough to the touch; new branches grow from the axils, as do, every so often, small spikes of lilac-coloured flowers among green bracts; since they are by no means decorative, they are best removed as soon as they appear to save the plant's energy.

Habitat: From Madagascar.

Minimum winter temperature: 13–16 °C (55–60 °F); in lower temperatures it will lose the aerial part, although this will regrow in summer, and if exposed to frost, it will die altogether.

Light: As strong as possible to prevent the stems from growing too long and the markings from fading; do not expose to direct sunlight, however, which will cause the leaves to grow smaller and thicker, and turn the basic green colouring to bronze.

Environmental humidity: Plentiful; if the air is too dry the leaves will drop off and the plant will lose its symmetry.

Watering: Water frequently in summer and sparingly in winter, when the plant may often wither for no apparent reason.

Soil: Humus-rich, made up of equal parts of compost, mature leaf-mould and peat with some sand added to stop the soil clodding too much around the roots.

Propagation: In time the plant will become considerably less attractive, and it is thus better to take frequent cuttings; place these directly in appropriate soil and keep under covers at a temperature of about 21 °C (70 °F), preferably in spring. New growth will sprout easily from old, but the plant will still benefit from the frequent clipping and fairly strenuous pruning, which will encourage it to produce new branches.

MARANTA LEUCONEURA (Marantaceae)

Etymology: Named after the doctor and botanist Bartolomeo Maranta (b. Venosa, 1500 – d. Molfetta, 1571).

Description: A herbaceous perennial with tuberose roots producing clusters of radical leaves and slender stems, usually prostrate, smooth at the internodes, where evident nodes appear; these carry further leaf-clusters and may root if conditions are right on contact with the ground or moist supporting structures. The foliage is usually delicate, with very lovely variegations; the leaves are elliptical and obtuse at the tip, with quite long stalks which are sheathing and alate; the new leaves sprout successively from these; they are curled at first, and broaden out as they emerge. The species has two major varieties: 'massangeana' and 'kerchoveana'. The variety 'massangeana' has velvety leaves with a silvery pattern at the centre which opens out in thin lines, shaped like a fish's spines, along the lateral veins; the areas in between the pattern are darker coloured, and almost brown at the centre near the main nervation, right to the green margins. Recent years have seen the appearance and spread of a very similar variety, which has just one very pale-green central stripe; the subtle fishbone pattern along the veins is crimson-red; the intermediate zones are greenish-brown, sometimes with darker central blotches. This has rightly been called *erythoneura* (red-veined) although in horticultural jargon it is often called *tricolor*; the lower blade of the leaf is somewhat reddish, as it is in the other varieties. This plant has plenty of branches and is often grown with the help of moss- or sphagnum-covered tutors which should, in theory, be kept moist; although slightly less fragile than the 'massangeana', it is still a whimsical plant and is in fact best suited to the greenhouse.

Habitat: All the varieties come from Central and South America where they grow in the undergrowth in the tropical forests of Guyana and northern Brazil, and often in even more northern regions. Like most members of the family, they are used to 12 hours of daylight and 12 hours of darkness and within these limits are subject to nyctonastia, i.e. their leaves straighten and remain pressed together when night is about to fall.

Minimum winter temperature: About 16 °C (60 °F).

Light: Plentiful, but not too much, and above all diffused; do not expose to direct sunlight; too much light will fade the colours of the leaves, as will too little light.

Environmental humidity: Should be very high, using any means available, but do not spray, because this may mark the velvety leaves.

Watering: Water plentifully in summer and sparingly in winter with adequate atmospheric humidity; the water must never stagnate, because this may rot the small root tubers.

Soil: Light, porous and coarse, made up of equal parts of leaf-mould and peat, with some sand or perlite added; ensure very good drainage; enemy number one for this plant is clodded and saturated soil. Often, and particularly if the air is too dry and the temperature too high, this will cause the aerial part to wilt as it is about to become dormant, but if the tubers are healthy and firm, the plant will start to vegetate after a fairly long period of dormancy.

Propagation: By division of the roots or cuttings, cutting the stem immediately below a node with a leaf-cluster and rooting it in light soil consisting of moistened sand and peat, under glass or plastic covers at a temperature of about 24 °C (75 °F). Air from time to time to stop condensation damaging the leaves, and remove the covers gradually when the roots have become established. Division of the roots may be carried out when the plant is dormant and has lost its aerial part, and in so doing the state of the tubers may also be checked. Remove all the dead or rotten roots and repot in appropriate soil, keeping slightly moist to begin with until the new growth appears.

MARANTA LEUCONEURA var. KERCHOVEANA
(Marantaceae)

Description: This species has oval, velvety-looking leaves; alongside the central nervations these have a series of chocolate-coloured markings which stand out against the green background and turn dark green as the leaf ages. It has a prostrate growth and the leaves may grow to a considerable size. These varieties, even when cultivated, flower readily; the flowers grow in scorpioid racemes, but these are whitish, small and short-lived and hence of little decorative value.
Habitat: From Brazil.
Minimum winter temperature: About 16 °C (60 °F), but will tolerate slightly lower temperatures, preferring cold to dry, overheated conditions.
Light: Fairly plentiful and always diffused.
Environmental humidity: As high as possible, but avoid staleness.
Watering: Water frequently in summer and sparingly in winter. Like the other varieties, it dislikes saturated soil and can only begin its dormant period with healthy tubers — thus preserving its vegetative capacities — if watered carefully so as to prevent rot.
Soil: Made up of leaf-mould and peat in equal parts with some sand added, but if the leaf-mould is not sufficiently loose, use a greater amount of peat.
Propagation: By division of the tuberose roots or by cuttings, with the same precautions as for the other varieties.

THE MONSTERA GENUS (Araceae)

Etymology: The name is of uncertain origin; it is henerally thought to derive from the Latin *monstrum,* in the sense, often used by the Romans—and even by Cicero and Catullus—of something 'strange, amazing, and incredible'; this may refer to the size and curious shape of the leaves of some species.
Description: The genus includes about 30 species, all climbers developing aerial, adventitious roots which act as supports and to supplement its food supply by clinging to trees or damp rocks. If there is inadequate support and humidity the plants will gradually produce smaller and less distinctive leaves, often echoing immature forms. Depending on the species the leaves may be lobate, laciniate, pinnatifid, or may also have the lamina unevenly perforated; alternatively the margins may be entire and the perforations fairly large and regular; this latter feature applies to several species, the foremost being *Monstera obliqua expilata,* where the lamina is little more than a thin segment at the veins and the margin so small that it often matches the holes. The genus includes one of the commonest of all indoor plants: *Monstera deliciosa,* more usually known as the 'philodendron'.
Habitat: All the species come from tropical America.
Minimum winter temperature: Some species will only grow in the hothouse, but the commonly cultivated types need a min. temp. of 13 °C (55 °F), although large fully-grown specimens grown in sheltered spots in the ground in milder climates will survive occasional drops in temperature.
Light: Should be plentiful to preserve large, distinctive leaves, but young potted plants dislike direct sunlight; adult plants in humid places only require shade in summer.
Environmental humidity: Very high; sponge the foliage frequently and, most important, provide supports which should be kept as moist as possible.
Watering: Water frequently and plentifully in summer, sparingly in winter; the water must never stagnate at the bottom of the pot, because this will rot the roots. The adventitious roots may be trained so that they absorb the necessary moisture from the dish beneath the pot or from the wet gravel, without the water reaching the bottom of the pot.
Soil: Very porous and coarse, made up of equal parts of not too mature leaf-mould and peat with some sand or perlite added and small pieces of chestnut detritus which will keep the mixture ventilated. The roots form a fairly small network, so it will not be necessary to use large pots where the soil may tend to clod; keep an eye on the stability of the plant.
Propagation: Reproduction is very simple, either by apical cuttings or pieces of stem with no special precautions except that of keeping the soil slightly moist to avoid rot; it is preferable to use a very porous soil — i.e. a mixture of sand and peat; this operation may be carried out at any time of year with a temperature of about 21 °C (70 °F) or more; the best season, nevertheless, is late spring so as to give the cuttings as much light as possible. Topmost cuttings are better for plants with fully-grown and already distinctive leaves, while plants with young-looking leaves will sprout from the node of pieces of stem; even in perfect conditions these will take some time to develop into fully-fledged plants.

MONSTERA ACUMINATA (Araceae)

Description: This species belongs to the group with entire leaves which are perforated on the surface in the adult stage. Several species have this feature and are often hard to tell apart, especially when young, when the leaves are quite alike, with an oblong-oblique lamina, acuminate at the tip, green all over and leathery-looking. It is probable that most species on the market are not even real species, but hybrids selected for their hardiness; the conspicuous heterophylly between young and adult forms of almost all the *Araceae* makes it particularly tricky to identify young potted specimens.

Habitat: The true *Monstera acuminata* comes from Guatemala; other similar species come from other parts of Central America.

Minimum winter temperature: 16–18 °C (60–65 °F).

Light: Because it is completely green this plant does not have specific light requirements, but if the light is poor the internodes will grow too long, and the leaves will remain or become small and lose their distinctive, irregular perforations.

Environmental humidity: Should be kept as high as possible, using any means available, including spraying and sponging the foliage; but the crucial point, which poses the greatest problem, is to keep the supports to which the aerial roots cling constantly moist.

Watering: Water plentifully in summer and sparingly in winter.

Soil and propagation: As for the genus as a whole.

MONSTERA DELICIOSA (Araceae)

Description: In the wild this plant is a climber with large lignifying stems; the leaves are very large, sometimes reaching a metre in length and a considerable width; they are leathery, conspicuously septate with the surface perforated both along the central vein and in the segments. The long, tough adventitious roots growing at the nodes help keep the stems upright by clinging to trees or other supports, and also absorb additional food both from the atmospheric humidity and from any organic matter with which they come in contact. The dimorphism between young and adult leaves is so marked in this species that the first stage was in fact included in a different genus with the name of *Philodendron pertusum*; it is still debatable whether this distinction is valid or not, but the fact remains that this very common indoor plant is still usually known as a 'philodendron', although the name belies the appearance when the plant has developed its distinctive leaves.

Habitat: From southern Mexico, and naturalized in many parts of Central America and Florida.

Minimum winter temperature: 13 °C (55 °F); will tolerate higher temperatures, but requires greatly increased atmospheric humidity.

Light: Plentiful and diffused, not direct sunlight; in poor light the leaves will first lose their perforations and then the segments of the leaves which will become entire and small. In our milder climates it may thrive outside in sheltered spots, and will do well outside in summer in semi-shade.

Watering: All other requirements as for the genus as a whole.

MONSTERA 'GUTTIFERYUM' (Araceae)

Description: This is a very controversial species in as much as some authors include it in the genus *Pothos* while others ascribe it to the genus *Raphidophora*. It is often tricky to identify these genera, because they have often been named before the plants flower and fruit, or when they are still too young. It is a climbing plant with fairly small, oval-acuminate, dark-green leaves with very depressed veins, growing on quite lengthy, conspicuously alate stalks. When mature the leaves become slightly larger and adventitious roots appear at the nodes.

Habitat: Not altogether clear. The theory that it comes from Malaya in tropical Asia may confirm the fact that it does not belong to the genus *Monstera*.

Minimum winter temperature: About 16 °C (60 °F).

Light: Does not require too much light, but in poor light the internodes will usually grow excessively long.

Environmental humidity: As high as possible, using any means available.

Watering: Water frequently in summer and sparingly in winter.

Soil: Well-drained and porous, made up of equal parts of leaf-mould and peat with a little sand added.

Propagation: By reproduction, either by top cuttings or pieces of stem, barely moist sandy soil at a temperature of about 21 °C (70 °F). During winter the stems usually grow too long indoors and the leaves remain under-developed, often because of inadequate atmospheric humidity; in spring it is thus advisable to prune the stems back to the lowest normal-sized leaf.

NEOREGELIA CAROLINAE (Bromeliaceae)

Etymology: Named after E. Albert von Regel (1815–1892), a Russian botanist. The genus was first called *Regelia*, then changed to *Aregelia* because there was already an homonymous genus in the family *Myrtaceae*; but on the basis of priority *Neoregelia* was accepted as the right name.

Description: A herbaceous perennial plant with strap-shaped leaves growing in rosettes, bronze-green in colour with spiny margins; the rosette is very wide and at the centre, during flowering, short, brightly-coloured bracteal leaves appear which take on a vexillary function; inside the 'vase' there are small, inconspicuous violet flowers with white margins. In the typical species the bracteal leaves are orange-red or crimson-red, but there are also several varieties, including 'Marechalii', which is smaller and crimson-pink at the centre, and 'Meyendorfii' with olive-green leaves and the centre varying from pink to brown, and the finest of all, 'Tricolor', with shiny green leaves with lengthwise white and yellow stripes with pink shading and crimson-red bracteal leaves.

Habitat: From Brazil.

Minimum winter temperature: About 16 °C (60 °F).

Light: Plentiful to preserve the colour of the bracteal leaves.

Environmental humidity: High, using any means available.

Watering: Water regularly in summer and sparingly in winter. Water may be kept in the middle of the vase-like foliage as long as the outer part of the rosette is in contact with matter which does not hold moisture which would rot the collar.

Soil: Light and very porous: two parts of peat or leaf-mould, one part compost and one part sand mixed with fern-roots and shredded sphagnum. Drainage must be very good, and the pot as small as possible.

Propagation: The basal shoots may be removed and repotted at about 21 °C (70 °F); they grow around the central rosette when this latter starts to wither and finally dies after flowering.

NEPHROLEPIS EXALTATA (Polypodiaceae)

Etymology: The name comes from the Greek *nephròs*, 'kidney' and *lépis*, 'scale', because of the shape of the indusium, the thin membrane which protects the spores.

Description: The typical species with pinnate and almost perfectly upright fronds is seldom cultivated, but has been replaced by a very large number of varieties with fronds of varying lengths, different growths; they also differ in the way they duplicate the segments which may become bipinnate or tripinnate, fairly septate, curly and downy in appearance. Despite these very numerous forms, the English-speaking countries usually group them under the generic term of 'Boston ferns' because of the long and unrivalled predominance of the variety *bostoniensis* in the last decades of the 19th century.

Habitat: The typical species and some primary varieties occur throughout the tropical and sub-tropical regions of the Old and New Worlds.

Minimum winter temperature: About 7 °C (45 °F); although some forms tolerate higher temperature, the maximum is about 16 °C (60 °F), because dry indoor atmospheres cause them to wilt and encourage the brown scale insect.

Light: Moderate and diffused; do not expose to direct sunlight.

Environmental humidity: High, using any means available.

Watering: Water regularly all year round, but do not allow water to stagnate because this will rot the rhizomes.

Soil: Light and porous, made up of mature leaf-mould and peat with some sand added. During the vegetative period it is advisable to use light amounts of liquid nitrogenous fertilizer weekly.

Propagation: The plants produce plenty of long, thin shoots from the base, with young plants sprouting from the ends; these may be removed and potted in late spring; environmental humidity must be high and the soil should consist of peat and sphagnum. Large clusters may be divided at the start of the vegetative period.

NIDULARIUM FULGENS (Bromeliaceae)

Etymology: The name comes from the Latin *nidus*, 'nest', because of the position of the flowers which appear half-hidden at the centre of the foliar rosette, among leaf-bracts.

Description: This genus is quite akin to *Neoregelia* and, indeed, many of the species belonging to it were taken from it. *Nidularium fulgens* is fairly easy to find on the market; it consists of a brightly-coloured rosette of flattened leaves with spiny margins, which are olive, or light-green in colour, with uneven darker markings and bright crimson central bracteal leaves among which grow the small blue flowers.

Habitat: From Brazil.

Minimum winter temperature: About 16 °C (60 °F), but they will tolerate lower temperatures.

Light: Strong, to keep the colours of the bracts even when flowering is over.

Environmental humidity: As high as possible, in relation to the temperature.

Watering: Water frequently in summer and sparingly in winter; be sure that the water never stagnates at the bottom of the pot or around the collar of the plant.

Soil: Light and very porous; an ideal composition is chopped fern-roots and shredded sphagnum in equal parts with some sand added; if these are not available use a mixture of mature leaf-mould and peat with a little sand, pieces of chestnut and charcoal chippings, reduce the amount of watering and never press the collar, thus allowing the water to run off.

Propagation: As for the entire family, the original rosette will die after flowering, but the plant produces shoots at the base which can be removed, if possible when they have started to lay roots, and potted in appropriate soil kept just moist at a temperature of about 21 °C (70 °F).

OXALIS HEDYSAROIDES RUBRA (Oxalidaceae)

Etymology: The name of the genus derives from the Greek *oxýs*, 'acid' because of the taste of some species.
Description: Compared to most of the other species, this one is somewhat anomalous, in as much as it is shrubby and upright, with thin stems and leaves composed of three leaflets, each of which is petiolate; their shape is ovate-acuminate and the lamina looks satin-like; it is wine-red in colour. They have nastic movements and are sensitive to touch to some extent. The flowers, which grow in pauciflorous cymes, are yellow.
Habitat: From Columbia, Ecuador and Venezuela, where it grows in the forests at a certain altitude, in the damp, but well-lit undergrowth.
Minimum winter temperature: 13–16 °C (55–60 °F).
Light: Very strong; except in the hottest months it may also be exposed to direct sunlight, but the environmental humidity must be increased accordingly; intense, diffused light is safer in our climate.
Environmental humidity: High, using any means available, especially in relation to the heat, but the plants should be placed in a well-ventilated spot because stagnating moisture will cause cryptogamic diseases.
Watering: Water regularly in summer, less often in winter.
Soil: Light and humus-rich, made up of equal parts of compost, mature leaf-mould and peat, with a little sand added to increase the drainage which must be extremely efficient.
Propagation: Reproduction by cuttings is quite difficult indoors because it requires a well-protected but well-ventilated place such as a frame in a greenhouse, with a high basic temperature; in confined places, moreover, the condensation caused by the heat may easily cause rot. When the plant has more than one stem, division may be carried out when the vegetative period commences; keep the level of atmospheric humidity very high and keep the mainly sandy soil barely moist.

PACHYPODIUM LAMEIRI (Apocynaceae)

Etymology: The name comes from the Greek *pachýs*, 'fat' and *podós*, 'foot', because the bottom part of the stem is fat and stocky.
Description: A shrubby or arborescent plant in the wild, some species of this genus are grown as young specimens and treated more or less as succulents. The stem of the cultivated species almost always has long, strong thorns; the leaves, which drop off gradually towards the base, form a topmost cluster in the form of a spiralling rosette; they are linear, leathery, growing directly between the thorns on a short stalk; the general growth pattern of the plant has earned it the name of 'Madagascan palm', although it has nothing in common with palms. In this species the thorns or spines, which are in effect stipules, are arranged in groups of three, with each leaf growing at the base of these groups; the lamina is green and shiny; the central vein is pale-coloured. The funnel-shaped, five-lobed flowers should appear in the form of apical cymes, but potted specimens rarely develop sufficiently to flower.
Habitat: From Madagascar.
Minimum winter temperature: About 10 °C (50 °F), but will also tolerate higher temperatures.
Light: Plentiful, including direct sunlight.
Environmental humidity: Not necessary.
Watering: Water regularly in summer; stop altogether in winter, and water with great caution in slightly higher temperatures.
Soil: Very porous but humus-rich, made up of very well decomposed compost with about 1/4 coarse sand.
Propagation: Reproduction by cuttings in pure, barely moist sand, having first dried out the cutting and stopped the latex which oozes from the cut with lukewarm water or cigarette ash. You will need a temperature of about 24 °C (75 °F) and it is advisable to wait until summer. Fresh seeds should be germinated in sand, in spring, at not less than 20 °C (68 °F), and transplanted at once.

THE PAPHIOPEDILUM GENUS (Orchidaceae)

Etymology: The name comes from the Greek *Paphie*, one of the attributes of Aphrodite, to the worship of whom the town of Paphos in Cyprus was dedicated, and *pédilon*, 'sandal' because of the distinctive shape of the labellum.

Description: This genus, made up of some 50 species, most of them growing on the ground, was once included in *Cypripedium* (the name in fact has the same meaning, i.e. 'foot of Cypris') but was separated from this grouping, although horticultural jargon still situates it there, because it has quite different features. First and foremost, the *Paphiopedila* are evergreen, but in addition the new leaves when budding appear folded in two, whereas in the *Cypripedia* they are convolute, i.e. turned in on themselves. No species in the genus has pseudo-bulbs and the leaves are leathery and linear with a marked crease at the centre; they grow in the form of a fan, overlapping (imbricate), sprouting directly from the rhizome. The flowers are bright, usually solitary, with an upright dorsal sepal and the labellum usually sack-shaped. The hybrids and cultivated varieties obtained are very numerous and some, with the due precautions, may also be grown indoors where, even if they do not bloom, they make pretty, decorative plants. The hybrids from this genus come in all forms, with variously blotched or marbled foliage, with, at the top of the list, *Paphiopedilum × maudiae* (*P. callosum × P. lawrenceanum*), whose flowers have a white dorsal sepal with green stripes.

Habitat: From tropical Asia, especially Assam, Indochina and Indonesia.

Minimum winter temperature: The authentic species usually need 16–18 °C (60–65 °F) but many hybrids can make do with a minimum of 13 °C (55 °F).

Light: These orchids are among those considered to tolerate poor light, but indoors the light should undoubtedly be quite good.

Environmental humidity: This is the greatest problem in growing orchids outside the greenhouse. Use any means available to keep it high.

Watering: As these plants have no storing organs they do not like a real peiod of dormancy, but make sure that the soil is never too wet, which might rot the very carnose roots, and let it dry out somewhat between one watering and the next.

Soil: For the ground plants, the best soil is that suited to epiphytes, consisting of fern-root fibres (2/3) mixed with 1/3 chopped sphagnum, with some charcoal chippings added. Drainage must be extremely good, and the soil must never become clodded or saturated.

Propagation: By division of the rhizomes before the vegetative period starts; make sure every part has the greatest possible number of shoots; the new plants should be kept moist, but water sparingly until they are well-established, at a temperature of about 21 °C (70 °F) with good environmental humidity.

▲ *Paphiopedilum × maudiae*

PEDILANTHUS TITHYMALOIDES VARIEGATUS (Euphorbiaceae)

Etymology: The name comes from the Greek *pédilon*, or 'sandal', and *ánthos*, or 'flower', describing the flower which has an involucre with a deep split and a short spur.

Description: A rather succulent, shrubby plant with fleshy stems which secrete irritant latex if damaged. The zigzagging stems form angles at the nodes where the ovate, alternate leaves are attached. The leaves have pronounced, irregular white markings which take on a pink or light red tinge in a good light. The flowers, which may have a red or purple involucre, grow in cymose inflorescences at the stem tips, but they hardly ever appear indoors and rarely even in greenhouses.

Habitat: From the West Indies.

Minimum winter temperature: 13 °C (55 °F); the plants tolerate slightly higher temperatures but often lose a good many leaves.

Light: Excellent, but some protection against very hot sun.

Environmental humidity: Undesirable, especially in winter, as this succulent plant is very prone to oidium. To prevent withering in warmer conditions spray the foliage.

Watering: Regular from March to October, infrequent in winter to prevent the plant starting into growth and becoming spindly.

Soil: Very free-draining and humus-rich, composed of well-composted farmyard manure or compost with some sand.

Propagation: By cuttings at any time of year, so long as a temperature of 21 °C (70 °F) is maintained. Use a very sandy mixture kept slightly moist by spraying, but do not water until you are sure roots have formed. Dry the latex that oozes from the cut surfaces on both the cutting and parent plant, with a pad of material dipped in hot water, or by stubbing with a cigarette end.

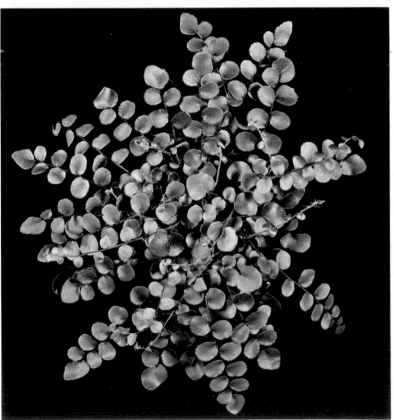

PELLAEA ROTUNDIFOLIA (Polypodiaceae)

Etymology: The name comes from the Greek *péllos*, 'dark', clearly referring to the dark colour of the fronds and rhachis.

Description: This small rhizomatose fern has semi-prostrate fronds when young and semi-upright only when more developed, but these never exceed about 30 cm in length (12 in); they consist of a blackish rhachis bearing alternate, single round leaflets when young, turning oblong when adult. The fronds grow directly from the rhizomes, and the plant is usually fairly tillered.

Habitat: From New Zealand originally where it grows in cracks in rocks forming creeping rhizomes around which water is unable to stagnate because of the natural environment.

Minimum winter temperature: 5–7 °C (40–45 °F) minimum is sufficient, but the plant will die if the maximum temperature rises above 21 °C (70 °F) in dry conditions.

Light: Good but diffused, and not in direct sunlight.

Environmental humidity: Should be high, with additional spraying of foliage, at fairly high temperatures, otherwise the leaflets will wither.

Watering: Water frequently in summer, and much less in winter, when the soil should dry between waterings, especially at low temperatures; but make doubly sure that the water never stagnates at the bottom of the pot, at any time of year.

Soil: May be made up of very fibrous compost, with an equal amount of peat and additional very coarse sand; it must never clod. There must be very good drainage.

Propagation: Reproduction by division in spring, making sure that every part has whole rhizomes with shoots. Watering should be done at the outset with great caution.

PELLIONIA DAVEAUANA (Urticaceae)

Etymology: This genus is named after the navigator Alphonse Odet Pellion (1796–1868) who later became a French admiral.

Description: A herbaceous perennial plant, forming a creeping cover, with flat, alternate, lanceolate and slightly oblique leaves which are crenate at the margins where the colour ranges from dark-green to bronze, while the uneven central area is very pale silvery-green overall. The stems are somewhat succulent, pinkish or reddish; the plant may be used as a hanging decoration.

Habitat: From Burma and Malaya, where it grows in the tropical undergrowth.

Minimum winter temperature: About 16 °C (60 °F).

Light: Diffused, not in direct sunlight, although quite good light is necessary to bring out the variegations to the full.

Environmental humidity: As high as possible.

Watering: Water frequently in summer and sparingly in winter, when the atmospheric humidity should be quite high. Bear in mind at all times that the stems are succulent and the roots very fine, which means that the water must never saturate the soil or stagnate.

Soil: Must be very porous and well aired, made up of leaf-mould and peat in equal parts with sand and shredded sphagnum added; plants will also grow in sandy soil covered with moss.

Propagation: Reproduction by stem cuttings which root very easily as long as the soil is very soft, even consisting solely of sphagnum and peat, and kept moist, with a temperature of about 21–24 °C (70–75 °F). Because of the fleshy (carnose) nature of the stems it is not advisable to put the cuttings under covers; try to maintain the level of humidity necessary by spraying, which will not cause too much run-off, thus drenching the soil.

THE PEPEROMIA GENUS (Piperaceae)

Etymology: The name comes from the Greek *péperi*, 'pepper' and *òmolos*, 'similar' because many species have botanical features akin to those of the pepper plant, or at least to much of the genus *Piper*.

Description: This is a huge genus, including more than 1,000 species; among these several are commonly cultivated. The plants are all herbaceous and perennial and may be either upright or creeping, with some epiphytes as well. They have very small root systems indeed; the leaves, coming in all shapes and sizes depending on the species, may be alternate, opposite or verticillate, and quite fleshy in texture; the stems, however, are invariably rather succulent, as are other parts of the plant, such as the nervations, even though the lamina appears to be thin. The attraction of many resides in the variegation of the lamina, which may be leathery or velvety; while others are prized for the way they grow. The inflorescences are formed by tiny flowers on spikes which are very often above the foliage, sometimes upright and curled into cymes like a small tail; in at least one species the spikes open to form clusters of small verticillate flowers which grow successively longer and look like a small pyramid. In the taxonomic system concerning the entire genus there is some confusion and very often the synonyms are used as actual names of species; but the commonest are generally well defined.

Habitat: Most come from central-southern America where they grow in the tropical forests, although there are also some Asian species which are not easy to cultivate.

Minimum winter temperature: About 16 °C (60 °F), although, if kept dry, some species will tolerate a few degrees less.

Light: Plentiful; no species tolerates direct sunlight, so the light must be diffused but as intense as possible. In poor light the internodes lengthen, the variegated species lose their variegation, the species which should, in ideal conditions, remain low and compact and almost acaulescent, develop stems which are often too weak to support the foliage, and hence take on an untidy appearance.

Environmental humidity: Varies greatly depending on the species; generally speaking the indoor species do not require much and, obviously, the requirement is less for the more succulent plants.

Watering: Water regularly in summer and sparingly in winter. It is often hard to judge the right amounts, but as one of the major dangers is causing the fleshy stems to rot, it is often advisable to let a few leaves wither rather than risk losing the whole plant.

Soil: All species require fairly light and porous soil where the water cannot ever stagnate; it may be made up of equal parts of mature leaf-mould and peat with a good amount of sand or perlite added to help keep the mixture well-aired. The pots can be small, and drainage good. It is as well to avoid soils with organic matter which is still decomposing, so as to prevent bacteria and fungi attacking the collar.

Propagation: All the species are reproduced quite easily by stem cuttings and most also by leaf cuttings. They do not need covers, given the presence of succulent tissues, but they do need a very porous soil; and for leaf-cuttings this should consist mainly of sand or perlite; water sparingly until the new plants have properly taken, with a temperature of 21 °C (70 °F) and more. Some variegated species, such as *Peperomia caperata triclor*, if reproduced by leaf will revert to being completely green, and it will then be necessary to take stem cuttings.

▲ *Peperomia caperata*

PEPEROMIA ARGYREIA (Piperaceae)

Description: This species, often known as *P. sandersii*, is almost stemless, with leaves in rosettes, with fairly long and fleshy stalks, dotted with reddish blotches; the lamina is thick, the leaf peltate (shield-shaped) and acuminate, slightly concave, with silvery stripes radiating out from the joint of the stalk towards the tip; the central stripes are almost straight, the outer ones curved, almost crescent-shaped. The other side of the lamina is pale-green.
Habitat: From Brazil.
Remarks: Cultivation is straightforward, as for other species, but indoors the stems tend to grow quite long and bend under the weight of the foliage; it is thus advisable to reproduce the plant periodically, by either stem- or leaf-cuttings. These latter may be planted in the soil with a small length of stalk at the base, from which the new plant will sprout; but simple pieces having a principal vein will also produce new growth from the base.

PEPEROMIA CAPERATA (Piperaceae)

Description: This species has small, green, rounded, peltate-cordate leaves with conspicuous corrugations between the nervations; the stalks are red or pink and the small white spikes of the inflorescences grow out above the foliage. This plant is also more or less stemless, but it is hard to keep it as such. There is a variety: *tricolor* with leaves with wide white margins which, in good light, take on pinkish colouring; it is much more delicate than the typical species, and cannot be reproduced by leaf-cuttings.
Habitat: From southern Brazil.
Remarks: Cultivation is the same as for the other species; this plant needs good light to avoid etiolation of the stems. Small and compact, it is ideal as a single plant, but its tendency to rot makes it unsuited to mixed groups of plants.

PEPEROMIA OBTUSIFOLIA VARIEGATA (Piperaceae)

Description: This species, which is often muddled with the very similar *P. magnoliaefolia*, is somewhat taller than the other species, easily reaching 1·50 m (5 ft) with large, carnose, ramifying stems which unfortunately tend to grow twisted in time. The succulent leaves are quite large, obovate, and, in the variegated forms, have a wide, white or cream-white margin which tends to vanish in the older leaves or in poor light.
Habitat: The typical green species is from Venezuela; the variegated forms are cultivated varieties which are often named according to their size or the intensity of their variegation.
Remarks: Although cultivation is the same as for the other species, this species is more succulent, so it is as well to keep a careful eye on winter watering. If kept dry it will tolerate quite low temperatures, and may be reproduced by stem-cuttings in spring to have young plants which are both upright and well-coloured.

▲ *Peperomia argyreia*

PEPEROMIA SCANDENS (Piperaceae)

Description: This is a small creeping species which may be used as a hanging plant; in the wild it produces roots at the nodes and with these may take root not only in the ground but also by clinging to various sorts of support, thus growing vertically. The stems are reddish, slender and carnose, with quite long internodes; the leaves are green and shiny, cordate and acuminate, and fairly small.
Habitat: From Peru.
Remarks: This plant is best grown as a hanging specimen, given that, indoors, it is very hard to have sufficiently moist supports without running the risk of rotting the succulent stems. In horticultural circles it is often muddled with *P. glabella*, a very similar species except for the fact that the base is tapered and not cordate, and the lamina is predominantly elliptical; in other respects it may be put to the same use. It is easily reproduced, and it is advisable to put more than one cutting in each pot to obtain more compact specimens, in view of their slender growth pattern.

PEPEROMIA SCANDENS VARIEGATA (Piperaceae)

Description: This plant, which grows very like the typical species, is in greater demand than some other varieties because of its attractive appearance due to the wide white margins of the small, cordate-acuminate leaves, which contrast sharply with the red stalks and reddish stems. Sometimes there may be entirely white leaves, and as in all cases where this occurs — it is known as albinism — reproduction by stem-cuttings is only possible if there are a couple of leaves with some green in them; in fact the total absence of chlorophyll prevents the formation of regenerative tissues.
Habitat: This is a horticultural variety.
Remarks: This plant will not lose its variegations even with diffused and not very intense light; it is thus very well-suited to being grown indoors, especially as a hanging plant; it is succulent, thus disliking too much watering, and can therefore be grown in baskets without much trouble. As for the typical species, reproduction is by stem-cuttings which take root very easily.

THE PHILODENDRON GENUS (Araceae)

Etymology: The name derives from the Greek *phílos* 'dear, beloved' and *déndron*, 'tree', because of the fact that most species are climbers and, in the wild (i.e. in tropical forests), twine round trees by means of aerial roots which appear at the nodes.

Description: This is a very large genus, including, it is reckoned, at least 275 species, although the exact number is quite vague, not least because there is such considerable dimorphism between the young stage and the adult plant that they are often classified as different plants when they are in fact single plants at different stages of development; and also because the habitat of many is so wide that there are local varieties with such diverse features that they are considered to be quite different. Things are further complicated by the large number of primary, original and natural hybrids, or hybrids produced in cultivation, some by mutation. The plants may be suffruticose, even semi-arborescent, climbing or upright; some are also epiphytes; their foliage is often very decorative in shape, size or growth pattern, although it is completely green in most species; not only are very few forms variegated, but these are also usually too delicate to be grown indoors. The leaves are always petiolate (stalked), the stalk being geniculate and often quite long, especially in the upright forms; it may or may not be vaginate at the base and alate, but not conspicuously; the new leaves are convolute at first, appearing in tight stipules which become caducous once the stalk is completely developed. The inflorescences are typical to the family, consisting of a spadix with unisexual flowers enclosed by a spathe on which the berries ripen. It is nevertheless very hard to get these plants to flower when cultivated, even in the ideal conditions of the greenhouse, and very fully-developed plants are needed to achieve this. The lamina may be entire, lobate or septate.

Habitat: All the species are from tropical and sub-tropical America.

Minimum winter temperature: Ranges from 13–16 °C (55–60 °F).

Light: Given that they grow in the undergrowth, the Philodendrons usually require not very intense light, but they like a reasonable amount of diffused light; do not expose to direct sunlight.

Environmental humidity: The level of atmospheric humidity varies from species to species, but no species thrives in conditions which are too dry; the climbing species need humidity not only to improve the look and condition of their tissues but also to help the growth of the adventitious aerial roots which grow at the nodes.

Watering: Water quite frequently in summer and sparingly in winter, with sufficient increase of atmospheric humidity.

Soil: Always very well-drained and porous, it may be made up for most species of leaf-mould and peat in equal parts with sand added. The roots are carnose, so the soil must never clod; keep the pots as small as possible, and ensure excellent drainage.

Propagation: Generally reproduction is by apical cuttings or cuttings using a part of the stem with a few nodes. Almost all the species will root in water, requiring a temperature of about 21–24 °C (70–75 °F) and very good light; if planted in firm soil, this must be very porous and kept just slightly moist to avoid rot. Rooting is a slow process, as for all the *Araceae*.

◄ *Philodendron 'Burgundi'*

PHILODENDRON 'BURGUNDY' (Araceae)

Description: This is a climbing species which grows very slowly and remains compact and low for some time. Its very large leaves are sagittate-acuminate, leathery, and green with reddish highlights; the base may be cordate or spear-shaped; the stems are wine-red, as are the petioles, which are alate, the central vein on the underneath of the lamina, and the stipules containing the new leaves.

Habitat: This is a commercial hybrid which is very common and sturdy, derived from numerous selected crossings with various species; in shape, colour and growth pattern it reveals features of *P. hastatum, P. erubescens, P. wendlandii and P. imbe.*

Remarks: Although it tolerates indoor conditions, if specimens are to be kept in good condition there must be plenty of light and quite a high level of environmental humidity, helped by frequent sponging of the foliage. Without these two requisites, the red colour will tend to fade, the internodes will lengthen and the leaves will become smaller. Cultivation and reproduction are as for the genus as a whole.

PHILODENDRON CORDATUM (Araceae)

Description: There is considerable confusion between *P. cordatum, P. oxycardium* and *P. scandens*; in effect, the two latter are synonyms and as well as being very alike, are also very similar to the first species. They are climbing plants with slender stems, not very large, heart-shaped, acuminate, leathery and shiny leaves which become larger when fully developed, reaching about 30 cm (12 in). They stand up well to hot and cold conditions, and the temperature may even drop to 10 °C (50 °F); they also tolerate quite poor light, although in these conditions the leaves never grow very large and the internodes tend to lengthen. These forms, which are so common in horticulture, are probably not the actual typical species, but crossings with hardier types.

Habitat: From Brazil.

Remarks: Cultivation is as for the genus as a whole, but bear in mind that in winter they should be watered even more sparingly than the other species, and that their root system is easily damaged by too much watering which will clod the soil around the roots; for the same reason stem-cuttings should be planted just beneath the surface of the soil so that the soil remains almost dry round the nodes, and provides a certain amount of moisture from lower down.

PHILODENDRON 'EMERALD QUEEN' (Araceae)

Description: A vigorous climbing plant with shiny green spear-shaped leaves, easy to find on the market because of its hardiness and its tolerance of relatively low temperatures and moderate light — which should, nevertheless, not be poor.
Habitat: This is a hybrid, but the parents are not known; it is probably the offspring of more than one species.
Remarks: Cultivation as for the other species, but even though it is very hardy, the leaves will become gradually smaller in poor light.

PHILODENDRON FRAGRANS (Araceae)

Description: This highly decorative plant is not common, although hybrids derived from it are to be found on the market. It is a very slow-growing climber, with large leaves, cordate at the base, with obtuse or slightly acuminate tips. The veins are depressed, and the lamina between them appears corrugated and is shiny green.
Habitat: From southern Brazil.
Remarks: This species requires higher environmental humidity than the others and will not tolerate low temperatures. The size of the leaves makes it ideal for large rooms, not least because in the wild it is creeping rather than climbing, and as a result large, strong supports are required to keep it upright.

PHILODENDRON HASTATUM (Araceae)

Description: A climbing species with rather fleshy leaves, having a bright green lamina, and sagittate in the early stages, and become spear-shaped and slightly wavy when adult. This plant is ideal for growing large specimens; it grows quite fast once well established and thus needs tall props. From it are derived numerous horticultural hybrids, in some of which the crossing with upright species has given rise to lower and more compact plants, which grow more slowly, but retain the hardy quality of the species as a whole.

Habitat: From Brazil.

Remarks: Cultivation as for the genus as a whole; this plant thrives in diffused but quite plentiful light which will stop the internodes growing too long and the leaves losing their distinctive look. Specimens grown in greenhouses have fairly upright stalks because of the light coming from above; indoors they will tend to grow like most climbers, developing foliage on just one side and bending the stems, which must for this reason be firmly attached to supports. This may be helped by turning the plant every so often so that it receives light all round.

PHILODENDRON LACINIATUM (Araceae)

Description: A climbing plant with rather slender stems and dark-green, five-lobed leaves; the lobes are often in turn lobed in older leaves; the petioles are long, the lamina has quite separate and curved lobes, with the apical one very acuminate and invariably larger and longer than the others; the veins are depressed and marked. This species is very similar to *P. squamiferum*, which has the same growth pattern and leaves of roughly the same shape, but the petioles are covered with setules ranging in colour from green to reddish. It is probable that specimens found in shops are neither of these species but the results of crossing; one of these, the variety 'Florida', is hardier and more compact and has intermediate features, with a light down on the stalks, and more conspicuously lobed leaves.

Habitat: *P. laciniatum* is from Peru, but its natural habitat stretches as far as Brazil; *P. squamiferum* is from Guyana.

Remarks: Hybrids found in shops stand up well to less than perfect surroundings; their cultivation is like that of the other species of the genus. There is a very strong tendency to turn towards the source of light and it is advisable to let this happen because it is hard to keep the plant growing upright, even with lighting from above; if you move the plant you will simply cause the stems and stalks to twist untidily. If, because of poor light, the leaves look small and stunted in winter, it is advisable to prune the plant, in spring, back to the lowest normal-sized leaf.

PHILODENDRON PANDURIFORME (Araceae)

Description: This species, often written *panduraeforme*, is a climber with unusually shaped leaves, i.e. pandurate, a term coming from the Latin *pandura* which was the name of a cithara, a three-stringed musical instrument, and, in botanical circles, means any leaf whose shape recalls that of a stringed sound-box, violin and so on. In this case the lamina has a large basal region with two wide lateral lobes and a long central lobe which broadens out again to the obtuse apex after tapering in the central part. The leaves are leathery and olive-green, and the plant is fairly uncommon, not least because it is not really happy indoors and is better suited to the greenhouse. If the air is too dry the leaves lose their handsome texture and poor light causes the leaves to grow small and somewhat dull, although in good conditions they will reach 30 cm (12 in). The temperature should not drop below 16 °C (60 °F), and there must be high humidity.

Habitat: From southern Brazil.

Remarks: Although more delicate than the other species as regards warmth and atmospheric humidity, it is cultivated in all other respects like the other members of the genus.

PHILODENDRON PENNATIFIDUM (Araceae)

Description: This plant is a large suffruticose species which, in the wild, may assume almost arboreal proportions; when cultivated it remains low, with a short trunk and an apical leaf-rosette with a long, channelled, red-dotted stalk; it is uncommon to find specimens where the stem exceeds a maximum of 50 cm (20 in) in height. The lamina is very pinnate, with the segments well divided and with a conspicuous depressed vein; it is green and in good light will show metallic highlights. It may be confused with similar species, and in particular with *P. bipennatifidum*, which has longer, narrower segments and, as the name implies, basal segments which are in turn pinnate. There are also various cultivated varieties; they are all large and bulky plants, due to their long petioles.

Habitat: The distribution area of this species stretches from Venezuela to Amazonia and in all probability the differences, which are sometimes considerable, between plants are due to the fact that there are various local varieties.

Remarks: This plant, like all the others of the same upright type, dislikes places where the light does not come from above, and will develop twisted stems. This may be partly remedied by rotating the pot every now and then so that the light falls on the whole plant. The temperature should never drop below 13 °C (55 °F) and the environmental humidity should be kept as high as possible, using any means available. Old plants will readily produce shoots at the base which may be used for reproduction, but they will be very slow-growing. Should you wish to reduce the size of the plant, it may be topped, and the uppermost part used as a cutting. In this case, and in due course, the old stem will produce new shoots at the base.

PHILODENDRON SCANDENS (Araceae)

Description: This species has caused considerable taxonomic confusion and a diversity of opinions among the various authors. Its synonym is *P. cuspidatum*, and the specific attribute indicates the major difference with *P. cordatum* because, in fact, the tips of its leaves are much more acuminate and, more precisely, cuspidate. This does not, however, stop many authors from considering this to be a young or local form of *P. oxycardium*, and yet, commercially speaking, all the species of this type are called *P. scandens*. It is a very hardy plant which will tolerate temperatures as low as 7 °C (45 °F) as well as fairly high temperatures, and will grow even in poor light, although in such cases the cordate and very acuminate leaves remain far smaller than normal. In good light they are bronze-green, specially while young; the stipules are pinkish; even in far from ideal conditions as far as atmospheric humidity is concerned they will produce very long aerial roots at the nodes. As in all the *Araceae*, the initial growth is slow, but once established, this pretty but not brightly-coloured plant, will cover whole walls in a short time.

Habitat: From the West Indies, and Puerto Rico in particular.

Remarks: Its tendency to rot and its tolerance of dry soil mean that this plant requires to be watered even more sparingly than the other species during the winter, especially at low temperatures. The plant may also be used as a hanging specimen, but it will grow less energetically if so used; overall, its cultivation is the same for the genus as a whole, but more straightforward, and this species requires the least attention of all.

PHILODENDRON SELLOUM (Araceae)

Description: This is a suffruticose plant which may grow in the wild either as an arborescent plant or as an epiphyte on trees, with its roots dropping right to the ground. These roots, which grow at the base of the parts left by the withered leaves on the large falling stem, are very sturdy and fleshy; in pots they tend to curl in on themselves and penetrate the ground around the edge of the pot. The petioles are very long indeed, and bear large leaves with a bipinnate lamina which is wavy at the edge of the segments. Because of its resistance to the cold (it will tolerate just a few degrees above zero (32 °F) and its broad growth pattern, it is particularly well-suited to large, cool, airy and well-lit rooms. There are a great number of varieties and hybrids with other species of the same type such as *P. bipinnatifidum*. But both varieties and hybrids are often hard to find names for.

Habitat: It has a vast distribution area stretching throughout south-western Brazil to all of Uruguay in hilly regions and, in the Sierra do Mar, also at quite high altitudes, which explains why it will survive in low temperatures.

Remarks: These plants require only very small pots, considering their size, and transplanting is only necessary when the stability of the plant itself is at risk. In our milder climates it may stay outside for most of the year, but in a semi-shady position; older, well-established plants may also be exposed to direct sunlight except in very hot, dry spells. The other requirements are as for the genus as a whole; reproduction may be carried out with shoots, where they appear, or by top-cuttings having some roots, if a plant is to be rejuvenated. This is only a slender possibility, however, in view of the slow growth of the plant.

PILEA CADIEREI (Urticaceae)

Etymology: The name comes from the Latin *pileus*, a felt cap worn by the ancient Romans on special occasions; the Latin term in turn came from the Greek *pilos*, which meant virtually anything made of felt, including blankets; in this plant it refers to the fact that the female flowers have the segments of the perianth covering the achene.

Description: This very well-known indoor plant is an evergreen perennial with opposite, petiolate, obovate and acuminate leaves with crenate margins. The lamina stands out between the depressed veins and is variegated in silver on a green background, which is darker in older leaves and light-coloured, sometimes slightly glaucous, in young leaves. New growth is contained in pinkish, caducous stipules. This plant is very easy and fast to reproduce, so much so that all the plants presently being cultivated come from one cutting which arrived in Paris from Annam quite recently; one of its features which is shared by few other plants is that it can produce roots from any part of its stem, although they grow most readily at the nodes, of course.

Habitat: From Indochina.

Minimum winter temperature: 10–16°C (50–60°F) minimum, but is easy prey to scale insects at high temperatures.

Light: Does not need to be very strong, and will tolerate moderate light, but do not expose to direct sunlight; it tends to twist its stems towards the source of light, so rotate the pot frequently.

Environmental humidity: Good, increased by spraying or sponging.

Watering: Water frequently in summer and regularly in winter, and slightly more if the temperature is not high.

Soil: Should be porous and humus-rich, made up of equal parts of compost and mature leaf-mould with peat and sand added. Drainage must be excellent so that the water never saturates the soil; do not use large pots.

Propagation: Reproduction either by top-cuttings or pieces of stem, with a temperature not lower than 18–21°C (65–70°F). Rooting may take place either in normal soil or in sand mixed with peat, or in water. To preserve the foliage and make the operation safer, put the cuttings in small pots under glass or plastic covers, but the soil must be very slightly moist and will need frequent airing to stop condensation rotting the leaves. In due course the plants will shed the leaves in the lower part of the stem which tends to become twisted; it is thus advisable to reproduce the plant regularly so as to have a constant supply of young plants; put several cuttings in each pot so as to have a more compact effect. Regular clipping of the young plants will make them produce ramifications and give tillered specimens.

PILEA REPENS (Urticaceae)

Description: This plant, which has been put on the market only recently is universally known by this name among horticulturalists, but there is some doubt as to whether it is the right name. Although there are more than 400 species of *Pilea*, they do not form a very closely studied genus, and there is a host of synonyms for every cultivated species, which confuses the taxonomic system even more. What is more, thanks to the way the tiny seeds are scattered, they very often cross, so that it is hard to identify the real species from natural hybrids. The species which we know as *Pilea repens* is probably a hybrid form of *P. spruceana*, often known also as *involucrata*, although, according to American authors, there really is a *Pilea repens*, whose description, however, does not agree with that of the cultivated variety. The plant has opposite, almost sessile, decussate (i.e. each pair crosses with the previous pair) leaves which are very close together with very short internodes; the lamina is ovate-acuminate in form, dentate at the margins and with three very depressed lengthwise veins, between which the tissue is slightly pubescent and bullate, with salient areas. The basic colour is green, but in good light it takes on a bronze colour, which is especially intense at the margins. Although single-stemmed specimens with fairly large and very attractive leaves may be produced in nursery greenhouses with very high humidity, intense and diffused light and careful reproduction, this is rarely a satisfactory indoor plant. It ramifies a great deal, and fails to give a tillered appearance; the leaves become smaller and lose their bronze and coppery hues, becoming green throughout.

Habitat: Apparently from Central America, while *P. spruceana* is from Peru. It may therefore be a local variety.

Minimum winter temperature: About 16 °C (60 °F).

Light: Diffused, not direct sunlight, but very strong to keep the colours of the foliage unchanged.

Environmental humidity: Very high, using any means available.

Watering: Quite frequently all year round, but the water must never stagnate at the bottom of the pot. The leaves wither very easily and often turn black from a fungal disease which develops if the soil is too saturated. It is also prey to the cotton scale insect.

Soil: Must be very porous and moist, but without stagnating water; it may be made up of equal parts of leaf-mould and peat, the latter in slightly larger amounts, with some sand added.

Propagation: As for almost all the species, reproduction by cuttings is very straightforward. Do not use covers and keep the soil just moist, in view of its liability to cryptogamic diseases. The temperature should be about 21 °C (70 °F) and cuttings may be taken at any time of year. As it ramifies naturally, there is plenty of opportunity for taking top-cuttings.

THE PIPER GENUS (Piperaceae)

Etymology: *Piper* is the Latin name, derived from the Greek *péperi* which in turn was probably Indian in origin and was used in Greece as early as the fourth century BC.

Description: Although this extensive genus consists of almost 2,000 species very few are cultivated and only two are suitable as house plants; one very attractive but delicate, the other hardy, but rare. Both are sarmentose, dioecious shrubs which have alternate leaves with stipules and cordate, acuminate blade. *Piper futokadsura* has dark green leaves and although not very showy it grows vigorously; unfortunately it is little cultivated. *Piper ornatum* is a very handsome plant with glossy, peltate, green leaves; the venation is emphasized on young leaves by irregular pink markings which become white on mature leaves. The underside of the leaf is dark red and the petiole is also reddish.

Habitat: *Piper futokadsura* is from Japan, *Piper ornatum* from the Celebes island.

Minimum winter temperature: 7–10 °C (45–50 °F) for the first species, about 16 °C (61 °F) for the second.

Light: Diffuse, well out of direct sun; the light need not be very strong.

Environmental humidity: Good, especially for *Piper ornatum* which likes a very humid atmosphere and frequent spraying of the leaves.

Watering: Fairly frequent all the year round; water rather less often in winter but never let the soil dry out.

Soil: Porous and light, composed of equal parts of leaf mould and peat with some sand or perlite.

Propagation: By stem cuttings, inserted in a porous mixture of perlite and peat, kept slightly moist at 21–24 °C (70–75 °F). Cover with glass or plastic but air frequently. Soil-layering is also possible. Place a pot near the parent plant and fasten down a root-forming node; detach when roots are well established.

PISONIA BRUNONIANA (Nyctagynaceae)

Etymology: Named after the Dutch naturalist Wilhelm Piso, who died in 1648.

Description: In the wild this is an arborescent plant which can grow to a considerable height; young plants are cultivated, although not very commonly, because of their low resistance to life outside the greenhouse. The leaves are alternate, petiolate, oval-oblong and acuminate. The lamina is entire, irregularly variegated in two tones of green, while the margins, which are quite wide, are cream-coloured, with pinkish highlights and hues in good light.

Habitat: It has a vast distribution area stretching from New Zealand to Tahiti, including several Pacific islands.

Minimum winter temperature: 13–16 °C (55–60 °F).

Light: Very good to keep the colours of the variegations unchanged, but do not expose to direct sunlight.

Environmental humidity: As high as possible, and the leaves should be regularly sponged and sprayed. If the air is too dry the leaves tend to fall off fairly easily.

Watering: Water regularly, slightly less in winter, depending on the ambient temperature. The water must never stagnate at the bottom of the pot.

Soil: Light and porous, made up of equal parts of leaf-mould and peat with some sand added; it is vital that the soil does not clod or become too wet, which would choke the root system.

Propagation: Generally by air-layering on plants which have lost their lower leaves and have a lignified stem. It is not advisable to take cuttings of semi-herbaceous parts of the stem, although it is possible if the temperature is 24 °C (75 °F) or more and if there is plenty of atmospheric humidity, but avoid stagnation. These conditions are hard to create indoors.

PLATYCERIUM BIFURCATUM (Polypodiaceae)

Etymology: The name of the genus comes from the Greek *platýs*, 'large' and *kras*, 'horn' because of the shape of the fronds.
Description: This genus of epiphyte ferns, including some 17 species, has two types of fronds, sterile and fertile. The fertile fronds come in various shapes, but are generally long, fairly pendent, lobate or bilobate towards the tip. *P. bifurcatum* is one of the most distinctive and easily obtainable species; being sub-tropical, it is grown more easily than others. Very akin to it is *P. alcicorne*, but this is very delicate, being tropical. The fertile fronds are pendent and may have several lobes, which explains the specific name.
Habitat: *P. bifurcatum* comes from Australia; *P. alcicorne* from Madagascar to Polynesia.
Minimum winter temperature: Unlike the other species, *P. bifurcatum* is semi-hardy and only requires shelter from frost, although a min. temp. of about 7–10 °C (45–50 °F) is advisable.
Light: Must always be diffused, not direct sunlight and fairly bright.
Environmental humidity: Use any means available but do not spray fronds, which are slightly downy and blotch easily.
Watering: Water frequently in summer and sparingly in winter.
Soil: Must be light and very porous; these plants are best if hanging, attached to pieces of treetrunk or bark, with the roots wrapped in shredded fern roots and leaf-mould enclosed in sphagnum and fixed to the support with wire. The plants may be grown in pots, as wide and low as possible, but quite small, with good drainage and a soil made up of fern-roots, sphagnum and peat.
Propagation: Remove and pot any basal shoots in peat and sphagnum at about 21 °C (70 °F) with higher atmospheric humidity and little watering; new shoots rarely appear in potted plants.

PLECTRANTHUS COLEOIDES 'MARGINATUS' (Labiatae)

Etymology: The name derives from the Greek *pléctron*, 'spur' and *ánthos*, 'flower', because the rear part of the corolla forms a small tube shaped like a spur.
Description: A herbaceous perennial plant which is low-growing and bushy; the stems are four-sided, the leaves opposite, downy, with a green centre, while the crenate margins are emphasized by a white or cream-coloured stripe. The central part often has two shades of green, usually quite dark and greyish, and irregular.
Habitat: From India.
Minimum winter temperature: 13–16 °C (55–60 °F).
Light: Very bright; does not tolerate direct sunlight, but strong, diffused light is essential for its survival during the winter months.
Environmental humidity: No special requirements; the plant is more attractive with a humid atmosphere, but more important than this is good ventilation, avoiding stale air.
Watering: Water frequently in summer and sparingly in winter.
Soil: Humus-rich and well-drained, made up of equal parts of compost and mature leaf-mould with peat and sand added so that it remains permeable.
Propagation: By cuttings in spring at a temperature of about 21 °C (70 °F) in porous soil made up of peat and sand or fine and mainly sandy earth. The cuttings produce roots in water too, with plenty of warmth and light. If planted directly in pots, they may be put under glass or plastic covers, but do not over-water the soil, and air often to prevent rot. The plants usually lose their lower leaves and become too long and untidy, so it is advisable to take cuttings at least once a year.

POLYSCIAS BALFOURIANA (Araliaceae)

Etymology: The name derives from the Greek *polýs*, 'many' and *skià* 'shade' referring to the abundant foliage of this shrub or small tree.

Description: In the wild this species is a shrub or small tree which may grow 8 m (25 ft), with leathery, rounded leaves, obtuse at the tip and crenate at the margins. The typical species is not cultivated, but the variety 'Pennockii' is commonly grown; this has unevenly variegated leaves coloured cream and pale-green, and dark-green at the edges.

Habitat: The typical species comes from New Caledonia, where there is also a variety, *marginata*, with irregular white margins; it is presumably the parent of the cultivated variety.

Minimum winter temperature: About 16°C (60°F).

Light: Very bright, in theory, with high atmospheric humidity; will also tolerate direct sunlight, although this is not possible as a rule in our part of the world, especially at the hottest time of year.

Environmental humidity: Maintain high, using all available means, but avoid staleness; as for most of the family, this plant requires high humidity with good ventilation. In dry air it is particularly vulnerable to attacks by mites.

Watering: Water regularly all year round but be careful to avoid stagnating water at the bottom of the pot.

Soil: Very permeable, made up of compost and mature leaf-mould in equal parts, with peat and sand added; it is most important to stop the earth from clodding by being saturated with water; in such cases the root system will be endangered and the plant may die.

Propagation: By semi-herbaceous cuttings in mainly sandy soil which is never too wet, under glass or plastic covers at a temp. of about 21°C (70°F), ventilating often to avoid rot. In very humid atmospheres do not use covers. Cuttings may be taken at any time of year, but it is best to wait for the vegetative period to recommence to be sure of having better light.

PSEUDERANTHEMUM ATROPURPUREUM TRICOLOR (Acanthaceae)

Etymology: The name comes from the Greek *pseudés*, 'false' and from the name of the genus *Eranthemum*, belonging to the same family, which is very akin and was once included in it.

Description: A suffruticose evergreen perennial with upright stems and opposite, petiolate, entire, elliptical leaves which are acuminate at the tip. The lamina, which is shiny and leathery, is unevenly variegated in olive-green, violet-red and pink; with too much light the foliage may revert to almost uniformly dark-red.

Habitat: From Polynesia.

Minimum winter temperature: 13–16°C (55–60°F).

Light: Very bright, but diffused, sheltered from direct sunlight.

Environmental humidity: Good, including sponging and spraying the foliage, but keep well ventilated. Air which is too dry and stagnating humidity both render the plant vulnerable to attack from brown scale insects, to which the family as a whole is liable. In summer will grow well outdoors, in semi-shade.

Watering: Water frequently in summer and sparingly in winter, when the plant will tend to lose many of the leaves near the stem.

Soil: Porous and light, well aerated, made up of compost, mature leaf-mould and peat in equal parts with some sand added.

Propagation: As for all the *Acanthaceae*, these plants have a particular tendency to lose the leaves along the stem, even when herbaceous, and hence lengthen the distance between internodes, which sometimes includes twisting. As reproduction is fairly easy, it is advisable to take cuttings periodically, so as to have young specimens; at the same time the old plants will ramify. Put three or four cuttings to a pot to obtain a better effect in light soil made up of barely moist peat and sand under glass or plastic covers at a temperature of about 24°C (75°F). Air often, and take cuttings, preferably in spring.

PTERIS ENSIFORMIS (Polypodiaceae)

Etymology: The name comes from the Greek *ptéron*, 'wing', referring to the rather light and elegant shape of the fronds.

Description: The genus includes more than 60 species, which vary greatly, and have numerous varieties. This is an attractive species, with two types of fronds: the sterile ones are shorter and wider; the fertile ones upright and slender. The variety 'Victoriae' has a white central stripe along all its segments, in both the fertile and sterile fronds, while the green margins are wavy.

Habitat: The typical species comes from India and parts of Australia.

Minimum winter temperature: 13–16 °C (55–60 °F).

Light: Diffused, moderate will do, but not too poor. Never expose to direct sunlight.

Environmental humidity: High, using all available means; spray the foliage frequently; if humidity cannot be raised, it is advisable to choose a cooler position.

Watering: Water regularly all year round; the soil must never dry out completely, but should remain constantly moist, with not too much water, which would endanger the rhizome; provide good drainage.

Soil: Very light, very soft, made up of a mixture of peat and leaf-mould with shredded sphagnum and charcoal chippings added; the rhizomes must be buried very lightly and may be covered by a thin layer of lightly pressed sphagnum; pots should be small, to stop the soil clodding.

Propagation: By division of the rhizomes in spring, keeping the atmosphere as humid as possible, without covers (which allow the water to stagnate); bury the rhizomes shallow, and keep covered with sphagnum.

Remarks: All species have the same requirements, including *P. quadriaurita*, growing throughout the tropical zones, and parent attractive varieties.

▲ *Pteris ensiformis 'Victoriae'*

▼ *Pteris quadriaurita*

147

RHAPHIDOPHORA DECURSIVA (Araceae)

Etymology: The name (sometimes incorrectly spelt Raphidophora) comes from the Greek *rhapis* or 'needle' and *phoréo*, 'I bear', because the cells contain needle-like oxalate crystals.

Description: A sarmentose plant with adventitious roots, which may grow upwards or have a creeping habit: it is not easy to train its twining stems to grow on supports. Closely related to the genera *Monstera, Scindapsus* and *Philodendron*, the plant has leaves which are different in shape at different stages. When young they are acuminate and entire, but when fully grown they become pinnatifid, with broad, sickle-shaped segments growing in a semi-alternate arrangement from the central vein and an oblong, acuminate central lobe usually at an angle to the leaf axis. The plant grows rather slowly. The leaves are very dark green and glossy.

Habitat: From a large area including Ceylon, India and Indochina.

Minimum winter temperature: 10–13 °C (50–55 °F).

Light: Adult plants tolerate moderate light, but in young plants the leaves will remain immature if they do not get enough light.

Environmental humidity: The plant likes a dry indoor atmosphere, but leaves will be improved by washing and spraying.

Watering: Plentiful in summer, well spaced in winter.

Soil: The plant is not fussy, but does need a free-draining mixture (to prevent the fleshy roots rotting) composed of equal parts of leaf mould and peat with some well-composted farmyard manure and sand. Size of pots depends on the irregular growth of the stems which sometimes makes the plant top heavy.

Propagation: By stem cuttings, either from the tip or from leafless sections of the stem itself. The first method is commonest if you want plants with characteristic leaves from the start; the second method will give side shoots with young, entire leaves. Cuttings can be taken at any time of year. They need a temperature of 21–24 °C (70–75 °F), and root slowly, like all *Araceae*. The rooting mixture must be porous, free-draining and kept slightly moist.

RHIPSALIDOPSIS ROSEA (Cactaceae)

Etymology: The name derives from the Greek *òpsis*, 'aspect, appearance', and the name of the genus *Rhipsalis*, because of the likeness of the two genera.

Description: This species, the only one cultivated, is made up of epiphyte cacti; the other species, *R. gaertneri*, is commonly ascribed to the genus *Schlumbergera*. The plants have triangular or flattened branches forming successive joints; the funnel-shaped, long-petalled flowers grow from the areolae at the tips; they are pink and appear in spring. There are several cultivars, even some obtained by crossing with related genera, and they are all very alike.

Habitat: From the tropical forests of Brazil.

Minimum winter temperature: 7–10 °C (45–50 °F).

Light: Very bright and diffused; in the intermediate seasons it may be exposed in direct sun for a few hours, but must be kept shaded in summer. Good light and observance of the winter dormant period are vital for good blooms.

Environmental humidity: High, using all means available, especially in winter, when the plant should be watered sparingly.

Watering: Water frequently in summer and sparingly in winter, and stop almost altogether at minimum temperatures.

Soil: Like all epiphytes these plants need very porous soil which must never become saturated; keep pots as small as possible, drained through at least three-quarters of the depth; the soil consists of leaf-mould and peat in equal parts with chestnut fragments and charcoal chippings added.

Propagation: By cuttings, taken at the joints and potted in pure sand; spray lightly every so often. Cuttings may be taken at any time of year, as long as the temperature is about 21 °C (70 °F).

Remarks: Like almost all related genera, these plants must always be kept in the same position as regards the source of light when the flower-buds start to appear; if they are moved, or turned round, these will fall off.

RHIPSALIS (Cactaceae)

Etymology: The name derives from the Greek *rhips*, 'rush, or rush-work', because of the slender interweaving branches.

Description: This genus, which includes at least 60 species, often hard to tell apart, consists of epiphyte cacti from tropical forests where there is high environmental humidity. The genus varies greatly, and has a rather muddled taxonomic system; the term *Rhipsalis* is often applied to plants belonging to very similar genera, which once belonged to this genus and have since been re-allotted. Most of the species have distinctive ramifications consisting of slender, articulated, aphyllous (leafless) stems which produce clusters of new branches at the joints; in some species these are tubular or triangular, in others flattened and crenate. The areolae are inermous (unarmed) and appear both on the edges and on the smooth part of the cylindrical ones; the dullish, not very conspicuous flowers and the mistletoe-like fruit grow from these.

Habitat: Although most come from the tropical forests of Brazil or other parts of Central and South America, the oddness of this genus lies in its being the only one in the family that is not exclusively American; there are species from Madagascar and Sri Lanka.

Minimum winter temperature: Usually 10 °C (50 °F) approx.

Light: Bright, but diffused; not in direct sunlight.

Environmental humidity: High, using all available means, although many species will tolerate dry indoor air quite well.

Watering: Water frequently and plentifully in summer, and very sparingly in winter; this period of dormancy is vital for flowering.

Soil: These plants are best grown in hanging baskets or attached to tree-bark; in such cases the soil must contain a good amount of sphagnum and may be made up of peat and leaf-mould. Cultivation in pots, however, requires excellent drainage, and a soil consisting mainly of shredded fern-roots with a little sphagnum and peat.

Propagation: By stem-cuttings or articuli cut at the joints, in sand and peat kept just moist at 21 °C (70 °F).

RHOEO SPATHACEA (Commelinaceae)

Etymology: The English botanist H. F. Hance (1827–1886) who named the genus did not give any explanation; it was probably not used until it had been adopted by the German G. W. Walpers (1816–1853).

Description: This species, often also known by the name of *Rhoeo discolor*, is monotypic, being the only one in the genus; it is an evergreen, herbaceous perennial with linear leaves in rosettes up to 30 cm (12 in) in length and slightly concave. The leaves are sessile, vaginal at the base, overlapping (imbricate); the lamina is green above and violet beneath; the inflorescences, consisting of small trimerous flowers with three white petals, grow between the axils; they are short-lived, and enclosed by two violet, concave bracts which half-close at flowering. As the plant grows the lower leaves are shed and the internodes lengthen to form a bare stem.

Habitat: From Mexico.

Minimum winter temperature: 10–13 °C (50–55 °F).

Light: Bright, if possible from above to keep the stems upright; if not, it is advisable to turn the pot every so often.

Environmental humidity: No special requirements; with some humidity the leaves will be more handsome and turgid.

Watering: Water frequently in summer, more sparingly in winter, when many of the leaves will wither at the base; but because it is dormant, frequent watering will encourage its growth too slowly and it will turn out spindly and stunted.

Soil: This plant has no special requirements: the soil may be made up of equal parts of compost, leaf-mould and a little peat and sand.

Propagation: Given the position of the blooms, they pollinate themselves quite easily and seed; seed is however less advisable than reproduction, given that this is so straightforward. Cut the stem below a node and plant it at about 21 °C (70 °F), keeping the soil just moist to avoid rot. By cutting the old stem at the base, sideshoots will appear, and can be kept or removed.

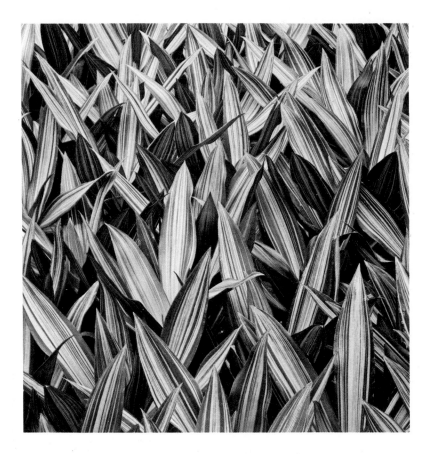

RHOEO SPATHACEA VITTATA (Commelinaceae)

Description: The same as the typical species, this variegated form has irregular white or yellowish markings lengthwise on the upper blade of the leaves.

Remarks: The plant requires even brighter light than the typical species, and likes direct sunlight even in the summer months, as long as it is exposed to it gradually, and kept out of the sun at the hottest times of day. It also likes higher atmospheric humidity and more warmth in winter, but in other respects it is grown like the typical species. Propagation only by agamic reproduction because the seeds only produce completely green plants.

RUELLIA PORTELLAE (Acanthaceae)

Etymology: The genus is called after Jean Ruel (1474–1537), herbalist to François I of France, who in 1536 compiled a treatise of Greek and Latin botanical writings called *De natura stirpium*.

Description: A creeping evergreen herbaceous plant, with opposite, downy, velvety leaves, variegated on the upper surface, with a white stripe along the central vein and white markings along the lateral veins almost to the leaf margin. The lower side is purplish-red. The small, single flowers with tubular corolla and expanded lobes are pink and appear in winter in the right conditions.

Habitat: From Brazil.

Minimum winter temperature: 13–16 °C (55–61 °F).

Light: Very good to prevent the stems getting leggy and losing leaves, as tends to happen in this family, and also to encourage flowering. The plant will tolerate direct sun.

Environmental humidity: Increased to the maximum; you may even like to put a pad of damp sphagnum under the creeping stems.

Watering: Plentiful in summer, regular in winter.

Soil: Humus-rich and light, composed of equal parts of leaf mould and peat, with a little extra sand to improve drainage and prevent saturation which is likely to make leaves drop. An effective drainage layer is needed.

Propagation: By stem cuttings kept at a temperature of about 21 °C (70 °F) with plenty of humidity. They need not be covered as this encourages mildew on the leaves. Cuttings can be taken at any time of year, but late spring and early summer are best.

Remarks: With all *Acanthaceae* the young plants have a much more attractive appearance, while older plants lose their lower leaves and grow rather crooked and ungainly. It is advisable to renew the plants periodically by taking cuttings to provide young, attractive plants. You can prune the plants after any flowering has occurred; water less frequently until new growth appears.

SAINTPAULIA (Gesneriaceae)

Common name: African violet.

Etymology: In about 1890 Baron Walter von Saint Paul-Illaire discovered a little plant near the Usambara mountains in Tanzania and sent the seeds back to his father in Germany. The plants did well, so the naturalist H. Wenland named them *Saintpaulia* in honour of the two Saint Pauls, and *ionantha*, or 'with flowers like violets'. This explains both the scientific and the common name, although the plants are not in fact even remotely related to violets.

Description: The plants now available are all hybrids, produced mainly by crossing the first known species, *Saintpaulia ionantha*, with more recently discovered species, particularly *Saintpaulia confusa*. Most cultivated plants have rosettes of leaves, usually stemless, but sometimes with a short rhizomatous stem, spathulate leaves with crenate or dentate margins and a long fleshy petiole. However there are some varieties with indented, undulate, almost sessile leaves, which generally have a pale mark at the base; these are generally known as 'girl' not because they are female, but because they are mutations produced from the first hybrids, the most famous being 'Blue Boy'. Leaf colour varies from pale to dark green, and the underside is sometimes purplish red. Nowadays plants can have simple or double flowers in all shades of pink, red and purple, sometimes white or mauve, but never yellow. Plants with double flowers are sterile; the flowers do not drop spontaneously, but have to be removed when they wither, as happens with most flowers which have double petals.

Habitat: All species come from Tanzania, especially the Usambara mountains, where they grow at altitudes of up to 2,000 m. *Saintpaulia ionantha* grows lower and so is accustomed to an average temperature of about 25 °C (77 °F). This makes it the easiest species to grow as a house plant and it is the parent species of all hybrids. Other hybrids like lower temperatures and more humid conditions.

Minimum winter temperature: About 16 °C (61 °F), or higher to produce good flowers. These are the only plants which like a higher temperature at night than during the day.

Light: Good, diffuse, out of direct sun. Duration of light is more important than intensity; this is why the plants flower well under artificial light. In winter some artificial light in the evening will encourage growth and shorten the winter rest period to a minimum.

Environmental humidity: Increased in every way.

Watering: Regular all the year round. Allow the soil to dry out slightly between waterings and never let it become waterlogged. *Saintpaulias* need two semi-rest periods, one during the summer when the temperature rises above 25 °C (77 °F), the other during the winter. You can make either period longer, or shorter depending on whether you want more flowers in summer or winter, by watering less frequently and stopping feeding. During the remainder of the year small amounts of fertilizer should be given regularly.

Soil. Very porous and humus-rich, composed mainly of equal parts of leaf-mould and peat with some sand or perlite.

Propagation: It is very easy to take leaf cuttings. Use a light mixture of moist peat and sand or perlite. Cut the petiole near the leaf base and insert in the mixture. Leave uncovered at a constant temperature of 18–21 °C (65–70 °F). New plants will also develop in clean water, but care must be taken to keep the water level only a little above the base of the cut stem. The plantlets which appear round the bottom of the cutting should be divided and planted separately in suitable-sized pots.

SANCHEZIA NOBILIS (Acanthaceae)

Etymology: This species is named after José Sanchez, 19th century Professor of Botany who taught at Cadiz, in Spain.

Description: A suffruticose evergreen perennial with oblong-lanceolate, opposite leaves which, in variety *glaucophylla* (the commonly cultivated type) have white or yellowish variegations along the nervations. The flowers grow on apical spikes and have a long tubular yellow corolla which emerges from red bracts; it rarely blooms when grown indoors.

Habitat: From Ecuador.

Minimum winter temperature: 13–16 °C (55–60 °F).

Light: Bright, to keep the variegations intact and get the plant to bloom, but diffused; do not expose to direct sunlight.

Environmental humidity: Very high; a dry atmosphere will cause the plant to shed its leaves, and represents the major problem in growing this species.

Watering: Water frequently in summer and sparingly in winter, so that the soil can dry out slightly between watering; stagnant water at the bottom of the pot and saturated soil will also cause the leaves to drop off.

Soil: Light and porous, made up of equal parts of mature leaf-mould and peat with sand added to keep it permeable and well-drained.

Propagation: By cuttings, under glass or plastic covers, aired every so often, in peaty and sandy soil kept just moist at a temperature of 21–24 °C (70–75 °F), remove the covers very gradually when the plants have rooted. Given that these plants – like the whole family – tend to shed their lower leaves, it is advisable to prune regularly during the vegetative period to encourage ramification; the uppermost parts thus removed may be used as cuttings.

THE SANSEVIERIA GENUS (Liliaceae)

Etymology: The name of this genus is due to a mistake made in the late 18th century which has never been corrected. The first known species was observed by the Neapolitan botanist Vicenzo Petagna, who sent it to the Swedish naturalist C. P. Thumberg, saying that he wanted to name it after P. A. Sanseverino, Count of Chiaramonte, who created a garden of rare plants in southern Italy. But because of linguistic and other difficulties Thumberg got it wrong and called it *Sansevieria*, because there was also a man named Raimondo di Sangro, Prince of Sanseviero, a soldier and inventor who had nothing to do with the botanist at all. Thus the plant, which should have been called *Sanseverinia*, has retained its incorrect name, although some authors today accept what should have been its rightful one.

Description: The genus includes some 60 species, all herbaceous, leathery, with underground rhizomes and caulinar, solitary leaves, or leaves growing in rosettes. These, in some cases, are tightly imbricate (overlapping) and form a short stem, from which they grow in the shape of a fan with vaginal leaves; at least one species produces stolons at the tips of which new plants grow. It is occasionally possible to find species with cylindrical and rigid leaves, such as *S. cylindrica*, or with slender, curving leaves such as the stoloniferous *S. parva*; but the commonest species is undoubtedly *S. trifasciata*, and some of its varieties and mutations are even more common, especially the variety *laurentii* which has the same upright growth pattern as the typical species, but has leaves with wide white or cream-coloured margins: many cultivated varieties are derived from this latter. The mutation 'Hahnii' with rosettes of short, tillered leaves is also quite common.

Habitat: Almost all the species are African: but there is one species, *S. zeylanica*, from Ceylon, and this is often muddled with *S. trifasciata*, which it closely resembles.

Minimum winter temperature: 10–13 °C (50–55 °F), but they will grow in higher temperatures, and also, if dry, in lower temperatures.

Light: All the species will grow in moderate light, but they will be more handsome in good light conditions.

Environmental humidity: No special requirements, but it is advisable to sponge the foliage.

Watering: Water intermittently in summer, so that the soil dries out between waterings, and even more sparingly in winter; rot is the major risk for these plants.

Soil: The soil must be more consistent than for other tropical plants, made up of two parts compost and one part mature leaf-mould, with some sand added to stop it clodding; use small pots.

Propagation: By division of the rhizomes in spring, watering sparingly to avoid rot. The leaves, cut into pieces and planted the right way up in sandy soil will produce roots and rhizomes from which new leaves will sprout. But this is a lengthy process and will require careful amounts of moisture to stop them rotting or withering. The variegated forms cannot be reproduced in this way because they will turn out like the typical species; here, the cuttings must have at least a small piece of rhizome with a shoot. Whole leaves may take root in water, although very slowly, but they will always turn out to be completely green.

SANSEVIERIA TRIFASCIATA (Liliaceae)

Description: A herbaceous rhizomatose plant with caulinar, upright, leathery, linear leaves which are slightly concave, and dark-green streaked crosswise and irregularly with grey-green or whitish markings. The flowers, growing on not very striking inflorescences, are greenish-white and scented at night. In the wild it grows quite large, and is used for its fibres, but in pots it stays much smaller. The variety *laurentii* is more common than the typical species; its leaf margins are large or small, proportionately, and white or yellowish in colour; there are many cultivated varieties, including 'Craigii' with long and slightly obovate leaves, and 'Goldiana' with wide cream-yellow stripes at the margins and irregular markings at the centre of the lamina.

Habitat: The typical species comes from the eastern region of South Africa, and the variety *laurentii* from Zaire and Tanzania.

Remarks: All the other conditions — light, temperature, watering and soil — are as for the genus as a whole, but *S. laurentii* cannot be reproduced by leaf-cuttings because it reverts to the typical form; in its case at least a small piece of rhizome with one or more shoots is needed.

▼ *Sansevieria trifasciata laurentii*

153

SANSEVIERIA TRIFASCIATA 'HAHNII' (Liliaceae)

Description: This mutation of *S. trifasciata*, which is grown in America, is quite different in habit from the typical species although the foliage has the same texture and colours. It is in fact a low plant with short lanceolate-acuminate leaves growing in rosettes; they develop spirally one after the other, growing towards the centre. The leaves are quite wide, concave, sometimes wavy, and striped crosswise in grey-green or whitish. The plant is very prolific and is easily tillered. The variety 'Golden Hahnii' is very common in shops, with the margins of the leaves variegated in yellowish or cream-white.

Remarks: Cultivation is as for the genus as a whole, but in this case too the variety 'Golden Hahnii' cannot be reproduced by leaf-cuttings, but only by division of the rhizomes; if the former method is used it will lose the lighter-coloured margins which are its brightest feature.

SAXIFRAGA STOLONIFERA TRICOLOR (Saxifragaceae)

Etymology: The name of this huge genus derives from the Latin *saxum*, 'stone' and *frango*, 'break', probably because some species penetrate rocks.

Description: Although it includes some 370 species, divided into 16 groups, this genus is of little horticultural importance, and consists mainly of hardy types. The only one grown in pots is *S. stolonifera*, also known as *S. sarmentosa*, a small acaulescent plant with soft, carnose, rounded and crenate leaves which are olive-green with white and reddish veins on the lower blade. The plant produces long runners (stolons) which carry small new plants at the tip; these root in the ground roundabout; it is more or less hardy, but do not expose to frost. The variety *tricolor*, sometimes used as an indoor plant, is much more beautiful and delicate; it grows similarly, but the green leaves have wide margins and are variegated.

Habitat: The typical species comes from China and Japan.

Minimum winter temperature: 5–10 °C (40–50 °F); it does not tolerate high temperatures, which will make it wither in no time.

Light: Good but diffused, shelter from direct sunlight.

Environmental humidity: As high as possible; very high humidity combined with a cool place is the only way of keeping the plant alive and avoiding repeated attacks from cotton scale insects.

Watering: Water sparingly almost all year round; in summer water slightly more, depending on the temperature.

Soil: Not humus-rich and very well-drained; it may be made up of very old compost and sand in equal parts, with stone chippings.

Propagation: By means of the young plants which grow at the ends of the stolons when they start sprouting roots; no special precautions when potting; keep cool and in a damp spot; or the runners may be trained to other pots where they will root naturally.

SCINDAPSUS AUREUS (Araceae)

Etymology: The name comes from the Greek *skindapsós*, describing an unidentified plant not unlike ivy. In common horticultural jargon the plant is called *Pothos*

Description: This is one of the commonest indoor plants, although indoors it grows and looks quite different to the wild state where it is a large climber with entire, cordate and inclined leaves when young, becoming lobate and laciniate when mature, more than 50 cm (20 in) in length; the lamina is irregularly variegated in yellow; the stem has adventitious roots at the nodes. Indoors the leaves are small, entire, and often lose their variegations, although such varieties as the 'Giant Leaf' have been obtained, which develops quite large leaves even when young. A highly prized variety is 'Marble Queen', with almost totally white leaves speckled with green but this type easily tends to reverse its coloration and needs frequent agamic reproduction.

Habitat: From the Solomon Islands.

Minimum winter temperature: 13–16°C (55–60°F).

Light: Not direct sunlight, but good diffused light.

Environmental humidity: Must be high, helped with sponging the leaves; the tutors must be kept almost constantly wet.

Watering: Water frequently in summer and sparingly in winter.

Soil: Must be very porous and coarse, made up of equal parts of leaf-mould, peat and sphagnum, including small pieces of chestnut, with shredded sphagnum and sand added. The roots are very carnose and rot easily; in addition the root system is not very extensive, so it is vital to give the adventitious roots sufficient moisture, as nurserymen who grow them against walls where they may develop fairly large leaves well know. The water should never stagnate in the soil, as it would tend to rot the roots.

Propagation: Reproduction by cuttings, buried very shallow and diagonally, around 21 °C (70 °F), but rooting will be slow. A safer way indoors is soil-layering.

SCINDAPSUS PICTUS ARGYREUS (Araceae)

Description: A perennial, evergreen, fairly slender climber, at least in the form *argyreus*, which many authors consider to be the young stage, incidentally. The leaves are small, very oblique and markedly acuminate, dark-green tending to blue-green, with irregular markings and thin silvery margins; the whole blade is glossy-looking; this very beautiful plant is little cultivated because it is rather delicate.

Habitat: From Indonesia.

Minimum winter temperature: About 16°C (60°F).

Light: Will survive in fairly poor light, but it must be diffused; never expose to direct sunlight.

Environmental humidity: High, using any available means.

Watering: Water plentifully in summer and slightly less in winter.

Soil: Light and porous, made up of equal parts of leaf-mould and peat, with a little sand added. However, given that it is very liable to fungal diseases which appear in the form of yellow or brown blotches on the leaves, it is advisable, if possible, to replace the leaf-mould with a pre-sterilized all-round compost or mould, reducing the amount of peat, since such mixtures are already quite peaty.

Propagation: Reproduction by cuttings entails a long rooting process and is not particularly easy, given the tendency of the stem to rot if the soil is too wet; but if kept too dry the leaves will wither. A safer way is by soil-layering, training one or more branches over a pot placed beside the mother plant and fixing it at the nodes with thin wires in light, sterile mould or soil. It will take some time for the roots to enter the soil, but once they have, cut off the branches and support the plants as necessary until well-established.

155

SETCREASEA PURPUREA (Commelinaceae)

Etymology: The meaning of the name of this genus is unknown; Karl Moritz Schumann (1851–1904), Professor of Botany at Berlin, who named it, never gave any explanation as to why.

Description: A herbaceous perennial plant with fairly succulent stems, upright at first, then creeping, and radicant at the nodes; the slightly carnose leaves may grow up to 10 cm (4 in) and are vaginal, growing spirally along the stem. The lamina is lanceolate, bright violet in colour in good light, tending to turn dark-green in poor light. The stems and leaves, which are both violet, are dotted with thin white hairs, especially at the nodes and on the leaf margins. The flowers, which are fairly large for the family, are short-lived like all the others and appear successively between two opposite, imbricate, acuminate bracts at the tip of the branches. These have three small sepals, and three lilac-pink petals. New growth appears beneath the bracts when flowering is over.

Habitat: From Mexico.

Minimum winter temperature: Will not survive frost; they may wither in low temperatures, but the roots will not die and if cut back to the ground in spring new growth will appear. If the temperature is too high and the light poor they will lose their colour and become spindly and green. In such cases prune them drastically and new shoots will appear.

Light: Very bright, except at the hottest times of day and in the hottest months they also like direct sunlight; in summer, however, they will be more luxuriant in semi-shade.

Minimum winter temperature: No special requirements.

Watering: Water plentifully in summer and very sparingly in winter, which is their normal period of dormancy.

Soil: They will thrive in theory in any good garden earth, but will be more handsome in humus-rich earth, i.e. with leaf-mould, sand and peat added. Given that they are semi-succulent, never let the water stagnate.

Propagation: Very simple, by cuttings. Plant the cuttings with no special precautions in pots with appropriate soil; just make sure to keep the soil moist but not wet to start with, so that the stems do not rot. Cuttings may be taken many times a year.

SPATHIPHYLLUM WALLISII (Araceae)

Etymology: The name derives from the Greek *spátha*, 'spathe' and *phýllon*, 'leaf' because of the spathe of the inflorescences which is leaf-shaped.

Description: A herbaceous, perennial, evergreen, acualescent or very short-stemmed plant; the leaves are oblong or lanceolate, acuminate, with a very marked central vein, green, shiny and leathery. The inflorescence, which forms the decorative part of the plant, consists of a white, concave and cuspidate spathe which turns green as it ages, and a shorter white spadix, tightly covered with hermaphroditic flowers, which are all fertile. The whole inflorescence often appears greenish in colour, then passes to white, and back to green before withering; the flowering cycle lasts one month or slightly more and occurs twice a year, in spring and autumn. Many hybrids and cultivated varieties are derived from it, often bearing more flowers or with slightly differently shaped and more colourful spathes; the commonest is 'Mauna Loa', which has a green spadix and large white spathes.

Habitat: From Colombia and Venezuela.

Minimum winter temperature: 16°C + (60°F).

Light: Diffused, not in direct sunlight, but bright while flowering; during the other periods light may be moderate.

Environmental humidity: Should be very high, and represents the major difficulty in producing plants indoors with fine blooms. Use all means available, but do not spray inflorescences.

Watering: Water quite frequently at all times, so that the soil never dries out completely, but do not saturate, which might rot the roots.

Soil: Must be light and porous, made up of equal parts of leaf-mould and peat with a little sand and charcoal chippings added to avoid rot caused by moisture.

Propagation: Reproduction by division at the end of winter. It is however hard to obtain good results outside the greenhouse because high humidity and light basic warmth is required.

STROMANTHE SANGUINEA (Marantaceae)

Etymology: The name comes from the Greek *stróma*, 'bed' and *ánthos*, 'flower' because of the bracteal inflorescence.

Description: Herbaceous perennial with large underground rhizomes, often ramified, from which sprout the vaginal leaf-stalks (petioles) which open gradually to form a fan, with each one growing from the alate petiole of the one before; from the centre grows an upright stele on which, at the nodes, grow new clusters of leaves. This species is very vigorous and its steles may grow to a considerable height; the leaves are long, lanceolate-acuminate, the upper blade shiny dark-green, with the central nervation pale-coloured in young leaves; the lower blade is blood-red. The inflorescences, which grow easily in greenhouses, and less so indoors, are formed by small white flowers surrounded by red bracts not unlike small spathes.

Habitat: From Brazil.

Minimum winter temperature: 16–18°C (60–65°F).

Light: Moderate light; never expose to direct sunlight.

Environmental humidity: Quite high. The foliage should be sponged and sprayed often, not least to avoid attacks from mites.

Watering: Water frequently and plentifully in summer, and sparingly in late-autumn to early-winter, during which the level of atmospheric humidity should be increased.

Soil: Light and porous, made up of equal parts of leaf-mould and peat, with sand or perlite to stop the rhizomes rotting.

Propagation: May be division of the rhizomes; each piece should contain more than one shoot, with a temperature of about 24°C (75°F) and high environmental humidity; if steles have appeared, cuttings may be taken immediately below a node which carries a leaf-cluster; put the cuttings to root in moist sand and peat, in small pots, under glass or plastic covers, at 24°C (75°F); remove covers gradually once they have taken root. It is advisable to wait until early summer has arrived.

SYAGRUS WEDDELIANA (Palmae)

Etymology: The correct name for this small palm should be *Microcoelum weddelianum*, from the Greek *mikrós*, 'small' and *kóilos*, 'hollow' or 'hollowed', because of the small hole in the fruit, but the plant has undergone many taxonomic changes and in horticultural jargon is still known as *Syagrus* or *Cocos weddeliana*.

Description: This is a small palm which in exceptionally good conditions may reach a height of more than a metre (3 ft), but is normally sold when 30–50 cm (12–20 in) in height, thus resembling a miniature form of a larger species. The fronds are curved and septate in slender segments; the stipe is covered by the persistent sheaths of the withered fronds.

Habitat: From the tropical forests of Brazil.

Minimum winter temperature: About 16 °C (60 °F).

Light: Quite good, but not too bright; it must always be diffused, and avoid direct sunlight.

Environmental humidity: Much less tough than other palms, this plant needs quite high environmental humidity, given its natural habitat. Spraying the foliage and placing moist gravel beneath the pot will moisten excessively dry conditions which are harmful; but be sure that the water never stagnates at the bottom of the pot.

Watering: Water regularly all year round and quite plentifully in summer; although the soil must never become saturated and clod around the roots, which would choke them, it must always be fairly moist; for this reason non-porous pots are often used, but the outlet hole must be kept clear, and the pot must be well-drained.

Soil: These plants are usually sold in very small pots and given the very slow growth rarely need repotting; if this should be necessary, however, disturb the roots as little as possible and add a mixture made up of compost, leaf-mould and peat in equal parts, with some sand added.

Propagation: Cannot be propagated indoors. Reproduction is by seed, which must be really fresh; germination is very slow. Once they have germinated, the plant will grow just as slowly, and it will take some time to obtain a specimen fit for sale; this makes the plant somewhat expensive.

THE SYNGONIUM GENUS (Araceae)

Etymology: The name is derived from the Greek *syn*, 'together' and *goné*, 'seed, generative organ', because of the ovaries, which are joined.

Description: This genus, which includes 20 species of climbing plants, is very akin to *Philodendron*, but, apart from a few cases, it is less vigorous. All or almost all the species and their varieties are fairly common as indoor plants; in fact they tolerate a dry atmosphere exceptionally well, although they are versatile enough for some species to be able to live immersed in water; in general they do not need strong light. The stems are invariably flexible, and climb by means of adventitious aerial roots which, in the wild, form supports against trees or rocks, but will also absorb moisture from the air, not unlike *Philodendron*, *Monstera* and other *Araceae*. In most species the leaves are sagittate when young, becoming pedate in adult plants, where they are often divided into 5–9 unequal parts, with lanceolate segments, the bottom ones often having two smaller side lobes, and the central one being the longest and largest. The stalks are vaginal and alate and each leaf, as it appears, is wrapped in the stalk of the one before; unlike the other genera, the leaves never have stipules. The lamina is multiveined, and one of the nervations runs parallel to the margin of the blade, while all the others merge with it. The inflorescences are typical of the family, formed by a spadix which is shorter than the spathe around it, but they practically never appear on cultivated specimens, whether adult and grown in greenhouses or not.

Habitat: All come from central and southern America.

Minimum winter temperature: 13–16 °C (55–60 °F).

Light: Quite bright but diffused, not direct sunlight. The variegated forms require more light than those with all-green foliage.

Environmental humidity: Although they will tolerate a dry atmosphere up to a certain point, they will be more handsome if there is a certain amount of atmospheric humidity; washing and spraying the foliage will also help.

Watering: Water frequently and plentifully in summer, and slightly less in winter, letting the soil dry out between waterings.

Soil: Like the family as a whole, they prefer porous, well-aerated soil, made up of equal parts of leaf-mould and peat with some sand added, so that it remains well-drained and will not rot the roots.

Propagation: By reproduction, either by top-cuttings or from pieces of stem. Plant the cuttings in appropriate soil, slightly sandier than for adult plants, at a temperature of about 21 °C (70 °F). If you want to use a confined place, and avoid dehydration and subsequent wilting of the lower leaves, use quite large plastic covers, and ventilate often; as a whole, though, these will not be necessary if the plants are kept moist by spraying, and only a few leaves will be lost. If covers are used, the soil should be just moist, and never wet.

Remarks: The versatility of these plants is such that if a branch is bent and immersed in water, it will continue to grow and produce aerial roots and foliage, although this will be much smaller. Sometimes they are used for aquarium plants, with small specimens which become progressively adapted to this environment. But these will not necessarily live long or grow any bigger.

SYNGONIUM PODOPHYLLUM (Araceae)

Description: This is perhaps the most commonly grown species grown on the market, with many varieties. When young it is a small plant with slender, green, spear-shaped leaves; its growth depends on the type of cultivation; in plants grown as climbers, with supports to which the aerial roots can cling, it will be more vigorous, while if cultivated as a hanging plant it will be weaker and almost without aerial roots. In good specimens the leaves become palmate-pedate and may develop up to nine segments. The typical species, however, is quite hard to come across, and is replaced by much more attractive varieties such as the natural one: *albo-lineatum*, which in the young leaves has white veins; the older leaves become completely green; or the mutation *albo-virens* in which the upper part of the lamina on young leaves is almost completely greyish-white or greenish with just the margin green. There are also many cultivated varieties on the market.

Habitat: The typical species is common in Central America; the variety *albo-lineatum* comes from Mexico.

Remarks: Cultivation and reproduction as for the genus as a whole.

SYNGONIUM PODOPHYLLUM 'TRILEAF WONDER' (Araceae)

Description: One of the numerous varieties of *S. podophyllum*; the form is the same as the typical species, but along the veins there are marked silvery-grey variegated areas, and the plant quickly develops foliage typical of the adult stage. Other varieties of the same species to be found on the market, which are not always easy to tell apart, are: 'Emerald Gem', with green leaves which are slightly more carnose and corrugated than the typical species, and 'Green Gold', with yellow-marbled foliage.

Remarks: Though slightly more delicate than the typical species in so far as they require better light to keep the variegations and higher environmental humidity, all these cultivated varieties will make good indoor specimens. They are mainly used as small or average-sized plants, often decumbent, not the most suitable condition for cultivation. The larger, variegated types almost all belong to the variety *albo-lineatum*, which is more vigorous than the typical species.

SYNGONIUM VELLOZIANUM (Araceae)

Description: Although this name appears in many European lists, sometimes as distinct from *S. auritum*, this species poses a minor taxonomic puzzle. It is a vigorous climbing plant with green, shiny carnose leaves which, in adult plants, are septate with three or five segments, three of which are lanceolate, with the central one possibly reaching 25 cm (10 in) in length, and the two basal ones oval, short, with an obtuse tip. In fact they look like two small ears, whence the specific name *auritum*, but common botanical features suggest that these are two different local varieties of the same species, and that the species *vellozianum* was introduced to Europe in 1800, and has not been cultivated in the United States, where its place was taken by the variety which H. W. Schott, director of the Schönbrunn Gardens (1824–1865) discovered in Brazil and gave the attribute already used by Linnaeus for a *Pnilodendron: auritum*.

Habitat: *S. vellozianum* probably comes from Jamaica and other parts of Central America; *S. auritum* would appear to come from Brazil, but authors fail to agree over this, and often suggest the contrary.

Remarks: This is a climber which grows exceptionally vigorously once past the early stage; both grow well in a dry indoor atmosphere and will produce a lot of growth with good light; they will also benefit from being put outdoors in summer in semi-shade. Cultivation for this genus also applies to these very decorative plants, even if the foliage is completely green.

GENUS TRADESCANTIA (Commelinaceae)

Common name: Spiderwort, Wandering Jew.

Etymology: This genus, named by Linnaeus himself after the English gardener and naturalist Tradescant, John the Elder, and his son, John the Younger, has common names in almost every language. John Tradescant the Elder, born in the latter half of the 16th century, was gardener to King Charles I of England and travelled widely, introducing many new plants; his son John completed his work and between them they brought all the American plants introduced into Europe for at least 3 decades in the 17th century. Those referred to as pot plants, thanks to the ease with which they were reproduced, took the names 'miseria', 'misère', 'wandering jew', 'spiderwort' etc.

Description: There are 60 species of *Tradescantia*, but some of them are only grown outdoors (these come from north America). Among the non-hardy types, some species are very akin to other genera, such as *Zebrina*, and often muddled with it; these are creeping plants with prostrate or semi-upright stems, radicant at the nodes, with lanceolate-acuminate leaves sheathing the stem; they ramify easily, with bracteal inflorescences with inconspicuous and short-lived blooms. *T. albiflora* and *T. fluminensis* are very alike and sometimes hard to tell apart. The typical forms are virtually never cultivated and are semi-hardy, but there are variegated varieties such as *T. albiflora albo-vittata*, with the even better variety 'Quick Silver' which are both very decorative. *T. blossfeldiana* has large stems and carnose, elliptical, olive-green leaves with the lower blade violet with white down; it bears many flowers. *T. navicularis* is a small succulent with carinate, tightly imbricate leaves growing in two parallel rows which completely cover the twisted stems. *T. sillamontana* is semi-upright, with oval leaves completely covered with white down and quite large, lilac-coloured flowers.

Habitat: All come from central-southern America: *T. blossfeldiana* from Peru; *T. sillamontana* from Mexico.

Minimum winter temperature: 5–10°C (40–50°F), will not survive frost.

Light: All require as much light as possible; *T. navicularis* will also tolerate direct sunlight.

▲ *Vriesea splendens*

▼ *Vriesea* hybr.

GENUS VRIESEA (Bromeliaceae)

Etymology: The name, often written *Vriesia*, was given in honour of Willem H. de Vriese (1806–1862), a Dutch botanist.

Description: These herbaceous and often epiphyte plants have the typical growth pattern of the family, with leaves in rosettes and tightly imbricate, forming at the centre the 'hollow' or 'vase' from which the inflorescence grows; this is bracteal and often brightly coloured. There are several cultivated species: some have bright and variegated leaves and are more or less grown for these alone; others are prized for their gay inflorescence; as well as the botanical species there are several varieties and hybrids. The commonest of the natural species is *Vriesea splendens* which has long semi-upright leaves, quite dark-green in colour, with uneven crosswise wine-red markings; the lower blade is also striped in the same colour, or in violet; the inflorescence is a fairly long flattish spike with bright red bracts which last for more than two months, and yellow flowers which die first. A large number of hybrids have also been grown from other species.

Habitat: From the forests of Central and South America; *V. splendens* is from Guyana; many others come from Brazil.

Minimum winter temperature: About 13°C (55°F); increase atmospheric humidity as much as possible in higher temperatures.

Light: Diffused; not in direct sunlight, but must be good, to keep the variegations and the colour of the bracts of the inflorescence.

Environmental humidity: As high as possible; like all epiphytes in the family, it is inadvisable to keep water in the central 'vase' when the plant is grown as a pot plant, unless the collar is surrounded by well-aerated and water-repellent soil.

Watering: Water regularly in summer, intermittently in winter.

Soil: As light and porous as possible, made up of equal parts of peat, sand and shredded royal fern roots; if these latter are not available, use not very advanced leaf-mould or chestnut fragments, but water less to avoid the risk of rot. Use small pots, with good drainage.

Propagation: These plants are hard to get to bloom outside the greenhouse and are usually bought with the spike of the inflorescence already formed. As in the family as a whole, the rosette which has flowered dies, but around it the plant will produce lower shoots which can be removed and rooted in fine, peaty soil kept just barely moist, at a temperature of at least 21°C (70°F).

ZEBRINA PENDULA (Commelinaceae)

Etymology: The name comes from *zebra*, but is not an accurate reference because the stripes are lengthwise.

Description: These herbaceous, perennial plants are very like *Tradescantia* and often muddled with it, so much so that it is also known by the common name of 'wandering jew'. In fact, apart from the slightly more ovate leaves and the corolla of the small short-lived flowers which is slightly tubular and does not have separate and free petals, the habit is the same with quite succulent, creeping stems, radicant at the nodes, and sessile vaginal leaves at the base. The upper surface of the lamina is shaded with dark-green to violet, and punctuated by two lengthwise silvery stripes; the lower surface is dark violet. There are several varieties: the delicate *quadricolor* has leaves with silvery highlights and white, pink and red stripes.

Habitat: From Mexico.

Minimum winter temperature: 10–13°C (50–55°F).

Light: Diffused but very strong, to stop the stems growing too long and prevent the leaves losing their colouring.

Environmental humidity: No special requirements, happy with moderate humidity, but likes well ventilated places.

Watering: Water plentifully in summer and moderately in winter, the period of semi-dormancy, in which it will almost certainly die if there is not enough light, especially at high temperatures.

Soil: Although it will adapt to almost all types of soil, better results will be obtained from a permeable mixture of equal parts of compost and mature leaf-mould with some sand added.

Propagation: Very easily reproduced by cuttings; it is advisable to reproduce these plants about twice a year to have healthy specimens; it will do to plant them in small pots with appropriate soil, several cuttings at a time, the most colourful if possible; water quite moderately to start with to avoid any risk of rot; the best temperature is about 18°C (65°F) and although no other precautions are necessary, good light will help the cuttings to root.

ZYGOCACTUS TRUNCATUS (Cactáceae)

Etymology: The name derives from the Greek *zygòs*, 'yoke' and *cactus*, referring to the way in which the articuli are joined together.

Description: This species of epiphyte cacti is often known by the old synonym *Schlumbergera bridgesii*, the genus to which it was first ascribed. The stems consist of carnose, flat articuli, with almost inermous areolae which only appear at the margins; the tip is fairly truncated; the ramifications grow from it. In the typical species the flowers are cherry-red; they grow from the apical areolae and their corolla tube has bracts coloured like the petals. It blooms in winter, and is often called the 'Christmas cactus'; here it differs from the genus *Schlumbergera* which flowers in spring and is thus called the 'Easter cactus'. Several varieties are cultivated, including *altensteinii*, which is often considered a separate species, with brick-red flowers and more crenate margins on the articuli; other varieties have blue-violet, lavender, orange-red, pink, white and even two-coloured (red and pink) flowers.

Habitat: From Brazil.

Minimum winter temperature: 10–13°C (50–55°F).

Light: Very bright, especially in autumn–spring, but not in direct sunlight; provide with as much as possible so that the flower-buds can form; as this is a short-day plant, make sure that in November and December the light is bright but does not last more than 12 hours; in the other 12 the plant should be in total darkness.

Environmental humidity: As high as possible.

Watering: Intermittently in autumn and early-winter, regularly in the other periods, but make sure that the water does not stagnate.

Soil: Very rich and porous, made up of equal parts of compost, leaf-mould and peat with some sand added to keep it permeable. Drainage must be very good; fertilize regularly with mainly phosphorus fertilizers to help the plant in the vegetative period.

Propagation: By cuttings taken from the articuli removed at the joints in just moist sand, at about 21°C (70°F).

Window-sill and balcony plants

ABUTILON × HYBRIDUM (Malvaceae)

Description: This group of hybrids consists of perennial shrubs with upright stems and alternate, usually green leaves, although there are also variegated forms with white and yellow stripes. The lamina is usually lobate and dentate, a feature inherited from the species *A. darwinii* which, together with *A. striatum* and *A. venosum*, is one of the main parents; for this reason, in the English-speaking countries, it is often called the 'drawing-room maple'. The flowers which generally appear in summer–autumn, but may occasionally appear in winter, are solitary and pendent, growing on long stalks at the leaf axils; they are campanulate in shape, with a small gamosepalous calyx and five petals which often curve inwards towards the apex; as in the whole family, the stamens are joined together to form a column which has the anthers at the tip, often growing out of the corolla.
Habitat: All the species are from tropical America.
Minimum winter temperature: 5–10 °C (40–50 °F).
Light: Very strong, but shelter from direct sun in summer.
Environmental humidity: Good, but avoid stagnation; these plants do not tolerate badly-ventilated places and high winter temperatures. In summer they should be put outside in semi-shade.
Watering: Water plentifully in summer and sparingly in winter.
Soil: Very rich, made up of two parts compost and one part mature leaf-mould, with sand added. Small plants should be repotted annually; with larger plants, replace the surface layer with fresh soil and include a small amount of fertilizer such as concentrated humus or seaweed. Like fertilizers may also be used in small, but regular amounts, once the vegetative period has started.
Propagation: Given that for tillering these plants will need pruning in spring and trimming later on, there is adequate material for cuttings. Place cuttings in a small pot with a mixture of leaf-mould and, under covers, at about 21 °C (70 °F). Ventilate frequently; remove covers gradually when new growth appears.

ACHIMENES LONGIFLORA (Gesneriaceae)

Etymology: The name comes from the Greek *chemàino*, 'in the cold', with the negative prefix a-, indicating that these plants do not tolerate low temperatures.
Description: Although this is the main parent of all the present-day hybrids, the typical species is not cultivated, because of its rather untidy behaviour; it has been widely crossed with *A. coccinea, A. grandiflora* and other species, giving more compact and flower-bearing varieties. These are herbaceous, perennial, rhizomatose plants with scaly rhizomes requiring a period of total dormancy for quite some time. The leaves are opposite, ovate-acuminate, with serrate margins; at their axil the solitary flowers grow on a long petiole; they have a small calyx with five sepals and a long, tubular, cylindrical corolla with five broad often irregular lobes. In the various cultivated varieties the colour of the flowers may vary greatly, in every shade of violet, pink, red and even white. The stems are upright, then become decumbent and need support.
Habitat: From Mexico originally, where they grow quite high up in the mountains, and from Central America.
Minimum winter temperature: The dormant rhizomes must be kept at a temperature of about 16–18 °C (60–65 °F).
Light: Good, diffused light, but not direct sunlight.
Environmental humidity: Very high during growth.
Watering: The rhizomes are put to vegetate in February or March in pots, about 6 cm (2·5 in) deep at about 18 °C (65 °F); to start with, water moderately and then gradually increase the amount as the growth develops. After flowering reduce the amount gradually and then stop altogether; the steles are cut and the rhizomes left dormant and completely dry in the pot.
Soil: Light and porous, made up of mature leaf-mould and peat in equal parts with sand or perlite added to increase drainage. If you see uneven growth in the plant, repot it when it is at least 5 cm (2 in) high, putting all the plants of the same height in the same pot.

ANTHURIUM SCHERZARIANUM (Araceae)

Description: A herbaceous perennial with carnose roots; when young it is stemless, but in time develops a short stem along which adventitious roots continue to grow, and which often produces new growth at the collar by tillering. The leaves, on long petioles, are dark-green, lanceolate and acuminate; the inflorescence has a long peduncle and consists of the slender, very long and semi-spiral yellow spadix; beneath it is the scarlet spathe, which may be uniform in colour or with white or pink streaks; varieties have been obtained with spathes which are white or various shades of red.
Habitat: From Central America, where it grows in hilly regions at 8–33 °C (45–90 °F).
Minimum winter temperature: 10 °C (50 °F); if the temperature rises above 16 °C (60 °F) during the semi-dormant period the plant will not bloom.
Light: Very bright, to preserve the blooms which may last as long as two months, and to get the plant to flower again; it may be exposed to direct sunlight for controlled periods only in winter.
Environmental humidity: As high as possible; the leaves must be sponged but do not wet the inflorescences.
Watering: Water regularly so that the soil is always just moist, and let it dry out slightly in the semi-dormant period.
Soil: Light, humus-rich and very permeable, made up of not very advanced leaf-mould and peat with some sand or perlite added. In very dry places add a little shredded sphagnum, while some quite loose sphagnum may be wrapped around the adventitious roots when they appear. When the flower-buds appear use small but regular amounts of liquid fertilizer.
Propagation: By apical cuttings, with adventitious roots, or by basal shoots. Reproduction may be carried out at any time of year, with a temperature of at least 21 °C (70 °F), in small pots, in a mixture of peat, sand and shredded sphagnum kept just moist; do not use covers — these may rot the cuttings.

APHELANDRA TETRAGONA (Acanthaceae)

Description: Although much less common than A. *squarrosa*, whose size and behaviour make it more suitable as an indoor plant, this species is very beautiful when it has enough space and light. It is in fact suffruticose, shrubby and grows quite wide; it may become untidy if not kept in shape; the leaves are opposite, green elliptical-acuminate and reach a length of 25 cm (10 in); the inflorescences are apical and consist of a cluster of spikes, with the central one longer and the others shorter and of unequal lengths, ramifying from the base; the flowers emerge from the green, upright bracts which grow tightly round the rachis; the corolla is formed by a long scarlet tube which tapers at the base and is bilabiate at the opening of the fauces.
Habitat: From South America.
Minimum winter temperature: This plant is best-suited to the hot-house, and needs at least a 16 °C (60 °F) minimum in winter.
Light: Diffused, not in direct sunlight, but bright to obtain good blooms, without which the plant is not particularly attractive.
Environmental humidity: As high as possible, with spraying of the foliage but not the inflorescences.
Watering: Water plentifully in summer and sparingly in winter. When the inflorescences appear use liquid fertilizer with a phosphorus and potassium base.
Soil: Very humus-rich, made up of equal parts of compost, mature leaf-mould and peat with a fair amount of sand added.
Propagation: Because, like the other species, this plant tends to become bare at the base, with long and untidy stems, it is a good idea to prune and trim regularly, not least because the inflorescences are apical and as a result the plant produces a greater number as it ramifies. Every so often it will be necessary to take apical cuttings to obtain new and more compact plants. The cuttings will root in sandy, light soil at 21 °C (70 °F) under plastic covers; air the plants and remove covers gradually.

167

ARISTOLOCHIA ELEGANS (Aristolochiaceae)

Etymology: The name comes from the Greek àristos, or 'best', and lochéia or 'childbirth', either because the flower's shape suggests a foetus curled up in the other's womb, or because in ancient times some known species were believed to be helpful in childbirth. The name, which was used by Hippocrates, probably also described other genera of the same family.

Description: A climbing woody plant with slender stems. The kidney-shaped, cordate, blunt-tipped leaves have long petioles, a wide depression at the base and rounded lobes. As in the rest of the genus, the flowers have no corolla and this function is performed by the unusually shaped calyx – a swollen, sinuous tube, yellowish in colour, opening out into a wide, circular limb, purplish-brown with white spots. Unlike many of the other species which have a very unpleasant smell, these single flowers are quite odourless.

Habitat: From Brazil.

Minimum winter temperature: About 16°C (61°F).

Light: Excellent, but diffuse, out of direct sun.

Environmental humidity: Good. If spraying, do not let the flowers get wet.

Watering: Regular all the year round, increased during particularly hot spells.

Soil: Light and well drained: two parts of fibrous compost to one part leaf-mould, with some sand. Pot size should take account of the plant's height and it will need supports to cling to.

Propagation: From seed in spring, sown in a light moist mixture at a temperature of about 24°C (75°F). As always with tropical plants the seed must be fresh as it soon loses its fertility. You can try air layering, soil layering and cuttings on young woody stems, but they are unlikely to root successfully.

ASPARAGUS PLUMOSUS (Liliaceae)

Etymology: The name of the genus has remained in its Latin form, for the species *Asparagus officinalis*, the edible asparagus, was well known to the ancient Romans.

Description: In the wild this is quite a large climbing plant with slender and very ramified stems; its roots are rhizomatose, the leaves reduced to scaly bracts and the small terminal branches transformed into very thin, almost needle-shaped cladodes, the overall appearance of which is like a feathery frond, as the specific attribute indicates. In this form it is not grown as an indoor plant, but there is a variety *nanus* which has been much used since the last century as a pot-plant, when it could live in houses without much heating. Today, given the spread of central heating, it is only suited to cool, airy verandas.

Habitat: From South Africa.

Minimum winter temperature: 5–10°C (40–50°F).

Light: Good, do not expose to direct sunlight.

Environmental humidity: No special requirements at the right temperatures.

Watering: Water plentifully in summer and sparingly in winter.

Soil: Although these are adaptable plants, and are happy in good garden earth, they will be more handsome with humus-rich soil made up basically of compost with some leaf-mould and sand added. It is important, however, that it is permeable and loose, so as not to allow any water to stagnate. Although the typical species has very sturdy roots, the variety *nanus* may live for several years without being repotted; when it becomes too gangling much of the roots may be cut away during the repotting operation; if this is not done the plant will tend to develop a felt-like mass which, in time, will damage the live roots.

Propagation: By division in spring, with no particular precautions, but do not saturate the soil with water, which might rot the roots.

ASPARAGUS SPRENGERI (Liliaceae)

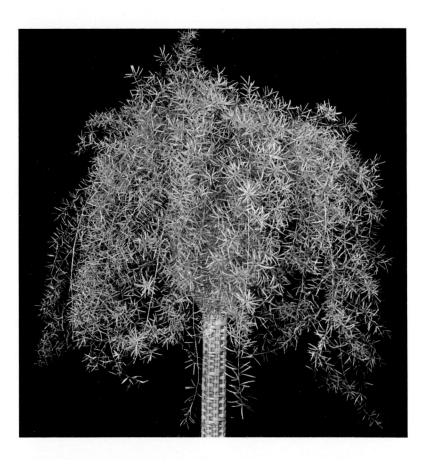

Description: This very common and semi-hardy herbaceous perennial, which can be grown outdoors in places with mild climates, has tuberose roots producing the drooping branches which ramify with small, flat, linear, bright-green cladodes. On these appear the flowers, which are small and inconspicuous, white, in racemose inflorescences, producing the small distinctive bright-red berries. This plant, likewise, will not tolerate artificial winter heating and is only suitable for verandas or cool, very well-lit places.
Habitat: From western Africa and Natal.
Minimum winter temperature: 5–10 °C (40–50 °F), but it will survive occasional frosts, as long as they are sporadic. In high temperatures it is vulnerable to attacks from scale insects.
Light: Bright and diffused; a slightly shady position is most suitable.
Environmental humidity: No special requirements at the temperatures given.
Watering: Water frequently in summer and sparingly in winter.
Soil: This species is also not demanding and is happy in any type of soil as long as it is sandy and permeable, but a humus-rich soil made up of compost with mature leaf-mould and sand added will certainly give better results. The roots of this species are very tough and spread quickly, and the small tubers even appear on the surface of the soil; it is not unheard-of for the roots to break earthenware pots. There is no point in excessive repotting, because before long it will in any event be impossible to give the plants enough room; cut back the root system drastically, and repot to the size desired. Growth will quickly appear with a good soil mixture.
Propagation: By division in spring, with no special precautions; however, this species produces plenty of fruit which germinate fast wherever they fall; as a result it is possible to reproduce by seed, but be sure that it is fresh, because it will germinate more rapidly.

ASPIDISTRA ELATIOR (Liliaceae)

Etymology: The name comes from the Greek *aspìs*, 'shield' because of the shape of the stigma.
Description: This very well-known plant which has been cultivated since the last century as an indoor plant nowadays no longer meets the requirements of this category. In fact, although it will tolerate moderate light, it withers in rooms with central heating, and is thus only suitable for unheated verandas, hallways and stairways. The plant is an evergreen perennial with creeping rhizomes from which the caulinar leaves grow; the lamina, on a long petiole, is entire, lanceolate-acuminate, leathery and dark-green. The bright violet flowers appear at ground-level, but are in no way decorative. There is a variety, *variegata* with white markings on the leaves, but this requires more light than the typical species.
Habitat: From the Far East, mainly China.
Minimum winter temperature: Needs protection from frost, but will remain more attractive in about 5–10 °C (40–50 °F).
Light: Its tolerance of poor light does not mean that it does not thrive in good, diffused light, but shelter from direct sunlight.
Environmental humidity: No problems here at the minimum temperatures; with higher temperatures increase humidity to avoid attacks from parasites; the foliage will benefit from being sponged regularly.
Watering: Water regularly all year round, and more intermittently in winter at low temperatures.
Soil: Although not at all demanding, the best soil is made up of compost with mature leaf-mould and a little sand added. It must however be permeable to prevent the rhizomes from rotting.
Propagation: By division at the start of the vegetative period, with no special requirements or problems.

BEGONIA × TUBERHYBRIDA (Begoniaceae)

Description: This vast group of hybrids produced by crossing different species is generally considered suitable for growing outdoors or on patios, terraces and open balconies, although the plants do not like very dry, hot weather. In a fresh, airy, well lit position where some protection against direct sunlight and a humid atmosphere can be provided they should produce a fine display of blooms. As so many different horticultural hybrids belong to this wide-ranging group, often the foliage is the only feature which shows they are of the same genus. The stems are fleshy and succulent. The leaves which may be broad or narrow are almost always oblique, and acuminate, and generally downy. The plant may be erect or pendulous in habit. The flowers are simple, double or multiple in a wide range of colours, although never blue. The commonest types include 'Bouton de Rose', 'Fior di Camelia', 'fimbriata', 'multiflora', 'pendula', 'crispa', and 'marmorata'. They all have a period of complete rest during the winter when the tuber must be kept completely dry in its pot, and protected from the cold until it is time to bring the plant back into growth.

Habitat: The original species, now unidentifiable, come mainly from the Andes; foremost among them is *Begonia boliviensis*, which is native to Bolivia.

Cultivation: The tubers, which are usually round and flat and slightly concave on the upper side, are brought into cultivation in spring. Half bury them in damp peat, leaving the hollow side from which shoots will sprout uncovered; the root system will form on the underside. During this first stage water moderately, maintain a temperature of about 21°C (70°F) and spray to provide a moist atmosphere; too frequent watering may make the tubers rot. When shoots appear stand the plant in a well-lit position out of direct sun, and when the roots reach 5 cm (2 in) in length put the plant in a mixture composed of equal parts of well-rotted leaf-mould and peat with a good proportion of sand to make it very porous. Throughout the summer water only when the mixture is fairly dry, but increase the level of humidity as much as possible and keep the temperature constant by means of shading and ventilation as required. When the plant begins to wither in the autumn water less and less often and then stop altogether, leaving the tuber to rest until it is time to bring it into growth again.

Propagation: Commercial growers start plants from seed to produce tubers, but amateurs usually start with ready-formed tubers sold during their rest period. The plants can easily be propagated from cuttings if grown in an almost dry sandy mixture at a temperature of 21°C (70°F), but plants produced in this way are unlikely to form a tuber capable of overwintering, although they will probably flower. Tubers bearing many buds can be divided, but the cut surface should be treated with fungicide powder and watering should be kept to a minimum until the cut is fully healed.

BEGONIA SEMPERFLORENS (Begoniaceae)

Description: This large and familiar group, technically described as *Begonia semperflorens cultorum*, is better known as the 'bedding begonias'. There are a great many hybrids from the major species, which has fibrous roots, is somewhat succulent, and has smooth, oval leaves and inflorescences in various shades of pink, white and red (there are also two-coloured varieties). They cannot be strictly defined as indoor plants. In horticulture they are treated as annuals, although they are perennial, and grown from seed each spring. There are, however, some extremely beautiful varieties which are well worth hanging on to; these are propagated from cuttings taken when the mother plant becomes weak or spindly; in a cool, well-lit spot — by a window for example — they will bloom almost continually, as their specific name implies.
Habitat: Originally from Brazil.
Minimum winter temperature: 10–13 °C (50–55 °F).
Light: As strong as possible, even in direct sunlight, except in the hottest months and at the hottest times of day. Under artificial light they will continue flowering in winter if placed very near fluorescent lighting for 16 hours a day.
Environmental humidity: Moist, but never stagnant. They should be well ventilated, but never sprinkled.
Watering: Water regularly in summer, and very sparingly in winter. Particular attention should be paid to the fact that the water must never stagnate at the bottom of the pot or in the soil.
Soil: Light and porous, made up of compost and advanced leaf-mould in equal parts with peat and sand added to make it more permeable.
Propagation: By apical cuttings from the stem, unenclosed in barely moistened sand kept almost dry, given that the main dangers are rot and fungal diseases, including oidium (powdery mildew). The temperature should be around 21 °C (70 °F) and cuttings may be taken at any time of year, given plenty of light.

BELOPERONE GUTTATA (Acanthaceae)

Etymology: The name comes from the Greek *bélos*, 'arrow' and *peròne*, 'clasp, buckle', because of the shape of the filament.
Description: A suffruticose evergreen perennial with ovate and slightly pubescent leaves; the terminal inflorescences are composed of spikes of tightly imbricate bracts, squarely arranged, with the small white flowers growing between them in succession; they have a long, bilabiate tubular corolla, with violet dots at the fauces. The bracts are green at first, passing gradually to a brick-red colour, and have earned the plant, in the English-speaking countries at least, the name of shrimp plant. They are persistent, whereas the flowers are caducous, dropping off gradually as they open, with the whole inflorescence eventually being shed.
Habitat: From Mexico.
Minimum winter temperature: 7–13 °C (45–55 °F); it will survive in lower temperatures, but will tend to shed its leaves; the same will happen if the temperature rises too high.
Light: Bright, although in summer it will flower better if in a shady spot; in other seasons it may be exposed to direct sunlight.
Environmental humidity: Quite high, but never stagnating; the plant must be well-aired.
Watering: Water frequently and plentifully in summer, very sparingly in winter; stagnating water at the bottom of the pot will produce diseased leaves which will blacken before dropping off.
Soil: Very porous and humus-rich, made up of equal parts of compost and leaf-mould, and some sand to obtain loose soil.
Propagation: By cuttings; rooting is quite straightforward with a temperature of about 21 °C (70 °F) and good environmental humidity; in spring it will be as well to prune the plants to encourage them to ramify and keep them compact, and this is also the best time to take top-cuttings, as long as there is adequate warmth. Do not put the cuttings under glass or plastic covers in smallish pots, because the lack of ventilation may cause death.

171

BILLBERGIA NUTANS (Bromeliaceae)

Description: A herbaceous perennial with the typical growth pattern of the genus; the slender grey-green leaves with silvery sheen are upright for the most part, with the tips curved, and form a narrow, tubular rosette with a deep central 'vase'. The leaves are rigid and thorny, and the plants tiller considerably, forming large clusters. The inflorescence rises from the centre of the 'vase'; it is tall and pendent, with bright crimson-pink bracts and greenish flowers. This species requires much less warmth than the others and may be grown outdoors in places with milder climates, but it must be in a humid spot.

Habitat: From Uruguay and Argentina.

Minimum winter temperature: 10–13 °C (50–55 °F).

Light: Very strong, diffused, not in direct sunlight.

Environmental humidity: High, but not stagnating; in order to thrive and avoid the risk of rot, this species needs a very airy environment.

Watering: Water frequently in summer and very sparingly in winter; but make sure that the water never stagnates either in the soil or at the bottom of the pot.

Soil: These plants can be seriously affected by moisture at the collar; in the wild they are epiphytes and the water runs off easily from their roots, and may stagnate in the 'vase'; this is not good when they are grown in soil, and only feasible if they are grown as hanging plants, on trunks or pieces of bark, with the roots in fern fibre and peat wrapped in sphagnum; in pots the soil should be made up of equal parts of leaf-mould, peat and shredded fern roots, with sand added; drainage must be very efficient.

Propagation: By division in spring at a temperature of about 18–21 °C (65–70 °F), with no particular precautions, but make sure the soil is just moist and spray the foliage.

BROMELIA BALANSAE (Bromeliaceae)

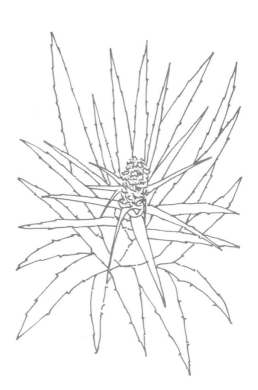

Etymology: The Bromelia genus, from which the name of the family is derived, is named after the Swedish botanist Olaf Bromel (1629–1705).

Description: This genus is less cultivated than others of the same family, because of the rigid, thorny leaves and the bulky size of the plant. The species in question has a large rosette of extremely rigid basal leaves, with wicked thorns growing in every direction; at the centre the inflorescence emerges; on its rachis there are bracteal leaves like the basal leaves, but shorter; these turn red before flowering and have a vexillary function; the real inflorescence, at the apex, consists of a ramified panicle of white flowers which are followed by small, oval, orange fruit in the wild and when grown in ideal conditions.

Habitat: From tropical America, from Brazil to Argentina.

Minimum winter temperature: About 16 °C (60 °F), although occasional drops in temperature will harm it.

Light: Very strong; it will tolerate direct sunlight, but not in the hottest months and at the hottest times of day.

Environmental humidity: As high as possible, but more important for these plants is good ventilation; it is thus only suited to large rooms, and in summer may be put outside, in a fairly shady spot in dry climates.

Watering: Water regularly all year round; these plants grow in the ground and are thus easier to grow than epiphytes, not least because their shape does not encourage stagnating water in the centre; but let the soil dry out slightly between waterings.

Soil: An appropriate mixture will consist of equal parts of compost, leaf-mould and peat with a good amount of sand added to make it permeable.

Propagation: By removing the basal shoots which form around the main rosette; pot at a temperature of 21 °C (70 °F) and, to start with, keep the soil just moist.

BROWALLIA SPECIOSA (Solanaceae)

Etymology: The genus is named after Johann Browall, Bishop of Abo, a naturalist (1707–1755), who was a friend of Linnaeus and a champion of his theories.

Description: A herbaceous perennial plant, usually treated as an annual, although cuttings may be taken in winter and kept in a cool, well-lit place. The plants have small lanceolate dark-green leaves; the flowers are axillary, with a fairly long peduncle and a small gamosepalous calyx; the corolla is a long, slender tube which opens out into five, joined, spreading lobes, which are bluish-violet and lilac underneath in colour. In a well-lit, sheltered and airy place the plants may be kept throughout the winter, and will also flower more or less all year round.

Habitat: From Columbia.

Minimum winter temperature: 10–13 °C (50–55 °F) to keep it as a perennial.

Light: Very strong, but sheltered from direct sunlight; in summer they will thrive outdoors in semi-shade.

Environmental humidity: Quite high, but the major requirement is an airy position, such as a fairly cool greenhouse or a veranda.

Watering: Water regularly all year round, but let the soil dry out slightly between waterings.

Soil: Very humus-rich, made up of equal parts of compost and mature leaf-mould, with a fair amount of peat and sand added to make it more permeable. Regular and light amounts of liquid fertilizer will help the flowering.

Propagation: If desired as an annual, it may be reproduced by seed in spring, in light, sandy soil; with early sowing it will flower in June and throughout the summer. If the right conditions for keeping it through the winter are available, cuttings may be taken in spring and in late summer with a temperature of about 18 °C (65 °F), without any special precautions. Plants kept as perennials should be trimmed often for a bushy, compact appearance.

BRUNFELSIA CALYCINA (Solanaceae)

Etymology: This genus is named after Otto Brunfels (1489–1534), the German theologist and naturalist, of Magonza, who in 1530 published the first work on plants with illustrations.

Description: A shrubby evergreen upright plant, ramified from the base, with elliptical-acuminate, short-stalked, glabrous and entire leaves; the flowers growing in axillary or apical inflorescences have a small white eye and five flattish petals with slightly wavy margins. In English this plant is called 'yesterday, today and tomorrow' because of the flowers which are intensive mauve-violet in colour when they open, then fade to pale lilac and turn completely white before withering. The smallest variety, which is thus best-suited to cultivation in fairly large pots, is the *floribunda*, which blooms in autumn–spring if kept warm enough.

Habitat: From Brazil.

Minimum winter temperature: Tolerates temperatures slightly higher than 0–10 °C (32–50 °F); in mild climates and sheltered places it may be outdoors, but it becomes semi-deciduous.

Light: As much as possible, but not direct sun; well ventilated.

Environmental humidity: At the temperatures shown, spray foliage, but not when the flowers appear.

Watering: Water plentifully, combined with liquid fertilizer during the vegetative period; water sparingly when the temperature drops to allow semi-dormancy; the ensuing vegetative period and flowering will depend on the winter temperature.

Soil: Well-drained, made up of compost and mature leaf-mould in equal parts, with peat and sand added. The pots should be gauged according to the size of the plant; better blooms will be obtained in proportionately small pots.

Propagation: Reproduction may be carried out by seed, but the commonest way is by cuttings of young semi-herbaceous branches in spring, in moist sand under plastic covers at 15–20 °C (60–70 °F). After flowering it is a good idea to prune and train.

CAMPANULA ISOPHYLLA (Campanulaceae)

Common name: Star of Bethlehem.

Etymology: The name is the diminutive form of the late Latin *campana* or 'bell', describing the flower shape of most of the genus's 300 species.

Description: This small, bushy, semi-erect plant is often allowed to grow so that the stems lie flat, rising at the tip; they are sometimes trained against supports. The rounded cordate leaves have crenate margins. The calyx is short and the corolla has a short funnel-like tube with five very expanded lobes. The flowers are usually light blue, though in the variety *alba* they are white. Both varieties flower profusely.

Habitat: Although commonly known as Star of Bethlehem, *Campanula isophylla* in fact comes from a small area along the Ligurian coast of Italy. It is sometimes mistaken for the rather similar species *Campanula fragilis* which comes from central and southern Italy and has the same requirements.

Minimum winter temperature: 5–7 °C (41–45 °F).

Light: Excellent; some protection from strong direct sun in summer will encourage finer blooms which may continue to appear until winter.

Environmental humidity: At the recommended temperature there is no problem; the plant will anyway not overwinter successfully if conditions are too warm.

Watering: Frequent in summer, very sparing in winter.

Soil: Rather chalky, well-composted garden soil with a little sand added. Do not allow the mixture to become waterlogged.

Propagation: By cuttings in early spring. Plant in a mixture composed of equal parts of sand and peat and keep in a cool position, sheltered from frost. Taking cuttings is good for the parent plant and encourages new shoots.

CATHARANTHUS ROSEUS (Apocynaceae)

Etymology: The name comes from the Greek *kathariòs*, 'pure' and *ànthos*, 'flower', probably referring to the white colour of this plant, better known by the old Linnaean name of *Vinca rosea*.

Description: A small, upright, carnose, herbaceous plant, sometimes tillering at the base. The leaves are oblong, and dark-green with a white central vein; the flowers have a small calyx and a corolla with a long thin tube which opens out into five divided and spathulate laminae; in the typical form these are pink with darker markings at the tiny orifice of the tube; but there is a variety, *alba*, which is all white, and another which is a more delicate shade of pink. Although perennial, these plants, which may be grown outdoors in summer, are usually treated as annual; in a cool, very well-lit and airy place they may be kept through the winter and will flower at other times of year, although after a few years they will have to be reproduced because they lose their beauty.

Habitat: Although sometimes known as the 'Madagascan periwinkle', these are worldwide plants and come from the tropics.

Minimum winter temperature: 13–16 °C (55–60 °F).

Light: Very strong, including direct sunlight, but slight shade in summer keeps the blooms longer, and preserves their colour better.

Environmental humidity: Fairly high, especially in winter.

Watering: Water plentifully in summer, and regularly but somewhat sparingly in winter: the water must never stagnate.

Soil: Humus-rich and loose; it may consist, basically, of compost with mature leaf-mould and sand added.

Propagation These are reproduced commercially by seed each year in spring, given that the flowering occurs mainly in summer–autumn; as mentioned, it is hard to keep these plants through the winter because of the amount of light and ventilation necessary; verandas and cool conditions might do the trick; it may be reproduced in spring by cuttings in a very damp place, planted in sand and peat, kept not too wet, at about 18 °C (65 °F).

CHLOROPHYTUM COMOSUM (Liliaceae)

Etymology: The name comes from the Greek *chlorós*, 'green' and *phytón*, 'plant', but in horticultural jargon the plant is often known as 'phalangium' from the name of an old genus *'Phalangium'*, now split up, to which a similar species belonged.

Description: This plant, which has been cultivated for a long time, is a herbaceous perennial with carnose roots; the basal leaves grow in a rosette and are markedly outward-turned; long pendent stolons grow among them; at their tip are small radicant plants which naturally reproduce the plant when they come into contact with the ground. The inflorescences, appearing in summer, have quite long steles and are formed by small greenish-white flowers. The variety *vitatum* is very commonly cultivated; it has a white stripe running lengthwise at the centre of the leaf.

Habitat: From South Africa.

Minimum winter temperature: The plant is semi-hardy and can be grown outdoors in our milder climates; although best protected from frost, it will survive occasional drops in temperature to below 0 °C (32 °F), as long as they are short-lived. Indoors it requires temperatures which do not rise above 10 °C (50 °F), and thus rooms which are unheated.

Light: Very strong, but direct sun will spoil the foliage.

Environmental humidity: No problems at minimum winter temperatures, but will benefit from being sprayed during summer; quite important to provide an airy spot.

Watering: Water regularly in summer and sparingly in winter; the roots are very carnose and thus liable to rot.

Soil: Any humus-rich soil, but the plant prefers two parts compost, one part mature leaf-mould and a good amount of sand.

Propagation: By means of the young plants growing at the ends of the stolons, which almost always have root-buds; plant directly in appropriate soil, with no special precaution, although it is better to wait until spring.

THE CLERODENDRON GENUS (Verbenaceae)

Etymology: Derived from the Greek *kléros*, 'fate, destiny' and *déndron*, 'tree', this name appears to have no significance, although it has been thought to refer to the fact that some species in the genus are used therapeutically, while others are poisonous, thus they were used as if lots were being drawn.

Description: The genus consists of suffruticose plants and shrubs; some shed their leaves, others are evergreen, and several are sarmentose; the leaves are opposite and verticillate, with the lamina entire or crenate at the margins. The flowers are usually in panicles or apical cymes, but in some species they are also axillary and have a persistent calyx and a tubular corolla with spreading laminae; the fruit, which follow the flowers in many species, are drupes (stone-fruit) forming in the calyx. The genus includes more than 100 species, some semi-hardy, and others suited to the greenhouse, depending on where they are from. In horticulture they are identified on the basis of these two groups rather than by their shrubby or sarmentose growth pattern, given that their cultivation is unaffected by this latter factor.

Habitat: All the species come from the tropical and semi-tropical parts of the world, but most are from Asia and Africa.

Minimum winter temperature: Ranges from 5–16 °C (40–60 °F).

Light: All species require bright light to flower, but not direct sunlight, especially in summer.

Environmental humidity: Quite high for all species, and as high as possible for the tropical types.

Watering: Water frequently in summer, and very moderately in winter, when the plants are semi-dormant.

Soil: Very humus-rich, made up of equal parts of compost, leaf-mould and peat, with sand added. Regular use of fertilizer during the vegetative period will encourage the blooms, and the pots must always be large enough for the size of the plants, since the Far East species in particular have fairly spreading roots.

Propagation: Reproduction either by semi-mature wood-cuttings in moistened sand and peat, at a temperature of 21 °C (70 °F) under covers to retain humidity, airing every so often, in late summer or autumn, or by herbaceous cuttings with the same conditions in spring. Reproduction is also possible by seed, but this takes some time to germinate, as do all lignifying seeds: sow under glass in spring. If older plants have basal shoots, these can be removed and potted, but transplant with a good amount of earth around the roots.

CLERODENDRON BUNGEI (Verbenaceae)

Description: This plant is often called by its old name: *C. foetidum*, which was given to it because the leaves, when rubbed, give off a very unpleasant smell, a feature common to a greater or lesser extent to the whole genus; this is a rather dwarf-sized shrub, reaching 1·50 m (5 ft) in height; it is thorny, with large ovate and acuminate leaves, dentate at the margins, dark-green on the upper blade with reddish hairs on the underside. The flowers grow in large umbrella-like corymbs; the calyx is small and the corolla tube long and slender, opening out into five linear segments; it is bright pink in colour.
Habitat: From China.
Minimum winter temperature: It will not survive frost, but also dislikes high winter temperatures; it is suitable for cool and airy verandas giving similar conditions to a greenhouse.
Light: Very strong, slightly shaded in summer.
Environmental humidity: No special requirements up to 10 °C (50 °F), but in higher temperatures the plant may wither.
Watering: Water frequently in summer and sparingly in winter.
Soil: Made up of compost and mature leaf-mould in equal parts; use half a part of peat to avoid excessive moisture during winter; the sand should be coarse to make the soil as permeable as possible so that the water will not stagnate.
Propagation: Given that it tillers easily with radical branches, the simplest method of reproduction is by division, carried out when the vegetative period starts, at a temperature of 21 °C (70 °F).

CLERODENDRON SPECIOSISSIMUM (Verbenaceae)

Description: This shrubby, ramified species is also known by its old name of *C. fallax*. The stems are four-sided, covered in white down, as are the large, cordate-ovate leaves; the margins are entire and the lamina is corrugated between the secondary veins. The carrying inflorescence is upright and consists of ramified panicles carrying scarlet flowers with a long, slender corolla tube and separate and evaginated lobes; stamens and pistils are as in most species of the genus.
Habitat: From Java, but its distribution area stretches as far as Ceylon; it grows in forest in mountainous regions, but in well-exposed places, as indicated by the pubescence of the foliage.
Minimum winter temperature: About 16 °C (60 °F).
Light: Bright, but diffused. In the intermediate seasons or winter it may be exposed to a few hours of sunlight in the morning.
Environmental humidity: As high as possible, but do not spray; this will mark the pubescent leaves.
Watering: Water all year round, but more intermittently in winter.
Soil: Made up of equal parts of compost, mature leaf-mould and peat with some sand added.
Propagation: By ligneous cuttings from semi-mature wood in autumn or by herbaceous cuttings in spring. In both cases a temperature of 21–24 °C (70–75 °F) is necessary, as are slightly moist soil made up and sand and peat, and a cover, but air often to stop the condensation rotting the herbaceous parts. The rotting process is a slow one.

CLERODENDRON THOMSONIAE (Verbenaceae)

Description: A sarmentose shrubby plant with opposite, oblong-ovate and acuminate leaves with the entire lamina grooved by evident nervations between which it is wrinkled. The inflorescences are axillary and terminal, very ramified and usually pendent; the flowers have a white calyx which is swollen and forms five very pronounced angles; it tapers towards the apex. From this emerges the terminal part of the corolla, a slender tube opening out into five brightly coloured crimson petals with stamens and pistil projecting. There is a variety, *variegatum*, which is even more beautiful, having leaves with greenish-yellow margins.
Habitat: From West Africa.
Minimum winter temperature: About 16 °C (60 °F); in lower temperatures it becomes partly deciduous and loses many leaves.
Light: Good, but diffused, not in direct sunlight; the plant is really best-suited to the hot-house.
Environmental humidity: As high as possible, using any means available.
Watering: Water regularly all year round, and slightly less in winter. The water must never stagnate at the bottom of the pot, so good drainage is important.
Soil: Equal parts of compost and leaf-mould with a little peat and sand added. Fertilize regularly during the vegetative period.
Propagation: Herbaceous cuttings in winter-spring with a temperature of about 24 °C (75 °F), under glass or plastic covers, in a mixture of peat and sand kept not too wet. Air often and remove the covers carefully and gradually. Adult plants should be pruned, removing branches which have flowered for some time; the plant may also be trimmed to keep its shape compact, and the branches should be trained and fastened to supports.

THE COLEUS GENUS (Labiateae)

Etymology: The name comes from the Greek *Koleòs*, 'sheath, scabbard' — the filaments of the stamens are joined in a fascicle.
Description: This genus includes a fair number of tropical species which may also be suffruticose, but those usually grown are all hybrids deriving from the species *Coleus blumei* mainly; these are herbaceous perennials, usually grown as annuals, with opposite, ovate-acuminate leaves, crenate at the margins and brightly coloured on the lamina. The stems are four-sided. Small spikes of inconspicuous violet flowerlets may appear, but should be removed before developing, because when the plant goes to seed it is very unattractive. It is possible to keep them through the winter in very well-lit places, but is generally better to reproduce the plant by cuttings, or sow seed each spring.
Habitat: *Coleus blumei* comes from Java.
Minimum winter temperature: About 16 °C (60 °F).
Light: Very strong, but avoid direct sunlight which often causes the plants to lose the colouring of their leaves and the tissues to thicken; slight shade is thus better. They are also ideal for growing in artificial light which facilitates overwintering.
Environmental humidity: Fairly high, using any means.
Watering: Water plentifully in summer and sparingly in winter.
Soil: Humus-rich and porous, made up of equal parts of compost, leaf-mould and peat, with some sand added.
Propagation: Reproduction by seed in spring; the seeds are subject to the normal rules regarding all fine seed; they vary a great deal, and from every sowing a quantity of different colours will be obtained, from which those to be kept can be chosen by thinning out and transplanting. If a certain type of plant is desired, use agamic reproduction by taking cuttings which will root very easily, even in water alone. In pots use sandy soil, not too wet, and provide a temperature of about 21 °C (70 °F). The plants must be regularly clipped to keep them compact, even dwarf specimens.

THE COLUMNEA GENUS (Gesneriaceae)

Description: The genus consists of evergreen, semi-woody plants, often epiphytic. The stems are usually flexible and grow flat, rising at the tip, though they may be erect at first. The entire, opposite leaves are small or medium-sized and sometimes long and narrow. The flowers, which grow in the leaf axils, resemble those of *Aeschynanthus*, but the calyx is much shorter and the tubular corolla has much more pronounced lobes at the tip; the top lobe is trilobate and concave, while the lower one is usually long and narrow. In different species the colours range from red to deep yellow, but plants available commercially are usually hybrids with scarlet or orange flowers.

Habitat: The species come mainly from Central America, with some from South America.

Minimum winter temperature: 12–15 °C (53–59 °F). Will tolerate slightly lower temperatures if kept dry during the winter.

Light: Excellent but diffuse, out of direct sun.

Environmental humidity: A high level, especially in warm conditions, increased by spraying and sprinkling the foliage.

Watering: Frequent in summer, very sparing in winter at low temperatures. Plants need a rest period in late autumn and winter since, with a few exceptions, most species flower in spring. As with all epiphytes, make sure water can drain away freely.

Soil: Very humus-rich and porous, composed of equal parts of leaf-mould and peat with some sand.

Propagation: Plants can easily be propagated by cuttings kept under glass or plastic at 21 °C (70 °F). Give frequent airings and wipe away any condensation to prevent damage to the slightly fleshy leaves. If the atmosphere is humid enough it is better not to cover the plants, even if a few leaves wither. Cuttings can be taken at any time of year so long as warm, light conditions can be provided.

CYPERUS ALTERNIFOLIUS (Cyperaceae)

Etymology: The name comes from the Greek *kypeiros*, a name already used by Theocritus and Theophrastus for the then-known species and probably also for other marsh-plants.

Description: A herbaceous marsh or semi-marsh plant with rhizomatose roots producing upright, hollow stems, up to 1·50 m (5 ft) tall, or more in good ground, carrying at the apex a crown of linear, upright or evaginated leaves, between which grow small depressed spikes of green flowers, with no perianth and scaly bracts. The plants tiller a great deal and are semi-hardy, suitable for cool, airy places. There is a variety, *gracilis*, which is smaller and more delicate, but in many cases plants bought do not belong to it and are simply young specimens of the typical species.

Habitat: From Madagascar.

Minimum winter temperature: May be grown outdoors in all places with mild climates; in occasional frosts it will wither but not die, growing again in spring; indoors, keep at 5–10 °C (40–50 °F) because it will not tolerate either excessive heat or dry air.

Light: Good but diffused, not in direct sunlight.

Environmental humidity: Very high, using any means available.

Watering: Water frequently and plentifully all year round; the ground must never dry out; this is one of the few plants which needs a few centimetres of water in the dish under the pot all the time. The pot may also be immersed in small basins.

Soil: Leaf-mould with a quarter part of sand so that the soil does not clod.

Propagation: By division in spring, or by cuttings, cutting a stem just below the crown of leaves and setting it to root in water in a small bottle with the leaves out of the water, but just touching it. The roots and new stems will appear and the plants should be transplanted in very light, sandy soil with plenty of water in the soil and around the pot. A temperature of about 21 °C (70 °F) is necessary.

CYPERUS DIFFUSUS (Cyperaceae)

Description: This species is of average height, reaching to not more than a metre (3 ft), and thus best-suited to being grown in pots. The involucral leaves of the stems, which wither fast in *C. alternifolius*, are more persistent; the linear leaves of the apical corona are wider, while the branching floral spikes are longer, handsome and often of a pale brown colour.

Habitat: From Mauritius.

Minimum winter temperature: 10–13 °C (50–55 °F).

Light: Bright but diffused, not direct sunlight.

Environmental humidity: Very high.

Watering: Water frequently; the soil must never dry out and the pot should be immersed quite deep in a water-filled receptacle.

Soil: Leaf-mould with one-quarter part of sand to stop clodding. It is a good idea to mix charcoal chippings in with the soil to prevent decomposition.

Propagation: By division in spring or by stem-cuttings, taken below the crown of leaves and set in a small bottle filled with water so that the water just touches the bottom of the leaves where the roots and new stems will appear. A temperature of about 21 °C (70 °F) will be necessary.

DAVALLIA BULLATA (Polypodiaceae)

Etymology: This fern is named after the Swiss botanist Edmond Davall (1763–1798).

Description: This fern has not very tall fronds, reaching up to 30 cm (12 in) in length, although they often remain much smaller; the long, flexible rhizomes are dark, with light-brown tips. Being creeping plants they may be grown as epiphytes in various ways, from pots to hanging baskets, or on pieces of treetrunk or bark.

Habitat: From Japan.

Minimum winter temperature: About 10 °C (50 °F).

Light: It will survive in fairly poor light, but it must always be diffused, and never in direct sunlight.

Environmental humidity: High, helped by spraying, especially during winter.

Watering: Water frequently and plentifully in summer and very sparingly in winter; if grown in hanging baskets at quite low temperatures, it will be enough to water by immersing the receptacle every 2 or 3 days, letting it drain well before putting it back in the basket.

Soil: Loose and very porous; if grown indoors in hanging baskets, sphagnum and shredded fern roots may be used; if in pots, use larger amounts of the latter. Of course, because this is inactive matter, fertilize with small but regular doses during the vegetative period, using mainly nitrogenous and potassic products. If fern roots are not available, use leaf-mould with equal parts of peat and sand; if this is the case, the drainage must be extremely efficient, and water with even greater care.

Propagation: By division of the rhizomes in spring, keeping the soil just moist, but spray frequently until the plant has clearly taken.

EUPHORBIA MILII (Euphorbiaceae)

Description: This plant, which in horticultural circles is still known by its old name of *Euphorbia splendens*, is also known as the 'crown of thorns', a name which is better suited to the typical species. There are in fact some varieties which can only be told apart by certain minor features; the typical plant has slender, twisted stems and branches with sharp thorns, green and somewhat caducous leaves, and inflorescences which are cyathia emphasized by two opposite, red bracts; it does not bear many flowers and the inflorescences are often pauciflorous. The variety *bojeri* has strong upright stems with grey thorns, more persistent leaves, crimson-red bracts and larger inflorescences; it is very ramified and tillered. The variety *hislopii* is quite like it, but has slightly larger leaves and the bracts are scarlet with paler centres.

Habitat: All the varieties come from Madagascar.

Minimum winter temperature: 10–13 °C (50–55 °F).

Light: Very bright, including direct sunlight, but in summer a certain amount of partial shade may stop the leaves withering.

Environmental humidity: Moderate, but the air must not be completely dry, especially in high winter temperatures.

Watering: Water frequently in summer and sparingly in winter, but never stop altogether as for other xerophilous plants; if the plant is not kept sufficiently watered and warm it will shed all its leaves and grow again in spring, but if treated properly it will even flower occasionally in winter.

Soil: Very humus-rich and porous, made up of equal parts of compost and mature leaf-mould with sand added.

Propagation: By cuttings planted in very sandy, almost dry soil at a temp. of 21 °C (70 °F); the cutting usually loses its leaves, which re-appear once it has taken root. When the stems are cut, keep an eye on the latex which will ooze in abundance from the cut; it can be stopped by running hot water over the cutting and applying ashes to the mother plant.

EUPHORBIA PULCHERRIMA (Euphorbiaceae)

Common name: Poinsettia, Christmas flower.

Description: In the wild this plant is a shrub reaching 3 m (10 ft) in height; it is ramified with alternate, dentate or slightly lobate, and sometimes slightly pubescent leaves; stems and branches have an apical crown of bracteal, lanceolate leaves which are usually red but may also be pink or white. The bracts surround the ramified inflorescence which is formed by numerous greenish cyathia with a large yellow nectary. For many years attempts have been made to produce low and tillered forms, and the last decade has seen positive results due to the use of dwarf-producing hormones. Plants on the present-day market may be easily grown on well-lit verandas, although it is not very easy to get them to flower again.

Habitat: From Mexico.

Minimum winter temperature: The typical species needs low temperatures; in high temperatures it will lose its leaves; modern cultivated varieties will nevertheless tolerate 16 °C (60 °F).

Light: Very bright, including direct sunlight, but not in the summer.

Environmental humidity: Keep as high as possible until the plant has finished flowering.

Watering: Water regularly, and stop almost entirely after flowering to allow the plant a period of dormancy; before this period, prune it quite considerably; start watering again when the new branches appear.

Soil: Very humus-rich, made up of equal parts of compost and mature leaf-mould, with sand added.

Propagation: By cuttings in spring, stopping the latex which oozes from the cuts with hot water or cigarette ash. You will need a temperature of 21 °C (70 °F) and very sandy soil kept fairly moist; do not use covers, even though this may cause some leaves to wither, or, if under glass or plastic, air frequently.

Remarks: These short-day plants need absolute darkness for 13 hours a day, at least in November, if they are to re-flower.

FATSIA JAPONICA (Araliaceae)

Common name: Aralia.
Etymology: The name is of Japanese origin.
Description: This plant, better known by its old name of *Aralia*, which is the name of another genus, is an evergreen shrub with upright and ramified stems, and is often tillered at the base. Its leaves are shiny green, and palmate-lobate; the inflorescences, which appear regularly in mild climates outdoors, are much branched; at the tip of each ramification there appears a spherical cluster of small, inconspicuous, cream-white flowers which, in suitable climates, are followed by green berries that later turn black. There is a variety 'Moseri', grown in the Moser nurseries at Fontainebleau in France, which is lower and has larger leaves, thus being better suited to indoors than the typical species which droops rapidly without enough air and light.
Habitat: From Japan.
Minimum winter temperature: This very hardy plant will grow outdoors in open ground wherever frosts are short-lived and occasional; indoors it will only survive in very cool, and preferably unheated, rooms in winter.
Light: Very bright, but always diffused; semi-shade outdoors.
Environmental humidity: Negligible; in high temperatures do not attempt to raise the level because the plant will die just the same; the foliage should be washed to keep it free of dust.
Watering: Water frequently in summer and moderately in winter.
Soil: More or less any type of soil will do, but for fine specimens use compost and mature leaf-mould with sand added.
Propagation: Plants that have shed their leaves may be air-layered in spring, cutting off the lower stems, when the layered part has been removed, so that the plant will ramify at the base; commercially however they are reproduced by seed, and this is the best method for producing attractive young plants. The seeds germinate easily if sown in sandy, moist soil in late winter.

FORTUNELLA MARGARITA (Rutaceae)

Common name: Kumquat.
Etymology: The name commemorates Robert Fortune (1812–1880), a Scottish naturalist who travelled in China and introduced a great many ornamental plants into the West.
Description: An evergreen shrub or small tree which may grow to about 2 m (6 ft 6 in), but will remain small if correctly pruned. When grown as a pot plant it must have a large enough container. Stems and branches are slender and erect, and almost completely free of spines. The green, glossy leaves are entire or slightly crenate, lanceolate and cuneate at the base. The flowers, which are single or clustered in pauciflorus inflorescences, grow in the leaf axils, and are white and highly scented. They are followed by little oval fruits, never more than 2·5 cm (1 in) in diameter, which are edible, skin and all, and have a distinctive scent and flavour. The fruit appears from October to the end of January, and ripens slowly.
Habitat: From Kwangtung in South China. The plant can be grown out of doors in milder European climates.
Minimum winter temperature: 0°C. The plant will tolerate short sharp spells of frost, and so is very suitable for unheated balconies and verandas.
Light: As much as possible, with airy conditions.
Environmental humidity: Not particularly important except in relation to temperature and ventilation.
Watering: Regular all year, increased during very hot spells.
Soil: Equal parts of fibrous compost and well-rotted leaf mould, with some charcoal.
Propagation: It is difficult to grow cuttings in ordinary indoor conditions, and growing from seed is a very slow process, with no guarantee about the quality of the fruit. It is therefore advisable to buy cultivated plants ready to bear fruit from a nursery. Because of the lack of insects indoors you should encourage pollination by dusting pollen on to the flowers with a soft feather.

THE FUCHSIA GENUS (Onagraceae)

Etymology: Named after the German Leonhardt Fuchs (1501–1566).

Description: This genus, which includes mainly shrubby plants, as well as a few arborescent ones, has about 100 species, but hybridization and crossing has been so abundant that probably none of the forms cultivated is a real species. The stems may be upright or decumbent; the leaves are single and entire; the flowers are axillary, usually pendent, either solitary or growing in racemes. The calyx is coloured, funnel-shaped, quite long, with four spreading sepals; the corolla emerging from it consists of 4 or 5 petals, usually variously coloured, with projecting stamens and pistils, which are generally quite long. They require cool, damp conditions.

Habitat: Most of the typical species come from Central and South America, where they may be found at considerable altitudes.

Minimum winter temperature: 5–10°C (40–50°F); in Mediterranean countries the major problem is to provide sufficiently cool temperatures during the hot, dry summers.

Light: Very strong, but not direct sunlight; keep in semi-shade.

Environmental humidity: As high as possible, but never allow to be stagnant; Fuchsias need airy places.

Watering: Water frequently in summer, with liquid fertilizers every so often, and very sparingly in winter; remember that the smallest amount of stagnant water will cause the leaves to drop off.

Soil: Good, humus-rich soil, made up of equal parts of compost and mature leaf-mould with sand added.

Propagation: By herbaceous cuttings in spring in light sandy soil at a temp. of about 18°C (65°F), under glass or plastic covers, removing the condensation regularly. Cuttings may be taken in summer from semi-ligneous parts or in winter with old wood. But always prune the plants in spring and trim them often.

Remarks: Although the blooms of many cultivated varieties are more brightly coloured, one of the best plants for well-lit indoor places, which will also survive slightly warmer summer temperatures than others, is *F. triphylla*, from the East Indies, and its cultivated varieties; the flowers grow in clusters; they are slender and long and coral-coloured; the corolla emerges only a short way from the calyx; the leaves are slightly velvety and red-veined. Cultivation is as for all the other types.

HEDERA CANARIENSIS VARIEGATA (Araliaceae)

Common name: Ivy.
Etymology: The name has kept its Latin origin.
Description: Practically all the species of the genus are hardy in most European climates, although this one is slightly more delicate, but will survive a certain degree of frost, as long as it does not last too long. It is vigorous and sarmentose, and in the early stages has not yet the clinging parts which appear when it has lignified, and consist of adventitious roots; when young it will not even ramify when trimmed, and as a result small specimens look somewhat spindly and more than one plant is usually put in each pot. The leaves are large, with plenty of grey-green and white variegations which differ from leaf to leaf; totally white leaves often appear at the tips of the branches. It is often found in shops under the name of 'Gloire de Marengo' and 'Souvenir de Marengo'; it is not suitable for heated rooms where it will wither fast as a result of the red spider or fungal diseases.
Habitat: From the Canary Islands.
Minimum winter temperature: It only needs protecting from frost; in winter the temperature should not rise above a max. of 10°C (50°F) indoors.
Light: Plenty of light, but remember that young plants and, in general, those grown in pots will not tolerate direct sunlight.
Environmental humidity: No problems if the temperature is kept low; all types of ivy benefit from having the foliage sponged and washed.
Watering: Water frequently in summer and moderately in winter.
Soil: Any good fertilized soil with sand added to stop it clodding.
Propagation: By cuttings; plant the tip of a branch in moist perlite or sand, keeping it damp; do not use covers, and keep the temperature at about 18°C (65°F), with plenty of light. The cuttings will take root in water in a warm, light room.

HEDERA HELIX (Araliaceae)

Common name: Ivy.
Description: We all know the common wood ivy, with its green, shiny, leathery, fairly lobate leaves and adventitious roots which cling to any available support or develop in the ground roundabout in the absence of supports. There are hundreds of varieties, not least because ivy produces mutations more easily than most other plants. Generally speaking, old plants in the wild produce fertile, upright, non-sarmentose branches with adventitious roots bearing umbels of small inconspicuous flowers followed by berries which are usually black, but may be yellow in some forms. It cannot be said that these are ideal indoor plants, because they need fresh, moist air, and will seldom thrive when enclosed. But especially in northern Europe and America many cultivated varieties have been created, usually with small, variegated, marbled leaves, or leaves with oddly shaped laminae which can be sometimes kept successfully in cool and very well-lit places, at least for limited periods of time, after which they must be put outside again. The more commonly found cultivated varieties are: 'Needlepoint', with trilobate, very acuminate leaves; 'Glacier' with grey-green, white-edged leaves; 'Elegantissima' with small, white-edged leaves.
Habitat: Found throughout Europe and Asia Minor, in Asia, the Canary Islands and North Africa.
Light: Diffused, but not too strong, and never in direct sunlight.
Environmental humidity: Negligible at required temperatures, but wash and spray the foliage especially in summer.
Watering: Water frequently in summer and sparingly in winter.
Soil: Compost with one part mature leaf-mould and sand added.
Minimum winter temperature: 0–7°C (32–45°F).
Propagation: By cuttings put in water, perlite or sand kept constantly moist, without covers and preferably taken in autumn or spring. Branches growing upright with no aerial, adventitious roots root only with difficulty.

HIBISCUS ROSA-SINENSIS (Malvaceae)

Etymology: The name comes from that used in Ancient Greece for a species of mallow: *ébiskos* and *ibískus* were terms used by Dioscorides.

Description: This species, one of the best-known of the genus, is suffruticose and, when potted, may grow to 3 m (10 ft); in the wild it takes on an arborescent appearance and will grow to 8 m (25 ft). The leaves are quite large, shiny, ovate, and with slightly dentate margins and acuminate tips; the flowers are solitary and axillary, very brightly coloured, campanulate, with five spreading petals from the centre of which the staminal column peculiar to the family emerges; along this are the stamens with five pistils at the tip. The typical species has scarlet flowers, but numerous hybrids have been created with single or double blooms in various shades of white, pink, yellow and orange. There is one variety, *cooperi*, with small leaves unevenly variegated in white and single, scarlet flowers. All the forms of *H. rosa-sinensis* have short-lived flowers which grow on the most recent growth; as a result it is advisable to prune and shape in late winter before the new branches appear; if you prune later than this, it will impede flowering; but the plants may be frequently clipped and trimmed.

Habitat: From China and Japan; the var. *cooperi* is Indian and more delicate.

Minimum winter temperature: May be grown outdoors in milder climates where there is no frost; indoors, in winter, keep the temperature at 5–10 °C (40–50 °F).

Environmental humidity: Good but never stagnant; the plants need air.

Light: Bright, and in theory the plants will tolerate direct sunlight, but the air may be too dry to permit this, and it is best to keep in a slightly shaded place.

Watering: Water plentifully in summer and sparingly in winter.

Soil: Rich and well fertilized, with mature leaf-mould and peat and a little sand added to keep it permeable.

Propagation: By semi-herbaceous cuttings in spring in sandy soil kept moist at a temperature of 21 °C (70 °F). Many leaves will be shed, but if covers are used there is risk of the whole cutting rotting.

189

HOYA CARNOSA (Asclepiadaceae)

Etymology: The genus was dedicated to Thomas Hoy, chief gardener to the Duke of Northumberland in the eighteenth century.
Description: An evergreen climbing plant which clings to supports or walls by means of tiny adventitious roots on its voluble stems. The oval, oblong, acuminate leaves are large and fleshy, covered with waxy tissues; they are glossy green, darker on the upper side and paler underneath. The plant has semi-spherical umbel inflorescences, composed of starlike, waxy flowers each attached by a stalk. Milky white with pink centres, the flowers appear in spring and summer and have quite a strong perfume at night time. The main stem of the inflorescence is multifloral; it should not be removed, nor should the flowers be cut off as this will prevent the plant flowering again.
Habitat: All species are from Asia and Australia. This species does not need much warmth.
Minimum winter temperature: 10 °C (50 °F).
Light: Maximum, to encourage good flowers. The parent species will tolerate direct sunlight, but needs an airy position.
Environmental humidity: Increased by spraying the leaves lightly. As the plant is succulent it does not like still, poorly ventilated conditions.
Watering: Regular in summer, very infrequent during the winter rest period. The roots are liable to rot, so allow the soil to dry out between waterings.
Soil: Humus-rich and light, composed of two parts of compost, one of leaf-mould and one of peat, with some sand to provide maximum drainage.
Propagation: Stem cuttings root readily at 18–21 °C (65–70 °F); use a very porous mixture with a large proportion of sand or perlite, and moisten it only occasionally. You can also propagate by soil layering. It is best to wait till growth has started.

HOYA LONGIFOLIA (Asclepiadaceae)

Description: This species, which grows more slowly than the previous one, has slender branches and carnose, linear long and acuminate, dark-green leaves which are concave on the upper blade and rounded on the lower. The inflorescences, which are less rounded in appearance, are numerous and formed by white, rather small flowers with flesh-coloured centres. As in the other species, the stem of the inflorescence reflowers and must therefore never be removed.
Habitat: From Sikkim, in the Himalayan region; it does not need much warmth, but will tolerate a certain degree of heat non-the-less.
Minimum winter temperature: 10–16 °C (50–60 °F).
Light: Very strong, and diffused.
Environmental humidity: High, but not stagnant; the best position is a well-ventilated one, because the plant is succulent.
Watering: Water regularly in summer and very sparingly in winter. If there is a risk of the water collecting in the pot, water more intermittently during the vegetative period as well.
Soil: Very rich and light, made up of two parts compost, one part mature leaf-mould and a half part of peat, with a fair amount of sand added to stop it clodding and becoming saturated with water.
Propagation: By top-cuttings from branches, which will root easily in sandy soil as long as the temperature is 21 °C (70 °F) and the soil kept only just moist, and almost dry; or by soil-layering, placing a flexible branch over an adjacent pot and attaching it to the soil at a node, by burying it just slightly. The plant grows rather slowly and in time will need supports to prop up the flexible branches.

IMPATIENS BALFOURI (Balsaminaceae)

Etymology: The name comes from the Latin *impatiens*, 'impatient', because with most species the capsules open at the slightest touch and scatter the seeds contained in them in this way.
Description: This species, which is not commonly grown, is, like all the others, a perennial, but treated as an annual because it is hard to keep it successfully through the winter. It is a fairly tall herbaceous plant, reaching 1 m (3 ft) in height, with carnose, ramified, upright stems which will need supporting in less than ideal growing conditions. The leaves are ovate-lanceolate and very acuminate; the flowers grow in very open racemes, with long peduncles, and are bilabiate; the lower petal is dark-pink or violet, the upper pale-pink or white, and the fauces are dotted with yellow.
Habitat: From the Himalayas.
Minimum winter temperature: 10–13°C (50–55°F).
Light: Good, but protect from direct sunlight; outdoors keep in semi-shade too.
Environmental humidity: Not of great importance, because it is hard to keep the plant through the winter; in summer keep in well ventilated places.
Watering: Very frequently and plentifully in summer.
Soil: Any good garden earth will do, with perhaps a little mature leaf-mould and sand added to avoid clodding; incidentally, this plant will also grow in pots which are too small for it, and does not need a large amount of soil.
Propagation: By seed in spring; it will grow very quickly and will flower all summer long and even into the autumn. If it survives the winter it will still be better to reproduce it in spring because only the young plants are attractive.

IMPATIENS WALLERIANA (Balsaminaceae)

Description: This is the name nowadays given to both the old species *I. holstii* and *I. sultanii*, although both names still occur in seed lists. They are very similar species, and their differences have been eliminated by innumerable hybridizations. Although perennials, they are often treated as annuals, especially the taller forms suitable for gardens; even when grown indoors it is preferable to reproduce them periodically by cuttings, because they become too unruly and large. They are herbaceous plants with very carnose and ramified stems; the leaves are alternate, with long petioles often producing drops of a sticky, shiny secretion; the flowers are solitary or grow in clusters, and are axillary with a slender peduncle; they are more or less flat, with a short tube ending in a spur and five very spreading, irregular petals. In the wild, they are very floriferous and hence known in English-speaking countries as 'busy Lizzies'; there are many hybrids, some of which are dwarf, with a host of colours from white to orange, pink, red, lavender, violet; even two-coloured forms in white and red, as well as forms with double petals.
Minimum winter temperature: About 13°C (55°F); in lower temperatures they may rot or suffer from powdery mildew; in higher temperatures they are prey to the red spider.
Light: Very bright but, unless grown in open ground or in humid climates, they will be more beautiful if partly shaded.
Environmental humidity: High, but never stagnant, because the stems may rot; they should be kept in well-aired places.
Watering: Water regularly in summer and sparingly in winter.
Soil: Made up of equal parts of compost and leaf-mould, with peat and very coarse sand or perlite added to stop the water collecting.
Propagation: Very straightforward by cuttings, which is the only way of obtaining plants identical with those already growing; the cuttings will take root in water, which is the simplest method for the amateur who will have trouble regulating the humidity.

JACOBINA CARNEA (Acanthaceae)

Etymology: The genus is probably named after the city of Jacobina, near Bahia in Brazil.

Description: A semi-shrubby plant, also known by its old name *Justicia magnifica*, which can grow very large unless pruned into shape. This is particularly important since the plant, like the rest of the family, loses leaves along the stems and becomes very untidy-looking. The reddish stems are four-sided; the opposite ovate-lanceolate leaves, attached by petioles, are acuminate, sometimes with undulate margins. The flowers, which range in colour from flesh pink to light red, cluster in inflorescences surrounded by bracts at the stem tips; the calyx is composed of five, long, narrow segments and a long tubular corolla which is bilabiate at the tip, with one lobe divided into two, the other into three. The erect flowers form a very compact spike. Flowering occurs mainly in summer and autumn, but in the right conditions may occasionally occur in spring and even sometimes in winter.

Habitat: From Brazil.

Minimum winter temperature: About 10 °C (50 °F). Higher temperatures will make the leaves drop faster than they would naturally do.

Light: Excellent, with some sunlight, although the plant needs shade in summer.

Environmental humidity: Very good. The foliage should be sprayed often, because the plant is liable to scale insect infestation.

Soil: Porous and humus-rich, composed of equal parts of well-rotted leaf mould, peat and some sand. Use pots of a suitable size, but remember that the plants flower better in small pots.

Propagation: By cuttings taken either from the tips or from sections of stem, kept at 21 °C (70 °F) under glass or plastic with some ventilation to prevent condensation. Though cuttings may be taken at any time of year, it is probably best to take them when you prune the plant into shape at the start of the growing season.

JASMINUM GRANDIFLORUM (Oleaceae)

Common name: Jasmine.

Etymology: The name is the latinized form of the Arab *yasmin*.

Description: Jasmines do not make very good house plants. Most species are hardy or semi-hardy and some of the more delicate types are difficult to find and tricky to grow. A possible exception is *Jasminum polyanthum* which flowers profusely, although unfortunately only for a very short time. If you have a cool, airy veranda or balcony you can grow *Jasminum grandiflorum*, a shrub which is initially upright-growing and then puts out long slender stems which need to be attached to supports. In warmer climates where it can be grown in open ground it gets very large, but when grown in a pot it can be kept under control by pruning. The stems are slender and angular, the compound leaves have five to seven elliptic leaflets growing in pairs from a central axis. The large white flowers, sometimes pink on the outside, have a small calyx and a tubular corolla with five lobes opening out to form a star. The flowers are scented and are grouped in inflorescences.

Habitat: From the Himalayas, in India.

Minimum winter temperature: The plant can stand several degrees of frost but prefers temperatures of about 5 °C (41 °F).

Light: Very strong. Although they like direct sun, pot plants need some shade when it is very hot to protect the flowers.

Environmental humidity: Not a problem at the recommended temperature.

Watering: Plentiful in summer, sparing in winter.

Soil: Well-composted farmyard manure with some sand. Feed regularly with liquid fertilizer during the growing season.

Propagation: By semi-woody cuttings taken in summer, inserted in sand and kept moist by spraying. Soil-layering is a surer method, however. Lay some branches across a pot full of moist, sandy mixture placed near the parent plant; cover with a shallow layer of the mixture and detach once roots have formed.

LANTANA CAMARA (Verbenaceae)

Etymology: In Late Latin the name was given to *Viburnum*, but since Linnaeus it has been used for this genus which has leaves rather like those of the present-day *Viburnum lantana*.

Description: Small, shrubby or semi-woody plants. The opposite, ovate, dentate leaves are wrinkled and rough with a rather downy underside. The small flowers have a tiny calyx and a corolla with a slender tube opening out into irregular lobes. They occur in inflorescences growing on long stalks from the leaf axils. The inflorescences are semi-spherical, flattened at the top and the flowers open in succession towards the centre. Flower colour varies a great deal. In the commonest form the flowers are yellow as they first open and gradually turn red or orange as the inflorescence grows. However there are many variations: a single plant may have different coloured inflorescences, either all red or all yellow. This plant, which can be grown outdoors if there is no risk of frost, is not really a house plant. If it is pruned into a compact shape it will flower for a very long time on a cool, sunny veranda or balcony.

Habitat: From the West Indies; also Mexico and Texas.

Minimum winter temperature: 5–10 °C (41–50 °F). At higher temperatures the plant will droop and be prone to pests.

Light: Very strong with direct sunlight if possible; make sure there is enough ventilation when it is very hot.

Environmental humidity: No problem at the recommended temperatures.

Watering: Frequent in summer, sparing in winter.

Soil: Good compost, containing a little clay and lime, with some sand to prevent it becoming too compact. Regular feeding during the growing season will encourage flowering.

Propagation: The forms most often available tend to be large and unwieldy. They should be clipped and pruned at least once a year in autumn or spring; cuttings will root readily if inserted in damp sand and peat and kept under glass at about 21 °C (70 °F).

MEDINILLA MAGNIFICA (Melastomaceae)

Etymology: The genus was named in honour of José Medinilla de Pineda, governor of the Marianne Islands in about 1820.

Description: This evergreen shrub is essentially a hothouse plant. It is sometimes sold already in flower as an ornamental house plant. and may last some time, but it is unlikely to flower again, as it needs very light humid conditions. A well-lit, warm veranda or sheltered balcony is the ideal place to produce flowering. The plant has large, opposite, sessile, leathery leaves with a white midrib. As in most of the family, the sunken secondary veins start from the midrib and curve towards the tip. The pendulous inflorescences are of the spike type and often grow very long. They bear a great many flowers, consisting of a corolla with five pink or coral petals, which open in succession; the pink rachis or axis extends below the large pink bracts. These bracts become winged and as the inflorescence grows they open out with spaces between them.

Habitat: From the Philippines and Java.

Minimum winter temperature: 15 °C (59 °F) or slightly more.

Light: Very strong, out of direct sun.

Environmental humidity: A high level, increased by every possible means. In spring, when in flower, the plant likes it drier.

Watering: Frequent in summer, sparing in autumn, gradually reducing the temperature to allow the necessary rest period during which flower buds form. When the inflorescences have formed gradually resume regular watering.

Soil: Very rich in humus, composed of equal parts of compost, ericaceous mixture and leaf mould with some sand and charcoal. Drainage must be good. Give small quantities of fertilizer regularly during the summer.

Propagation: By semi-woody cuttings in spring, inserted in damp sand and peat at 21 °C (70 °F) under glass or plastic. Give frequent airings to prevent rotting. Cuttings may not take successfully except in better-ventilated greenhouse conditions.

193

NERIUM OLEANDER (Apocynaceae)

Common name: Oleander.
Etymology: The name comes from the Greek *nerón*, or 'water' because in nature this plant grows freely besides rivers and streams.
Description: A shrubby plant, with leathery, entire lanceolate leaves, often growing in whorls. It does not usually make a very good house plant. In summer it has dazzling flowers growing in cyme-type inflorescences at the stem ends. The calyx is small, the corolla tubular at the base, broadening to become funnel-shaped and then opening out into five large, blunt-tipped limbs. The fruit is a kind of pod which splits open when ripe; the two follicles roll up, freeing the light seeds, which have a ring of fine filaments so that they can be disseminated by the wind. In existing forms the flowers are a wide range of colours – white, pink, red and yellow. There are also double forms in which the dead corolla does not drop automatically but has to be removed. All parts of the plant are poisonous. Although it cannot stand frost except for very short spells and needs shelter in winter, in cold climates it is unlikely to flower unless placed in a sunny position in the open air during the summer. The variety *variegata* which has yellowish or white-speckled leaves is more suited to verandas or balconies because it looks more attractive there even when it has few flowers.
Habitat: The plant grows spontaneously all round the eastern Mediterranean and has become established in the rest of the Mediterranean region and most subtropical countries.
Minimum winter temperature: 5–10 °C (41–50 °F). In warmer conditions infestation by scale insects is likely.
Light: Full sun.
Environmental humidity: No special requirements.
Watering: Plentiful in summer, reduced in winter.
Soil: Well-composted garden soil with a little sand.
Propagation: By semi-woody cuttings during the summer; cuttings will root in clean water in a warm, bright position.

PAPHIOPEDILUM INSIGNE (Orchidaceae)

Description: This is one of the few species of the genus which likes cool greenhouse conditions. It flowers profusely and is easy to grow with the right amount of light, warmth and humidity. Usually cultivated for cut flowers, it can easily be grown if you have an unheated veranda, but indoor winter temperatures are too warm for it. The plant has narrow, green, fairly long leaves and often forms large clumps. The characteristic flowers grow on a reddish, downy scape. The oval dorsal sepal which curves slightly forwards is yellow with brown spots at the base and white at the tip. The petals are yellow with brown veins and the yellow-green tip is tinged with red-brown. There are a number of varieties which differ only slightly from the parent species and form the group still commonly known to florists as *Cypripedium*. Flowering generally occurs in winter.
Habitat: The distribution area reaches from Nepal to Assam, in the Himalayas; the plant likes low temperatures because it is accustomed to altitudes of up to 2,000 m (6,600 ft) above sea level.
Minimum winter temperature: 5–10 °C (41–50 °F) maximum. Flowering will not occur in warmer conditions.
Light: Good, but diffuse. The plant should be well shaded in summer if it is very hot.
Environmental humidity: As high a level as possible.
Watering: Frequent in summer, sparing in winter, but never stop watering altogether, as these plants do not have pseudobulbs. Make sure water never collects round the fleshy roots.
Soil: Although these are terrestrial plants they grow among rocks in very well-drained soil, so they need much the same type of mixture as epiphytic plants, composed of two parts osmunda or fern fibre to one part sphagnum moss. Feed regularly during the growing season as this mixture is poor in nutrients.

THE PASSIFLORA GENUS (Passifloraceae)

Common name: Passion flower.

Etymology: The generic name dates from the Spanish *conquistadores'* discovery of the plant in Latin America in about 1600. The missionaries who went with them thought they could discern in the flower's shape the instruments of Christ's passion: the halo of filaments at the centre represented the crown of thorns; the style the pillar at which he was scourged; the stigmas the three nails; the stamens the sponge soaked in gall. In the species then under observation the corolla has five red marks which look like five wounds. The choice of name, from the Latin *passio*, or 'passion', and *flos*, or 'flower', was thus an obvious one and was confirmed by Linnaeus.

Description: The genus, which includes some 300 species, contains herbaceous, shrubby and tree-like plants, but cultivated species are all climbing suffrutescent plants which cling to supports by means of tendrils. There are various leaf types; they are normally alternate and may be entire, lobed or digitate. The flowers usually occur singly in the leaf axils. The calyx has a short tube with expanded sepals and the petals open out at its mouth below a showy crown of filaments, sometimes double or triple; the stamens have the filaments fused to form a tube in which the ovary is inserted. The fruit is a berry and is edible in some species.

Habitat: From tropical and semi-tropical regions of America, from Brazil to Mexico.

Minimum winter temperature: Some species are semi-hardy and can be grown outdoors in a sheltered position, although they cannot stand frost. More delicate species need a minimum temperature of 10–15 °C (50–59 °F).

Light: All species need very good light to flower and most like sun, though they may need some shade if it is very hot.

Environmental humidity: Good; dry air makes the leaves shrivel and drop.

Watering: Frequent in summer, sparing in winter especially at low temperatures.

Soil: These plants are not fussy about soil; it should contain plenty of humus but not be too rich in nitrates, which cause excessive leaf growth at the expense of flowers. A suitable mixture would be well-composted farmyard manure, rotted leaf mould, peat and sand. An effective drainage system is vital and the pots used must be large enough for the fairly extensive root system. Feed with phosphates and potash during the growing season to increase flowering.

Propagation: All species can be grown from seed, which germinates easily in a light, sandy mixture. Sow from October to February and plant the young plants in pots in spring. Cuttings may be taken in late spring or summer and should be kept warm under glass or plastic. Not all species root easily, so with more delicate species soil layering may be a better method; bury semi-woody branches shallowly in a small pot near the parent plant.

PASSIFLORA CAERULEA (Passifloraceae)

Description: This vigorous climber which sometimes grows to 10 m (33 ft) is probably the best known and most popular species. It can be grown outdoors in many areas, but is also suitable for a cool, airy, well-lit veranda or balcony where it may flower throughout the summer with adequate ventilation. The leaves are digitate, with five lanceolate segments. The soft branches turn woody very slowly. The flower petals and sepals are white with a tinge of green, the crown of filaments is blue at the tip, white at the centre and brown at the base; the yellow anthers are hammer-shaped, the ovary is prominent and the styles are large and very conspicuous.

Habitat: From Brazil.

Minimum winter temperature: 5–10 °C (41–50 °F); the plant will tolerate slightly lower temperatures in a sheltered position and can also spend the winter in warmer conditions though its appearance will suffer.

Light: In a damp climate it likes full sun, but it will flower in semi-shade, especially in a hot, dry summer.

Environmental humidity: No problems at the recommended temperatures.

Propagation: Seeds of this species germinate readily under glass in autumn or late winter. Softwood cuttings root easily in summer under glass but need frequent airings to prevent condensation.

Remarks: When grown in a pot the plant needs pruning into shape to encourage it to branch out densely instead of getting straggly. The branches can be trained to twine round semi-circular supports, producing compact specimens. A hybrid 'Imperatrice Eugenia' (*Passiflora caerulea X triangularis*) is also sometimes available; this is a more delicate plant with pink-tinged flowers and makes a better pot plant.

PASSIFLORA QUADRANGULARIS (Passifloraceae)

Description: One of the species with very showy flowers. A large, strong climber with entire, ovate-cordate leaves. The large, scented flowers have ovate sepals and petals, the sepals white, the petals reddish. The crown consists of five rings of white and purple-red filaments; it is slightly raised and so large that it practically hides the sepals and petals. The edible pulpy yellow-green fruits may grow 25 cm (10 in) long in nature, but are unlikely to appear on indoor plants, except in a greenhouse.
Habitat: From tropical America where it is known as 'granadilla'.
Minimum winter temperature: 10–15 °C (50–59 °F).
Light: Very strong, but it does not like summer sun if the air is too dry.
Environmental humidity: As high a level as possible.
Watering: Frequent in summer, sparing in winter.
Soil: Humus-rich and porous, composed of compost with some well-rotted leaf mould, peat and sand. Use large, well-drained pots and provide supports big enough for the plant's vigorous growth.
Propagation: By hardwood cuttings kept under glass or plastic at about 21 °C (70 °F), taking care to remove the cover as soon as condensation forms. The best mixture to encourage rooting is sand with a little peat if possible. Perlite may also be used.
Remarks: If you want to make an attempt at producing fruit, although any fruit which does appear is unlikely to ripen, you will have to pollinate the flowers artificially with a soft brush when you think the stigmas are ready to receive the pollen grains.

PASSIFLORA RACEMOSA (Passifloraceae)

Description: This species, also known to nurserymen as *Passiflora princeps*, has smooth leaves, usually trilobate, but sometimes entire. The axillary flowers at first grow singly or in pairs but towards the branch tips they are grouped in pendulous raceme-type inflorescences. The slender petals are light crimson and expanded or outward-turning. The crown has short, erect filaments, purple with white edges on the outside and red on the inside where the filaments are very short.
Habitat: From Brazil.
Minimum winter temperature: 12–16 °C (53–61 °F).
Light: Excellent; but in summer some protection should be given against very hot sun.
Environmental humidity: Good, increased in every way.
Watering: Frequent in summer, sparing in winter.
Soil: A mixture of well-composted farmyard manure with some leaf mould, peat and sand. As for other species, excellent drainage is required and the pots must be large enough for the plants' growth.
Propagation: By semi-woody cuttings, taken preferably in summer, and placed in sand or sand and peat under glass or plastic. Air frequently and remove the covering gradually once rooting has occurred.

PUNICA GRANATUM NANA (Punicaceae)

Common name: Pomegranate.
Etymology: The name comes from the Latin *punicus*, or 'Cartha-ginian', probably because, although the plant came from western Asia, the Romans were introduced to it by the Carthaginians.
Description: Spiny shrubs or small branched trees, with glossy green, entire, oblong leaves. The flowers have a persistent, red, leathery calyx, from which, fused with the ovary, the fruit develops. The petals, which are usually red, are caducous. Some varieties have double or white flowers. The plant is deciduous and the parent type does not make a good pot plant. However the variety *nana*, which is unlikely to grow more than 1 m (3 ft 3 in) in height and in any case does not mind quite drastic pruning, does well indoors in a well-lit, airy position and can often be left outdoors; adult plants will even survive short spells of frost. This dwarf shrub produces miniature flowers and fruit in summer.
Habitat: The distribution area is from Asia Minor to India.
Minimum winter temperature: 5–12 °C (41–53 °F); at higher temperatures the plant tends to continue growing, putting out tender, weak branches which do not have the strength to flower.
Light: Very strong, with full sun; if the plant is grown in a small pot, it needs some shade when the weather is very hot.
Environmental humidity: Fairly high in summer if it is very hot. Good ventilation is necessary.
Watering: Frequent in summer, sparing in winter.
Soil: Any good compost, preferably slightly sandy to improve drainage and reduce waterlogging to a minimum. Regular feeding during the growing season is helpful.
Propagation: Plants can easily be grown from seed in spring, but germination is slow, as with all woody plants: it is a good idea to soak the seed in warm water for forty-eight hours beforehand. The young plants should be protected from cold for the first two years. Cuttings may be taken in summer, but they do not root easily.

RECHSTEINERIA CARDINALIS (Gesneriaceae)

Etymology: The name commemorates the Swiss priest and botanist Rechsteiner (1797–1858). The species is still often called by its old name *Gesneria cardinalis* although it has not belonged to that genus since the first half of the nineteenth century.
Description: A tuberous plant which needs a period of complete rest; it is grown for its flowers which appear in spring or summer depending on when the plant is started into growth. It has fairly short, herbaceous stems and green, velvety, rounded, cordate leaves, with crenate margins, attached by petioles. The in-florescences of showy flowers occur at the stem tips; the calyx is bell-shaped and the long tubular, bright red corolla is slightly curved and bilabiate.
Habitat: From Central America.
Minimum winter temperature: The resting tubers should be kept dry at about 15 °C (59 °F) to make sure they do not rot.
Light: Very good during growth, but out of direct sun.
Environmental humidity: Very high, increased to the maximum.
Watering: When the tubers are brought into growth in late winter or spring, water moderately at first, then more often until you are watering frequently during the summer. When flowering is over and the plant begins to droop water more sparingly until the next rest period when you stop altogether. Feed regularly with small amounts of fertilizer during the growing season.
Soil: Very humus-rich and porous, composed of one part of compost and one of leaf-mould to two of peat with some sand or perlite and charcoal to keep the mixture fresh and light.
Propagation: From seed; the very fine seed is pressed onto the surface of a light mixture and kept under glass at 21 °C (70 °F) in winter. Young plants which have not formed a tuber in the autumn should be kept in growth, not left to rest. It is also possible to divide tubers which have started to sprout into a number of pieces, each bearing at least one bud.

THE RHODODENDRON GENUS (Ericaceae)

Etymology: The name comes from the Greek *rhódon*, or 'rose', and *déndron*, or 'tree'. Linnaeus gave the name to this genus although the Greeks called the oleander *rhododéndron*.

Description: This enormous genus which includes over 500 species and countless hybrids is divided into two subgenera. The first, *Eurodendron*, covers all the species and hybrids known to gardeners as 'rhododendrons', the second, *Azalea*, includes all the species commonly called azaleas although in scientific usage they keep the generic name since there is now no such thing as an 'azalea' genus. These shrubby, or sometimes tree-like plants have leathery, entire, alternate leaves and are usually evergreen. The flowers are clustered in umbellate raceme inflorescences at the stem tips. Plants cultivated nowadays are usually hybrids and it is difficult to find true botanical species.

Habitat: Mainly from Asia, though there are some European species, a small number from North America and one from Australia. Most grow high up in the mountain ranges of the Himalayas, or on lower ranges in Asia, the Alps or the mountains of Central Europe. Although there are some species from hot countries, they usually come from a cold climate and so flourish all over Northern Europe, though they are hard to grow further south.

Minimum winter temperature: All rhododendrons are hardy and will tolerate temperatures below freezing point, but they cannot stand winter temperatures above about 15 °C (59 °F). In a warmer, dry atmosphere they soon die.

Light: Excellent. When grown in open ground in a suitable climate they like direct sun, but may need some shade in a very hot, dry summer.

Environmental humidity: A high level all the year round. At low winter temperatures there is no problem, but moist, cool, airy conditions are vital in summer.

Watering: Frequent in summer, with some spraying of the foliage, sparing in winter; applications of liquid fertilizer in spring and summer will make the plants stronger and encourage more flowering.

Soil: All rhododendrons like very acid soil; this, together with cool, fresh conditions, is their main requirement. Pot plants need a totally lime-free mixture such as beech leaf mould, chestnut mixture, ericaceous mixture and peat. If using chestnut mixture leave in the larger chips to provide ventilation and drainage.

Propagation: By softwood cuttings taken in summer, inserted in damp chestnut mixture or sand and peat and kept in a shady place under glass. Semi-woody cuttings may also be taken in winter in the same way; keep them at 18 °C (65 °F) and dust the ends with hormone rooting powder which encourages the formation of roots. Air layering is also possible with large plants, but it is a slow process, as always.

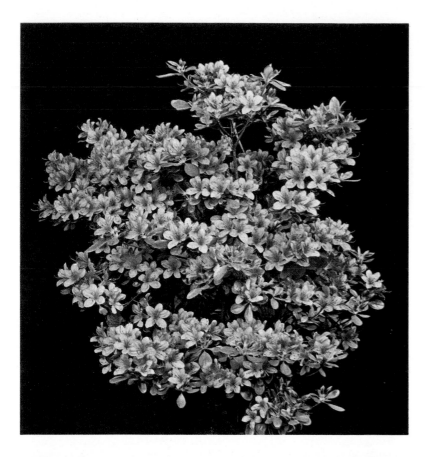

THE RHODODENDRON GENUS (Ericaceae) SUBGENUS AZALEA

Description: The main difference between these shrubby plants and the first subgenus is that azaleas may be deciduous or have semi-persistent or evergreen foliage; their smaller leaves are usually coarse and sometimes downy, but hardly ever glossy and leathery. The flowers are smaller too, and in the commonly cultivated hybrids they are of various shapes, including bell-shaped, and may be either single or double. Evergreen forms are usually grown as house plants, since deciduous forms are completely hardy and need to be grown outdoors, besides being unattractive when they lose their leaves. Among the commonest are the numerous cultivars derived from hybrids of *Rhododendron simsii*, known to nurserymen as *Azalea indica*. They are usually forced into early flower in winter and the single or double blooms come in a wide range of colours, from white to shades of pink, red and mauve. Other evergreen hybrids are descended from many other species and have an exceedingly complex genetic make up. They usually have quantities of single flowers and are very hardy; they can easily be made to flower again. There are also dwarf hybrids of Japanese species, known as 'Kurume', with small, bell-shaped flowers.

Habitat: Most parent species of modern hybrids are Asian in origin, from China and Japan.

Minimum winter temperature: 7–13 °C (45–55 °F).

Light: Excellent but diffuse, with protection against direct sun.

Environmental humidity: A high level; dry air causes leaves and flowers to drop and prevents the flower buds opening.

Watering: Frequent in summer, regular in winter, sparing at minimum temperatures. Do not allow water to collect.

Soil: Acid, composed mainly of ericaceous mixture or chestnut with some peat. Good drainage is required and the soil should never get saturated and heavy.

Propagation: By semi-woody cuttings in summer, kept under glass with plenty of ventilation. It is a good idea to use a hormone rooting powder.

Remarks: Often forced, well-tended azaleas will flower again, not the next year, but the year after at the normal flowering time. The flower buds are more likely to open when a mild winter spell is followed by a few days of cold which rouse the dormant buds. If brought back to a warmer temperature the plant will flower readily and more profusely.

SOLANUM WENDLANDII (Solanaceae)

Etymology: The generic name is the Latin term used by the Romans to describe the invasive and poisonous species *Solanum nigrum*, commonly known as black nightshade.

Description: The genus includes over 1,000 very different species, from useful plants like the potato and the tomato to highly poisonous ones like *Solanum nigrum*, and a number of ornamental species of which *Solanum wendlandii* is one of the finest. It is a sarmentose shrub with a great variety of leaf shapes, the leaves being segmented near the base, then becoming trilobate and finally entire and oblong-acuminate towards the tip. The mauve flowers, clustered in large inflorescences at the stem tips, have a corolla with a short tube opening out into flat, slightly lobed limbs. Stems and branches are slightly spiny and tend to grow vigorously, but can be kept under control by regular pruning which encourages more shoots — and eventually more flowers, since the inflorescences occur at the ends of the stem.

Habitat: From Costa Rica.

Minimum winter temperature: 7–13 °C (45–55 °F).

Light: Excellent, with some sun; pot plants especially should be protected from direct sun.

Environmental humidity: At minimum winter temperatures normal conditions should be adequate, but good ventilation is required.

Watering: Frequent in summer, sparing in winter.

Soil: A fresh, humus-rich, free-draining mixture composed of compost or well-composted farmyard manure with a little well-rotted leaf mould, peat and sand.

Propagation: By semi-woody cuttings in late summer kept under glass or plastic in sand; give frequent airings to prevent the fungus diseases which may develop in a very still atmosphere.

STEPHANOTIS FLORIBUNDA (Asclepiadaceae)

Etymology: The name comes from the Greek *stéphanos*, or 'crown' and *ótos*, or 'ear', because of the appendages of the crown of stamens. There may be another explanation: Theophrastus gave the name *stephanotis* to a kind of myrtle used for crowns, so perhaps this climbing plant served the same purpose.

Description: The genus is entirely made up of twining, sarmentose, evergreen climbers with leathery, opposite leaves; the flowers are clustered in umbrella-like cymes and have a funnel-shaped corolla with five expanded lobes. This is the only cultivated species. It has glossy, elliptic leaves and heavily scented, waxy white flowers. The tube of the corolla is slightly swollen at the base above the small green calyx with open sepals. The plant flowers from early summer until autumn. As in the rest of the family, damaged tissues secrete a thick, white latex.

Habitat: From Madagascar; the common name is 'Madagascar jasmine'.

Minimum winter temperature: 15–18 °C (59–65 °F).

Light: Excellent; direct sun in winter, some shade in summer.

Environmental humidity: Good, but not excessive. These plants are succulent by nature and like well-ventilated, airy conditions.

Watering: Frequent during the period of growth; combine with applications of fertilizer and spray lightly, taking care not to damage the flowers. Water less frequently in winter but do not dry out.

Soil: Free-draining, composed of equal parts of compost and leaf mould with some sand. Grown in a greenhouse with plenty of space the plants may grow to 5 m (17 ft) or more, but they stay much smaller when grown in pots. They need a support and can be trained round a semi-circular frame.

Propagation: By semi-woody cuttings inserted in sand and peat and kept under glass at least 24 °C (75 °F), preferably in spring. The latex can be dried with hormone rooting powder. Plants should be dipped and pruned to encourage new branches.

STRELITZIA REGINAE (Musaceae)

Common name: Bird of paradise flower.
Etymology: W. Aiton (1731–1793), director of the Botanical Gardens at Kew, named the plant after Charlotte of Mecklenburg-Strelitz who became Queen of England in 1761.
Description: This splendid plant usually grown for cut flowers is only suitable for large, airy, very light verandas or balconies because its extensive rhizomatous root system needs large pots or tubs to have room to grow. The leaves, which grow on long petioles from the roots, are oblong with a strong mid rib and sometimes grow 32 cm (12 in) long. The strange inflorescence grows on a long scape, enclosed by a spathe-like bract which opens out to allow a succession of five or six flowers to emerge; these have orange-yellow lanceolate sepals and a corolla composed of three azure blue petals, one shorter and hood-shaped, the other two fused in an arrow-head shape. Flowering continues from October to May, depending on temperature. In a warm enough climate the plant can be grown in open ground, with some temporary protection against winter cold.
Habitat: From South Africa.
Minimum winter temperature: Adult plants can tolerate occasional spells of slight frost, but for flowering a temperature of 10–15 °C (50–59 °F) is required.
Light: Excellent, with light shade in summer to protect the leaves.
Environmental humidity: Not a problem at the recommended temperatures, but avoid a very still atmosphere. Provide as much ventilation as possible from May till the end of summer.
Watering: Plentiful, combined with feeding, except in May and June when the plant needs a rest period.
Spil: Well-composted farmyard manure with some sand added. Effective drainage must be provided.
Propagation: By dividing the clumps in early summer. Growing from seed will give plants capable of flowering in five to six years.

STREPTOCARPUS X HYBRIDUS (Gesneriaceae)

Common name: Cape primrose.
Etymology: The name comes from the Greek *streptós* or 'twisted', and *karpós*, or 'fruit'—the seed capsules are rolled up in a spiral.
Description: There has been a great deal of discussion about the classification and division of the hundred or more species of perennial herbaceous plants belonging to this genus, although it is really an academic question, since only hybrids and cultivars are grown nowadays. The fibrous-rooted plants are grown for their showy, trumpet-shaped flowers with a tubular corolla opening into irregular limbs. The flowers, which come in a variety of colours, grow from the centre of a rosette of leaves, either singly on a long stalk or in cymose inflorescences. Plants sold are usually unnamed and they are often treated as annuals because it is difficult to provide the cool, moist, well-lit winter conditions they need, except perhaps in an enclosed veranda or sun-room.
Habitat: The parent species are from southern Africa; their distribution area reaches from Tanzania to South Africa.
Minimum winter temperature: 5–7 °C (41–45 °F).
Light: Excellent, diffuse, out of direct sun.
Environmental humidity: A very high level increased in every way, especially in winter when watering is less frequent.
Watering: Regular in summer, combined with applications of liquid fertilizer; sparing in winter. Hybrids usually flower from May to September, and so normal watering should gradually be resumed from March.
Soil: Humus-rich and light, composed of equal parts of leaf mould and peat with some sand and charcoal. Do not saturate.
Propagation: Usually from seed; very fine seed should be sown in the proper way at a temperature of 18 °C (65 °F) in late winter or spring. It is also possible to take leaf cuttings with a small piece of petiole attached; insert gently in a porous mixture like sand or perlite, kept moist at a temperature of 21 °C (70 °F).

STREPTOSOLEN JAMESONII (Solanaceae)

Etymology: The name comes from the Greek *streptós*, or 'twisted', and *solén* or 'tube', describing the shape of the corolla.
Description: The genus consists of this one species. The rambling evergreen shrub of slender growth is usually trained against supports. The small, oval leaves are wrinkled: the orange flowers grow on stalks from the leaf axils in corymb inflorescences. The calyx is tubular, like the long corolla, spiralling at the base and opening into five large, blunt-tipped lobes. The flowers appear in spring. In a warm enough climate the plant can be grown outdoors, as it tolerates near-freezing temperatures.
Habitat: From Colombia.
Minimum winter temperature: 7–10 °C (45–50 °F).
Light: Very good, with light shade in summer, especially if the atmosphere is rather airless.
Soil: Free-draining, composed of two parts well-rotted leaf mould to one of peat with some sand. The pots should be well-drained and large enough for the plant, which can be pruned to prevent it becoming unwieldy, either in summer after flowering or at the beginning of winter. Pruning will also encourage the growth of young flower-bearing branches.
Propagation: By semi-woody cuttings in spring, inserted in porous soil at about 21 °C (70 °F); it is a good idea to use hormone dusting powder.

TIBOUCHINA SEMIDECANDRA (Melastomaceae)

Etymology: The name comes from the native Guyanese name. The genus used to include the now vanished *Lasiandra* and this plant is still sometimes listed as *Lasiandra macrantha*.
Description: A shrub which has oblong, ovate, bronze-green, downy leaves, about 15 cm (59 in) long, with three to five very pronounced veins. As in many other members of the family, the midrib is straight, while the secondary veins curve from the base to the tip. The purple flowers have a hairy calyx and grow in raceme inflorescences at the stem tips. The corolla has a slender tube which opens into five large obovate petals. The flowers are rather short-lived; but with the right amount of light and warmth they will appear intermittently all the year round, whereas at low winter temperatures flowering usually only occurs in late summer and autumn. The more compact variety *floribunda* also flowers as a young plant.
Habitat: From Brazil.
Minimum winter temperature: Although the plant can stand occasional frost and can be grown outdoors in a mild enough climate, 12–15 °C (53–59 °F) will give better results.
Light: Very strong, but out of direct sun.
Environmental humidity: As high a level as possible throughout the growing season, and fairly high in winter; the plant needs a well-aired position.
Watering: Frequent in summer, combined with feeding; sparing in winter.
Soil: Very rich in humus, composed of equal parts of leaf mould and peat with some sand to improve drainage.
Propagation: By semi-woody cuttings taken in summer, and kept under glass or plastic in a warm, shaded position. The plants sometimes get untidy-looking and must be kept in good shape by pruning, severe if necessary, in spring.

▲ *Tillandsia cyanea*

▼ *Tillandsia cawligera*

THE TILLANDSIA GENUS (Bromeliaceae)

Etymology: The name commemorates Elias Til-Landz, the Swedish botanist (1640–1693).

Description: This enormous genus includes about 500 species and many hybrids. However, they have such special requirements that even in a greenhouse only a few can be grown successfully. They are epiphytes and, although they vary in appearance and habit, all need such a high level of environmental humidity that it is very difficult to provide suitable conditions. Some species simply consist of very slender branches or thin branching stems. They have almost no roots and hang from the branches of trees, hence the common name Spanish moss. Other more substantial species are grown for their very beautiful flowers. *Tillandsia cyanea* is typical of this group: it forms rosettes of long, narrow, greyish leaves, and the inflorescence is made up of pink, overlapping bracts among which the showy, bright blue flowers appear. Although often grown singly, the plant puts out new shoots very readily. There are several varieties, including *luxurians* which has a number of inflorescences to each rosette and *major* which has larger flowers.

Habitat: All over tropical and subtropical America, from Florida to Argentina; *Tillandsia cyanea* has a large distribution area reaching from Guatemala to Ecuador.

Minimum winter temperature: 13 °C (55 °F). As higher temperatures dry out the air, unless you can increase the level of humidity sufficiently it is best to stick to the recommended minimum temperature or only slightly above it.

Light: Very strong, but out of direct sunlight.

Environmental humidity: Increased in every way; stand the pots in trays of wet gravel and spray frequently.

Watering: Frequent in summer, sparing in winter. Remember that the plants absorb moisture from the air through their leaves. Do not let water collect in the soil or at the bottom of the pot.

Soil: The plants can be grown in hanging baskets or even on pieces of bark; fasten the roots in position with nylon string or copper wire and wrap peat and osmunda fibre and then sphagnum moss round them so that they can grow as in nature. This system is recommended for greenhouses, but is more difficult in an ordinary room where the dry atmosphere will soon dry out the arrangement. If grown in pots the plants need a very deep drainage layer and a growing mixture suited to epiphytes, composed of equal parts fern fibre, peat and sand with a little chopped sphagnum moss. Feed regularly in small quantities throughout the growing season.

Propagation: As with all bromeliads the rosette of leaves dies down after flowering; meanwhile a number of side shoots will have appeared round the base and these can either be removed and potted or left to grow on after the dead rosette has been carefully cut away. Some species have a succession of sheathed leaves which form fairly long branches and can be propagated by cuttings kept at about 21 °C (70 °F) in damp sphagnum moss; repot once they have taken root.

VERBENA PERUVIANA (Verbeaceae)

Etymology: The name comes from the Latin term used generally to describe the sacred boughs of laurel, myrtle and so on carried by priests and used at sacrifices and other ceremonies. It was not this plant's name.

Description: Most verbenas grown by gardeners are treated as annuals, although in fact perennials, because they cannot tolerate frost and lose their looks unless they have suitable winter conditions. However, this small, trailing species with easily-rooting stems can be kept in a well-lit, airy, rather cool position. The almost sessile, oblong, irregular leaves are crenate, dentate or lobate in some varieties; the underside is downy. The spikes of flowers are borne on erect stalks; they have a small calyx and tubular corolla opening into narrow, irregular, scarlet limbs. Although the flowers are small the plant is very free-flowering and attractive.

Habitat: Despite its name, the species is not simply Peruvian, as it is also found in southern Brazil, Uruguay, Paraguay and all over the pampas.

Minimum winter temperature: 7–13 °C (45–55 °F).

Light: Very strong, with light shade for pot plants in summer as direct sunlight makes the air too dry.

Environmental humidity: No problem at the recommended temperatures.

Watering: Frequent and plentiful in summer, sparing in winter.

Soil: Very porous and rich in humus, composed of equal parts of compost and well-rotted leaf mould with some peat and sand. Use wide, shallow pots because of the plant's creeping habit. If grown in a hanging basket the stems grow flat, rising at the tip.

Propagation: By dividing the clumps in late spring. Keep in a warm, shaded position. When roots have developed the branches can be cut back from time to time to keep the plant a good, bushy shape.

ZANTEDESCHIA AETHIOPICA (Araceae)

Common name: Trumpet lily, calla or arum lily.

Etymology: The present name commemorates Francesco Zantedeschi, the Italian botanist (born 1797). Linnaeus called the genus *Calla*, which survives as a common name. When the genus was divided C. S. Kunth gave these plants the name *Richardia* which is still often used, although it was changed in 1826 by Kurt Spregel because another genus already had the same name.

Description: A rhizomatous, herbaceous, perennial plant. The leaves, which grow from the roots, have a long spongy petiole and hastate or sagittate blade. The plant is grown, sometimes commercially, for its inflorescences, which consist of a spadix with the stamen-bearing flowers at the top and the pistil-bearing ones at the base; they are enclosed by a large, showy, white spathe, sometimes coloured in other species. There are a number of varieties including 'Perle de Stuttgart' and 'Little Gem' which are smaller than the parent species and make better pot plants. They may flower all the winter on a cool, light veranda or sun room. The more delicate, coloured species are summer-flowering, but the white is half-hardy and in an enclosed position needs a complete rest during the summer; start the rhizomes into growth in August or September.

Habitat: From South Africa.

Minimum winter temperature: About 10 °C (50 °F).

Light: As strong as possible.

Environmental humidity: The plants are semi-marshy: grow in large pots in trays with a few centimetres of water.

Watering: Once the rhizomes have been brought into growth, gradually increase watering so that the soil stays wet. As summer approaches reduce the frequency, then stop watering and leave the rhizomes completely dry for at least two months.

Soil: Humus rich and light: equal parts of leaf-mould and peat with a good proportion of sand and some pieces of charcoal.

Propagation: By rhizome division at planting time.

Succulent plants

AGAVE VICTORIAE-REGINAE (Amaryllidaceae)

Etymology: The name comes from the Greek *agauós*, or 'admirable', because of the plant's beautiful appearance when in flower.
Description: A low, stemless, slow-growing plant with stiff, leathery leaves, closely overlapping to form a rosette. The leaves are dark green, marked with irregular, converging white lines, and keel-shaped underneath. The margin, edged with fine white lines, is not armed, but at the tip there is a short, stiff, very tough, blackish spine. As the plant grows slowly small specimens can be kept in relatively small pots for years.
Habitat: From northern Mexico.
Minimum winter temperature: 5–10 °C (41–50 °F).
Light: Very good, to prevent the leaves getting weak and losing their markings. Although the plant can do without direct sun for long periods it likes sunlight if introduced to it gradually. Otherwise the inadequately protected leaf tissues may scorch.
Watering: Regular in summer, very sparing in winter.
Soil: Very well-rotted compost with some sand to make the mixture porous and light and so prevent waterlogging and rotting.
Propagation: By means of the offsets which develop occasionally round the central rosette. Plants kept in pots which look too small produce more offsets.

THE ALOE GENUS (Liliaceae)

Etymology: The name probably comes from an Arab or Hebrew term meaning 'bitter'. Already in the first century A.D. Dioscorides used the Greek word *alóe* for a species of this plant.
Description: Evergreen, succulent plants with acuminate leaves usually arranged in a rosette; in young plants they may grow in two opposite lines, acquiring their spiral formation with age. Most species have spines along the margins. They are often confused with *Agaves*, though in most of these new leaves grow rolled up at the centre while in *Aloes* they are already opened out when they emerge. Most of the plants grow bushy and develop stems when mature. They produce spikes of very showy, red or orange, tubular, pendulous flowers. One of the commonest species *Aloe arborescens* grows spontaneously in a mild, Mediterranean climate and sometimes reaches enormous heights, with long, spiny leaves curving outwards. There are smaller species, more suited for growing in pots, such as *Aloe brevifolia* and *Aloe variegata* (commonly known as partridge-breasted aloe), which barely reaches 30 cm (12 in); it has spineless, fleshy, over-lapping leaves with irregular markings; sharply creased down the centre, they grow grouped in a three-sided arrangement.
Habitat: All species come from Africa, but some now grow spontaneously in the Mediterranean region.
Minimum winter temperature: 5–10 °C (41–40 °F).
Light: Very strong, with full sun, although pot plants need light shade when the sun is very hot in summer.
Watering: Regular in summer, very sparing in winter.
Soil: Humus-rich, but it should not contain insufficiently decomposed organic material; use well-rotted compost with some sand.
Propagation: By means of the side shoots which form at the base or by branch or stem cuttings. Allow the cut surface to dry and then place in just moist sand in a warm, shady position, preferably in early summer.

APOROCACTUS FLAGELLIFORMIS (Cactaceae)

Common name: Rat's-tail cactus.

Etymology: The name comes from the Greek *áporos*, or 'impenetrable', coupled with 'cactus', probably because in most species the long trailing stems form an inextricable tangle on the ground.

Description: This plant has long, cylindrical stems which trail or grow horizontally, rising at the tip. The ribs are close together and crowded with areoles bearing fine reddish spines which cover most of the stem. There are small, pink, bell-shaped flowers.

Habitat: From Mexico.

Minimum winter temperature: 4 °C (39 °F).

Light: Very strong, with direct sun if possible.

Watering: Regular in summer. Water when the soil seems dry, which may mean daily if the plant is getting full sun. Do not water in winter to allow the rest period which is necessary to produce flowers.

Soil: Well-rotted compost with a good proportion of sand. When using large pots include some crushed stone or brick for maximum drainage.

Propagation: When taking cuttings allow the cut surface to dry off completely in a shady place before placing on just moist sand or sand and peat; to avoid rotting do not cover until roots appear. Aerial roots often form on the stems but do not develop enough to root independently.

CARALLUMA BURCHARDII (Asclepiadaceae)

Etymology: The name's origin is not known, but it is believed to come from the native South African name.

Description: The genus includes some fifty species. They are all very bushy, succulent, rather small plants with leafless, branching, erect stems and flowers grouped at the tip, unlike related genera which have flowers at the base. This species has irregular grey or olive-green four-sided stems with small downward-pointing teeth sticking out at the angles. The flowers are small with a starlike corolla forming five lobes, whitish inside, brown outside.

Habitat: Most species are South African, but one comes from southern Spain; this species is from the Canaries.

Minimum winter temperature: 7–12 °C (45–53 °F).

Light: Full sun.

Watering: Regular in summer, gradually reduced in autumn. Do not water during the winter; resume the normal pattern in spring. If the winter temperature is too high and the plant starts to wither, it is better to spray it lightly rather than start it into growth again by watering.

Soil: Very porous, composed of compost with some sand and crushed stone. A good, deep drainage layer is necessary.

Propagation: By stem cuttings, or by breaking off a branch at the joint during the summer. Place in just damp sand and spray occasionally; keep in a warm, shaded position.

CEREUS PERUVIANUS MONSTROSUS (Cactaceae)

Etymology: The name comes from the Latin *cereus*, or 'torch', because of the shape and habit of the upright, columnar stem. The common name is torch thistle.

Description: This used to be a very large genus but it has been split up several times on the basis of different botanical features and now consists of relatively few species. *Cereus peruvianus* is the commonest and most popular. In nature it can grow into a tree some 10 m (33 ft) high, but cultivated plants stay much smaller and grow very slowly. The stem is green or blue-green with five to eight ribs. The areoles have a few brown spines and the flowers, which do not appear very easily in cultivation, are green-brown on the outside and white inside. The variety *monstrosus* is often preferred as a pot plant, especially in its dwarf form *nana*; it has bunched tufts of adnate branching stems with many tips which grow into strange contorted shapes.

Habitat: From south-eastern Brazil, though most plants sold have probably been bred by growers.

Minimum winter temperature: 4 °C (39 °F).

Light: Very strong, with full light.

Watering: Regular in summer, whenever the soil seems dry; none in winter at the minimum temperature, but very occasionally watering may be needed if it is a little warmer.

Soil: Composed of well-rotted compost with a little sand. Pot size depends on the plant's growth, and repotting is required every two or three years to stop the cactus becoming top-heavy.

Propagation: If the plant branches out, cuttings may be taken from side stems, preferably in summer. Allow the cut to dry, place in lightly sprayed sand to prevent rotting, keep in a shady position at a high temperature. Plants can be grown from seed following the usual method for very fine seed, but growth is very slow.

CHAMACEREUS SILVESTRII (Cactaceae)

Etymology: The name comes from the Greek *chamaí*, or 'on the ground', combined with the generic name *Cereus*, describing the plant's trailing habit.

Description: This species, the only member of its genus, is a very common type of cactus, partly because it flowers very easily. It has low, trailing, twisted, multiple stems, pale green in colour and almost covered by soft white spines which grow from the numerous areoles. The funnel-shaped, glossy, red flowers are about 5 cm (2 in.) long and appear in early summer. There are a number of varieties which differ slightly from the typical plant; the form *cristata* in which the stems grow in a curious fan shape is much more delicate and produces far less flowers.

Habitat: From Argentina.

Minimum winter temperature: About 4 °C (39 °F).

Light: Very strong, preferably with direct sun.

Watering: Regular in late spring and summer, whenever the soil seems dry, gradually reduced in autumn. Do not water at all during the summer.

Soil: Well-rotted compost with about a fifth of sand.

Propagation: Very simple; by taking cuttings from the small stems, which break off very easily. Insert in some sand and spray lightly from time to time; they need plenty of warmth and shade. The operation is best done in summer.

THE CRASSULA GENUS (Crassulaceae)

Etymology: The name comes from the Latin *crassus*, or 'fat' describing the fleshy leaves of all species.

Description: The genus includes over 300 species of widely varying habit, appearance and requirements. The different species often grow in very different positions. Usually they have small, inconspicuous flowers and, apart from *Crassula falcata*, which has showy red blooms, they are not grown for their flowers. The flowers, which are grouped in cyme or corymb inflorescences, are usually pink or white with five petals, stamens and carpels. The opposite leaves are usually sessile, but may be attached in various other ways. In a great many species they are closely overlapping and because they are fleshy form a kind of column. In other species, such as *Crassula orbicularis*, they are arranged in flattened rosettes. Others, like *Crassula perfossa*, have perfoliate leaves in which the base is completely joined round the stem, which thus appears to pass through and pierce the leaf. The commonest cultivated species are shrubs like *Crassula arborescens* which is woody at the base.

Habitat: All species are from southern Africa.

Minimum winter temperature: 7–10 °C (45–50 °F); semi-shrubby species tolerate slightly lower temperatures.

Watering: Regular from spring to autumn, sparing in winter at minimum temperatures.

Soil: Humus-rich, but it should not contain insufficiently decomposed organic matter. Use compost with a little well-rotted leaf mould and sand for a porous free-draining mixture.

Propagation: Cuttings can easily be taken from most species; insert in just moist sand at a temperature of at least 21 °C (70 °F) and spray for light humidity until roots develop. Species which form rosettes often put out runners with new plantlets at the end which can be used for propagation.

▲ *Crassula falcata*

▼ *Crassula corymbulosa*

211

DOLICHOTHELE LONGIMAMMA (Cactaceae)

Etymology: The name comes from the Greek *dolikós*, or 'long', and *thelé*, or 'breast', because of the long tubercles growing on the stem.

Description: This cactus is easy to identify because from the earliest stages the stem is completely covered with long, fleshy, conical tubercles ending in areoles which have a ring of pale, flexible spines. The epidermis is green with transparent spots. The flowers are yellow.

Habitat: From Mexico.

Minimum winter temperature: 4 °C (39 °F).

Light: As much as possible with full sun.

Watering: Regular in summer, whenever the soil looks dry, gradually reduced in autumn; do not water at all during the winter.

Soil: Very porous, composed of compost with some sand and finely crushed chalk or brick. Repot fairly regularly because the strong, fleshy roots tend to grow through the drainage holes.

Propagation: Old plants may put out sideshoots which can be removed and treated as cuttings; insert in sand, keep very warm and spray lightly from time to time. However, as a rule plants are grown from seed in spring, following the usual method for very fine seed. Growth is very slow.

THE ECHEVERIA GENUS (Crassulaceae)

Etymology: The generic name commemorates the painter Atanasio Echeverria y Godoy who visited Mexico from 1787–1797 and did illustrations of many local plants.

Description: Herbaceous, perennial, evergreen succulents with fleshy, usually flat, leaves arranged in a rosette. Stemless at first, they usually develop a short stem and where the old withered leaves are attached new plantlets appear and sometimes put out branches and adventitious roots, especially when the stem is semi-trailing, as in many species. The flowers, usually clustered in rather long racemes, are red or orange, or often red or yellow. *Echeveria elegans* has light blue-green, almost flat leaves with a thick bloom, and coral-pink flowers. *Echeveria derembergii* has round or slightly cylindrical rosettes with short, fleshy, red-tipped leaves and short racemes of orange flowers. There are many hybrids, as the plant often cross-breeds spontaneously.

Habitat: All species are from Mexico.

Minimum winter temperature: 4–10 °C (39–50 °F), or slightly lower.

Light: Very strong; the plants usually need full sun or very intense, diffuse light. This is the main problem when growing them indoors.

Watering: Frequent in summer, as little as possible in winter when many of the lower leaves will shrivel. The plants soon pick up again in spring if kept in a cool, bright, frost-free position.

Soil: Compost with some sand to give a porous mixture. *Echeveria derembergii* does better if some well-rotted leaf mould is added.

Propagation: Very easy, by taking cuttings or by removing sideshoots, often with ready-formed rudimentary roots. Early summer is the best time. Keep warm and dry to stop the new plants rotting. It is also possible to remove leaves and lay them on moist sand to produce new plants at the base. As the plants tend to deteriorate during the winter it is a good idea to renew your stock periodically so that you always have young, attractive specimens.

ECHEVERIA GLAUCA (Crassulaceae)

Description: Probably the hardiest, most popular species. Its rigorous, sturdy growth in fact makes it difficult to grow indoors, as it will not tolerate high winter temperatures though it will do all right in, say, an unheated spare room or some other cool, bright position; it will thrive on neglect until it starts into growth again in spring and can be put out into the open for the summer. It has rosettes of large, grey-green, spatulate leaves with a small point at the centre and a narrow red margin which appears in a good light. It gradually develops a stem with a tendency to grow horizontally, from which many little rosettes of leaves grow. If left they grow larger at the tips of stoloniferous branches and root whenever they touch the soil. The inflorescences may be long, with flowers which are red outside and yellow inside. It is not generally known that the inflorescence is very longlasting if used as a cut flower and, although not very showy, it can make an unusual feature in an arrangement.
Habitat: From Central Mexico.
Minimum winter temperature: It must be protected from frost, but withers at temperatures over 10 °C (50 °F).
Light: Very strong, preferably with full sun.
Watering: Regular in summer, practically none in winter, especially at low temperatures.
Soil: Compost, with some sand to prevent waterlogging.
Propagation: By means of the new rosettes of leaves, which should be kept in a very warm, shaded place until they take root. Several rosettes can be planted together in the same pot as most *Echeverias* do not need much room to spread. They are often used to create a good border round other plants.

ECHINOCEREUS DELAETII (Cactaceae)

Etymology: The name comes from the Greek *echínos*, or 'hedgehog', and *Cereus*, as this genus used to be classed as *Cereus* but was later classified separately because of certain botanical differences.
Description: The genus consists of a number of very varied species, some upright and cylindrical in habit, others longer and creeping. This particular cactus is a low, clumpy plant which does not grow more than 20—25 cm (8—10 in) high. The stem is pale green with as many as twenty ribs. The areoles which grow on them bear many radial spines, four central spines and a great many long, white, hairlike bristles covering most of the stem. It looks like a small version of *Cephalocereus*, or 'old man cactus', but it grows more quickly and puts out a number of sideshoots at the base making it more compact and attractive to look at. It has small, pink flowers.
Habitat: From Mexico.
Minimum winter temperature: 4 °C (39 °F).
Light: Very strong, preferably with direct sun.
Watering: Regular during the growing season, but reduced in autumn; do not water at all during the winter.
Soil: Well-rotted compost with quite a lot of sand. Add a little powdered chalk to make the bristles strong and help them keep their colour.
Propagation: By cuttings preferably in summer, removing the sideshoots which form at the base. Lay them on lightly sprayed, just moist sand or stand them upright supported by a small stick, but do not insert the tip in the sand. Keep warm in a shaded position.

EUPHORBIA RESINIFERA (Euphorbiaceae)

Description: Most of the 1,000 and more species belonging to this genus are true succulents and a great many are cactiform. Many make good pot plants, though for some small, delicate species a greenhouse is almost essential. *Euphorbia resinifera* is a very branching, bushy plant which may form large clumps. The grey-green stems, which remain fairly short in cultivated plants, are four-sided with short, tough, brown spines occurring in pairs on the raised angles. As the plant grows very slowly it can be left in a pot for years. The yellowish flowers are inconspicuous, so the plant is just grown for its general appearance. As in all related species, damaged stems secrete a thick latex known as euphorbium which used to be used as gum; it is an irritant substance which causes blistering.
Habitat: From Mexico.
Minimum winter temperature: 4–6 °C (39–43 °F).
Light: A very well-lit position, with full sun.
Watering: Regular from spring to autumn. Do not water in winter at minimum temperatures, but in warmer conditions an occasional watering may be given.
Soil: Well-rotted compost free of all insufficiently decomposed organic material and some sand. Keep an eye on the drainage and repot if you suspect waterlogging.
Propagation: By cuttings taken from stems or branches. Let the cut dry before inserting in just moist sand and peat. Keep very warm in a shady position. Dry the latex on the cut with a wad of material dipped in hot water, or stub with a hot cigarette end.

FAUCARIA TUBERCULOSA (Aizoaceae)

Etymology: The name comes from the Latin *fauces*, or 'jaws' because the fleshy, concave, leaves have tooth-like appendages along the margins.
Description: These small, evergreen, almost stemless succulents have large, fleshy, dark-green leaves which are keeled and tri-angular and occur in pairs at right angles to the pairs on either side of them. They have dentate margins with projections which look like spines but are soft and unarmed. The upper side is irregularly marked with wart-like, whitish tubercles. The plant grows very bushy and flowers quite freely, bearing yellow flowers at the centre of the two top leaves.
Habitat: From South Africa.
Minimum winter temperature: 7–10 °C (45–50 °F).
Light: Very strong, in the sunniest possible position, although light shade may be required in very hot weather, especially in a poorly ventilated position.
Watering: Like the rest of the family, these succulents are very prone to rotting, so should be watered very cautiously even in summer, making sure the soil is really dry before giving more water. Do not water at all in winter and also make sure the plant is not left in a damp place, particularly at minimum temperatures.
Soil: Very porous. Use well-rotted compost and some sand, but also add some fine stone chips to keep the mixture well-aired.
Propagation: By dividing the clumps at the roots. Shoots growing from the base can be treated as cuttings; insert in pure sand, kept very warm and almost dry, and spray occasionally until the roots are properly formed.
Remarks: All species of this genus tend to become infested by mealy bugs and should be treated with white oils from time to time, making sure you reach the points where the leaves are attached. Wash with water after a few days.

THE HAWORTHIA GENUS (Liliaceae)

Etymology: The name commemorates Adrian Hardy Haworth (1768–1833), the English botanist and expert on succulents; he wrote a number of monographs on the subject.

Description: A large genus which also includes a great many hybrids, as cross-breeding between different species and also with the related genus *Gasteria* occurs very easily. Most species have rather flat, rosette-forming leaves, but they often grow bushy and form colonies. In many species the thick, fleshy leaves are leathery and dark green, often marked with whitish tubercles or warts and sometimes inserted spirally with grooves on the surface. In many the tip of the leaf is perforated on the upper side with translucent marks and lines which let light through to the tissues below. The inconspicuous inflorescences consist of long spikes of small bell-like flowers, white, green or pink in colour. All these plants do well indoors and although not very showy in appearance they are small and easy to grow.

Habitat: All species are from South Africa.

Minimum winter temperature: Ideally about 10 °C (50 °F), but the plants can tolerate warmer conditions.

Light: Good but diffuse. Direct sunlight turns the leaves a reddish or bronzy shade which makes the variegation disappear. It also dries them so that they become less succulent and attractive-looking.

Watering: Regular in summer, very sparing in winter depending on temperature. They will tolerate completely dry conditions especially at the recommended minimum.

Soil: Humus-rich, composed of compost with a little well-rotted leaf mould and sand to improve drainage.

Propagation: In their second year the plants readily become bushy, so shoots growing from the base or sideshoots can be removed, preferably in early summer. Keep almost dry until they root.

HUERNIA HYSTRIX (Asclepiadaceae)

Etymology: The genus is named after Justus Huernius (1587–1652), a Dutch missionary and the first collector of plants from the Cape of Good Hope.

Description: The genus consists entirely of succulent plants which have fleshy stems with raised ribs bearing small teeth. In this species the stems are very angular; they are dark or grey-green, turning bronze in the sun, with caducous spines on raised teeth. The flowers are bell-shaped with fused petals opening into a flattened limb with five acuminate lobes. They are purplish-brown with yellow spots.

Habitat: From the province of Natal, in South Africa.

Minimum winter temperature: 5–7 °C (41–45 °F).

Light: Needs full sun to flower.

Watering: Regular in summer, sparing in winter; do not water at all at minimum temperatures.

Soil: Well-rotted compost with a fair proportion of sand for a free draining mixture.

Propagation: As these plants sprout easily and the stems branch out, propagation is simple. Use shoots which have already rooted or take cuttings; this involves breaking off branches and planting them in pure sand during the summer. Keep in a shaded position and spray lightly, but avoid very moist conditions which might cause rotting.

KALANCHOE TOMENTOSA (Crassulaceae)

Etymology: The name is commonly thought to be Chinese in origin, although it has been suggested that it may have been a pure invention on the part of its originator, Michel Adanson (1727–1806), the French botanist and zoologist, author of a number of treatises including a Natural History of Senegal.

Description: This very handsome succulent has an erect, fleshy, branching stem covered with down. The leaves, which are ovate-acuminate, or lanceolate when mature, and slightly concave on the upper face, are completely covered with thick white down. Towards the tip the margins are slightly·dentate with brown markings. The flowers, which are unlikely to appear except in very adult plants, are whitish with brown markings. However the plant's real beauty is its foliage.

Habitat: From Madagascar.

Minimum winter temperature: 7–10 °C (45–50 °F); at lower temperatures the plant loses leaves.

Light: Very strong, with direct sun except in summer when it likes shade.

Watering: Frequent in summer, practically none in winter, depending on temperature.

Soil: Well-rotted compost with a little sand for a porous, well-drained mixture.

Propagation: Cuttings may be taken from the tip when a plant has lost leaves and needs renewing; place in a very sandy mixture at about 21 °C (70 °F) in the shade, preferably in late spring or early summer. It is also possible to propagate by leaf cuttings during the summer; break off a leaf, lay on just moist sand and keep at a high temperature in a shady position.

THE LOBIVIA GENUS (Cactaceae)

Etymology: The name is an anagram of Bolivia, where some species were originally found.

Description: The genus includes several species of globular or cylindrical, often dwarf cacti. The number of ribs and number and type of spines vary. Flowers may appear from any of the areoles on the stem, not just at the tip, and they again vary greatly in colour; although often red they also occur in various shades of pink, orange, yellow and violet and in some forms white. Identification is often difficult, but all species if properly grown are very free-flowering and most readily form clumps, making propagation easy.

Habitat: The species have an enormous distribution area, stretching from the Bolivian Andes to Peru and Argentina.

Minimum winter temperature: 7–10 °C (45–50 °F), but if kept completely dry they will tolerate slightly lower temperatures.

Light: Very strong with full sun, although light shade in very hot weather makes the flowers last longer and keeps the stems a better colour.

Watering: Frequent in summer, none in winter at minimum temperatures, though an occasional watering may be given in warmer conditions.

Soil: Fairly rich, composed of some well-rotted leaf mould and sand with compost. In nature the plants grow not in predesert conditions but in savanna-like territory with grasses and shrubs which eventually form humus in the soil.

Propagation: By removing sideshoots from the base in summer. They should have already formed roots but, if not, dry off the cut or the place where the shoot has been broken off and place in clean sand in a shady position.

THE MAMMILLARIA GENUS (Cactaceae)

Etymology: The name comes from the Latin *mamilla* or 'breast' because all species have tubercles, sometimes very prominent.

Description: This genus of over 350 species is one of the largest in the cactus family and also one of the most widely cultivated. The small, rather spiny plants are globular, often becoming cylindrical with age, and they readily put out branches and form clumps. The areoles usually occur at the tip of the tubercles, but there are small felt-like reliefs in the axils and branches and flowers grow from these, not from the areoles as in other cacti. The flowers usually appear on the upper part of the stem, arranged in a ring round the cephalium or apex. When an axillary areole has flowered once it will not flower again, so it is essential for plants to continue growing. Although there are a number of different forms in the various species three main groups can be distinguished. The first type consists of globular plants which are slightly cylindrical when mature; the tubercles have areoles at the tip with many slender, mainly radial spines which sometimes become woolly and almost hide the stem; the axillary areoles are small and sunken. In the second type the stem is again globular at first and then cylindrical, but the tubercles are cone-shaped with a wide base; the areoles at the tips have a few strong spines and leave the epidermis uncovered, while the axillary areoles are felt-like and clearly visible. The third type has fairly slender, completely cylindrical, very branching stems with short tubercles; the areoles at the tip are completely covered with fine, radial, intersecting, though not very long, spines which again more or less cover the stem. In this last type branches are not attached very firmly and will break off at a touch.

Habitat: Most species come from the southern United States and Mexico.

Minimum winter temperature: 4–10 °C (39–50 °F); if temperatures are allowed to go any higher the plants will not get the necessary rest period and will not be able to flower.

Light: Very strong. When the stem is protected by spines or bristles the plants will tolerate direct sun, but the second type, with uncovered epidermis, needs protection as too much sun and heat damages the tissues.

Watering: Regular from March to October, none in winter, especially if the plant is being kept at a low temperature with a view to making it flower.

Soil: Well-composted farmyard manure or compost with some sand. A little powdered chalk is good for the spines, as with all cacti.

Propagation: Some species, particularly those with slender, cylindrical stems, readily put out branches, and offsets can easily be removed in summer; put to root in a shady position in almost dry sand or sand and peat. Other species, particularly those with conical tubercles and short spines, hardly form clumps at all except in old plants. They must be grown from seed if available, sown in spring by the usual method for very fine seed.

▲ *Mammillaria zeilmanniana*

▼ *Mammillaria theresae*

NOTOCACTUS SCOPA var. RUBERRIMUS
(Cactaceae)

Etymology: The name comes from the Greek *nótos*, or 'southern', and *cactus*, perhaps because the genus comes from South America.
Description: This genus has a characteristic globular stem which becomes cylindrical when mature; it has very close, slightly spiral ribs densely covered with areoles from which soft, hairy, white spines grow, surrounding the central brown spine and covering the stem almost completely. The flowers, which grow towards the tip, are satiny yellow, darker at the centre. The plant is free-flowering even indoors, so long as it gets the winter rest period it needs. In the variety *ruberrimus* the areole's central spine is crimson.
Habitat: From southern Brazil.
Minimum winter temperature: 4–7 °C (39–45 °F).
Light: The sunniest position available.
Watering: In summer whenever the soil looks dry; with small plants in a sunny position this may mean every day. As a rule do not water in winter, although in warm conditions an occasional watering may be required.
Soil: Very porous, composed of well-rotted compost with a fair amount of coarse sand and fine stone chippings for perfect drainage. Repotting is only needed when growth makes the plant top-heavy.
Propagation: Eventually this species makes offsets at the base which can be used for propagation. Remove and place to root in pure sand or sand with a little peat, kept barely moist to prevent rotting. At the end of winter seed may be sown in a fine, sandy, just moist mixture at 21 °C (70 °F). Keep the young plants in a shady position for the first year at least. As is usual, germination occurs easily, but growth is slow and often affected by drying out or rotting.

OPUNTIA MICRODASYS var. ALBISPINA
(Cactaceae)

Common name: Prickly pear.
Etymology: The name comes from the ancient Greek city Opus, capital of Locris: Pliny gave the name *Opuntia* to an unidentified spiny plant which grew there. However, this plant was in no way related to the present genus, which is American in origin and was unknown at that time.
Description: The genus consists of a large number of species with plants of varying appearance, the 'joints' of which may be cylindrical, short and globoid, or flattened. In the Mediterranean area many species grow outdoors, often spontaneously, but these are usually too large for house plants. *Opuntia microdasys* is almost a miniature species, with small, flat, oval joints, and makes an excellent pot plant. There are a number of varieties: *albispina* has tufts of white glochids (barbed bristles); *lutea* has yellow glochids, while in *rufida* they are reddish brown. The joints are modified stems which perform the functions of leaves. The funnel-shaped red and yellow flowers are unlikely to appear on pot plants and only occur on fairly old specimens.
Habitat: From Mexico.
Minimum winter temperature: 4–10 °C (39–50 °F).
Light: Full sun if possible.
Environmental humidity: Dislikes a damp atmosphere.
Watering: Frequent in summer, whenever the soil seems dry. Do not water at all in winter, but spray occasionally if the joints start to wither in warmer conditions.
Soil: Compost with a fair amount of sand.
Propagation: Slice off a joint, allow the cut to dry for a few hours and place in sand to root at about 21 °C (70 °F). Spray the sand.
Remarks: All *Opuntias* are prone to scale insect infestation and should periodically be treated with white oil.

PLEIOSPILOS SIMULANS (Aizoaceae)

Etymology: The name comes from the Greek *pléios*, or 'many, much', and *spílos* or 'mark' because of the translucent dots all over the leaves.

Description: These plants are very similar to *Lithops* and like them are often given the common name 'living stones'. They have two or at most two pairs of very fleshy leaves which are flat on the upper face and rounded or keel-shaped underneath. Each pair grows from the centre of the previous pair, which then soon withers. The plants are completely stemless and often form clumps. The flowers grow at the centre and may be white, yellow or orange.

Habitat: From South Africa.

Minimum winter temperature: 7–10 °C (45–50 °F).

Light: Very strong, even with full summer sun.

Watering: These plants are among those most susceptible to rotting caused not only by too-frequent watering but even by a rather humid atmosphere. In summer plants which get full sun can be watered whenever the soil gets dry, but in winter they must be kept completely dry and the tissues must not be allowed to absorb and store too much moisture from the air.

Soil: Very porous and free-draining, composed of compost with a good proportion of coarse sand. Do not cover the collar with soil but surround it instead with fine stone chippings so that water cannot collect.

Propagation: Clump-forming plants can be divided; repot offsets in a suitable mixture and keep almost completely dry at first. However, plants are more often grown from seed sown in March in a fine, sandy mixture, following the usual method for very fine seed. The seedlings grow very slowly and must be kept in the shade until fully formed and watered only by an occasional spraying.

SEDUM RUBROTINCTUM (Crassulaceae)

Etymology: The name comes from the Latin *sedeo*, or 'I sit', describing the way many species become established on walls or rocks, growing into cushion-like formations. They are often known as stonecrops.

Description: The genus contains about 600 species of drought-loving succulents, but not all make good pot plants as they are hardy by nature and often only suited to a cold climate and stony setting. One of the most attractive of the half-hardy species which do not tolerate frost is *Sedum rubrotinctum*, often wrongly known by its old name *Sedum guatemalense*. It is a small branching plant with fleshy, cylindrical, close-growing leaves which generally only appear towards the stem tips, while new branches develop from the lower, leafless part. The leaves are glossy green, turning a reddish bronze in a good light. Pot plants which get full sun are at their best in spring and autumn but lose their fine colour with too much summer sun. The plant has small, yellow flowers with five petals which grow in cymeose inflorescences, but they are not a particularly attractive, or important feature.

Habitat: From Mexico.

Minimum winter temperature. 4–7 °C (39–45 °F). At higher temperatures the plant is liable to mealy bug infestation; it also continues to grow and loses its compact shape.

Light: Excellent, preferably with full sun.

Watering: Regular in summer, none in winter at the recommended minimum temperatures. In warmer conditions some spraying will keep the plant healthy without causing continued, stunted growth.

Soil: Porous: compost with some sand and fine stone chippings.

Propagation: It is very easy to take cuttings. Place cuttings from branch tips in a suitable mixture and keep very warm and almost dry. The leaves break off easily and will also root and put out new plantlets at the base if placed on just damp sand.

SETICEREUS HUMBOLDTII (Cactaceae)

Etymology: Although this cactus is still known by this name among nurserymen and growers, it is classed as a member of the *Borzicactus* genus; the name commemorates Antonio Borzì (1852–1921), the Italian botanist who founded the botanical gardens at Messina and Palermo in Sicily.

Description: The plant has long, erect, fairly slender stems which are dark green with whitish spots. It has at least ten ribs. The oval areoles grow on protuberances; they are covered with yellow felt and have many fine radial and central spines. The long, tubular flowers have relatively unexpanded petals and are crimson to pink in colour. Flowering is nocturnal. Because it has a slender stem and tends to grow a lot the plant may become semi-creeping.

Habitat: From Peru.

Minimum winter temperature: 5–10 °C (41–50 °F).

Light: Very strong. The plant likes sunlight and in a shady position the stem grows even thinner than usual.

Soil: Compost with some sand. Very effective drainage is required.

Propagation: Adult plants branch out, so cuttings can be taken in summer. Let the cut dry to prevent any rotting and place in just moist sand and peat in a shaded position. In young plants the tip can be sliced off and used as a cutting, which will stimulate the growth of sideshoots on the parent plant.

STAPELIA GIGANTEA (Asclepiadaceae)

Etymology: Linnaeus gave the genus its name in memory of Joh. Bodaeus von Stapel (died c. 1636), the Dutch physician who produced an edition of Theophrastus's main work on plants.

Description: The genus consists of about seventy-five species of succulent plants. They have large, angled, leafless, sometimes downy stems with dentate angles. The flowers grow at the stem base and have a tubular or funnel-shaped corolla, with five fairly long expanded lobes which are pointed and often hairy. Many species have a crown at the mouth of the tube. *Stapelia gigantea* is one of the finest, with upright, branching velvety stems and very prominent angles. It has enormous flowers which in nature may grow to 45 cm (18 in) in diameter, although they stay much smaller in cultivation. The funnel-shaped corolla has five broad, pointed lobes and is pale yellow, marked with small, irregular, wavy, crimson lines. Unfortunately most species, and this one in particular, are pollinated by carrion-feeding insects, especially blow flies, so the flowers give off an abominable smell of rotting flesh to attract them.

Habitat: From southern Africa.

Minimum winter temperature: 7–10 °C (45–50 °F). At higher temperatures the plants are liable to mealy bug infestation, which may also occur in summer in a dry, poorly ventilated atmosphere.

Light: The plants like direct sun, but when grown in pots they may need some shade against very hot sun in a dry summer.

Watering: Frequent between March and October, practically none in winter at the recommended minimum temperature.

Soil: Very rich in humus and free-draining, composed of well-composted farmyard manure with some sand.

Propagation: As the plants readily form clumps and branch out, propagation is easy during the summer. Break off branches, insert in sand and keep in the shade, spraying lightly so that the soil does not get too wet. Transfer to a pot when roots form.

THE TRICHOCEREUS GENUS (Cactaceae)

Etymology: The name comes from the Greek *thrichós*, or 'hair', and *cereus*, describing the hairy areoles which occur on these succulents.

Description: These columnar cacti are often branching or put out shoots at the base. Most have short spines clustered closely on the areoles which occur on the ribs. The number of ribs varies, but is always large. The flowers, usually nocturnal, appear on the areoles where a thick, woolly growth first develops as an indication that flowers will follow.

Habitat: All species come from South America, from Bolivia to Argentina and Peru.

Minimum winter temperature: 4 °C (39 °F). If kept completely dry the plants will tolerate occasional drops in temperature.

Light: Full sun.

Watering: Regular throughout the growing season, none in winter. Flowering depends on a rest period without watering at low temperatures.

Soil: Compost mixed with at least one sixth of sand as a very porous, free-draining mixture is required. Repotting is needed because sideshoots develop, not because of upward growth.

Propagation: By cuttings, using the branches which develop at the base. Let the cut dry off in a shady position before inserting the tip in sand. Spray lightly until roots appear and keep in the shade at about 21 °C (70 °F). Offsets often have roots even before they are detached and can simply be potted in a suitable mixture and watered with great care.

Collectors' plants

Most tropical and subtropical plants would undoubtedly do better as greenhouse plants than as house plants. Some will adapt to indoor life, even if they become rather less attractive or flower less readily, but others really hate dry, airless conditions. Enthusiasts eager to grow such plants have to find some way of creating the necessary hot or intermediate greenhouse conditions. You can build out a small lean-to greenhouse or plant window beside a house window (or windows) on a balcony or at ground level. The window can then be opened in winter to let some heat from indoors into the glassed section. Temperature can be regulated and increased as necessary by means of a convector heater turned on for a suitable number of hours a day depending on the outside temperature. Obviously a small greenhouse of this type needs some means of ventilation, just like a normal-sized greenhouse, and some method of shading in summer. Tropical plants cannot support too much direct sun; to avoid this, stippled glass or plastic material such as 3 mm 'plexiglass' can be used. Besides providing the right temperature for each species it is important to create a humid atmosphere by spraying and sprinkling, and by watering the floor.

Most of the plants discussed like intermediate greenhouse conditions so it should not be too difficult to maintain a suitable temperature. However orchids, for example *Cattleyas*, grown in intermediate greenhouse conditions need slightly higher temperatures than usual with a winter minimum of 14 °C (57 °F) at night; they like airier, shadier conditions in summer. Various shapes and sizes of plants are listed, so the collector can choose those best suited to the available space and to the amount of warmth that can be provided. Some are small enough to be grown in a well-lit terrarium.

BEGONIA BOWERI (Begoniaceae)

Description: This miniature plant is a dwarf rhizomatous evergreen which has ovate-oblique green leaves with irregular reddish-brown markings on the crenate, ciliate margins. It grows very bushy and the rhizomes spread to form large, not always very compact plants. Because of its attractive appearance and size many hybrids and cultivars have been bred from it, including 'Bow-Joe' (Boweri x 'Joe Hayden'); the second parent of this variety is another hybrid of *Begonia mazae x Begonia reichenheimii* and has star-shaped, bronze-coloured leaves which are transmitted to its descendants. 'Bow-arriola' is a hybrid which has small, dark-green, star-shaped leaves with purple markings along the margins and veins.

Habitat: The species comes from the forests of the Chiapas and Oaxaca provinces of southern Mexico.

Minimum winter temperature: About 16 °C (61 °F), or slightly lower if it is impossible to provide adequate environmental humidity.

Light: Diffuse, out of direct sun. The plant will tolerate moderate light but the petioles will get very long.

Environmental humidity: Good, maintained at a high level in every way.

Watering: Frequent during the growing season, so long as the soil is never allowed to get waterlogged, which causes rotting of the rhizomes; sparing in winter.

Soil: Humus-rich and porous, composed of equal parts of leaf mould and peat with some sand or perlite. Sodden, heavy soil is the worst enemy of all *Begonias*, although they need a moist atmosphere, so excellent drainage is essential.

Propagation: By rhizome cuttings planted in sand and peat kept just moist at about 24 °C (75 °F). No covering is required. Large clumps can be divided.

BEGONIA SERRATIPETALA (Begoniaceae)

Description: This splendid, fibrous-rooted begonia is not at all easy to grow and really needs greenhouse conditions. It has a very fleshy, almost succulent, branching stem. The rather small, oblique leaves with very pronounced venation are deeply lobed, with dentate, curly-edged lobes. They are iridescent olive green in colour with red or pink spots on the leaf blade between the secondary veins. The main difficulty about growing the plant is that its very fine roots soon drown if the soil is too wet and the fleshy stems also rot easily, while the foliage likes a very moist, hot atmosphere. This means it is really only suitable for a hot greenhouse and needs special conditions and care.

Habitat: From New Guinea.

Minimum winter temperature: 16–18 °C (61–65 °F).

Light: Good, to preserve the beautiful pink spots, but without any direct sun.

Environmental humidity: Very high, increased in every way. Do not spray the leaves as this may cause fungus disease. Good ventilation is required to prevent stems and branches rotting in a too sill atmosphere.

Watering: Regular in summer, sparing in winter.

Soil: Very porous and preferably sterile, composed mainly of peat with some well-rotted leaf mould and sand. It is best to use a ready-sterilised proprietary brand of some very light mixture containing sand or perlite.

Propagation: By cuttings taken from stem or branches. Insert in a very sandy, sterile, barely moist mixture and keep at a temperature of at least 24 °C (75 °F). Although the cuttings like a moist atmosphere it is not a good idea to use a glass or plastic cover unless very large and well ventilated. A small enclosed space creates a still, damp atmosphere which will certainly cause rotting.

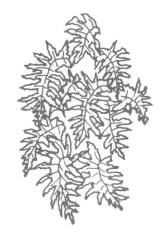

▲ *Cattleya* hybr.

▼ *Cattleya guttata leopoldii*

THE CATTLEYA GENUS (Orchidaceae)

Etymology: The name commemorates William Cattley (died 1832), a keen English collector of orchids and rare plants.

Description: This genus includes some forty species and countless hybrids and cultivars produced by intergeneric cross-breeding with *Laelia*, *Brassarola* and others. It is certainly one of the most popular and widely grown of orchids, and is also grown commercially for its long-lasting cut flowers. In fact these flowers are what many people first think of when they hear the word 'orchid'. Although modern cultivated forms are the result of successive hybridizations, the commonest parent species include: *Cattleya guttata leopoldii*, which has inflorescences composed of many rather small and scented blooms which have bronze-coloured, crimson-spotted petals and sepals, and a small purplish-red lip; *Cattleya mossiae* has large, scented, rose-purple flowers with broad, wavy-edged petals and sepals and a long pink, yellow-spotted lip which is tubular at the base, opening out into a frilled limb; *Cattleya trianae*, widely used for breeding because it is winter-flowering, has very large flowers with narrow sepals and large pink wavy petals; the purple, yellow-throated lip has a short tube and large frilled limb. In spite of cross-breeding with other different coloured genera, most hybrids are still characteristic shades of purple and rose-purple, although there are some highly prized pure white forms. Although *Cattleyas* have such beautiful flowers, at different seasons of the year depending on parentage, they tend to be rather clumsy and unattractive when not in flower. Often they have very long pseudobulbs and need a lot of attention to keep them growing tidily. They frequently require supports and even if suitable conditions can be provided they still take up space.

Habitat: For practical purposes the species can be divided into two groups: unifoliate plants with a single leaf at the tip of the pseudobulb, which are usually from Central America, Venezuela and Colombia; and bifoliate plants with two or three leaves growing from the pseudobulbs, which are mainly from Brazil.

Minimum winter temperature: 14 °C (57 °F), that is, intermediate greenhouse conditions.

Light: Excellent, but shaded in summer to prevent the leaves yellowing or scorching.

Environmental humidity: Very high. In nature the plants are epiphytic and develop a special tissue known as velamen on their roots, which can absorb moisture from the air.

Watering: Never overwater and let the soil dry out slightly between waterings. To allow a slight rest period after flowering (generally in late spring, though the season varies) let the plant partially dry out every two years, when repotting becomes necessary, and especially for three weeks afterwards, but do not allow it to dry out completely.

Soil: Ideally the plants should be grown in hanging baskets which allow water to drain away freely, but as this is not always possible even in a greenhouse they are often grown in pots. In this case the best mixture is three parts of crumbled fern fibre, osmunda if possible, to one of chopped sphagnum. Feed regularly with small doses of liquid fertilizer during the growing season, as the recommended potting mixture contains very little humus and is therefore poor in nutrients.

Propagation: Usually by division when repotting. Divide the rhizome behind the third or fourth pseudobulb and repot in a suitable mixture. The rhizomes should always be laid on top of the mixture with just the roots growing into it, otherwise rotting may occur. As already explained most plants need stakes to support the pseudobulbs and foliage and these should be placed in position when repotting as they may damage the roots if inserted later.

THE CYMBIDIUM GENUS (Orchidaceae)

Etymology: The name comes from the Greek *kymbé*, or 'cup', because of the shape of the lip.

Description: This genus of orchids includes epiphytic, semi-epiphytic and terrestrial plants with large egg-shaped pseudo-bulbs from which the linear or lanceolate leaves grow in a fan shape. In some true species the flower stalks are pendulous and sometimes as much as 1 m (3 ft 3 in) long, bearing up to thirty blooms, but in cultivated species they are upright or arching. In the flowers the dorsal sepal is erect and to some extent turned forward; the linear or lanceolate sepals and petals are about the same length, though the petals are sometimes shorter. The short, trilobate lip with raised side lobes is usually spotted at the top and attached along its length to the gymnostem. The true species are not usually found in cultivation but there are, at a conservative estimate, at least 1,500 hybrids; one reason for this is that the cut flowers may last as long as a month, making the genus a favourite of commercial growers. The plants do best in a cool or intermediate greenhouse.

Habitat: Most species are from Asia, especially India, although some are from Africa or Australia; they grow at high altitudes.

Minimum winter temperatures: About 10 °C (50 °F) during flowering (December to April); during autumn the night-time temperature should be about 4 °C (39 °F) to form flower buds.

Light: Excellent, out of direct sun.

Environmental humidity: As high a level as possible, but the plants like a fresh, airy atmosphere.

Watering: Regular all the year round, very slightly less frequent in autumn when flowering occurs.

Soil: Very rich in humus, composed of equal parts of compost, leaf mould, fern fibre and peat. Very good drainage is required with a deep layer of drainage material. Use large enough pots for the roots.

Propagation: By division. Remove four or five of the new pseudobulbs in autumn and place in damp sphagnum moss to root.

DIONEAE MUSCIPULA (Droseraceae)

Common name: Venus fly-trap.

Etymology: The name comes from the Greek *Dionaia*, one of the names given to the goddess Venus.

Description: This small, herbaceous, perennial insect-eater is fairly common in Northern Europe, and in a damp enough climate may not need to be grown in a greenhouse. The plant has tubers from which rosettes of leaves up to 20 cm (8 in) tall grow. The leaves have a flat, expanded petiole, and the rather fleshy bilobate blade has a single mid rib which is retractable. The margins are fringed with soft, spinelike teeth. When an insect touches the upper face, attracted by the red glands all over its surface, the two sides of the leaf snap shut and the teeth along the edges become closely enmeshed. The glands secrete an acid fluid containing pepsin to digest the insect's organic tissues, which are slowly absorbed by the whole leaf face. A spike of small, white flowers grows from the middle of the rosette of leaves and when correctly pollinated produces black, glossy seed capsules.

Habitat: The plant is endemic in the south-east of America: the narrow strip of humid sandy savanna in North Carolina.

Minimum winter temperature: 5–10 °C (41–50 °F).

Light: Very strong, with direct sun if the atmosphere is humid enough; in a poorly lit position the upper leaf face remains green and the glands fail to turn red.

Environmental humidity: As high as possible.

Watering: Very frequent in summer, regular in winter, but less often at the recommended temperatures. Do not allow any water-logging, as in nature these plants grow in moist, but well-drained soil. If possible avoid hard water, using instead rain water or water which has been boiled and filtered.

Propagation: Plants can be grown from seed, which will germinate easily under glass on damp chopped moss or by division in spring, keeping the new plants under glass.

DROSERA SPATHULATA (Droseraceae)

Common name: Sundew.

Etymology: The name comes from the Greek *droserós*, or 'dewy', because the glandular hairs on the leaf tissues make the plant appear to be covered with dew.

Description: The genus consists entirely of annual or perennial herbaceous insectivorous plants which grow in damp positions and catch insects by means of the glandular hairs covering their leaves. Usually red or pink, these secrete drops of a clear, sticky, sugary fluid which looks like water and traps insects. When one is caught the hairs fold over. The fluid becomes acid and slowly dissolves the animal protein, which is then absorbed by the plant tissue. In this way the plant, like all others of the same type, satisfies its need for nitrogen, which is in short supply in its natural environment. The leaves are arranged in a rosette and flowers may appear among them; they are usually white and grouped in scorpioid cyme inflorescences. *Drosera spathulata*, one of the most attractive species, suited to all temperate climates, has a rosette of flat, spatulate leaves.

Habitat: From Australia.

Minimum winter temperature: 5–10 °C (41–50 °F).

Light: Very strong, but it needs shade in hot weather, because it does not like a dry atmosphere.

Environmental humidity: Very high.

Watering: Frequent and plentiful. The soil must never dry out. If possible use soft water obtained by boiling, or use distilled water.

Soil: Use peat with sand for drainage, covered with sphagnum moss, still growing if possible.

Propagation: Plants are grown from seed if available; sow on damp chopped sphagnum moss and peat and keep under glass at about 15 °C (59 °F). If the plant does well and puts out shoots from the roots, these can be removed in spring and put to root in the same mixture; keep under glass at about 21 °C (70 °F).

HELICONIA JACQUINII PENDULA (Musaceae)

Etymology: The genus is called after Mount Helicon in Greece, where, legend has it, the Muses lived.

Description: This large herbaceous plant, which closely resembles the banana tree is evergreen and rhizomatous with robust stems and unusually long leaves. In the parent species the inflorescences which appear among the foliage are erect, consisting of stiff, sheathed spathe-like bracts arranged alternately in two lines on either side of the wavy rachis or axis. The flowers which grow inside the bracts are half-hidden and inconspicuous and the bracts are the real attraction, ranging in colour from salmon pink to crimson, and green at the tip. In this variety, as the name suggests, the inflorescence is pendulous.

Habitat: From the Fiji Islands, but found in other Pacific islands too.

Minimum winter temperature: 16 °C (61 °F).

Light: Very strong, but without direct sunlight.

Environmental humidity: High and increased as much as possible, though good ventilation is needed to prevent the air stagnating.

Watering: Regular all the year round, but slightly less frequent in winter. Let the soil dry out partly between waterings, and never allow it to get waterlogged as this can make the rhizomes rot.

Soil: Rich in humus, composed of well-rotted leaf mould with half the amount of compost and peat and some sand for maximum drainage.

Propagation: By rhizome division in spring. This is not possible unless you have a greenhouse, as the plants are too large for makeshift glass or plastic covers, which would in any case make the atmosphere too humid.

ONCIDIUM KRAMERIANUM (Orchidaceae)

Etymology: The name comes from the Greek *ónkos*, or 'hook', because the lip has an outgrowth at the base.

Description: This enormous genus of over 600 species and a great many hybrids consists of epiphytic plants which mainly have pseudobulbs with leaves sheathing the base and one or two leaves at the tip. The flowers are very varied, as is the general habit of the plants; there are some upright, dwarf species, while others are exceptionally large with very long inflorescences. The genus's distribution area is very extensive, covering different conditions, from sea level to heights of 4,000 m (11,000 ft) so there are species suited to cool, intermediate and hot greenhouses. *Oncidium kramerianum* is an intermediate greenhouse plant, not unduly large, with very unusual flowers, and although now rather rare it is still a collector's favourite. It has small, rounded, slightly angular pseudobulbs with a single leaf. The flowers have a linear, erect, dorsal sepal and petals resembling an insect's antennae. The large sickle-shaped, frilled wing sepals are yellow with brown spots, or orange with yellow spots; the very expanded lip is yellow and wavy with a band of red-brown markings at the edge.

Habitat: From Ecuador and Columbia.

Minimum winter temperature: 14 °C (57 °F).

Light: As bright as possible without direct sun.

Environmental humidity: A high level. In summer spray twice a day to keep the air humid and counteract the heat.

Watering: Regular in summer, reduced in winter, but do not allow waterlogging.

Soil: Composed of equal parts of fern roots, preferably osmunda, and chopped sphagnum. Repot once a year about March and feed lightly during growth. This plant does not have a well-defined growing season and may flower several times a year.

Propagation: By division when repotting. With small plants put single pseudobulbs to root in moist sphagnum kept very warm.

THE PAPHIOPEDILUM GENUS (Orchidaceae)

Description: Some plants of this attractive-leaved genus can be grown indoors, although they may not flower, and *Paphiopedilum insigne* can be kept on a cool veranda if the atmosphere is humid enough; but there is no doubt that it is much easier to grow many beautiful hybrids and make them flower in intermediate or hot greenhouse conditions. All hybrids and cultivars are terrestrial plants with rather long, narrow, sometimes lanceolate leaves growing from the base and arranged in a fan shape or rosette, often with paler markings or marbling. The flowers always have the pouch-shaped lip characteristic of the genus, hence the popular name slipper orchids. They vary in shape and colour from the rounder, more compact forms derived from *P. bellatulum* to those from *P. rothschildianum*, with slender, acuminate petals.

Habitat: Most hothouse cultivars are derived from species from Assam, Burma and Borneo.

Light: Diffuse and not too strong, with plenty of shade in summer.

Environmental humidity: Always very high.

Watering: As these terrestrial plants do not store food they should not be given a complete rest period. Water less frequently for about a month and a half after flowering, which is also the best time for the plant's annual repotting.

Soil: Although the plants are terrestrial, use the same mixture as for epiphytes, composed of two parts of fern fibre (preferably osmunda) to one of chopped sphagnum. Since the plants do not have a rest period and the roots are very fleshy a less porous mixture might cause rotting of the roots or collar. A good deep drainage layer is needed, and pots of a suitable size for each plant should be used. The recommended potting mixture is poor in nutrients, so during the growing season feed with liquid fertilizer at regular intervals, and water in between, preferably with soft water.

Propagation: By clump division in spring. Water moderately until the new plants are well established.

PEPEROMIA VELUTINA (Piperaceae)

Description: A very attractive, though delicate species. The fleshy, red, branching stems tend to grow trailing rather than upright if they do not get enough light. The leaves are fairly small, though if properly tended they may grow 5 cm (2 in) long. Their growth depends on humidity as well as light. The ovate, velvety blade is bronzy-green with a pale band along the mid rib and narrower stripes along the side veins. The underside is reddish. The plant is very delicate and sometimes does not do very well even in a greenhouse, but it is very beautiful.
Habitat: From Ecuador.
Minimum winter temperature: 16 °C (61 °F).
Light: Very good, but diffuse, without direct sun. If possible overhead light is best, otherwise the plants will need to be turned frequently, as the stems tend very much to grow crooked.
Environmental humidity: Very high, but the level cannot be increased by spraying as this will mark the leaves' velvety texture.
Watering: Like all members of the genus this species is fairly succulent, so water regularly in summer and sparingly in winter, making sure the soil never gets waterlogged.
Soil: Humus-rich and porous, composed of equal parts of well-rotted leaf mould and peat with some sand to stop the mixture becoming too heavy.
Propagation: By stem cuttings, inserted in just moist sand and peat or perlite at about 21 °C (70 °F). Do not cover, as this may cause rotting. Leaf cuttings are also easy: remove a leaf and lay it on some moist potting mixture. Do not cover with the mixture but use a small stone to keep the leaf base in place. Use large-grained perlite rather than sand for drier, lighter conditions.

THE PHRAGMIPEDIUM GENUS (Orchidaceae)

Etymology: The name comes from the Greek *phrágma*, or 'shelter, defence', and *pédilon*, or 'sandal', probably because the sound resembles the name of the closely related *Paphiopedilum* genus. The name also describes the flower's slipper-shaped lip.
Description: This genus, which is, as has been said, closely related to *Paphiopedilum*, consists of rhizomatous plants which form large clumps of long, narrow leaves growing from the roots. The flower stalks usually bear racemose inflorescences rather than single blooms. The dorsal sepal is erect and turned forward, with similar wing sepals. The lip is shaped like a pouch or slipper, but in most species the petals are the characteristic feature – long, slender and pendulous and often even twisted or spiral. This genus is less common than *Paphiopedilum*, partly because its blooms do not last as long either on the plant or when cut, but there are a number of hybrids, many derived from *Phragmipedium caudatum* which has pendulous, twisted petals sometimes 70 cm (27 in) long.
Habitat: Most species are from southern America and are the American equivalent of Asia's *Paphiopedilum*.
Minimum winter temperature: 13–16 °C (55–61 °F).
Light: Good, but diffuse, out of direct sun.
Environmental humidity: As high as possible.
Watering: These plants do not need a clear-cut rest period. They should be watered regularly in summer and rather less often in winter, so that the soil can dry out slightly in between. Avoid waterlogging by half filling the pot with drainage material.
Soil: The mixture should be composed of two parts crumbled fern roots to one of chopped sphagnum moss. Feed regularly with small amounts of fertilizer during the growing season. In a very hot atmosphere, if care is taken over the amount of water given, you can use equal parts of chopped sphagnum moss and leaf mould with some sand and small pieces of charcoal.
Propagation: By clump division in spring.

SARRACENIA DRUMMONDII (Sarraceniaceae)

Etymology: The name commemorates Michel Sarrasin (1659–1734), who introduced the plants into Europe.

Description: These plants are insectivorous. They are stemless, rhizomatous, herbaceous perennials which have variously coloured pitcher-shaped leaves (or ascidia) growing from the roots and ending in an expanded or forward-turning lid (or operculum) with winged appendages along its length. The flowers have five fleshy, persistent sepals and five deciduous petals. The ascidia have nectar-producing glands outside and also, more closely distributed, inside, where slanting hairs entice insects towards the funnel. As the upper part is very smooth the insects often fall into the sticky fluid secreted, which destroys the insect, trapped as it is by the long downward-turning hairs growing on the lower parts of the leaf-wall. Insects are not digested, but the tissues absorb their chemical components, which provide a good supply of nitrogen for the roots. This species has upright ascidia some 60 cm (24 in) high; they are funnel-shaped, narrowing at the base, and green in colour with dark red veins. The plant has purple, drooping flowers.

Habitat: From the swamps of southern Georgia, northern Florida and Alabama.

Minimum winter temperature: The plant tolerates temperatures around freezing point, but can be grown at a minimum of 4–7 °C (39–45 °F).

Light: Excellent, but with some protection from strong direct sun, especially in summer, to obtain a cooler, more humid atmosphere.

Watering: The soil should never be allowed to dry out, though this species does not like waterlogging either. It cannot stand hard, alkaline water, so should be watered with rainwater or boiled, filtered water mixed with some distilled water.

Soil: Very acid: two parts peat to one of sphagnum moss.

Propagation: By rhizome division in spring; keep the soil fresh and the atmosphere very humid.

THE SELAGINELLA GENUS (Selaginellaceae)

Etymology: The name comes from the Latin *Selago* which was used for a type of *Lycopodium*, a genus of closely related plants belonging to the same class.

Description: These small, very ancient, herbaceous plants are classed before ferns, although their archaic forms coexisted in the Devonian period about 200 million years ago. The present-day forms have small stems with little, scale-shaped leaves which have an appendage (or ligule) at the base to absorb water. The very branching stems may grow trailing or partially upright. The plants are often used for decoration in greenhouses, where they can be placed under the benches to enjoy the very moist atmosphere there. As pot plants they are extremely delicate and do best in a terrarium. The most beautiful species is *Selaginella martensii*, which has fleshy, scale-like leaves growing very close together on rather short, semi-erect, very branching stems which look like fern fronds. In most other species the leaves grow further apart and the stems are less branching, so the general appearance is not as attractive.

Habitat: Species are found in all tropical and sub-tropical regions of the world; *Selaginella martensii* is from Mexico.

Minimum winter temperature: 10–16 °C (50–61 °F) according to species. However, if you cannot provide plenty of humidity it is better not to let the temperature get too high.

Light: Good, but not too strong and with no direct sun at all.

Environmental humidity: Increased in every way possible.

Watering: Frequent: the soil must never dry out, but nor should water be allowed to collect, as this may kill the delicate and not very vigorous root system.

Soil: Very porous and rich in humus, composed of equal parts of peat and chopped moss and sphagnum.

Propagation: In most species propagation is easy, as adventitious roots form spontaneously on the small stems; these are removed and can be made to root if there is enough humidity.

SMITHIANTHA X HYBRIDA (Gesneriaceae)

Etymology: The name commemorates Matilda Smith (1854–1926), the flower painter who from 1878 to 1923 did illustrations for the *Botanical Magazine*.

Description: The genus consists of eight species of perennial, rhizomatous plants with scaly rhizomes and stems which usually occur singly. The opposite leaves, which are borne on petioles, are cordate at the base and velvety on the upper face. The pendulous, stemmed flowers grow in terminal inflorescences; the long, tubular, usually oblique corolla has fairly expanded lobes and is spotted at the throat. The flowers come in various colours. The species have been much hybridized, either with each other or with other gesneriads, so there are now a large number of compact-growing cultivars, and this is a definite improvement, as their natural habit is rather untidy. All these plants have a period of total rest, usually during the winter, when the small rhizomes should be kept dry and then brought back into growth. However, in hybrids the rest period may occur at any season and this means you can have plants in flower all the year round.

Habitat: All true species are from Mexico and Central America.

Minimum winter temperature: Dry rhizomes should be kept at about 13 °C (55 °F), plants in growth slightly warmer.

Light: Excellent, as soon as growth appears, but without direct sun.

Environmental humidity: Very high throughout the period of growth.

Watering: Moderate when the rhizomes are first brought into growth, then regular throughout the growing season. When the plant begins to droop after flowering reduce watering and stop altogether for at least two months.

Soil: Very light, composed of two parts of peat to one of leaf mould with some sand; a sterile, all-purpose potting compost with a little sand or perlite would be suitable.

Propagation: Plants can be reared from seed in spring, using the usual method for very fine seed. Cuttings may also be taken in spring and kept at 21 °C (70 °F) under glass or plastic, with frequent airings. The rhizomes can be divided when they are brought into growth; although they are not big they readily produce new plants, even from pieces which you might expect to be much too small.

VANDA 'NELLIE MORLEY' (Orchidaceae)

Etymology: The name is of Indian origin.

Description: These epiphytic orchids have an erect, leaf-bearing stem without pseudobulbs. Although there are only about sixty species, there are a great many hybrids, so the total number of forms is hard to calculate. The plants may be low and erect or very large and even climbing with aerial roots. The flat, linear, carinate or rounded leaves vary in size and are arranged alternately on either side of the stem, sheathing at the base. The flowers are grouped in axillary racemes. The similar-looking sepals and petals are extended but taper at the base into a wedge shape. The lip is spurred and trilobate with two small, erect, lateral lobes and a much smaller central lobe pointing forwards. Most types now found in cultivation are hybrids. 'Nellie Morley', one of the finest, is an old-established favourite. It has leathery, linear leaves. The racemes consist of large, fleshy, rounded flowers with pale pink petals and sepals spotted all over with red. The small lip is red with paler edges.

Habitat: All species are from India, the East Indies and the Philippines, but they are also widely grown in Hawaii.

Minimum winter temperature: 15 °C (59 °F) for most hybrids; some species need slightly lower temperatures.

Light: Very strong, but diffuse with protection from strong sun.

Environmental humidity: Very high.

Watering: Frequent in summer but avoid watterlogging; very sparing or none at all during the winter, especially with cylindrical-leafed species which need a period of complete rest.

Soil: Very porous to prevent rotting, composed of two parts crumbled fern roots to one of chopped sphagnum moss. If the plant needs a complete rest period the potting mixture will need to be moistened after it, by standing the pot in a bowl or bucket of water.

Propagation: By stem cuttings; cut below a node with aerial roots and new growth will appear at the base of the cutting. Offsets growing at the base can also be used to provide new plants.

In a cool climate an unheated room can be used as a cool greenhouse, if you have a room which you are not able to heat but which is large, airy and humid enough to grow plants in. The main requirement is good light so the room should preferably be south-facing. For best results cool greenhouse plants usually just need some protection against freezing temperatures, particularly long spells of frost; if possible a minimum temperature of about 4 °C (39 °F) should be maintained so some form of heating will probably be required during cold spells. As this temperature is obviously too low for living accommodation your cool greenhouse will have to be a separate room or unit. Environmental humidity is not essential, as it is in intermediate or hot greenhouses, and may in many cases be harmful at low temperatures, but good ventilation is vital and so is excellent light, perhaps even with direct sun in summer.

In most cases a cool greenhouse can be made from a glazed balcony or sun room with sliding windows, or windows which open very wide. The glass should not be completely transparent however, as even succulents, including delicate types, which in nature are used to similar conditions, cannot tolerate exposure to direct sunlight through glass without acquiring usually permanent scorch marks, because of the high proportion of infra-red rays which pass through. Polythene in particular is lethally transparent to these rays and also lets through a dangerous amount of ultraviolet rays. Stippled greenhouse glass, although much heavier and so more difficult to handle, is the most suitable material as it has maximum transparency to rays of the visible spectrum. The amount of ventilation also varies according to climate; more is required in hot, dry conditions.

The best plants for this setting are the more delicate succulents, some of which are described in the following pages. However, the plants listed as suitable for glassed-in verandas include many which will also do well in cool greenhouse conditions, depending on the minimum winter temperature they require.

ARGYRODERMA ROSEUM (Aizoaceae)

Etymology: The name comes from the Greek *argýreos*, or 'silvery', and *dérma*, or skin, because of the silvery-grey colour of the leaves.

Description: A small, succulent plant which looks like a stone split down the middle and in fact belongs to the group of so-called 'living stones'. The two fleshy leaves are flat inside and rounded outside. They gradually open to allow a new pair of leaves to grow at right angles to the old leaves which gradually wither away. The mauve-pink flower also emerges from the centre on a short stalk. When it appears the succession of leaves stops and the plant puts out one or more sideshoots which start up the cycle again. In this species the epidermis is bluish grey.

Habitat: From South Africa.

Minimum winter temperature: 7–10 °C (45–50 °F).

Light: Very strong, ideally with full sun.

Watering: Regular from April to September, whenever the soil seems quite dry; do not water at all during the winter, as these plants, like other related species, are extremely sensitive not only to moisture in the soil but also to damp air, and rot easily.

Soil: Very porous, composed of compost with some sand. If possible surround the collar with stone chippings rather than with potting mixture.

Propagation: Even with plants which form clumps, propagation by means of offshoots is fairly difficult and requires a very well-heated, shady position in summer, with almost dry sand. If seed is available, plants can be reared in this way, following the usual method for very fine seed.

THE CLEISTOCACTUS GENUS (Cactaceae)

Etymology: The name comes from the Greek *kleistós*, or 'closed' combined with *Cactus* because the flowers scarcely open.

Description: These columnar cacti usually have rather slender branching stems with many ribs on which the spiny areoles occur close together. The spines are often white or yellow and bristle-like; sometimes, as in *Cleistocactus straussii*, they grow so thickly that they completely cover the epidermis below. The rather small flowers are yellow, orange or red. The plants are elegant when young because of their slender growth; when mature they put out sideshoots and offsets at the base.

Habitat: From South America: Argentina, Uruguay, Paraguay and Bolivia.

Minimum winter temperature: 4 °C (39 °F).

Light: The sunniest position available.

Watering: Regular throughout the growing season, which starts with the appearance of a denser growth of spines on the cephalium; do not water during the winter, especially at minimum temperatures, though an occasional watering may be required in warmer conditions.

Soil: Composed of compost and sand; a little powdered chalk will be good for the plant.

Propagation: Stem cuttings can be taken when the plant branches out. Cut a sideshoot or an offset at the base and place in just moist sand in a warm, shady position once the cut has been allowed to dry.

COLLETIA CRUCIATA (Rhamnaceae)

Etymology: The name commemorates the French botanist Philbert Collet (1643–1718).

Description: The genus is composed of spiny shrubs. This species is the strangest of all. Stem and branches consist of a succession of flattened, triangular spines arranged alternately opposite or decussate in relation to the previous and following pairs. These perform the function of leaves which only appear on the young plants and are tiny and caducous. The small, white, bell-shaped flowerets which grow in groups at the base of the spines have a strong vanilla-like perfume. The plant often flowers twice, in spring and autumn. In ideal conditions the flowers are followed by small capsules containing two or three seeds. The shrubs grow very slowly so they can be left in pots for a long time in a cool, bright position.

Habitat: From Uruguay.

Minimum winter temperature: 7–12 °C (45–53 °F); at higher temperatures the plant may wither.

Light: Excellent, but protect young plants from direct sunlight.

Environmental humidity: Fairly good, but this should not be a problem at the recommended temperatures.

Watering: Regular in summer, sparing in winter.

Soil: Any good compost, so long as it is free-draining and does not get heavy and waterlogged. Either well-rotted leaf mould or well-composted farmyard manure with some sand would be suitable.

Propagation: Plants can be grown from seed, sown in a sandy mixture at a temperature of at least 20 °C (68 °F) and kept under glass; air the seedlings and wipe away any condensation. The seeds do not always germinate successfully and the small plants develop their characteristic appearance very slowly. It is not easy to take cuttings, which again root very slowly. If attempting this, use a very sandy mixture and keep in a cool position under glass to create a humid, but not stagnant atmosphere.

THE CONOPHYTUM GENUS (Aizoaceae)

Etymology: The name comes from the Greek *kónos*, or 'cone', and *phytón*, or 'leaf', because of the form of some species.
Description: These small succulents which also belong to the group of 'living stones' occur in two forms. The first form looks like a round, flat stone with a small slit at the centre from which the flower grows and which opens like a ring to allow new growth through; this type, unlike plants of related genera, does not have two fleshy leaves, but a single globe, apparently with a hole in the top. The second form also consists of a single globe divided at the tip into two short lobes which look like two leaves; the flower again appears at the centre. The epidermis tissues are often perforated with transparent spots which allow light through to the tissues below. The flowers may be white, yellow, orange or violet.
Habitat: From South Africa.
Minimum winter temperature: About 10 °C (50 °F).
Light: Very strong, with full sun.
Watering: Very sparing even during the summer and none at all during the winter. In spring start watering gradually when the plant looks almost dried up and the tissues are cracked; new growth will then appear at the centre of the old plant and often new plantlets will develop round it, forming small colonies.
Soil: Very porous, composed of very well rotted compost without undecomposed organic matter which might cause rotting, and some sand. As a precaution, plant in this mixture to within about 1 cm ($\frac{1}{2}$ in) of the collar and then finish off with a layer of stone chippings which will repel water and so prevent any waterlogging.
Propagation: If the plants develop offsets the clumps can be divided. Pot any offsets which have properly-formed roots separately and keep very warm and almost dry in a shady position until they are established.

FENESTRARIA AURANTIACA (Aizoaceae)

Etymology: The name comes from the Latin *fenestra*, or 'window'; it describes the plant's epidermis which is transparent and translucent on the upper side, like a window, so that the plant tissues can get the light they need with such a reduced stem. Tissues of this type are described as fenestrated, and in this case the adjective has become the generic name.
Description: Small, succulent plants with short, sprouting stems which in their natural setting are often almost completely buried, although in cultivation they may grow about 5 cm (2 in) above the ground. Like *Lithops*, they belong to the group of so-called 'living stones', but they are even more delicate and difficult to obtain. The genus consists of just two species. *Fenestraria aurantiaca* is the commoner of the two. It has small, short, grey-green stems which take on a reddish hue in the sun. The translucent, pearly tip is flat or just slightly curved. The flowers are golden yellow, but are unlikely to appear in pot-grown specimens.
Habitat: From South Africa.
Minimum winter temperature: 7–10 °C (45–50 °F).
Light: Very strong, in the sunniest position available.
Watering: Regular from April to October, none in winter. If the plants are kept in warmer conditions, though this is not recommended, and show signs of withering, they should be finely sprayed occasionally rather than watered or sprinkled, so that water cannot run between the stems and rot them at the base.
Soil: Like related genera, these plants are highly sensitive to excessive humidity, so they need a very porous mixture composed of compost with some sand and stone chippings round the collar. Use small pots with an excellent drainage system.
Propagation: Although the plants are usually clump-forming, division is not at all easy. It can be attempted using practically dry sand at a temperature of at least 24 °C (75 °F) in a shady position during the summer; give an occasional fine spraying.

LITHOPS HELMUTII (Aizoaceae)

Etymology: The name comes from the Greek *lithos* or 'stone', with the ending *ops*, or 'look', because the plants look like small stones. Their common name is in fact 'living stones'.

Description: These plants are an amazing example of mimicry and of adaptation to environmental conditions. In stony deserts their structure protects them both from excessive heat and from the attentions of hungry animals. All species have much the same form — a fleshy body almost completely buried which, at ground level or slightly above, splits into two segments separated by a narrow division. The tips are truncated, flat or rounded, and the upper side is perforated with translucent lines or spots allowing sunlight through to the lower part of the stem. The flowers appear in the centre, between the two segments, which spread out to give the buds room to open; this also allows two new segments to form at the centre which gradually replace the old parts as they die away.

Habitat: From the pre-desert regions of South Africa.

Minimum winter temperatures: 5–7 °C (41–45 °F).

Light: Very strong, even with full sun.

Environmental humidity: Very harmful as it causes rotting.

Watering: Regular, whenever the soil gets dry, until the two sections of the stem are turgid and flowers appear in summer or autumn. After flowering or when the new internal segments are forming stop watering till the old formations have completely died away, then water cautiously until growth has definitely started again. Usually the rest period falls in winter.

Propagation: If correctly tended old plants should put out new shoots. These can be removed with a small piece of stem and put to root in pure, lightly sprayed sand and kept at a high temperature, but out of direct sun. Plants can be grown from the very fine seed, in the usual way, by sowing in spring at a temperature of at least 21 °C (70 °F). As with all succulents the seeds germinate very easily but a great many of the young plants are lost.

LOPHOPHORA WILLIAMSII (Cactaceae)

Etymology: The name comes from the Greek *lóphos*, or 'crest', and *phoréo*, or 'I bear', describing the raised woolly, spineless areoles.

Description: A very slow-growing plant with globular or semi-spherical stem and spineless, woolly areoles on rounded protuberances. They are almost smooth at the base of the stem, but covered with thick down towards the slightly concave tip where the small, pink flowers appear, followed by pink fruit with black seeds. Old plants put out new shoots, but they grow so slowly that this does not very often happen. The plants contain hallucinogenic alkaloids from which a bitter, emetic drug is extracted; in the plant's native lands it was used in religious ceremonies by the ancient Aztecs and by some North American Indian tribes.

Habitat: From Texas and Mexico. It has a number of local names including 'peyote', and 'xicori'. The Apaches know it as 'ho' and the ancient Aztecs as 'teonanacatl'.

Minimum winter temperature: 4–7 °C (39–45 °F).

Light: It likes full sun or very strong, diffuse light.

Environmental humidity: No special requirements.

Watering: Regular in summer in a sunny position, whenever the soil gets dry. Do not water during winter, but if the stem starts to shrivel spray lightly, especially at temperatures higher than recommended.

Soil: Very porous, composed of compost and about a quarter of sand. The plant is very sensitive to moisture round the collar so provide a top layer of stone chippings which will not retain water. Use larger pots because of the plants' large, extended roots.

Propagation: From seed sown in a just moist sandy mixture at about 20 °C (68 °F). Protect young plants from sun for at least a year. Old plants which have put out new shoots can be used for propagation, but rooting does not occur easily and the young stems are very liable to rotting.

239

SOEHRENSIA FORMOSA (Cactaceae)

Etymology: The name commemorates J. Soehrens, a collector of South American cacti.

Description: These cacti are closely related to the *Lobivia* genus. They have a very large, globular stem with a great many ribs bearing the felt-like areoles which have strong, yellow, downward-curving spines. Generally there are five radial spines on the lower part of the areole with a longer central spine. The bright red flowers are closely clustered at the tip of the plant.

Habitat: From north-western Argentina.

Minimum winter temperature: 5 °C (41 °F).

Light: Very good, if possible with full sun.

Watering: Regular from March to October, less frequent in autumn and none at all in winter, except for an occasional watering if the temperature is above the recommended minimum.

Soil: Free-draining, composed of very well composted farmyard manure with some sand. The pots used should be large enough for each specimen but not so large that the weight of soil becomes excessive.

Propagation: These cacti hardly ever form clumps, so plants must be reared from seed in spring. Sow on fine, sandy mixture at 21 °C (70 °F) and keep moist in a shady position until germination, then gradually provide more air and light, although the seedlings should be kept out of direct sun for at least a year. Growth is very slow.

STULTITIA CONJUNCTA (Asclepiadacea)

Etymology: Unknown.

Description: Very similar to *Stapelia* but much rarer. A creeping, herbaceous plant with large, fleshy, trailing stems, grey-green in colour and leafless, with pointed reliefs in place of leaves. The flowers are not unlike those of *Stapelia*: a tubular corolla opens into an almost regular pentagon, with five tapering cream-coloured limbs and a very pronounced brown-spotted corona round the throat.

Habitat: From South Africa.

Minimum winter temperature: About 7 °C (45 °F).

Light: Excellent but diffuse, out of direct sun.

Environmental humidity: It dislikes humid conditions.

Watering: From spring to autumn water whenever the soil gets dry, but do not water at all for the rest of the year.

Soil: Well-rotted compost with a little well-rotted leaf mould and a third part of sand. The collar is particularly liable to rotting, so put a layer of free-draining stone chippings round it, as this will not hold any water.

Propagation: By means of sideshoots which grow easily and have usually already formed roots when the time comes to remove them. They then simply need to be potted and watered very sparingly.

Growing techniques

LIGHT AND TEMPERATURE

There are five generally accepted factors of plant growth: light, warmth, water, food and air. All five relate to nutrition and plant metabolism, but are so closely interrelated and interdependent that they cannot really be discussed separately. Your first consideration must therefore be to ensure that no single factor outweighs the others. For example, increased light and warmth cause faster transpiration, so a plant needs more water; with poor light and low temperatures a plant needs much less watering because its vital activities will be slowed down. If it gets only a moderate amount of light in relation to warmth and water the plant will survive, but its tissues will be weakened because they cannot build up the necessary food. Obviously plants have different needs as regards these five elements; the correct balance between them will vary according to the species and its original natural environment.

Although plants' needs differ according to their original habitat, they are still interrelated, and the factors of plant life and growth cannot therefore usually be ranged in order of importance. However, without a doubt insufficient light for the plants is the main difficulty that indoor gardeners encounter. Not only are there practical difficulties to be overcome, but there is also the problem of understanding the different factors involved and their interdependence. For example, our idea of what light is, is usually so intuitive that we never stop to think about it in relation to plants, a form of life very different from our own. Light, as the human eye perceives it, is only a tiny part of the immense field of energy which makes up the spectrum of electromagnetic radiations containing cosmic rays, gamma rays, X-rays, ultra-violet rays, visible light, ultra-red light and radio waves and others which merge into areas still unknown to science. Visible light to us means the solar spectrum, consisting of wavelengths which we perceive as different colours, and which we conventionally divide into bands blending with the nearest ultra-violet and infra-red rays to form solar light. The wavelength of light is measured in units known as 'angstroms' after the Swedish physicist A. J. Angstrom who lived in the first half of the nineteenth century: one unit is equal to one hundred-millionth of a centimetre. Vision is a sense peculiar to animal life, but it is not the same in all animals; some insects use only part of the spectrum the human eye can perceive, and possibly some kinds of animals use other forms of energy far beyond our perceptions, amounting almost to radar. Plants' vital activities take place within the visible range, but although it seems certain that chloroplasts have structural similarities with cells of the vertebrate eye, they use solar energy quite differently, since it manifests itself as a series of photochemical reactions. Essentially plants tap the various wavelengths not for vision but for energy, using a range of frequencies determined by their needs and not coinciding with those to which the human eye is most sensitive. Although this topic will be further discussed in the section on artificial-light gardening, it is worth explaining here that the vital process of photosynthesis principally occurs between 4,000 and 5,000 angstroms, but also to a great extent between 6,000 and 7,000, that is in the blue and red region; if this curve is contrasted with the eye's range of vision, it will be seen that its minimum coincides with the wavelengths which we most use: green and yellow.

This explains why you should not trust your own senses when deciding how much light plants need: plants use different wavelengths from us and in different ways. A place with enough light to read by may not be light enough for a plant to produce and use chlorophyll. You should therefore always try to give your plants as much light as possible (though not direct sunlight), otherwise you must expect stems to get leggy and leaves to lose their distinctive features, as tends to happen, for example, with *Monstera*, which if it does not get enough light tends to lose first the holes and then the indentation in its leaves, which become small.

It is impossible to lay down hard and fast rules; nor is it much good going round the house with a photometer hopefully looking for the right place for your plants. In general choose the best-lit positions and then proceed by trial and error, since

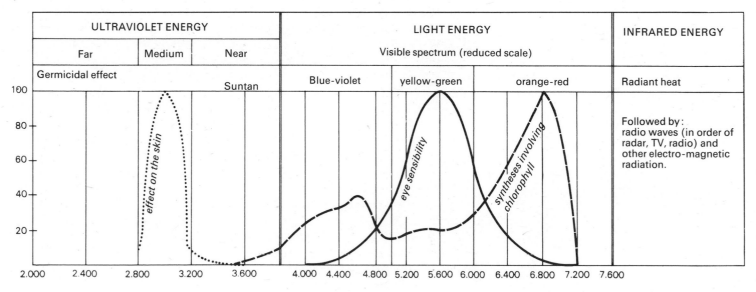

ULTRAVIOLET ENERGY			LIGHT ENERGY			INFRARED ENERGY
Far	Medium	Near	Visible spectrum (reduced scale)			
Germicidal effect		Suntan	Blue-violet	yellow-green	orange-red	Radiant heat

Wavelength in Angstrom

plants are often surprisingly adaptable. However there are some general rules which can be altered as necessary to suit particular circumstances.

1 Plants with completely green foliage tolerate moderate light more willingly than other plants. The darker the green of the leaves the better the plant will tolerate poorly lit conditions, though in a really bad light the tissues are often weakened and the plant gets spindly. Remember that plants use light to make food, but in the dark they use up their supplies in growth. In a poorly lit position they go on growing even if they have little food, but the new growth is feeble and attenuated.

2 Variegated plants with white or yellow-patterned foliage need much more light than green plants. Variegation has several causes; it may be due to a proliferation of cells without chloroplasts being superimposed on normal cells containing chloroplasts and masking them, or to viruses which prevent chlorophyll forming, or to any one of a number of other causes. The effect is always much the same: a partial or total lack, real or apparent, of chloroplasts in the cells which should be responsible for photosynthesis, with the result that only the green parts perform this function, and have to expend more energy on it. Since a smaller number of cells have to make more effort, they must be given every chance; that is, they must be given more light. Otherwise the plants will react by eliminating the cells without chloroplasts. They will lose their variegated markings and become completely green, so that the demands on them are less.

3 Plants with grey, silver or brown-coloured leaves often come from tropical undergrowth where the light is fairly dim and diffuse. The real reason for their colouring is not fully understood but it may sometimes be a protective device to

help the leaves merge with their surroundings. Such markings are also often combined with tomentum or hairs which control the turgescence of the stomata in a very humid atmosphere. Once a plant has developed these tissues it needs to use them, so unfortunately though these plants can tolerate poor light they also need the moisture-laden atmosphere found in their original habitat.

4 Plants with red or purple variegation or colouring need plenty of light. Their leaf tissues contain the same type of pigment as flower petals, usually anthocyanins, which mask whatever chlorophyll is present and only develop in very strong light. If there is inadequate light, the chlorophyll will reassert itself and the leaves will turn green again, just as a flower which blooms in the shade when it really needs sun will be much paler in colour than it should be.

5 Plants which have tissues to protect them against ultra-violet rays, for example, a white or silvery tomentum or down, or a waxy bloom, need direct sunlight. Otherwise they lose their defence mechanisms and become weak and feeble in appearance and growth. This category includes succulents, plants from high altitudes where the incidence of ultra-violet rays is high, and most plants which grow near the sea.

As regards temperature, plants of course have different requirements in winter and to some extent summer. In a hot, dry summer all you can do as a rule is protect plants against high outdoor temperatures by shading them from direct sunlight even if they like it at other times of the year, spraying the leaves frequently with water and, above all, moving delicate plants away from windows which reflect too much heat and glare. In winter the problems are more complex, and the best solution generally is to choose species which can adapt to the temperature you can provide. Remember that if a plant likes low temperatures, it will also want an airy position and its need for light will increase proportionately. Tropical plants, which thrive at temperatures above 16–18 °C (61–65 °F), do not need much ventilation; if the air is humid enough they only require a minimum of ventilation to prevent mildew and fungus diseases. It is more important to avoid sharp changes in temperature, although there should be a variation of about 5–10 °C (9–18 °F) between night and day, as is usual in nature. Generally speaking the minimum temperatures suggested for different plant species are for optimum greenhouse conditions and correspond to the three kinds of heated greenhouses – hot, temperate and cool – and possible intermediate variations. Indoor plants usually get less light and humidity, so these recommended temperatures should be reduced by two or three degrees for high temperatures, but can be kept the same for temperate and cool greenhouse plants which like as much light and air as possible. As a rule plants do not like sudden sharp temperature changes, which are fatal for some like *Codiaeum* and affect others in varying degrees; they should be avoided as far as possible. This does not mean you should never open a window in winter if you have tropical plants in the room; a normally heated house will soon warm up again after an airing, and the plants are unlikely to be affected. But a sudden drop in temperature before the heating goes on for the winter, or a cold spell after it has been turned off can be very harmful, especially when it lasts several days. If the heating is turned on again during a cold spring the alteration of cold days and hot air will be particularly damaging to plants which have just been through a long gloomy winter. Spring, traditionally the kindest season for outdoor plants, is often disastrous for long-suffering house plants, which only start to pick up when temperatures become more settled. You can help by only opening the windows during the warmest part of the day, making sure that plants do not stand in direct sunlight unless they really like it and are introduced to it gradually, otherwise the weak tissues may scorch, leaving permanent marks.

WATER: HUMIDITY AND WATERING

Water is vital to plants. Like other organisms plants are largely composed of water: they may contain 80% water in their storage organs, and in succulents possibly as much as 95%. Water conditions plant life in two ways: in the first place it serves to dissolve mineral salts in the soil which are absorbed by the roots and are essential to plant nutrition; in the second place, as moisture in the air it keeps the stomata turgid so that the processes of respiration and transpiration are possible. This important element also decisively influences the plant's vegetative cycle. In the tropics where light and heat are constant, water alone, as moisture in the air or in the soil, governs the incidence of rest or semi-rest periods, or the lack of such periods: the seasons are determined not by changes in temperature or in the hours of daylight, but by the amount of rainfall and humidity.

All tissues contain water. In higher plants it is normally absorbed through the roots and circulates through the stem and branches as sap, consisting of water and dissolved substances; it is then partly released through the leaf tissues by transpiration. This process creates a small microclimate round the foliage, which in normal circumstances in nature is adequate because it bears some relation to the surrounding atmosphere and climatic conditions. However in an artificial setting with unnaturally dry air it has little effect. As most house plants come from hot humid regions 50%–60% of atmospheric humidity is the minimum they will tolerate and an even moister atmosphere is often necessary for strong healthy plants. In damp climates the problem of dry air is caused mainly by central heating and can sometimes be solved just by opening a window to offset the drying effects of the heating system. However in climates of the Mediterranean type, it is a question of creating indoors a microclimate suitable for different species' requirements.

In the first place you should if possible stand vessels of water on top of radiators. Use large, shallow containers as the amount of evaporation which occurs is in direct proportion to the surface area in contact with the air (this is, of course, why the air is so damp near large stretches of water, including the sea). Stand plants in groups rather than singly as much as possible. Not only will they look more attractive like that, but the combined effects of evaporation and transpiration will create a more concentrated atmosphere round them. The simplest way of grouping pots is in large containers, trays or flower holders with a layer of wet gravel on the bottom, making sure however that the pots are not actually standing in water and getting waterlogged. Alternatively you can stand the plants on plastic supports, bricks or any other waterproof stand (not metal) over the water. The evaporation will create a moister atmosphere round the plants.

You can also encourage the aerial roots that are found in many plants, such as *Monstera* and *Philodendron*, to grow down towards the water so that instead of becoming woody and straggly they take a part in feeding the plant. Once the plants are dense enough to hide what you are doing you can often slip the shorter roots into little glass or plastic tubes with pierced rubber or plastic caps kept full of water and attached to the stem with plastic-covered wire. This gives the aerial roots a good supply of moisture, whereas if you are using a moss-covered support you will find it difficult to keep the moss permanently damp indoors. An additional advantage is that if you are away for a few days the plants will survive without watering. Small plants and plants which like plenty of moisture can be arranged in plastic trays containing a layer of damp (but not wet) perlite, preferably a large-grained type with pores so that the air can circulate. This classic method of sub-irrigation is used in nurseries where the pots are sunk in damp peat on the greenhouse benches. The trays must be plastic because with so much moisture metal will give off salts which could be bad for the plants. The plants will absorb

A pot plant obtains nourishment in the normal way; the essential nutrients are dissolved by watering which must take into account the plant's rate of absorption.

All tropical plants need a high level of environmental humidity, which can be achieved by placing pots in large containers on a layer of wet gravel. The pot base is not left standing in water to become waterlogged, but the water slowly evaporates round the plants creating a moist atmosphere.

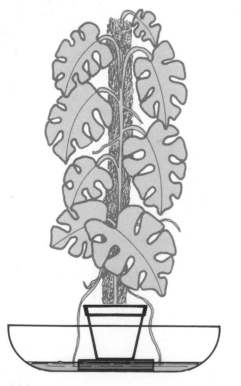

Below: Adventitious aerial roots should be trained down into a container of water while the pot itself is raised so that the soil does not become waterlogged.

some water directly through the pots' clay sides or drainage holes and so will need much less watering. Packing damp peat round the pots works very well in greenhouses which have heating under the benches to increase the rate of evaporation over a large area, but with smaller containers the peat simply impedes evaporation, so that it is difficult to control the amount of moisture: often the roots get too wet and rot as a result. As perlite is an inert material any roots that grow out through the drainage holes in the pot, as some are bound to do, will play a comparatively small part in the nutrition of the plant; the root system inside the pot will be self-sufficient enough to survive if the external roots are removed during repotting. If you are using peat, on the other hand, any roots that creep out of the pot will find a good growing medium and you must make sure that they do not develop too much; otherwise when they are removed the roots still in the pot may be left without root hairs and so will be unable to survive independently after repotting.

Foliage must be kept very clean so that the stomata do not get clogged up. Large smooth leaves can be washed, the rest should be sprayed. You will need a good spray which does not drip as it is such a chore moving pots to wipe up round them. Water is the only recommended cleaning fluid, and should be either distilled or boiled and carefully decanted to avoid leaving unattractive white marks on the leaves. This is especially important for leaves with a velvety texture. If you cannot get distilled water, use the water from the drip tray when you defrost your fridge (this is in fact distilled water too) or boil a saucepan full of water for half an hour and when cool pour carefully into a bottle: this simple operation will give enough water for several sprayings. Avoid any other liquid: milk, beer or even worse oil may give the leaves a deceptively attractive shine, but they are very bad for the tissues as they clog up the stomata and prevent respiration, transpiration and so on. Use cleaning fluids containing pesticides sparingly, because they too are oily and should be removed the next day by carefully washing the leaves with clean water. In healthy, well-kept plants the leaves should be in such good condition anyway that they do not require these extra attentions and the amount of shine will vary according to species. A plant which does not naturally have

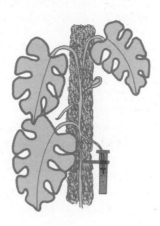

glossy leaves will look unnatural and plastic if it is given an artificial shine.

Watering is always the main problem for indoor gardeners. It must be said again that there are no set rules, except in the broadest sense, yet there will always be someone who wants to know if their plant needs a glassful of water or a litre a week. Of course some species like a moister potting mixture than others, but it is impossible to be more precise. Pot size and material, type of potting mixture, drainage, light, heat and humidity are all unknowns, and only by careful observation of all the factors involved can you decide how much water is needed. Generally speaking, frequent plentiful watering means the potting mixture should never dry out completely. Only a few plants need this amount of moisture, so take care, remembering that the definitions assume optimum conditions of light and heat. Often the potting mixture seems dry on top, but is much moister lower down. You can easily test this, unless you are concerned about your fingernails, by sticking your finger a couple of centimetres down into the soil. Regular watering means that the potting mixture needs to dry out slightly between waterings, though obviously not to the point when the foliage starts to droop. This is the commonest watering pattern and suits the needs of the largest number of species; unfortunately it is the most difficult to master as plants with tough foliage do not show signs of thirst for some time. You cannot judge by the colour of the potting mixture as this depends on the ingredients and is also affected by other variables.

Learn by experience and careful observation. Generally speaking a plant which needs regular watering should be watered when the potting mixture is dry more than two centimetres below the top. Moderate watering means water should be given less often, and this applies to such plants as those with tougher leaves and a slower rate of transpiration, especially during their semi-rest periods or if they are grown in large pots. However these less frequent waterings should be combined with an increased level of humidity in the air, at any rate for tropical plants. The leaves of such species as *Scindapsus, Philodendron* and particularly all members of the *Marantaceae* family should be sprayed frequently to keep them in good condition during the periods when they require less watering, so that the foliage

Above: When a plant has short aerial roots and thick foliage the root tips can be inserted into small tubes of water attached to the stems and hidden among the leaves; this allows the roots to absorb the moisture they need.

Below: Plants with large leathery leaves should be wiped regularly with a damp sponge; other foliage should be sprayed and sprinkled to keep the stomata turgid and the tissues dust-free. Use plain water for this.

stays healthy and beautiful while the root system develops new tissues in a well-ventilated growing medium. Only succulents and a few other plants need little watering, allowing the soil to dry out almost completely, but this only applies during their rest periods and at certain temperatures. However even at higher temperatures spraying succulents' stems and foliage is better than watering them more frequently, which can encourage rotting and tends to cause spindly, irregular growth. The few general rules about watering that do exist are all important. Above all each pot must have an effective drainage system, taking into account the pot size, so that the potting mixture does not get saturated at the bottom and drown the root hairs. Use a watering can with a long spout if possible and water slowly round the edge of the pot to avoid washing the collar bare, while at the same time moistening the clay sides of the pot. Remember that the new roots which are responsible for absorbing water usually grow sideways and reach out towards the sides of the pot. Watering in this way means that the parts of the root system which need most water get it, while the older parts, especially round the collar, which are more likely to rot, are left comparatively dry. Another advantage of this method is that the porous sides of the pot which tend to absorb water from the soil will themselves be moistened so that the delicate root tips which reach that far are not likely to get parched.

Water slowly and stop frequently, so that you can see when the water starts to trickle out through the drainage holes. This is the moment to stop, as pouring in more water will simply wash away the soil and its mineral salts. If when you have poured in a certain amount of water no trickle appears, stop anyway, as different potting mixtures have different rates of absorption. However if this happens repeatedly and the pot seems to retain too much moisture, it is worth removing the plant to check if the drainage hole is blocked, which can have fatal results for the plant. If on the other hand the water runs through immediately, the potting mixture has probably dried out too much and shrunk, especially if it contains a large proportion of peat or leaf mould. You should then give the plant a soaking: stand it in water to within a couple of centimetres of the rim and leave it for several hours until you can be sure that the soil is once again moist all through without being wet on top. Take the pot out of the water, let it drain well and put it back in its usual position. You can then resume normal watering. Watering from below is sometimes the only way, as in the situation just described, but is not advisable as normal practice. For one thing it is difficult to control the amount given, as obviously the soil at the bottom absorbs more moisture than the soil at the top. The salts tend to rise to the top rather than sinking to the bottom and gradually accumulate in the top layers. Although when watering from above the potting mixture round the plants is constantly washed away, this can be remedied with periodic applications of manure or fertilizer to redress the balance between different essential elements. However when some salts accumulate in the top layer of soil this creates an imbalance which is hard to put right, with disproportionate amounts of the most soluble elements. Moreover, because of this the root system tends to stay near the surface instead of growing downwards and making full use of the available space.

There are some exceptions, for example cyclamens, where the bulb (or corm) is so prone to rotting that watering from below is preferable in order to keep the collar relatively dry at all times. These plants in any case do not have a very deep root system and its functions can perfectly well be performed just below the surface: this is why they are often grown in fairly wide, shallow pots.

The importance of water temperature has been exaggerated, as the water is not likely to be so cold that it will damage plants. It is true that it should ideally be at room temperature but whether this is possible depends on how many plants you have, as does the question of whether the water can be left to settle for twenty-four hours in an open container to get rid of the chlorine which is added to water supplies nowadays. If you have a lot of plants, you most likely will not have room in your house to make these provisions. The best solution is probably to leave at least one full watering can standing overnight and use this water for the most delicate plants. You can then refill it with ordinary water for the others. To get the right temperature you can of course add some water from the hot tap, with the additional advantage that it will have lost some of its lime content in the course of

Always water carefully round the edge of the pot without disturbing the plant collar; this also moistens the pot's porous sides.

heating up. Although plants prefer rain water, you may as well forget this if you live in a city, where the rain is likely to be polluted so that it has no advantages over tap water. However a spell of heavy and prolonged rainfall will eventually wash the air clean, so it might then be worth collecting some rain water and using it, preferably for acid-loving plants like azaleas and hydrangeas, and also for ferns. Remember that plants are highly adaptable and will usually thrive on water which does no harm to people; they will also survive on water which is not strictly speaking fit for drinking so long as it does not contain detergents or other harmful substances.

If the soil gets too dry water runs straight through it. Soak the pot in water almost to the rim, until the surface of the mixture is moist again.

NUTRITION: POTTING MIXTURES

Plants draw their nourishment from salts dissolved in water and absorbed by the root hairs. This solution travels up the stem and along the branches by complex mechanisms of pressure and particularly tension. As it circulates round the plant and to the green parts, the process of photosynthesis supplies it with substances which are created with the help of energy from sunlight. As it descends, the solution nourishes the plant and carries food to the storage organs. This brief outline of the process shows that earth itself is not strictly speaking indispensable to plant nutrition and growth; apart from its chemical composition, it simply supplies the roots with support and anchorage. Plants can in fact be grown in any material, including inert material, so long as the necessary mineral salts are added in the right proportions for each species. There are about ten elements or nutrients essential to plants, and a number of other elements known as trace elements which are only needed in very small quantities. These trace elements are very necessary, and if they are deficient growth may be stunted, but they are not as important as the main elements: smaller amounts are required and the effects of deficiency are less drastic. Even in soil the essential nutrients may not always be present in balanced quantities. However if one particular nutrient is totally lacking in any given environment, often plants which grow there will not merely have become able to do without it, but will be quite incapable of growth in soil which does contain it. Thus on the one hand there are plants which like acid and cannot stand lime, and on the other plants which only grow well on limestone. The main essential elements include nitrogen, phosphorus and potassium.

Nitrogen is necessary for the formation of protein substances and is very important for the development and growth of the green parts: plants can only assimilate it in the form of nitrates. Phosphorus is essential for the formation of flowers and fruit-bearing shoots and the development of the root system; it can only be absorbed in soluble form, and excessive amounts of various elements, including calcium and iron, in the soil precipitate it, making it insoluble and impossible to absorb. Potassium is essential to the processes concerned with breaking down nitrates and synthesizing starch; without it nitrogen cannot be fixed. If one or more of the elements is deficient the plant as a whole cannot function properly and will exhibit abnormal growth. The essential elements also include carbon, oxygen and hydrogen, which form carbohydrates or sugars and are necessary for the process of photosynthesis; carbon and oxygen are absorbed from the surrounding air in the form of carbon dioxide by means of the plant's green parts; hydrogen is absorbed by the roots from the water in which all the other salts are dissolved. This gives particular importance to the acidity or alkalinity of the soil (or more generally of a solution), that is to say its pH value, or the negative logarithm of the concentration of hydrogen ions, measured by a scale from 0 to 14 on which distilled water shows as 7, indicating a condition of neutrality. Between 0 to 6·5 a certain level of acidity is said to exist, while from 7·5 to 14 the alkalinity increases. The pH value of the soil is a major consideration for outdoor gardening, but is less important for pot plants, especially indoor house plants. In potting mixtures specially prepared for house plants such components as leaf mould and peat, which are very acid, will play a large part, so special precautions will only have to be taken for those plants which really cannot tolerate lime.

Pot plants are grown in comparatively small amounts of potting mixture, and in a situation very different from natural conditions. The essential nutrients are gradually exhausted as they are absorbed, and may also be washed away by watering. The physical structure of the soil also gradually deteriorates and it can become useless as a growing medium if it gets so clogged that it loses its porosity and if its humus content, which cannot be automatically replaced, is reduced.

These problems can to some extent be overcome by periodic applications of manure or fertilizer and repotting if necessary, but the most important consideration is the initial composition of the mixture to make sure that the plants have a good growing medium from the start. The indoor gardener who has not got an outdoor garden or a patch in the open will obviously not be able to make his own compost, the basic ingredient made from layers of ordinary soil, manure, dry leaves and plant waste, chemical fertilizers and so on; although this type of compost is a part of many potting mixtures it is not suitable on its own for growing house plants. In England and America loam, a type of soil made from rotted turves, is widely used because of its fibrous texture. These potting mixtures are usually bought in small quantities, and it is difficult to know their exact composition. One important consideration is the stage of decomposition the organic matter in the mixture has reached, as indicated by increasingly dark colour, because some plants, for example bulbs and succulents, like as their base old soil with no organic residue, almost completely mineralized. Other common ingredients, especially in mixtures suitable for tropical plants, include leaf mould made from decaying dry leaves at varying stages of decomposition as indicated by the state of the leaf fragments and remains in the mixture; oak and beech which have a high acid content are the best leaves to use. Remember that the fleshier the roots are, the less rotted the potting mixture should be, as large fragments will help to create a better ventilated growing medium. If woody material is used, it is generally sieved to remove larger pieces and leave in smaller chips which help to prevent the rest caking. The large pieces make good drainage material. Almost all mixtures contain a certain amount of coarse sand from a fresh water source, which prevents the other ingredients caking together in a solid mass and keeps the mixture porous. Perlite (or agriperlite) can perform the same function as sand.

This is volcanic rock expanded and exploded by a heat process creating white, light, absorbent particles of various sizes which store up water and release it slowly. Both sand and perlite are inert materials, but when using them you should remember that sand repels water, but perlite absorbs it and is not suitable for such plants as succulents. Peat is a basic growing medium for a great many tropical plants. It comes from the more recent carboniferous formations of marshy plants, particularly sphagnum moss, and is available in various forms, sometimes already with added manure and usually in a dry state. Sphagnum peat is a very good compost material for acid-loving plants. Usually obtained from moorland areas, it is fibrous, light and extremely acid. It should always be damped before use as it tends to be resistant to normal watering. A useful corrective to limy soils and especially suitable for lime-hating plants, it is rich in humus, improves soil texture and decomposes very slowly. With its long white filaments, sphagnum moss is highly absorbent: it can hold up to four times its own weight in water. It has many uses, especially as it is unlikely to be attacked by micro-organisms, and can be broken up small and included in the potting mixture of plants which like constant moisture. It is normally used on its own or combined with other materials to provide a growing medium for the fleshy roots of epiphytic plants; sometimes it is added on top of the main potting soil to provide humidity and slight evaporation, but in this case care must be taken not to pack it too tightly round the collar, for that could encourage rotting. Other types of moss are sometimes employed but do not have the same qualities. For epiphytic plants, especially orchids, the best material is osmunda fibre or fibre from other ferns, broken into small pieces, moistened and used alone with sphagnum moss. Make sure the fibre has been carefully separated from the rhizomes which can vegetate and become quite invasive; cut the fibre into pieces of suitable size depending on use. Osmunda is difficult to get, and some experience is needed to prepare and use it correctly.

A substitute for these materials is lichen from hills or mountains, wood clearings, rocks or dead tree trunks. Lichens are organisms consisting of unicellular fungi and algae living symbiotically; some form crusts and obviously cannot be used as a growing medium, but there are also branched species resembling mosses. Less absorbent than sphagnum moss, easier to handle than osmunda, these lichens are useful for growing plants with very fleshy roots whether or not they are epiphytes. Often potting mixtures include a little well-crushed charcoal; this serves to absorb some of the gases which may be released by the process of decomposition, prevents unpleasant odours and generally keeps the soil well aired. Of course you can simply buy ready-made general-purpose potting mixtures. These sterilized, very light mixtures which contain a large proportion of peat are suitable for a great many house plants so long as sand or perlite is added. As they are so light they should not be used for large plants which might become top-heavy. In general they are useful for cuttings or small pots containing plants which like a light soil rich in humus.

Pots and containers are made in various shapes and sizes and of different materials. They must have a drainage hole or an effective drainage system.

POTS AND CONTAINERS

House plants are generally grown in pots so that individual needs as regards potting mixture, watering and feeding can be met. Clay pots with sloping sides are most commonly used, as wide across the top as they are deep, with a reinforced rim which also makes the pots easier to pick up, and with drainage holes for surplus water. Pots are available in a range of sizes up to 30 cm (1 ft) in diameter; above that heavier or stronger containers are needed to bear the extra weight of soil. For large plants wooden tubs sealed with a protective coat of waterproof varnish are very handsome, but because of their size they are usually better on a veranda or terrace, or in a very large room, rather than in the average indoor setting. However plant trolleys on castors are now available in a range of sizes, which solves the problem of moving large pots. As well as the traditionally shaped flower pot, there are other shapes including broad shallow bowls ideal for growing several species of plants together, and half-pots, which are half the normal depth and are particularly useful for bushy plants. Round pots, narrow at the neck, are very attractive especially for plants with a single upright stem. Unfortunately these pots have their disadvantages, although they hold a larger quantity of potting mixture. The main problem is that only a small surface area is in contact with the air, so that it is difficult for the rest of the soil to be well aerated; then when the time comes for repotting the pot will have to be broken as the rootball will have grown too big to pass through the neck. The main advantage of clay (or terracotta) pots is that, as they are porous, they allow air through into the soil, which is beneficial to the root system. However, to offset this, the porous material is also very absorbent and draws quite a lot of water from the soil; this does not matter if the root system has not yet reached the sides of the pot, but can be fatal if the plant is pot bound, especially if it is standing in a sunny position.

Old pots should be thoroughly cleaned before being used again. Wash them out and scrub with a stiff brush; ideally you should use a weak solution of copper sulphate to eliminate all traces of mildew or bacteria. New pots, on the other hand, should be left to stand in water for some time before use until they are well soaked and have stopped making that characteristic hissing noise which you will be able to hear; if you do not take this precaution they will simply suck all the moisture out of the soil when the plant is watered for the first time.

Nowadays plastic pots are popular as clay pots are becoming increasingly difficult to come by. As they are so light, 10 cm (4 in) is the maximum diameter which can be used, since with larger plants there is a risk of overbalancing. As plastic is not porous less water is required and unless you are careful you may find that the soil stays permanently wet. As the pots do not stain and are not liable to mildew, plastic is ideal for sub-irrigation; the layer of peat or other material on which the pots stand should be kept only slightly moist and watering should be drastically reduced. Plastic pots are also very suitable for cuttings which like plenty of moisture, so long as the potting mixture used is not too dense. Self-watering pots are also plastic. These are available in different shapes and sizes, with different watering devices. In some the soil is separated by a fine net from the base containing the water, and the moisture rises by capillary action; others have a small grating or openings in the sides through which strings or cords are inserted and these absorb water slowly. The main weakness of these pots, which would otherwise be very useful, especially when you have to go away on holiday, is that they supply the same amount of water all the year round and never allow for the rest or semi-rest periods which most plants need.

Plants grow well in other types of containers besides traditional flower pots, so long as certain precautions are taken. Clearly, hanging baskets and other similar types of holders which are both attractive and particularly well suited to the needs of such plants as epiphytes are on the whole unsuitable for indoor use. These

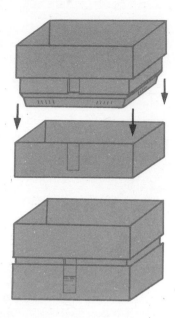

containers are meant to prevent water collecting and draining away too quickly, and this aim can be achieved provided you are willing to take the trouble to find a suitable position, but they are mainly used when constant slightly moist conditions are required and this is more or less impossible without a greenhouse, as the soil will dry out too quickly in normal indoor conditions. Metal containers should never be used because, as the damp soil causes them to oxidize, they may give off salts harmful to the plants. If you must use one, line it with heavy plastic pierced over the drainage hole. The drainage hole is in fact the secret of successful growth; there must always be a hole to let surplus water escape easily, otherwise the root system will soon suffer. Cover the hole with a curved crock or piece of broken pot so the soil cannot trickle out and then cover it with a suitable layer of drainage material, depending on the size of the pot. If the container you are using has no hole and it is impossible to make one, put a good deep drainage layer of stones and gravel so that the soil will be well above any water which might collect on the bottom. With all types of container, remember that the amount of watering necessary depends on whether or not the pot is made of porous material.

Above: One type of 'self-watering' pot. The water is kept at a set level and absorbed by capillary action.

Below: New clay pots should be thoroughly soaked in water before use so that the porous material does not absorb moisture needed by the root system from the soil.

Above: Cover all drainage holes with a good layer of drainage material so that the soil cannot be washed away and the roots are not in contact with any water which collects round the base.

Centre: Use the right-sized pot. A large plant in a small pot may over-balance and will not get adequate nourishment. If the pot is too large the root system may be damaged by the mass of soil. The middle pot is the right size.

REPOTTING

Pot plants need repotting more often than you may think, either because of growth or because the potting mixture is so exhausted that even with extra fertilizer it can no longer supply essential nutrients and so needs changing. In this context growth may mean two things: the plant may have become pot-bound, with the roots twined round the pot and often thickly matted on the outside so that the roots inside cannot breathe and grow; or, though the pot may still be big enough for the roots themselves, the stems, especially in plants with aerial roots, may have grown so long that a larger heavier pot is needed for balance. However remember that plants usually do better in pots which perhaps look too small for them rather than in over-large ones. The ideal of course is a perfect match between the plant, both roots and aerial parts, and its container. A too-large pot not only looks unattractive because it tends to make the plant in it seem puny, but can be positively harmful. The roots will certainly have room to develop, but they may not have the strength as they will be weighed down by a large amount of soil which most likely will be too wet anyway; a large proportion of the available salts will be wasted as the root hairs will not be able to reach them. When a plant needs repotting use a pot one size larger than before so that there is just a shallow layer of new potting mixture round the roots to allow them to grow easily.

The technique of repotting is very simple. When you are certain that a plant needs more space, choose a pot one size larger than the previous one, making sure that it is properly cleaned if it is old, or well soaked with water if it is new. The plant should be lightly watered so that the potting mixture is just damp: this prevents the soil crumbling away and disturbing the roots. The fresh potting mixture should also be damped so that it can be pressed down properly and is ready to absorb the final watering. Lift the pot with your right hand and place the fingers of your left hand on either side of the stem to support it. Then tap the rim of the pot lightly on the edge of a table or some other hard surface. If the plant is pot-bound the entire rootball will slip out into the palm of your hand; if you have made a mistake some of the soil will come away on its own and fall out. In this case all you need do is renew the drainage layer and put the plant back in the same pot, filling any spaces with fresh earth; leave it until it really does need more space. If a larger pot is required, make a good drainage layer suitable for the pot size and put a little potting mixture on top of it. Do not disturb the topsoil of the plant but simply remove about one inch of the old root ball at the bottom with a suitable implement and then lower it into the pot. Holding it in position so that the stem is at the centre of the pot, trickle fresh potting mixture in round it using your other

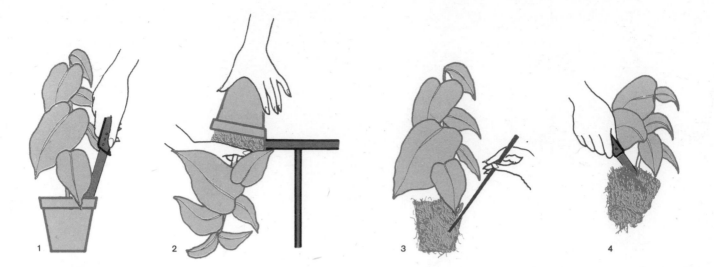

1   2   3   4

When repotting a plant first check whether the potting mixture comes away easily on its own. If it does not:

1 Run a knife blade round the side of the pot

2 Tap the rim of the pot on a hard surface, holding the plant with one hand until it slips out of the pot

3 Using a small stick carefully remove some of the old mixture and if possible the drainage crocks from among the roots

4 If the outer roots are dead and felt-like cut away until the new tips of living roots show

5 Now place the rootball in its new pot on a layer of drainage material covered with some potting mixture. The collar should be slightly lower than the rim. Run fresh potting mixture in round the edges and press down lightly

6 Start again if the plant is too high;

7 Or too low

8 The correctly potted plant.

hand or a small trowel, shaking the pot gently now and then so that all spaces are filled; press the mixture down lightly but do not pack it too tight. The plant collar should be slightly below the rim of the pot to avoid spillage when watering. The correct position for the plant is often the most difficult thing to judge. If it is too high you will have to go back to the beginning; if it is too low and you do not want to start again it is better to leave some extra empty space rather than packing more earth round the stem which can encourage rotting.

If the roots are thickly matted it may be advisable to cut some of them away with a sharp knife, stopping the minute you see the paler tips of growing healthy roots. Roots also need to be cut away fairly drastically when plants develop such an extensive root system that it is difficult to give them a large enough pot; in fact some plants have been known to break the pot, for example the so-called asparagus ferns, the *agaves* and some other plants. In this case cut away quite a lot of root, leaving the young tender roots intact as far as possible, and repot in a good new potting mixture in the same pot. Although the plants may lose some leaves they will soon start to grow again vigorously. After repotting always give a good watering to settle the soil so that any spaces fill up. You may find that the roots cling so tightly to the sides of the pot that it is difficult to get the rootball out. In this case use a small stick to push from below, through the drainage hole; at worst you may need to run a narrow-bladed knife round the sides of the pot to loosen the roots. In no circumstances should you tug hard at the stem to get the plant out as it can snap off. With large pots and plants rest the pot on its side on the ground, push through the drainage hole and pull gently at the stem until the rootball slips out.

With climbing plants growing on a support two people may be needed for the job, one to hold onto the plant and keep it at the right height. In special circumstances you may need to do a repotting operation in reverse, into a smaller container, when a plant is wasting away because of root damage or even root loss if the trouble is not spotted soon enough. Remove the plant from its pot, shake out the soil and with it any rotten roots, and carefully cut away any other dead-looking roots; then repot it in a much smaller container with very porous, just damp, potting mixture. Water very sparingly and carefully for some time.

With regard to firming the soil, the only case in which it should be necessary to do this is when the stem of the plant is rather long and overbalanced and just a cane or a stick is not sufficient to support it. It is only necessary to remove old soil from the surface of the pot when repotting-up ferns, as they do not like to have

any root disturbance whatsoever. After potting, leave enough space at the top of the pot to allow for watering. This is usually about $\frac{1}{2}$ inch for smaller pots and about $\frac{3}{4}$ inch to one inch for the larger pots and containers. One must be extremely careful not to overpot. Repotting can be carried out only if the plant is pot-bound. Overpotting occurs when the plant is put into a much larger pot than it needs, in this case the roots have too much soil to contend with and so eventually die.

PROPAGATION

One of the greatest pleasures of growing house plants is the possibility of creating new plants from your existing ones and observing the stages of their development. This is often a necessity, given that the life cycle of a plant is not so very different from that of any other living organism: youth, maturity, ageing and death. In nature some plants live far longer than a human generation (some trees are said to last 3,500 or 4,000 years), but the length of life varies according to species, starting with annual plants whose life cycle in effect lasts a single season.

However with pot plants the ageing process is often hastened by adverse conditions. The survival of the species is ensured in two ways. The first involves the sexual organs, fertilization and the formation of seed: this is known as sexual reproduction. In nature and in higher plants this is the commonest method of survival, as all these plants produce seeds. The second method does not involve the plant's sexual parts but its vegetative tissues or parts of them which can regenerate themselves and produce growth above or below ground. This ability, which occurs in nature in the lower plants as unicellular and multicellular budding, is known as asexual reproduction. In higher plants there are several types of spontaneous asexual reproduction: by means of runners, suckers, bulbils, or buds which form on the aerial parts (in this case the plants are inaccurately though vividly described as viviparous). However asexual reproduction is of greater importance when it comes to artificial propagation, and can occur by division, cuttings, air layering, soil layering and grafting. With sexual reproduction the enormous number of possible combinations which may result from the pairing of chromosomes in the formation of a new individual means that the offspring will never be identical with its parents but will differ from them, in accordance with the complex laws of heredity. In asexual reproduction on the other hand the offspring breeds true to the parent plant, and since it develops from the same vegetative tissues is a perfect duplicate. Some method of vegetative propagation is essential when it comes to multiplying plants which have variegated markings caused by gemmate mutation, or spores which have developed different characteristics of form or appearance. In any case, except with herbaceous plants growing plants from seed is a much longer process, often requiring special equipment.

Although growing plants from seed in a house or flat is not common practice because of the problems of providing enough space and suitable conditions, the basic principles still apply. Method of sowing depends on the size of the seed. Very fine seed should not be covered but should be pressed lightly onto damp soil – a light, fine mixture with some sand added is suitable. Larger seed should be covered with one to three times its own depth of seed mixture. It is essential to maintain even, moist conditions, as the seeds may not germinate if the mixture is allowed to dry out even for a single day. For this reason the seed tray or container is usually covered with glass or plastic to prevent rapid evaporation, although any condensation which appears should immediately be wiped away. Because of the constant moisture the seed mixture can easily develop mildew or fungus diseases, so it should be sterilized or consist of an inert material like perlite or of crumbled sphagnum moss which is unlikely to be attacked by micro-organisms. The germination periods of seeds vary and the length of time they remain capable of germination also differs from species to species. The seeds of tropical plants need to be very fresh and should be sown as soon as possible after gathering. The seeds of woody plants on the other hand are often very slow to germinate, while annuals sprout and grow most quickly.

The simplest method of vegetative propagation is undoubtedly division. With ornamental house plants this method is only used for plants which have leaves or stems growing directly from an underground stem or from tuberous roots like the

Propagation by root division is mainly used for plants with tuberous roots or caulinary leaves. Remove the rootball from the pot and gently shake free of earth. Choosing a suitable place, so that each piece has at least one bud, cut with a sharp knife and repot each section separately.

There are various ways of taking cuttings.
1 A geranium stem provides three types of cutting: from the tip, from a node and from a section of stem
2 A semi-hardwood cutting is more likely to root if cut just below a node. Remove the two bottom leaves or pairs of leaves and insert the two lower nodes at the edge of the pot with the tip near the drainage system so that waterlogging cannot cause rotting
3 With semi-hardwood plants it is advisable to take a cutting with a heel, i.e. with a small piece of bark attached to the node; this also encourages hardwood cuttings to root
4 A cutting can often be taken from a single bud by cutting it away from the shoot in the form of a shield bud and attaching it to the stock. This is the usual procedure with camellias.

Marantaceae or some *Liliaceae* such as *Asparagus, Aspidistra* and *Sansevieria*. Root division should always be carried out during the rest period just before the plant starts to grow again. Delicate foliage will need a very humid atmosphere to keep it healthy and this can be provided by some form of propagator until the roots have settled down again and begun to supply the necessary food. A simple plastic bag, or glass or plastic containers are possible substitutes for full-scale greenhouse equipment, but whatever method you use remember to remove the plant gradually from its enclosed situation, as once the leaves are used to moist surroundings they may wilt in a drier atmosphere unless broken in gradually. The removal and potting of shoots which appear at the base of plants, as happens with *Bromeliaceae, Agave, Aloe* and others, is a form of division if the shoots have already rooted. However if the buds do not have roots they should be treated like normal cuttings.

Taking cuttings is the most common and popular system used by growers of house plants. A great many plants are propagated by this method in nurseries too as it is a quick way of producing young attractive plants of a good shape and size. The procedure involves encouraging part of a plant – the tip of a stem or a cutting from it, sometimes even a leaf – to form roots. Although it is possible to take hardwood cuttings, it is not very easy where more exotic plants are concerned, so with house plants it is preferable to take herbaceous cuttings from soft stems and branches. This is not simply a way of getting new plants, but is often a necessity

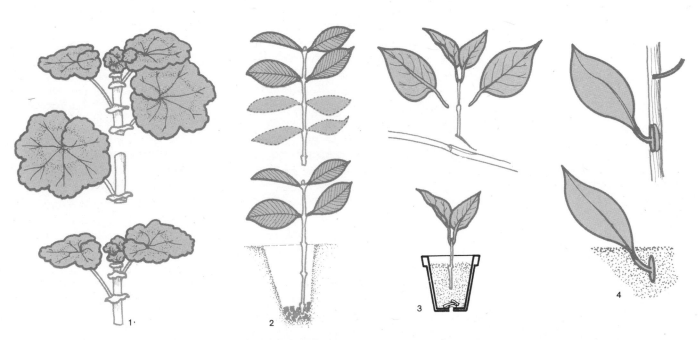

because so many house plants eventually get straggly and lose their lower leaves; taking cuttings from the tips will provide new plants with leaves right down to the base. The critical period before the roots develop comes after the cutting has been made but before the callus, a protective tissue covering the tip from which the roots will grow, has formed. This requires a moist, well-aerated growing medium. In all living organisms the formation of scar tissue depends on the presence of oxygen; even in humans wounds cannot heal if they are bandaged so that air cannot get at them. The quality of the growing medium is thus a decisive factor. It must be sterile and should not contain any organic material which in such moist

Above: A humid atmosphere is necessary to prevent the leaves shrivelling and encourage rooting. This can be achieved by means of a plastic bag supported above the cuttings. Make sure ventilation is provided if excessive condensation forms as a result of evaporation.

Below: Begonias can be propagated by leaf cuttings. Make nicks in the main veins and place so that the veins are in contact with some damp, very porous potting mixture. New plantlets will grow at each cut if the level of moisture and ventilation is right.

conditions might encourage mildew or rotting; for preference use inert materials like perlite or sand, probably with some crumbled peat added. With tropical plants which do not have a real rest period cuttings can be taken at any time, so long as an average temperature of at least 21 °C (70 °F) can be maintained. Usually however it is better to wait until growth starts again as cuttings taken in winter will have poorer light, making rooting slower and perhaps causing stunted growth once the roots have formed. Obviously in a greenhouse there are two ways of ensuring success: by heating the growing medium to a higher temperature than the surrounding air, and by providing a very humid atmosphere so that the foliage remains turgid and the leaves do not drop off. The first effect is difficult to achieve indoors, but as a substitute for the second you can again use a plastic bag as a propagator, allowing an occasional change of air to prevent mildew and removing it gradually at the end.

Many plants, especially those like *Hedera* and *Philodendron* which have adventitious roots, will put out roots in a glass of clean water if they have plenty of warmth and light. This also happens with semi-hardwood cuttings from plants like oleander and *Tradescantia virginiana* (spiderwort). Roots which develop in water however have a quite different capacity for absorption from cuttings grown in soil, as the tissues can take in different amounts of oxygen and hydrogen in a different form; when they are eventually potted it is difficult to start them growing. However it is a good idea for the beginner to try his hand at this: seeing the roots develop in a transparent container and observing the leaves at the same time is an experience which comes in useful when assessing the progress of cuttings grown in soil where obviously the roots cannot be seen. For cuttings from succulent plants moist conditions would be fatal. Instead they should be left in a shady well-aired position for a day or two to dry out until the cut has almost healed, then planted in almost dry sand and simply sprayed from time to time. Plants with prominent leaf veins do not like too much moisture either, or to be more precise they like a slightly damp but very well-aired atmosphere, so small propagators do not suit them. Plants of this type are ideal for leaf-cuttings, the classic method of propagation for succulents like *Crassulaceae* (the leaves should be broken off rather than cut and then placed on just moist sand) and also for *Peperomia, Gesneriaceae, Saintpaulia* in particular, and all tuberous-rooted *Begonias*. Cut off a leaf, leaving a small piece of stem attached, and plant it up to the leaf base in a very porous, barely moist growing mixture: a combination of perlite and peat is best, but perlite may be used on its own. With *Begonia rex* the leaves can be cut into pieces with a vein to each, and the pieces are then weighed

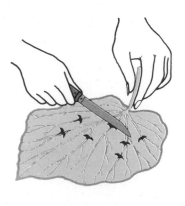

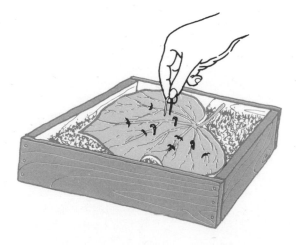

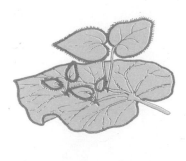

down lightly to keep them in contact with the soil. Plantlets will appear at the base of the stem or vein as the case may be. The main problem is maintaining the right degree of moistness in the growing mixture so that the leaf or piece of leaf does not dry out or rot. Warm surroundings are a help, so the operation is best performed in late spring or early summer. *Sansevieria* also produces new plants from pieces of leaf placed in small pots of sandy mixture, but they take some time to root and unless at least a sliver of the rhizome is attached to the cutting the plantlets will revert to type and lose their variegated markings.

Soil layering is not a very common technique in indoor gardening. Plants like *Chlorophytum* or *Episcia*, which put out new plantlets at the end of runners, take root so easily that they are usually treated as cuttings. However when a plant is slow to root or liable to rotting, like *Scindapsus, Philodendron* and most climbing *Araceae*, you can stand a small pot near the plant and draw one or more branches across it, using hairpins or some other device to peg them down at a knot, or covering them very slightly with soil. If they are kept slightly damp they will put out roots and can then safely be detached.

Air-layering is another technique which can be used for house plants, but it is a slow process, only used for woody plants which do not provide successful cuttings and never for herbaceous plants where these difficulties do not arise. It

Above: All plants which put out runners or roots at the nodes can be propagated by soil layering. Strawberries are a borderline case, but *Scindapsus* and similar plants can be encouraged to root in this way.

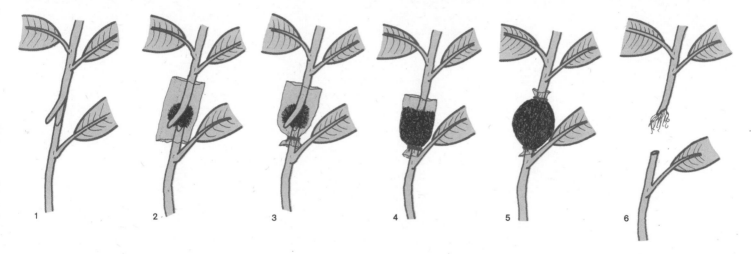

Above: Air layering is the method used for woody plants which are unlikely to root easily as cuttings.
1 Cut a slit in the stem below a node
2 Place some sphagnum moss in the cut so that it cannot close up again; with difficult plants dust the wood with hormone rooting powder
3 Wrap a piece of plastic round the stem and fasten firmly below the cut
4 Fill the space with moist sphagnum moss and press down firmly but not too hard
5 Tie the plastic firmly above the cut
6 When you see roots appearing through the moss remove the plastic and cut the stem through below the roots. In the illustration the moss has been removed to show what is happening, but it is best to leave it in position so that the young root system is not disturbed.

involves making a small clean cut sloping upwards in the stem, just below the last knot before the leaves begin, and reaching about half way through the stem. The cut is held open with a little sphagnum moss or a small piece of inert material such as a wood chip, depending on the thickness of the stem; it is important not to force it or the wood may snap completely. Wrap a layer of damp moss round the cut and cover it with a strip of transparent plastic tied firmly above and below the moss. The plastic must be dark-coloured as this helps the roots to form, but it must also be transparent to allow you to see when they grow through the moss. When they are fully formed remove the plastic and cut the stem below the moss, taking care not to disturb it or damage the new root system. Repot in a suitable mixture. As the sphagnum decomposes it will gradually become part of the soil. The process, as has been said, is a slow one and may take three to eight months, but it is the best way of renewing a *Ficus* which has lost its leaves or obtaining new specimens from other woody plants.

PLANT DISEASES AND PARASITES

House plants are not subject to very many diseases because they usually enjoy such dry atmospheric conditions. Some – *Begonia* is a typical example – may be attacked by oidium which covers the leaves with whitish mildew caused by the proliferation of a type of fungus which develops even at a relatively low level of humidity. The disease can be checked by treating the plant with a sulphur-based fungicide which may also contain pesticides. To reduce unpleasant side effects when dusting with fungicide powder place the plant in a plastic bag, if size allows, and dust it carefully through the bag opening, paying particular attention to the leaves most affected. Do not take the plant out of the bag until the dust stops flying about and settles properly. You can follow the same procedure with aerosol sprays, remembering that pests tend to congregate mainly on the undersides of leaves, so you should lay the pot on its side and put it foliage first into the bag. Many aerosols contain a propellant which can damage leaves if sprayed too close, so the bag should be large enough to make allowance for this. This method of application prevents the product escaping over too wide an area and removes the risk of inhaling toxic substances.

In house plants, deficiency diseases and pests are much more common. Deficiency diseases, as the name suggests, are caused by lack of essential nutrients, or the absence, partial or total, of one of the basic factors of plant growth. Insufficient light produces crooked stems, spindly growth and loss of leaves. Lack of air in the soil, so that the root system cannot expand, leads gradually to weakening and rotting of the roots, resulting eventually in the death of the entire plant; an early sign is yellow drooping leaves, and before that the experienced eye may notice that the tissues are looking opaque and unhealthy. Nitrogen deficiency characteristically appears as chlorosis, resulting in small pale green leaves. Chlorosis may also be due to iron deficiency and occurs in very limy soils when iron is no longer soluble and cannot be absorbed: the leaves first go yellow between the veins which stay green, and some dead tissues may appear. Well-spaced applications of water containing iron compounds, available under various trade names, may check the disease but will not cure leaves which are very far gone. Phosphorus deficiency manifests itself in the weakening of the whole plant, lack of new shoots and buds and often in over-dark foliage. Phosphorus is easily washed away by watering so plants which do not have a clear preponderance of foliage, and flowering plants especially, should be fed with fertilizers containing a good proportion of phosphorus. Other deficiencies are more difficult to diagnose, so it is always best to use a balanced compound fertilizer.

It is hard to say which pests cause most trouble to the indoor gardener; mites or mealy bugs. There are a great many species of mite, but the red spider mite is the one which most attacks house plants. This pest has a round body about half a millimetre in diameter, four pairs of legs and is red, orange or brownish in colour. The epithet 'spider' refers to the delicate web which it spins on leaves, particularly on the underside and on the tips of shoots, as an indication of its presence. It has a sucking organ with which it pierces plant tissues and draws out sap, causing enormous damage, and its rapid rate of reproduction makes it even more harmful. The leaves take on a dusty look and lose their colour, and finally turn papery and shrivel up. This pest likes dry air, and its favourite victims are plants which need plenty of humidity, *Marantaceas* being a classic example. It is difficult to combat, as pesticides effective against it are all extremely toxic and unsuitable for indoor use. You should prevent the mites appearing in the first place by increasing the humidity and washing and spraying the foliage frequently; if you notice an attack early enough you can sometimes get rid of it by placing the plant under a strong jet of water at room temperature to wash away adults and larvae. Mealy bugs are tiny white insects; as larvae they are bare and almost transparent, but later they secrete a cotton-wool-like substance which forms a coat round them. They are fairly mobile and attack a great many plants indiscriminately, though with a marked preference for *Dieffenbachia, Aglaonema* and *Gynura*. Their nests in the axils of winged stems or at the junction of leaves in *Saintpaulia* and many *Grassulaceae* and *Aizoaceae* are very difficult to eradicate. They are particularly active in hot, airless conditions. The best remedy is white oils, but though these can be used with care on smooth leaves they are obviously not good on velvety textures. Fumigation is out of the question inside the house, although it is feasible in a greenhouse, so the only possible method is to keep a careful watch for the insects' appearance and then destroy them with a cotton wool swab soaked in methylated spirits before they have a chance to multiply. The same method can be used to get rid of scale insects, which are fortunately much rarer on house plants.

The adult insects owe their name to the hard waxy scale covering them and also protects the eggs; the larvae are bare and transparent. They mainly attack plants which like airy cool conditions but are not getting them, and so are common on ferns, generally *Araliaceae* and some *Acanthaceae*. As they are almost immobile they can easily be destroyed when they first appear, but if they attack on a large scale and are not eliminated in time they are very harmful, as they secrete honeydew, a deceptively attractive-sounding sticky fluid which clogs the leaf tissues. If no action is taken, much of the plant will be affected and it may even die. Aphids, also known as plant-lice or greenfly, are a common garden pest, but are not usually such a problem with house plants. They appear from time to time on the young shoots of some more common plants, but they can easily be eliminated by spraying them with water in which a little tobacco is soaked until the liquid turns brown. Another fortunately rare pest is white fly; the larvae hatch under the leaves and the adult insects flutter out whenever the plant is touched.

These insects are common pests; indoors they may attack *Fuchsias* and other plants which like moist, cool conditions. If necessary you can use a pesticide spray of a less toxic type, but since these insects do not attack tropical plants the easiest thing to do is to move the affected plant outdoors to stand on its own for a while in the fresh air. Soil-living insects do not usually appear indoors, but sometimes leaf-mould contains earthworms. These useful creatures out of doors, where they ventilate the soil, are very harmful in pots, although they do not eat plant tissues, because they can block the drainage hole and clog the soil by breaking it down and destroying the root hairs growing in it.

There are special powders available which can be added to the potting mixture when it is prepared as a preventive measure to destroy eggs, but if worm casts on the surface of the soil have convinced you that one or more adult earthworms are living in the pot, the best thing to do is have a worm hunt; take the plant out of its pot, remove the worms and check the state of the roots and the drainage hole at the same time.

FERTILIZERS

Pot plants have a far greater need of fertilizers than plants grown in open ground because of the small amount of soil round the roots and the way watering washes away nutrients. Most pot plants do not have a marked rest period, so although it is advisable to feed them less in winter, during the rest of the year small weekly doses of fertilizer are a good idea. The only fertilizers suitable for house plants are ready-made-up compounds which are simply added to water and then applied when the plant is watered. The only exception is when preparing a mixture for repotting plants: you can add a little manure in powder form, so long as you are very cautious and halve the amount suggested on the packet. Concentrates of manure and seaweed, for example, are excellent but as they are very strong, and different plants tolerate different amounts of them, they may damage the roots.

Both chemical and organic fertilizers are available in water soluble form and should preferably be alternated. Most proprietary fertilizers can be used. Most, if not all of them, contain the correct amounts of trace elements as well, but in the case of particular deficiencies you should look for a fertilizer suitable for that specific case. Some contain iron compounds to prevent chlorosis, but these should not be used too freely. Many give their basic formula on the packet or label: the proportions of the three main elements are indicated by three numbers, the first giving the amount of nitrogen, the second the amount of phosphorus, the third the amount of potassium. This means that a fertilizer with the formula 15:20:26 is particularly suitable for plants in poor condition as it contains a high proportion of potassium; 14:28:18 shows a large dose of phosphorus, good for flowering plants; foliage plants need a fertilizer containing more nitrogen (i.e. with the first number the highest). It is important not to give over-large doses.

Packets of powdered fertilizer usually contain a measure, while the bottle top is used as a guide for liquids. In summer as much as 2 g a week may be given, according to size of plant and so on, but in winter the amount should be reduced drastically. It is better to give plants small regular amounts of fertilizer rather than a large occasional dose, so that the plant absorbs the essential nutrients gradually without excesses. Foliar feeding, which has been popular for some time, is useful in spring when growth has begun and the plant is active, and it can be combined with giving the leaves special hormone preparations. However these techniques should be used carefully as, applied at the wrong time, they can stimulate growth when the necessary light or temperature are not available.

HYDROPONICS

Hydroponics is the answer to many problems, including the difficulties of preparing potting composts and watering plants during holidays, but it does not appeal to everyone. Although the name comes from the Greek word meaning water, nutrient solutions containing all the necessary salts are in fact the basis of hydroponics. The French botanist H. L. Duhamel-Dumonceau first experimented with growing plants in water in 1705, using pure water. In 1858 Julius Sachs, a leading scholar in the field of plant physiology, arrived at a formula for solutions which provided plants with the nutrients necessary to develop according to their normal cycle. Later scientists, notably the American W. F. Geriche, perfected what is basically the present system. He invented the term 'hydroponic culture' now mainly used to describe the cultivation of plants without soil on a large scale for commercial or experimental purposes. As has been explained, chemical composition apart, soil only serves as a support and anchor for plants, and hydroponics is proof of this. All that most or even all plants need to live and grow is a supply of a watery solution containing hydrogen and essential nutrients. Photosynthesis does the rest and the metabolic cycle takes place normally. Of course the root system undergoes some drastic changes and develops tissues which can absorb oxygen from water instead of soil. This means that while it is easy enough to change a conventional pot plant over to water culture, the reverse operation is not always successful, and the same problems arise as with cuttings which have rooted in water.

Almost any type of container can be used for the hydroponic system, though transparent glass is not recommended. The roots develop far better in the dark and in fact if the watery solution gets too much light unattractive algae may appear and can harm the plant. The three basic requirements are some kind of support to keep the plant reasonably upright and stable; an airspace between the neck of the container and the solution so that the necessary oxygen reaches the liquid below; above all, once the level of the solution has been decided and its relative density measured, it must be kept constant to avoid an excessive concentration of nutrients. The cells of plant tissues are in fact enclosed by two membranes, one impermeable and the other semi- (or differentially) permeable. The inward movement of water, that is to say the absorption of necessary liquid, takes place by osmosis, caused by the different concentrations of the two liquids on either side of the membrane. Like any pressure it produces tension, in this case on the

Hydroponics
1 Special containers for growing plants by hydroponics are available; water-filled base is covered by a grid
2 Remove the young plant carefully from its pot
3 Wash the roots free of earth with slightly warm water
4 Arrange the plant on the grid
5 Place the grid over the container, making sure the latter contains the right amount of water.

membrane itself, and if the pressure becomes too strong the cells break away, causing the death of the tissues. To prevent the solution becoming too concentrated before it is changed altogether, it must be kept at the same level by adding pure water, given that the salts cannot evaporate and that the plant absorbs only a small amount of them compared with its absorption of water, some of which of course is lost through transpiration. Special containers are now widely available, often made of dark-coloured glass. They are in two parts: the container or pot itself and the top half which has a kind of grid and screws onto the bottom half or stands on top of it. Take the plants you are going to use out of their original pots, remove the soil and wash their roots carefully, getting rid of any dead or unhealthy parts. This whole operation will be simpler if the soil is completely dry so that most of it falls away easily without breaking the stronger roots. When they are quite free of soil rest the plants on the grid with their roots through the holes at the bottom. Place on top of the container, which should already have been filled with liquid up to the right level, which is usually marked; it must again be said that the liquid should never reach the grid itself. Pack some damp sphagnum moss lightly round the collar of the plant, and if necessary prop up the stems with large pebbles, pieces of stone or some other inert material. At first it is best to use pure water, so that the plant can develop a root system accustomed to living in liquid (in exactly the same way that fertilizers are not given an ordinary plant for some time after repotting), but after perhaps a fortnight or a month, when you can see that new roots have developed properly, replace the water with the solution, at the same time removing any dead or rotten roots.

Preparing the solution is no problem, as you can buy special tablets which are dissolved in a specified amount of water, usually a litre (nearly a quart). You will then need to renew the solution after the period stated on the packet (this varies according to make), topping up the solution to the correct level with pure water meanwhile as necessary. When you are more experienced and can work out the best way of supporting the stem, you can use any container which appeals to you, so long as you follow the basic rules.

Plants which can be recommended for hydroponic culture include all *Araceae*, especially if they have adventitious roots, as well as *Dracaena, Cordyline* and others. This method of cultivation seems particularly suited to plants with fleshy roots which can absorb enough moisture by means of their specialized tissues, whereas the root hairs of plants with slender, fibrous roots are often not well-enough developed.

Bulbs grown in water, for example flowering hyacinths grown in special bulb glasses, are not really part of hydroponics, because instead of absorbing nutrients from the liquid they draw on the food reserves of the bulb itself, which are brought into use at the right time. After flowering they have to be thrown away, as they will not have enough strength left for the new growth which can be expected from ordinary bulbs grown in natural conditions.

In artificial-light cultivation, even an ordinary lamp will encourage growth in winter. However, tungsten filament bulbs may scorch foliage so they must be kept some way away from plants.

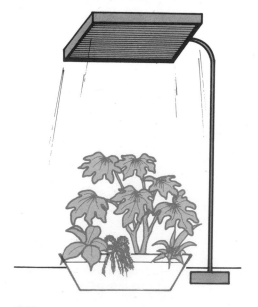

ARTIFICIAL-LIGHT CULTIVATION

It has already been shown how important light is for plants, not in terms of its luminosity but as a component of energy, which allows nutrition, growth and other vital processes, both permanent or temporary, such as flowering, to take place. Two aspects of light are important to plants: intensity and duration. Many plants in fact need a certain daily period of light in order to flower. They are conventionally divided into short-day plants which flower, or rather form flower buds, when the nights are longer than the days, and long-day plants which can only flower if the nights are shorter than the days; and indeterminate plants which are not affected by the hours of daylight and do not have a set photoperiod. These terms are not entirely accurate as it is the period of darkness not of light which matters. In a short-day plant the processes involved in the formation of flower buds will be slowed down or inhibited if the darkness is disturbed even for a short spell or by the feeblest glimmer, while the slightest break in darkness encourages long-day plants. Tropical plants are usually indeterminate, as in their original habitat days and nights are the same length all the year round, but because of this they suffer from the lack of light during our winters when daylight not only lasts less long but is weaker too. Since plants essentially use light photochemically it seems obvious that whatever the source of energy emission, they can use it, provided it is on the right wavelength; they can make more use of a weaker light source with longer exposure, as in photography.

In the last decades of the nineteenth century the first attempts were made at growing plants by artificial light, but there were no means of putting theory into practice. In the early 1890s experiments were made with arc lamps, but they had to be abandoned because the lamps gave off an intolerable amount of heat which made the plants wilt. Such experiments continued but with little success. Even ordinary incandescent lamps provide too much infra-red light or radiant heat. If you want to use them to supplement daylight in winter (which is often beneficial when the days are short), make sure they are 80 cm to a metre away from the plants, according to wattage, as if they are too near they may scorch the foliage. It was not until 1938 that fluorescent tubes were introduced in the United States and partly solved the problem; research is still going on into improved techniques for making them better. These tubes, which are often mistaken for so-called neon lights, consist of a glass tube coated with a fluorescent material by small quantities of phosphorus. They contain nitrogen and other gases, often argon or neon, and a small amount of mercury. Under the influence of an electric discharge, obtained by using a condenser, the mixture ionises, which in turn renders the wall covering luminous. These tubes, which are also known as cold-light sources, often emit a small amount of infra-red rays but, despite their larger surface area, give off far less heat than ordinary filament lamps. Even when they have been lit for several hours they may be touched without danger, and leaves will only scorch if they are actually against them. In horticultural establishments mercury fluorescent lamps are often used but these are all of a very high wattage and give off an enormous amount of heat, so they have to be hung very high up in very airy surroundings, possibly with ventilators, and are certainly not suitable for domestic use.

Fluorescent lamps on the other hand can be used anywhere provided certain points are kept in mind. Firstly, they are produced in standard sizes and the length of tube is related to the wattage, while voltage depends only on the condensers used and the starter which conducts the discharge into the tube. Consequently to pass from one voltage to another it will not be necessary to change the tube, but only the condenser or starter, while increasing the wattage involves altering the whole installation, complete with lamp fittings and reflectors, if used, of the right length. Light does not travel along the tube in a straight line and at the same

A unit with sliding glass panels and fitted with two 40 watt fluorescent tubes can house delicate plants which like a high level of environmental humidity. Ventilation must be provided to prevent mildew. Plants which like more light can be placed on stands to bring them nearer to the tubes.

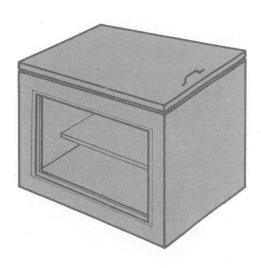

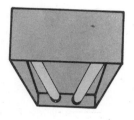

A shelf unit fitted with fluorescent lights is ideal for growing seedlings and cuttings, as in the lower shelves the lamps create a kind of 'bottom heat' which keeps the soil at a higher temperature.

intensity, but in waves with the greatest intensity in the middle and minima at the two ends where the fittings are. To increase the illuminated area it is necessary to use two or more tubes placed end to end, or better still, a longer tube with higher wattage to avoid having two less well-lit sections next to one another. If you want more powerful light you will need to put several tubes side by side to increase the amount of energy in the central section. Tubes are available in standard sizes of 20 watt (50 cm long), 30 watt (90 cm) and 40 watt (1·20 m). Two tubes of this last size are the most common form of installation used for growing house plants. 74 watt tubes (2·40 m long) are obviously preferable for lighting a long surface and are more effective than two 40 watt tubes placed end to end. There is a special name for each type of tube, whatever the make. The main types are cool white, soft white, daylight and warm white. The terms 'warm' and 'cool' refer not to the amount of heat released, but to the kind of light the tubes give. Sometimes the term 'de luxe' is also used, especially for daylight tubes, which means that the fluorescent part contains a substance which gives off more red colour. Some firms have for a number of years manufactured tubes known as 'growth lamps', giving out more light in the wavelengths which plants use most for photosynthesis. However these lamps are not essential, and two or more tubes of other types can be used to cover the maximum number of wavelengths within the spectrum which plants utilize. For example, you could combine a daylight tube with a warm white or a soft white one. The table gives a rough guide to percentages. These are approximate because they vary a little from make to make.

Percentage of light energy in different fluorescent tubes						
	Angstroms	cool white	daylight	warm white	growth lamps	
					normal	wide spectrum
ultraviolet	>3·800	1·65	2·10	1·50	1·40	3·15
violet	3·800—4·300	7·55	9·60	5·15	9·70	12·50
blue	4·300—4·900	20·70	27·80	12·80	27·05	14·30
green	4·900—5·600	24·65	27·30	20·20	14·00	14·50
yellow	5·600—5·900	18·30	14·50	23·45	1·45	9·75
orange	5·900—6·300	17·75	13·15	24·15	6·05	15·90
red	6·300—7·000	8·40	4·30	11·45	39·55	21·80
infra-red	7·000—7·800	1·00	1·25	1·35	0·80	8·10
total		100	100	100	100	100

Given the nature of the different bands, normal growth lamps, which have a high percentage of red, will obviously give a pinkish light, whereas the wide-spectrum lamps are almost completely white. Both cool white and daylight tubes will have a distinctly bluish tinge, while with warm white the light will be whiter but the tube will look pink. Calculating the necessary intensity of light is a complicated operation as the unit of measurement, the lumen, is based on what the human eye perceives, i.e. on received radiant intensity, whereas so far as the photochemical reactions of plants are concerned the amount of radiant energy is what matters. With wavelengths as discontinuous as those of growth lamps, in particular, measurement cannot be exact. Observation and experience have to make up for imperfect data. Generally speaking two 40 watt fluorescent tubes will be sufficient to light a surface measuring roughly 1·35 m by 600 mm (4½ ft by 2 ft). If the plant is 40 cm (15 ins) away from the tube it will get light equivalent to an indoor window sill (without direct sun) and if it is 10 cm (4 ins) away it will be equivalent to an outdoor balcony (again without direct sun). If you wish to increase the intensity of the light or the width of the lighted area, each tube placed

Usually two pairs of tubes with some filament bulbs of low wattage are required. The bottom shelf can be used for plantlets which have already rooted and for a small unit with the necessary fittings. A reflector with two 20 or 30 watt tubes attached to an adjustable metal stand may be placed above flowering plants standing on a tray of wet gravel or moss.

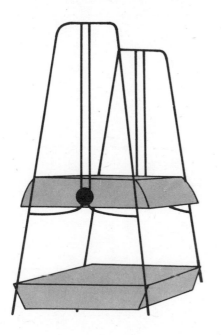

beside the others will give about 25 cm (10 ins) more light. To increase the length of the lighted area use longer tubes. The distance between tubes should be about 15 cm (6 ins) centre to centre, but obviously this depends on the type of light fitting being used. If using several single tubes it is best to observe this distance, however. When growing plants with no other source of light, the light should be left on from thirteen or fourteen hours a day to as much as sixteen hours for plants which need high intensities or are meant to flower. You can work out the cost if you multiply the numbers of watts by the hours of lighting and then by the price per kilowatt. You will get maximum intensity and best results if the fitting has an opaque white reflector to transmit light. If using a shelf system, paint it with white paint and provide a guard so that the light does not diffuse beyond the set limit. You may be able to buy suitable fittings complete with shelves, trays and sometimes small extra incandescent lamps. If these are not obtainable use your imagination, and get in a carpenter or electrician if you have not got the necessary skills yourself.

You will easily be able to find a suitable place for shelves or units. Remember however that the upper part of light fittings contains the condensers which generate most heat, so you must take care not to stand anything on top of them which might come to harm if you are using the shelves for any other purpose. Plants however, will benefit from this background heat if they are placed on trays of damp gravel or perlite so that there is slight evaporation, and this is an ideal position for cuttings to develop roots. More delicate plants benefit not only from the light but also from the moister air if they are enclosed by sliding glass panels like a miniature greenhouse. However the beginner is not advised to attempt this as he or she will often not know how to control air change and may find there are problems with mildew and rotting. Your first installation should be as simple as possible, until you get more experienced, and it is better to go in for plenty of spraying and watering rather than letting the whole range of plant diseases get a hold.

Many plants can be grown this way. *Saintpaulia* will flower readily and you may get good blooms from other *Gesneriaceae* too. Many *Begonias* grow superbly and may flower; larger types will obviously have to be propagated by cuttings from time to time when they get too big. Less well-lit positions, at the tube ends, are suitable for *Marantaceae* as well as *Fittonia* and *Piper*. *Peperomia* needs a very well-lit spot and should be moved as near the tubes as possible to prevent the stems growing too long and being affected by the very moist conditions required in the trays. Even orchids may flower, but they definitely need to be enclosed to get enough humidity, and some ventilation may be necessary. At least two pairs of 40 watt tubes will be needed. Succulents will need the same, but they should always be placed in cooler rooms where the heating is much lower. With some spraying and occasional watering they will pass the winter happily, but they should not be encouraged back into growth too soon.

Glossary

Acaulescent   Describes a plant with such short internodes that it appears to be stemless.

-aceae   As a word ending, the Latin suffix used to form family names. There are a few exceptions to this rule.

Achene   A dry, indehiscent fruit containing a single seed.

Adnate   Describes an organ which grows attached to another.

Adventitious   Describes an outgrowth or organ which occurs irregularly in an unusual position.

Agamic   Used to describe asexual reproduction by vegetative propagation.

Alternate   Arranged singly at different heights on the stem or branches.

Amorphous   Without a well-defined form.

Ampullaceous   Flask-shaped, like many aquatic plants.

Androecium   The male part of a flower. The term is also used to refer to the stamens collectively.

Angiospermae   One of the main divisions of the plant kingdom, consisting of plants in which the seed is enclosed by a fruit.

Anther   The part of a stamen which contains pollen.

Apetalous   Without petals.

Apex   The tip of an organ.

Aphyllous   Without leaves.

Apical   Situated at the top, or apex, of stems, branches etc.

Arachnoid   Covered with cobweb-like filaments.

Areole   A small space on a surface, for example the area occupied by groups of spines or hairs on cacti.

Armed   Equipped with various defensive and protective organs; the term is usually applied to plants with thorns or spines.

Articulate   A jointed organ which can easily be separated into a number of pieces.

Articulation   Generally speaking a joint; more specifically a section of a swollen or flattened stem with very constricted nodes, as found in some cacti.

Ascidium   A pitcher-shaped leaf, most often found in insectivorous plants.

Asepalous   Without sepals.

Axil   The angle between the upper side of a petiole or branch and the stem which bears it.

Axis   The main, central part of a plant or organ; with whole plants this means the stem, but the term can also be applied to a branch, inflorescence or leaf.

Berry   A fleshy, indehiscent fruit containing one or more seeds.

Bifurcate   Describes an organ, usually a branch or a leaf, which forks into two separate parts.

Bigeneric   Produced by crossing two different genera.

Bilabiate (or Labiate)   Divided into two asymmetrical and often dissimilar, lip-like parts.

Bipartite   Divided into two parts almost to the base.

Bipinnate   Describes an organ, generally a leaf, consisting of a petiole branching out into secondary petioles each bearing a number of leaflets.

Bisexual   Describes a flower which bears both stamens and pistil.

Bract   A modified leaf. Bracts usually surround flowers or inflorescences, and vary in size, colour, shape and function from species to species.

Bracteate Having bracts.

Bud The rudimentary growth of stem, branch or flower.

Bulb Short, very swollen underground stem with a single central bud.

Bulbil Either a small bulb; or, in many plants, a small aerial bulb which forms in the axils of leaves or bracts, or on the leaves themselves, and serves as an organ of asexual reproduction.

Bullate Describes a leaf which is blistered or puckered.

Bushy Describes a plant shaped like a bush with a number of branches growing from the same root.

Caducous Describes non-persistent organs or parts of a plant which fall early.

Callus A protuberance; the protective tissue which forms over a wound to heal it.

Calyx Outer covering of the flower bud, usually green in colour, which serves to protect the flower's internal organs. It may be caducous or persistent, and consists of the sepals which can be free or fused; if fused, the calyx is described as gamosepalous.

Campanulate Bell-shaped.

Canaliculate Grooved, generally lengthwise.

Capillary Hair-like.

Capsule Dry dehiscent fruit, usually containing more than one seed.

Carinate Shaped like the keel of a boat.

Carpel In higher plants, the female reproductive organ, consisting of a modified leaf. It forms an ovary containing the ovules, sometimes a slender elongated style, and the stigma which receives the pollen.

Caudex Usually the stem or trunk, especially of palms. Also the persistent base of a plant which loses its aerial parts each year.

Caulis Stem.

Cephalium The apex of certain cacti, covered with spines and hairs, where the fruit is produced.

Chromosomes Elements of the cell nucleus which are the bearers of the hereditary genes.

Ciliate Having fine hairs like eyelashes.

Cirrus (or Tendril) Clinging organ in some climbing plants, which coils round supports or grips by means of suckers.

Cladode Flattened branch with the functions of a leaf.

Clavate Club-shaped, tapering towards the base.

Climber A plant which grows upwards but cannot stand on its own and so clings to supports by some natural means.

Collar The junction of root and stem.

Compound Composed of a number of parts; used to describe a leaf with several leaflets on the same axis.

Connate United.

Corolla The petals collectively: the more or less brightly coloured and developed part of a flower which provides protection and serves to attract insects. The petals may be free, in which case the corolla is dialypetalous, or fused in which case it is gamopetalous.

Cotyledon Rudimentary leaf contained in the embryo which has a nutritive function;

the essential division of the Angiospermae into two classes, monocotyledons and dicotyledons depends on whether there is a single cotyledon or a pair.

Cristate Crested. Describes an organ which has an appendage shaped like a crest with deep, irregular indentation.

Cuneate Wedge-shaped, attached by the point.

Cyathium A kind of inflorescence typical of *Euphorbia*, with male flowers arranged round a female flower and surrounded by showy bracts.

Deciduous Falling; describes plants which lose their leaves in winter.

Decumbent Lying flat with rising tip.

Dehiscent Describes a fruit which opens spontaneously to free the seed.

Dioecious Describes plants which have male and female flowers on separate plants.

Diploid Cell containing a double number of chromosomes compared with the gametes; all somatic cells of the vegetative tissues are of this type.

Embryo All the elements contained in the seed which form the beginnings of the future plant.

Endemic Describes a species which is characteristic of a limited, well-defined area.

Ensiform Sword-shaped.

Ephemeral Short-lived, usually for a single day.

Epigean Used to describe a plant's aerial organs, particularly the stem; generally, whatever grows above the ground.

Epiphyte A plant which grows on another larger plant, but derives no food from it.

Face Either side of a leaf blade.

Flower Collectively, the organs involved in reproduction, consisting of the sexual organs and others which provide protection and serve to attract insects.

Frond Fern leaf.

Fruit The seed-containing organ which develops when the ovary has been fertilized, consisting of the seeds, which are the transformed ovules, and the pericarp which encloses them. A fruit is described as dry or fleshy according to the consistency of the pericarp.

Frutex A shrub.

Gametes Haploid germ cells which produce a new individual after fertilization.

Gymnospermae Plants without ovaries which bear naked ovules and later seeds on the surface of cone scales.

Gynaecium The female part of the flower, consisting of the pistil.

Haploid Cell with the base number of chromosomes constituting the chromosome set typical of each species; only sex cells or gametes are of this type.

Heterophyllous Having different-shaped leaves on the same plant.

Hybrid A plant grown from fertilized seed produced naturally or artificially by crossing plants of two different forms, species or genera. Usually a hybrid is indicated by the names of its parents separated by a small cross x. If it is fairly well established it may have an epithet of its own, again preceded by an x. A cultivar, produced by crossing cultivated varieties, is indicated by an invented, non-Latin name placed between inverted commas. The names of intergeneric hybrids are formed by a combination of syllables from the parents' names preceded by a large cross, X. Hybrid examples. Garden pansy: Viola x wittrokiana (*V. tricolor hortensis*) ; Red flowering crab-apple: Malus x purpurea.

Hypogean   Describes the plant organs beneath the ground.

Imbricate   Overlapping like roof tiles.

Indehiscent   Describes a fruit which does not open to release the seed but stays with the seed until germination, or rots away.

Inflorescence   An arrangement of flowers grouped on a stem. In a cyme the main stem ends in a single flower with subsequent flowers branching out in succession below it. In a raceme the stem continues to grow upwards while putting out sideshoots. There are various other kinds of inflorescence with different arrangements of flowers or secondary stems.

Internode   The length of stem between two nodes.

Lacinia   A deep incision dividing an organ, usually a leaf, into long, narrow, irregular lobes.

Latex   A milky fluid, exuded by the tissues of some plants when damaged, which is contained in narrow, often reticulate, lactiferous vessels. A feature of a number of genera, including *Ficus, Euphorbia* and *Papaver*. Its consistency, colour and other characteristics vary, but it is often poisonous or an irritant.

Layer   A trailing stem which strikes roots when it comes into contact with soil either artificially or naturally.

Leaf   Outgrowth from the stem or branches, attached at a node. It consists of the leaf-base by which it is attached and the petiole, of varying size, which joins the base to the expanded part; this last being known as the lamina or blade. Various terms are used to describe the different types of leaves, depending on the shape of the blade or parts of it.

Liana   A woody plant with flexible stems which cannot grow upright but clings to or twines round supports.

Limb   The free upper part of a gamopetalous corolla.

Long-day   Describes plants which will only form flowerbuds when the period of light each day is longer than the period of darkness.

Monoecious   Describes a plant which bears both male and female flowers.

Mutant   A plant arising from a sexual and therefore inheritable mutation.

Mutation   Sudden variations which appear in a plant. They may affect the whole plant, including the sexual organs, in which case they are inheritable and can be reproduced by seed, or they may just appear in a single part of the plant in which case they can only be reproduced by vegetative propagation.

Node   The point where a leaf or bud joins a stem or branch.

Opposite   Describes two organs placed on either side of a stem at the same level.

Palmate   Describes a leaf with veins or lobes arranged in a fan shape like the fingers of a hand.

Pauciflorus   Describes an inflorescence with few flowers.

Pedicel   The stalk of a single flower in an inflorescence.

Peduncle   The stalk of an inflorescence or a solitary flower.

Peltate   Describes a leaf which has the petiole attached to the centre of the lower surface rather than the margin.

Perfoliate   Describes organs, usually leaves, which grow so closely round the stem that they seem to form a single unit through which the stem passes.

Perianth The petals and sepals, or corolla and calyx, together. Known as a perigone when it consists of tepals.

Petiole A leaf stem.

Phyllode A broad, flattened, leaf-like petiole.

Pistil Female part of the plant, forming the gynaecium. It may consist of a single carpel or a number of fused carpels.

Pollen Grains which form in the anthers and produce male gametes.

Pollination The transfer of pollen from the anther to the stigma. The terms anemophilous, entomophilous and hydrophilous are used to describe pollination brought about by wind, insects and water respectively.

Pseudo bulb The short swollen stem of certain bulbs, particularly orchids, resembling a bulb, although it does not grow underground. It serves as an organ of storage and nutrition.

Rachis The axis which bears flowers or leaflets; the petiole of fern fronds.

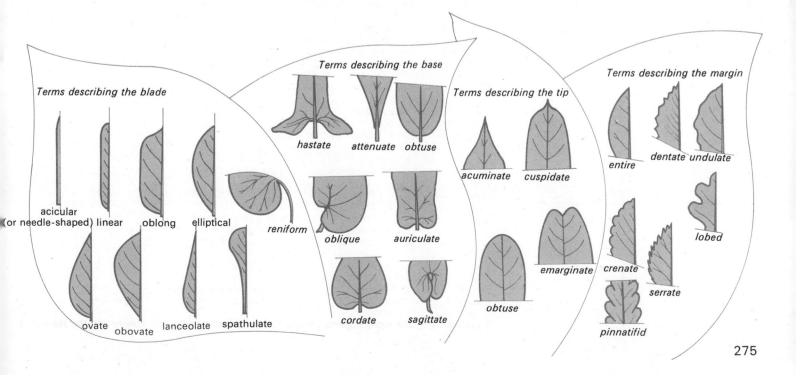

Terms describing the blade

acicular (or needle-shaped) linear oblong elliptical reniform

ovate obovate lanceolate spathulate

Terms describing the base

hastate attenuate obtuse

oblique auriculate

cordate sagittate

Terms describing the tip

acuminate cuspidate

emarginate

obtuse

Terms describing the margin

entire dentate undulate

lobed

crenate

serrate

pinnatifid

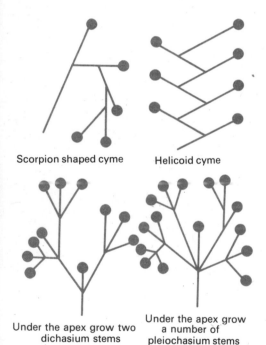

Scorpion shaped cyme | Helicoid cyme

Under the apex grow two dichasium stems

Under the apex grow a number of pleiochasium stems

Raceme (or indeterminate) inflorescences

Rhizome Modified underground stem which sometimes becomes epigean; it has reduced scale leaves and bears buds and roots at the nodes.

Sarmentose Any long slender stem which cannot grow upright may be described as sarmentose, but the term is generally applied to plants which have no special clinging organs and must be fastened artificially to supports, in contrast to climbing plants which cling spontaneously.

Scape An aphyllous flower stem, sometimes with scales or bracts, which grows directly from the plant's base.

Sepals The parts of a flower which make up the calyx.

Sessile Describes any organ which lacks the normal connecting part – a leaf without a petiole, a flower without a peduncle, a stigma without a style or an anther without a filament.

Sexual reproduction Propagation by means of the sexual organs, which after fertilization produce the seed from which the new plant will grow.

Sheath A leaf with a wide base encircling the stem. The term may be used for the whole leaf, or the petiole of the base alone.

Short-day Describes plants which will only form flowerbuds when the period of darkness each day is longer than the period of light.

Shrub A woody plant branching out from the base.

Sinus A depression, especially at the base of a leaf.

Spadix A flower spike with fleshy swollen stem from which the flowers grow.

Spathe A showy, often colourful bract which grows round the base of a spadix, frequently enclosing it.

Spore An asexual, usually unicellular reproductive structure.

ament

corymb

head

simple

cluster or raceme

umbel

spike

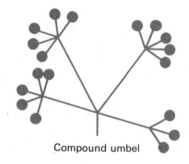

Compound umbel

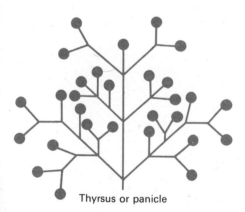

Thyrsus or panicle

Compound spike

Stamens   The parts which make up the androecium, bearing the pollen-containing anthers, usually at the end of a filament.

Stem   The plant's central axis which bears all the appendages, branches, leaves and flowers.

Stigma   The enlarged end part of the pistil which receives the pollen grains.

Stipules   Appendages at the base of the petiole; they may be single or in pairs, caducous or persistent, and sometimes develop into membranes which enclose the whole growing tip.

Stolon   A runner; a stem which grows out into a long shoot, usually creeping, and puts out adventitious roots at the nodes. This is one method of natural vegetative propagation.

Stoma   An opening between two guard cells in the epidermis of a leaf, which connects the air spaces inside the leaf with the external atmosphere and controls the exchange of gases.

Strobilus   Cone; inflorescence of *Coniferae*, consisting of usually woody carpellary leaves which protect the seeds.

Sucker   An underground side shoot which grows from the plant's roots or rhizome, puts out roots and becomes an independent plant.

Suffrutescent   Describes a plant with a woody stem at the base and a herbaceous apex.

Syconium   An inflorescence typical of the genus *Ficus* consisting of a fleshy receptacle containing unisexual flowers.

Symbiosis   The mutually advantageous association of two organisms, ranging from the enjoyment of reciprocal benefits to the formation of a single individual.

Syncarpous   Describes a fruit with persistent bracts composed of adnate carpels united with the fleshy axis; this type of fruit is typical of *Ananas*.

Tepals   The name used collectively for sepals and petals when they are similar in size colour and texture, as occurs typically in monocotyledons.

Trigonal   Having three angles or corners.

Tunicate   Having scales which cover and protect all the parts below.

Unisexual   A flower which has either stamens or pistil, but not both.

Vaginate   Generally describes a petiole with an expanded or winged base forming a sheath round the stem.

Verticel   A whorl; an arrangement of three or more leaves or stems growing from the same node.

Voluble   Broadly speaking describes any plants with weak stems but without special clinging organs which twine round available supports to hold themselves up; more specifically the term is used for herbaceous plants to distinguish them from lianas.

Winged   Describes an organ with a flattened, wing-like outgrowth. The term may be used to describe certain petioles and some fruit and corollas.

Zygote   Egg cell fertilized by the fusion of two gametes of different sexes.

Acknowledgements

The publisher would like to thank the floriculturists Redaelli and Giovanni Fumagalli of Milan, Italy, who kindly allowed Giuseppe Mazza to photograph their finest specimens, together with the following companies: Fernand Delrue of Menton-Garavan, France; Fiori del Lago of Capolago (Varese) Italy; Frattini of Masnago (Varese) Italy; Haller of Brugg, Switzerland; K. und M. Karst-Bürgi of Rupperswil, Switzerland; Idea Verde of Olgiate Olona (Varese) Italy; Luthi of Lengnau, Switzerland; Panzeri of Milan, Italy; Plantanova of Milan, Italy; Podere Toselli of Lainate (Milan) Italy; Riva of Milan, Italy; Romano of Milan, Italy; Ronco of Bordighera, Italy; Sozzi of Cernusco sul Naviglio (Milan) Italy; Villa of Trezzo d'Adda (Milan) Italy; Zama of Faenza, Italy.

The publisher would also like to thank Prof. Giovanni Dal Grande of the istituto Professionale per l'Agricoltura of Minoprio (Como) Italy; Prof. Joh. Diedrich Supthut of the Städt Sukkulentensammulung of Zurich, Switzerland; Prof. Marcel Kroenlein of the Jardin Exotique of the Principality of Monaco; and the staffs of the Palmengarten of Frankfurt, West Germany, the Blumengarten of Zurich, Switzerland, and the Department of Botany at the University of Zurich, Switzerland.

A special note of thanks to the late eminent authority Julien Marnier-Lapostolle of the 'Les Cedres' garden of Saint-Jean-Cap-Ferrat, France.

The crystal-vase arrangements on pages 35, 57 and 59 are by the Floricoltura Giuseppe Zama of Faenza, Italy; the bonsai on page 61 by Adriano Sartirana of Milan, Italy, and Gunter Ruhe of San Rocco di Camogli (Genoa) Italy.

The free compositions and ikebana are by Mrs. Keiko Ando Mei of Milan, Italy.

Index